The Williwaw War

The Williwaw War

The Arkansas National Guard in the Aleutians in World War II

Donald M. Goldstein

AND

Katherine V. Dillon

The University of Arkansas Press

Fayetteville 1992

96   95   94   93   92   5   4   3   2   1

This book was designed by John Coghlan and Ellen Beeler using the typefaces Janson and Simoncini Garamond.

The paper used in this publication meets the minimum requirements of the American National Standard for Permanence of Paper for Printed Library Materials Z39.48-1984. ∞

Library of Congress Cataloging-in-Publication Data

Goldstein, Donald M.
     The Williwaw War: the Arkansas National Guard in the Aleutians in World War II / by Donald M. Goldstein and Katherine V. Dillon
          p. cm.
     Includes bibliographical references and index.
     ISBN 1-55728-242-0
     1. World War, 1939–1945—Campaigns—Alaska—Aleutian Islands.   2. Arkansas. National Guard. Coast Artillery, 206th—History.   3. Arkansas. National Guard. Infantry, 153rd—History.   4. World War, 1939–1945—Regimental histories—United States.   5. Aleutian Islands (Alaska)—History.   I. Dillon, Katherine V.   II. Title.
D769.87.A4G65 1992
940.54'28—dc20
                                                                                            91-42730
                                                                                                 CIP

Contents

Preface

The Aleutian Islands were the site of a largely forgotten campaign in World War II. An archipelago extending close to two thousand kilometers west of the Alaskan peninsula, the chain comprises about one hundred islands. One of these is Unalaska (Amaknak Island) where Dutch Harbor is located. On these remote islands, the cold winds from Siberia and the ocean currents flowing down from the Bering Sea meet the warm air masses and currents flowing across the Pacific. Their interaction produces the williwaw—winds of high velocity—and dense fogs, rain, mists, and snow, making life miserable for the foot soldier.

Those who served in the Aleutians and especially those who saw combat, will never forget the treeless terrain and the extreme weather, the poor visibility, icing damage, frostbite, and other hazards of operation.

Despite the elements, the Americans and the Japanese saw a great strategic value in the Aleutians. Occupation by either nation would threaten the mother country of the other. Before the infamous attack on Pearl Harbor, the United States accomplished limited defensive construction of Unalaska; however, after the Japanese raid on Dutch Harbor and their troop landings on Attu and Kiska, there was a tremendous build-up.

The 206th Coast Artillery of the Arkansas National Guard was federalized on 6 January 1941, and after training at Fort Bliss, Texas, it began to deploy to the Aleutian Islands and the mainland of Alaska in August of 1941. Under the command of Col. E. C. Robertson, who was later to be deputy commander of all army forces at Fort Mears (the main army post at Dutch Harbor), seven batteries plus a headquarters were deployed.

The unit consisted of searchlight and radar batteries, automatic weapons units, and antiaircraft batteries. These soldiers went to such places as Mt. Ballyhoo, Morris Cove, Eiders Point, Haystack Hill, Power Hill, Signal Hill, Hill 100, Hill 300, Captains Bay, Bunker Hill, the Spit, and last, but not least, Hog Island, where, because of the harsh weather, three of them died. They carried equipment up rough terrain, strung communications wire, built outposts, bunkers, and dugouts, and, as one soldier so aptly put it, they "dug and dug and dug," often fighting the awful winds, the cold, the fog, and the chill. For many of the men, this was the first time away from home. They came from everywhere in the state of Arkansas: Little Rock, Fort Smith, Fayetteville, Arkadelphia, Conway, Monticello, Pine Bluff, Eureka Springs, Hot Springs, Blytheville, and Texarkana, to name a few. They came from colleges, farms, and cities and from almost every walk of life.

They were at Dutch Harbor when the Japanese raided it on 3 and 4 June 1942. For thirteen months, the men of the 206th, and her sister outfit, the 153d Infantry, prepared Dutch Harbor for a possible invasion. In August 1943 the Japanese were driven out of Attu and Kiska, which they had captured after the Dutch Harbor raid. However, the 206th remained for almost a year to insure that all was safe.

Asked for a brief summation of their Aleutian service, few indeed admitted to any pleasant memories. But many conceded it had been "a learning experience," while others pointed out that their Aleutian assignment had probably saved their lives. As Sgt. Earl Gill remarked, "I . . . considered the fact that being in 'cold storage' so to speak for 32 months probably kept me from much of the concentrated 'hot' war in North Africa, Europe, and the South Pacific." For some, the camaraderie made it all worthwhile. "It brought me ever closer to my school-day friends . . . ," observed S. Sgt. Murrel W. Buzzan, "and some who joined us along the way made life-long friends." Probably Sgt. James H. Ryals said it best: "I wouldn't take $1 million for the experience, but I wouldn't give a nickel to do it again."

The men of the 206th and 153d left Arkansas as boys and returned as men. They went to a forgotten place to fight a forgotten war. What they did was not romantic; it was dull, boring, hard, and cruel, but it had to be done. Not much has been written about the long days and nights spent in Alaska by a bunch of young men from Arkansas. What they did made no headlines in the newspapers across the country. They have never been given credit for their accomplishments, and few, if any, historians have ever mentioned their role in repelling the Japanese forces in the only campaign fought on North American soil during all of World War II.

This is their story.

Introduction

Every year they assemble on Labor Day, usually in Little Rock, occasionally in another town or city, but always in Arkansas. Each year they grow a little balder or grayer; a little stouter or a little thinner. In the last few years, the steps have been a little slower, and gaps have appeared in the ranks. It was becoming apparent to these men that eventually no one would be left who remembered, no one would be left who experienced at first hand the events that drew them together, no one would be left to tell the children and grandchildren how it had been in the Aleutian Islands back in World War II.

Many Americans did not even know that the war had touched the North American continent. Comparatively few books and articles among the vast literature of World War II dealt with the Alaskan theater in any depth; still fewer, if any, so much as mentioned the 206th Coast Artillery Regiment (Antiaircraft) of the Arkansas National Guard.

So a movement to have their memories put into written form began, under the guiding hand of William H. Bowen. His younger brother, John, had died in the line of duty in the Aleutians, so he had a particular interest in the project. He traveled to Dutch Harbor to see the place where his brother had died and realized that here was a story to be told, not only of John Bowen but of all John's buddies, living and dead.

William Bowen had read *Miracle at Midway* by Gordon W. Prange, with Goldstein and Dillon, which had dealt briefly with the Japanese attack on Dutch Harbor in the context of their major campaign against Midway and the U. S. Pacific Fleet. So the 206th veterans formed a committee, led by Aubrey T. Albright and Paul D.

Beasley (who had been the youngest man in the regiment) to raise the funds for an on-site visit to their old haunts at and near Dutch Harbor and to defray the costs of research. They contacted us to write the book, and they secured a grant from the Arkansas Endowment for the Humanities, to whom we are much indebted for their support.

The project began in 1989, with a targeted publication date of June 1992, the fiftieth anniversary of the attack on Dutch Harbor. While this book is not a complete history of the war in the Aleutians, it covers the main events. Basically it is the story of one outfit, the 206th, and tangentially of its sister regiment, the 153d Infantry, also from Arkansas.

Neither of these regiments participated directly in combat, but they saw plenty of action in the larger sense. As the title of this book implies, their war was as much against the weather as against the Japanese. Probably every man who served outside the continental United States in World War II would claim that his theater was the worst from the standpoint of climate. But these veterans of the Aleutians will bet their environment against the searing sun and desert of North Africa or the jungles, enervating heat, and malaria of the South Pacific. In the Aleutians they fought blinding, waist-deep snow; sleet that struck as from a sandblaster; fogs so thick and persistent that fliers claimed it was clear enough for takeoff if they could see their copilots; the williwaw, that incredible wind that seemed to blow from every direction at once, and that blew away anything not fastened down. Some men broke under the strain, and suicides were far from uncommon. But the Arkansas men hung in there grimly, enduring the weather, the grinding boredom, the feeling of uselessness as time went by and they were not called upon to fight, except for that brief encounter on 3–4 June 1942.

This book is based upon interviews with survivors; diaries, letters, scrap books, and a series of exhaustive questionnaires to which these men were kind enough to reply in depth. Secondary sources include books, articles, and newspapers, many given to us by the men of the 206th and by individuals at Dutch Harbor who kindly cooperated in this study. We are deeply grateful to all of them.

As mentioned, this book is not intended to be a history: the historical background included herein is strictly for the purpose of putting the experiences of the Arkansas men in context. Yet, in a larger sense, this book is not the story of the 206th and 153d only; it is the story of every GI who served throughout the war honorably without ever having the opportunity to fire a shot.

This book is dedicated to the men from Arkansas, the living and the dead, who served in the Aleutians during World War II, and also to every GI who filled a post of little glory, performing the unsung tasks that had to be done. Without them, victory would not have been possible.

Donald M. Goldstein, Ph.D.
Associate Professor of Public and International Affairs
University of Pittsburgh, Pittsburgh, Pennsylvania

Katherine V. Dillon
CWO, USAF (Ret.)
Arlington, Virginia

1

"Well Above the Average"

From Little Rock, Arkansas, and nearby Levy and Dermott, the young men of Battery A, 206th Coast Artillery (Antiaircraft) of the Arkansas National Guard converged upon the Little Rock armory on 6 January 1941. By 0800, the entire strength of 6 lieutenants and 196 enlisted men had assembled, looking expectantly at their commanding officer, Capt. Carl F. Schiebner. They knew what had happened, of course. It was no secret that the Arkansas National Guard had been called up into federal service; however, Schiebner would explain what mobilization involved and the effect it would probably have on their lives. A number of men were granted immediate leave to put their affairs in order.

Similar scenes were being enacted at various other locations in Arkansas as other units of the 206th assembled to get the word—the Headquartery Battery, Medical Detachment and Band at Marianna; Headquarters, 1st Battalion, Batteries D and F at Russellville; Batteries B at Monticello, C at Jonesboro, G at Helena, H at Hot Springs, and Headquarters 2d Battalion at El Dorado.[1]

Despite the briefing by Schiebner and other conscientious officers, it is doubtful if any of the guardsmen truly understood the seriousness of the situation. Gloom and pessimism are not the usual states of mind of healthy young men in their late teens and early twenties. There is no hint in the recollections of surviving 206th members of any consciousness that the tremendous events occurring throughout the world might touch Arkansas and disarrange their lives. Being inducted was the chance one took in signing up, and it would only be for one year.

Yet it would be a prime error to dismiss these men as unthinking hillbillies. Back on 8 September 1930, after training at Pensacola,

Florida, a commendation of the 206th said in part: ". . . the officers had attracted to their colors a class of enlisted men well above the average."[2] This was just as true in 1941 as it was in 1930. The 206th drew heavily upon Arkansas's institutions of higher learning, so many of its enlisted men were students at the college level. Others were well-established citizens. In addition to the regimental chaplain, Maj. John Williamson of Little Rock, seven clergymen belonged to the 206th, all serving as enlisted men.[3]

For a number of men, the Guard was a family matter. For instance, H Battery had sixteen sets of brothers and several cousins on its roster.

Why should any of these people want to join the National Guard? The Guard's most potent selling point was financial. These young men of Arkansas loved their country no less and no more than their counterparts throughout the United States, but the overwhelming majority had not signed up from patriotic motives. They joined for various reasons. A few rugged individualists had personal motivation. Pfc Ruben O. Oxner wanted "to get off the farm." Sgt. Russell R. Haden gave "Adventure, I guess" as his rationale. The Guard offered companionship with one's peers and occasional trips to other parts of the United States for maneuvers or bivouacs. Others joined the Guard to avoid the draft, not out of cowardice, but because they preferred to serve with their friends in familiar places. But for the majority, money was the deciding factor. For men putting themselves through college, the Guard's one-dollar-a-drill pay offered an honorable, not-too-onerous means of earning the few extra dollars that made all the difference in those years when the Depression was just winding down.[4]

Having joined, in general the men served conscientiously. In fact, when in September 1939 the 206th received new equipment, the troops were so eager to test it that they persuaded the regimental commander, Col. Elgan C. Robertson, to hold a week's maneuvers that winter at Camp Quapaw, Arkansas.[5]

Robertson was a veteran of World War I, when he commanded an artillery battery. After the Armistice, he became active in the American Legion, serving as Arkansas's department commander from 1923 to 1924. He had commanded the 206th since 27 February 1924. In civilian life he was president of the First National Bank of Marianna, and in 1941 was vice president of the Arkansas Bankers'

Association. In the normal course of events he would have moved up to the presidency, but the call-up of the 206th interrupted this progression.[6]

Most of the junior officers and enlisted men had too little contact with Robertson to form a definite opinion about him, but T. 4 Nathan R. Patrick wrote, "I especially admired our commander, Colonel Robertson, because I thought he was very military and sincere about our mission and seemed very much to be interested in the welfare of his men."[7] T. Sgt. John H. Harp was "personally inspired" by Robertson, "and was very glad he was promoted to General before his service was over."[8] WO Bernard E. Stout conceded, "Our old colonel, in spite of his faults, had the attitude, 'I may slap my own around but I won't let anyone else do it.'"[9]

In its current incarnation, the 206th CA (AA) Regiment dated back only to late 1923, but it was the heir to a rich tradition, beginning in the eighteenth century and into the early nineteenth with the old territorial militia. When Arkansas was admitted to the Union in 1836, the state constitution specifically provided for reorganizing the territorial militia into the state militia. All free white males who had lived in Arkansas for at least two months were eligible, but they had to join a regiment close to their homes, except in case of invasion or insurrection.

During the Mexican War, the regiment was called up as the First Arkansas Volunteer Cavalry. It served honorably throughout that conflict, and it saw combat at Buena Vista on 23 February 1847. With the outbreak of the Civil War, Arkansas joined the Confederacy, and its militiamen fought in various minor engagements. On 22 June 1868, Arkansas was once more admitted to the Union.

On 1 May 1898 at Manila Bay, Stokely Morgan of Camden, Arkansas, fired the opening shot of the Spanish-American War; however, no Arkansas State Guard units participated in that conflict.

The National Guard system came into effect in 1912, and State Guards became National Guards, with consequent reorganization and changes of unit designation with which we will not confuse the reader. Arkansas guardsmen served during the Mexican border disturbances, and in World War I three Arkansas National Guard regiments were called to active duty, all under the 39th Division.

In 1923 the 206th CA (AA) was organized from various companies. The personnel met every Thursday, and during the summer two-week training exercises were held at such locations as Fort Sill, Oklahoma, Fort Snelling, Minnesota, Fort Barrancas, Pensacola, Florida, and Camp Joseph T. Robinson (Camp Pike), North Little Rock. In 1937 some elements of the 206th were federalized and sent to Osceola, Arkansas, to help control heavy flooding of the Mississippi.[10]

At the time our story opens, the Arkansas National Guard consisted of four major organizations—the 153rd Infantry Regiment, the 142nd Field Artillery Regiment, the 154th Observation Squadron, and the 206th Coast Artillery (Antiaircraft) Regiment. When the latter was called up in 1941, it was a sound organization, its enlisted men were loyal to one another, and in general they were satisfied with their officers, who, in the words of S. Sgt. Murrel W. Buzzan, "were our friends and neighbors at home. They were all OK." Buzzan served at regimental headquarters, so he probably had more direct contact with the staff than did most enlisted men.[11] Pvt. John W. Davis of Battery C recalled that his captain had been his football coach in high school, and he frequently found himself addressing the officer as "Coach" rather than "Captain" or "Sir."[12]

This happy state of affairs was not destined to prevail undiluted. With expansion of the military came the dreaded "Ninety-Day Wonders"—young men sent through three months' training at Officer Candidate School and sprung loose on troops who were at best skeptical. As Pfc Lawrence Richardson of Battery F acknowledged, "I admired all the officers that were with us upon induction into the service. These were replaced by 90-day wonders who did not know as much as most of us. Many of our noncoms had 2+ years of college and were the true leaders of our unit."[13]

Warrant Officer Stout was even more blunt: "The passage of the Selective Service and resulting draft law brought a 'rash' of new enlistments and 'correspondence course' officers, many of whom had no more business of being officers than a tomcat. . . . Fortunately, the 206th had a good cadre of experienced non-coms and older officers so the expansion went smoothly."[14]

So did the move from Arkansas to the regiment's destination, Fort Bliss, at El Paso, Texas. By 14 January 1941 the regiment had made all preparations and was ready to begin the three-day journey. Early that morning the advance guard of Battery A—Captain

Schiebner, 1st Lt. Ralph Blanz and 65 enlisted men—left Little Rock with "eighteen pieces of motorized equipment and five private cars." The rest of the battery—five officers and 126 men—"boarded a Rock Island Special awaiting at the station."[15]

At Hot Springs, Sgt. Alford "Pook" Parker, and other members of Battery H climbed aboard a Rock Island train that would take them to Little Rock, where they would join the other Guardsmen. They followed the northern route to Oklahoma City, thence to Tucumcari, New Mexico, where they set their watches back an hour.[16]

Cpl. R. R. "Dick" Ballew of Battery C remembered the move vividly, for he was one of the truck drivers in the motor convoy from Jonesboro. He was assigned to the "Height Finder" truck, a long-wheel-base GMC vehicle. Others drove "Dodge Recon wagons" and "the new Mack trucks that pulled the 3-inch anti-aircraft guns . . . " This convoy was under the leadership of Sgt. Damon Mathis. The main body of Battery C moved out by train, sped on their way by "quite a turnout of townspeople, parents, relatives and girl friends . . ."

The trucks spent the first night on the road in Prescott, Arkansas. "Some place down the line"—Ballew did not recall just where—Battery C's convoy joined forces with Battery D from Russellville. Somewhere between Dallas and Fort Worth, one of Battery D's drivers almost lost a 3" antiaircraft gun when the tongue between the truck and gun worked loose. The gun ran onto the median strip. The driver was not aware of his loss until a jeep caught up with him and its driver broke the news.

Another incident Ballew never forgot was passing between Midland and Odessa, Texas, when natural gas was being burned off. It "looked like a forest of trees on fire."

The army had established an antiaircraft training center at Fort Bliss in September 1940. There the 206th found itself in the company of three other National Guard Coast Artillery (AA) Regiments—the 200th from New Mexico, the 202nd from Illinois, and the 260th from the District of Columbia, plus the 63rd Coast Artillery Regiment of the Regular Army, transferred from California.

Fort Bliss was an old, established Army post with brick quarters surrounded by grass and trees for its own personnel. But the

National Guard units in training there rated no such grandeur. Ballew's "new home was out in the dust and cactus on a slope of land in front of the Franklin Mountain range."[17]

This was the Logan Heights Cantonment, where the 206th was housed along with the other Coast Artillery units.[18] There they lived in tents, quite plush as tents go. They had board floors and sides. George Nettles, who sent periodic dispatches from Fort Bliss to the Camden *Times*, could give the home folks a reassuring picture: "All tents are equipped with electricity and cots, mattresses, three blankets and a comforter."[19] Sgt. James M. Massey of Battery G received a bleak first impression: "It was a desolate-looking place, snowing when we arrived, flakes big as a half-dollar."[20] Sgt. Earl Gill of Battery B was less than happy with the cantonment: "We were living in six-man tents, a wood frame with a tent stretched over it. I recall the wind became so strong a few times we found ourselves bracing the frame to keep it from swaying or being flattened. They were built rather hurriedly and really were not that sturdy."[21]

In an amazingly short time, with the resilience of youth, the men had begun to make themselves at home. "Things here are at last becoming normal," Cpl. David B. Alspaugh of Battery B wrote to his family in Smackover, Arkansas. "We are still taking shots. . . . The part of the camp we are in is a new addition. They are still working on the streets and buildings around here. The tents are heated with natural gas."

He had been to El Paso—"truly a beautiful city"—for the first time, and attended "the prettiest theatre" he had ever seen. And he had climbed "the highest mountain" in the Franklin range.[22]

On 21 January, the same day that Alspaugh wrote home, Nettles informed the Camden *News* that the ration allowance per man was 40.8 cents a day, and they expected crockery dishes the next week. To today's ear, that ration allowance sounds like slim pickings, but considering that on the open market eggs were selling for thirty cents a dozen, ham for thirty cents a pound, and chuck roast for twenty-four cents a pound, obviously the soldiers wouldn't starve. A newspaper picture showed a typical Fort Bliss breakfast tray of that pre-cholesterol-conscious period. GI Joe ate eggs, which were generally fried, with plenty of bacon, toast lathered with real butter, and, if he felt peckish, a few pancakes. He drank coffee with table cream and/or glasses of whole milk.[23] The soldiers thrived on this diet and worked it off in training exercises.

What took more getting used to was the West Texas climate and scenery, so different from that of Arkansas. Some took to it immediately; others hated it. The opinions of survivors concerning the weather ranged from "excellent" to "miserable." About one aspect they were agreed—the winds and the consequent sandstorms were bothersome. Cpl. Neal P. Kinney of Battery D pointed out that "there were no windbreakers such as trees. That's what I missed, Arkansas trees."[24] When on 26 January several men took over Nettles's column, one of their remarks was this: "Hoping Camden's still there and wishing heartily for the sight of a tree. . . ."[25] That complaint was destined to be a plaintive *leitmotif* in the 206th's subsequent history.

Pfc Dennis P. Abell of Headquarters pointed out that the Arkansas men were not used to the high altitude and dry air. As a result, "everybody had sore throats for a while."[26] 2d Lt. Raymond Byergson estimated that "about ⅓ of the personnel had some kind of respiratory infection."[27] Shots, too, took their usual toll. On 10 February, Alspaugh informed his family that he had just been discharged that morning from the hospital, where he had been for a week, having become "violently ill" immediately after his last typhoid shot.[28]

Whether suffering from a sore throat, a shot reaction, or some unspecified problem, Pook Parker had barely settled into his tent when he had to go on sick call, whence he was sent to William Beaumont General Hospital for a brief stay that changed his life. There on duty in Ward 3 was a "little, black-haired, black-eyed Second Lieutenant nurse named Vola Marie Burgess."

Parker fell in love with an almost audible thud. For a convalescent male patient to be attracted to a pretty nurse is by no means an unusual phenomenon, but Parker was quite sure that this was no passing fancy. While he was in the hospital, he was promoted to sergeant, and his pay rose from forty-two dollars to fifty-five dollars per month. Emboldened by this financial windfall, he proposed to Vola. "Don't you know it's against the rules for a Second Lieutenant to even date an enlisted man?" she retorted.

It was a long way from "yes," but it wasn't an unequivocal "no."

Encouraged, he suggested that "we sneak around and maybe go to a movie and see what the others might say." She must have been attracted to Parker, for she agreed to this disarming proposition. They dated occasionally in civilian clothes, and "the others" paid no attention to them. They came up with a solution to the problem of rank—she would resign her commission, and they set the wedding date, appropriately enough, for 14 June 1941—Flag Day.[29]

2

"Training Began to Pick Up"

W e started some training," wrote Sergeant Massey in his notes
for February 1941, "still trying to get better organized." As
Massey carried out his duties in his usual conscientious way, he carried a special burden. His father had been stricken with what would
be his last illness. Massey was devoted to his father, and worry and
grief shadowed his days at Fort Bliss.[1]

In line with getting "better organized," on 25 January 1941 the
army activated the 39th Coast Artillery Brigade to serve as the command and control element for the one Regular Army and the four
National Guard Coast Artillery Regiments in training at Fort Bliss.[2]

Battery K's history had little to say about that month, other
than listing mobilization promotions and selections for various Post
training schools. It recorded with some pride that on 26 February a
number of men began a math class, "of their own free will . . ."[3]

"The entire unit went through what was essentially boot training during the first few weeks—marching, military courtesy, small
fire-arms, guard duty, KP, etc.," recalled Sergeant Gill. "Many in
the unit, as I, had not been in long enough to receive the usual basic
training of a soldier."[4]

Some took specialized courses, such as automotive mechanics,
camouflage of guns and tanks, first aid and giving shots, fire control,
and cooks' and bakers' school.

Other subjects included map reading, aircraft recognition, and,
naturally, care of weapons. "At the base we practiced gun maintenance and use of the 3" guns," stated Cpl. Joseph G. "Jodie" Jones
of Battery B. "We also spent lots of time in convoy just learning
how to drive down a highway. We also drove in blackout on the

desert. . . . It was rumored that we used a year's allotment of gasoline in six months." He added, "I doubt that it was all rumor."[5]

The 206th had a special relationship with the 200th National Guard regiment from New Mexico. The 200th had trained for years as a cavalry unit, but upon mobilization had been designated Coast Artillery (AA). "Thereafter, one mission assigned to the 206th CA (AA) was to provide training cadre to instruct the men of the 200th on the operation and maintenance of the various types of equipment."[6]

Cold and windy February gave way to cold and windy March when, in Massey's words, "Training began to pick up. Classes every day."[7] March brought another chore—the absorption and training of four hundred draftees being sent to the 206th. These men were as green as unripe apples and would need indoctrination in every imaginable aspect of military life, including identification of insignia, as testified by a little incident that occurred while the men were en route to Fort Bliss. Guards were posted at the doors of all the cars in the troop train. One private, on duty during breakfast hour, feared he might miss the meal and looked around for a likely temporary relief guard. Sure enough, here came a young man in uniform. The gold oak leaves on his shoulders conveyed nothing to the private, who stopped him hopefully. "Hey, buddy," he said, "they are eating breakfast back yonder; how about standing here till I get back?"

The major, a medical officer, understood the inductee's total ignorance of the trappings of rank, and he obligingly stood guard for twenty minutes while the private ate his breakfast. On 11 March the draftees reached Fort Bliss, where the 206th Band welcomed them.[8]

In a less hospitable mood were some of the veterans who would have the job of turning the newcomers into soldiers. "We got in our draftees Saturday night. We started training them this morning," Corporal Alspaugh informed his family. "They are sure a dumb lot. Most of them are farmers." Most seemed young, "but some of them are old . . ." Coming from Alspaugh, just twenty years old at the time, that adjective should be taken with a shaker of salt. He had a further tale of woe on 22 March: "The selectees are really dumb and green. We have one that doesn't know right from left. Some of them can't read or write or tie a tie. . . ."

A month later Alspaugh was thoroughly fed up. He had been selected to train "the slow group," and they were a sore trial to him:

". . . I sure get tired of telling them things over and over. The men in the slow group are sure dumb. Most of them quit school in the 3rd or 4th grade and you have to use very simple language in instructing them. Most of them are also 29 to 35 in age and just can't seem to learn. . . ."[9]

Corporal Jones, however, could sympathize with these green-horns, who were coping not only with a whole new way of life but with the relentless wind-sand-sun combination of Texas weather. "The wind was strong enough to blow sand. This sand would charge the screens on our tents and trucks with enough electricity to give a strong shock when touched. I remember feeling sorry for our draftees that were going through basic training. Some of their faces were sun- and wind-burned beyond belief." He added indignantly, "A drill sergeant today would be court martialed for such treatment."[10]

However, either the inductees were smarter than Alspaugh gave them credit for, or else they received superior indoctrination, for training continued apace, and "the 206th rapidly rose in its efficiency ratings," and its members were firmly loyal to one another.[11] In mid-March the unit went to New Mexico and set up its guns. "It sure was desolate-looking over there," Alspaugh told his family. ". . . We have also been drilling on our guns at night with the searchlight."[12]

Over the ensuing months much of this activity took place in New Mexico, at the firing range near White Sands. "Training rigorous now, constantly on bivouac in the sandy desert," Massey noted in April. He had been on emergency leave, during which he was promoted to sergeant. "I would draw sixty-four dollars a month, more money than I dreamed of making."

Occasionally the outside world intruded into their self-absorbed scene. Massey requested transfer to the army's air arm, but "they won't take a married man for pilot training."[13]

"There are many planes landing here en route to England. Most of them have the R.A.F. insignia on them," wrote Alspaugh on 30 March. "They are all camouflaged. About 24 landed here at different times this week." He added a homesick P.S.: "Sure would like to see some green grass and trees."[14]

These were in short supply at their desert location where the 206th practice firing at towed targets. "On bright, sunny days—and there [were] lots of these kinds of days—an airplane would pull a long red sleeve and our 3" guns, after tracking the sleeve with the 'Height Finder,' would shoot the sleeve as it fluttered across the sky. Thank goodness," Ballew added, "we never hit a plane."[15]

At least one Battery—D—never had the opportunity to hit either the aircraft or its sleeve. John W. Weese, who had just been promoted to First Sergeant of Battery D, remembered the "bivouacs in the desert where our 3" guns and allied equipment would be dug in, set up, and moved 2 or 3 times in a 24-hour period." He related, "We were finally sent to the 3" firing range to fire on towed targets. Other regiments were also on the range and scheduled to fire before the 206th. The day we were to start our firing runs, orders were received to cease all firing to conserve ammunition. As a result, we wound up in the Aleutians firing at Jap planes without having ever fired our 3" guns at a moving target."[16]

1st Sgt. Donnel J. Drake of Battery A, an individual blessed with almost total recall, recollected, "The battery personnel continued training on the searchlight/sound locater equipment, battery/regimental close order drill/parades, desert training involving combat situations between opposing forces in the field involving U. S. Cavalry units." On one such occasion in late March, the AA "had established a certain light position some thirty miles in the desert north of Fort Bliss." About 0200, they were alerted "that a cavalry unit was advancing up an arroyo near the searchlight position." Nine of the searchlight men ambushed the cavalry. After the umpire determined what firepower had been involved—"eight rifles, a BAR and a pistol"—he ruled that the cavalry had lost ten men.

To the men of A Battery the ten cut-outs looked like "ten ghosts riding ten white horses"—they "were covered with dust, having been in the saddle all day and night." Both men and mounts were hungry and thirsty. Fortunately the cavalrymen had a supply of oats with them, and their erstwhile "enemies" gave them water. The searchlight men had no human food to offer beyond candy bars, but arranged that the field kitchen give the troopers breakfast. When the chow truck arrived, the "dead" men did full justice to "a hot meal consisting of biscuits and SOS*, fresh fruits, coffee and sausage."[17]

---

* GIese for creamed chipped beef on toast. This can be a delicious dish, but somehow most military cooks never got the hang of it. Don't ask us to spell out the initials!

In a dispatch to the Camden *News*, undated but from the context written in April, Sgt. G. E. Scott advised that the 206th had one of the best ratings at the center, which "partly can be accounted for because of the high type of enlisted personnel. Most of the men were either attending college, college graduates, or have at least a high school education."[18] A high school education was by no means a "given" in those days.

Not all of their experiences during training were pleasant. Corporal Kinney never forgot a humiliating, indeed bizarre, incident when he pulled honor guard duty one evening. He and soldiers from several batteries stood at attention for an inspection by the battalion commander. This officer moved down the line, pausing briefly to ask a question of each man. Reaching Kinney, he inquired, "What is our national anthem?"

"*The Star-Spangled Banner,* sir," replied the corporal.

"Sing it!" commanded the officer.

The inane question had surprised Kinney; this ridiculous order nearly floored him. He proved himself a true American by stammering, "Sir, I don't know all the words."

That didn't get him off the hook. "Then hum the national anthem where you don't know the words," pursued the officer relentlessly.

Wrote Kinney years later, "Well, being nineteen years old, scared stiff, this being my first time on Honor Guard, I somehow was able to get through the national anthem, but my voice and legs were sure trembling."

The officer moved on to the next victim, leaving behind him a young man shorn of all respect for his battalion commander, and with a psychological trauma that never quite left him. To what purpose? "I . . . still can't see any military training in it," Kinney observed with commendable moderation.[19]

April was a particularly active month. On the eighth, the 206th participated in a bang-up celebration of Army Day. Maneuvers were conducted to "protect" El Paso and Juarez, Mexico, with both U.S. and Mexican troops participating. In the afternoon Fort Bliss held a big parade. The celebration climaxed that night with the entire metropolitan El Paso area blacked out at 2130.[20]

Easter fell on 13 April. About seven thousand men, including Alspaugh, attended "a beautiful Sunrise Easter Service . . . at the base of the mountains." That day Alspaugh wrote to his mother with obvious pride, "This regiment was commended by Maj. General Swift, commanding officer of this post, for its cleanliness and initiative in cleaning up the camp. He said it was the most clean and homelike camp that he had ever seen."[21]

On 26 April "the regiment minus the necessary troops for security at camp" went to Carlsbad Caverns. This trip was partly for training and partly for pleasure. That night the men "put on a demonstration for the people," and the next day they visited the awesome caves. "At the time we were going through the caverns," recalled Cpl. Earl P. Hargrave of Battery F, "we were told that all the people in the group were from Arkansas, including the park superintendent who was with us."[22] Sergeant Gill remembered that the entire regiment pitched some nine hundred pup tents on the local football field. "Rained all night—sleeping in those pup tents did not prove to be a great amount of protection from the elements."[23]

April brought its unpleasant incidents. "We had a real 'duster' last Friday," Alspaugh informed his family on April 23. "The wind blew 50 miles an hour. You couldn't see over 10 feet in front of you part of the time. It blew down our $10,000 tent theater and tore it to bits."

This was a real annoyance, because attending the movies was a favorite form of recreation, but the problem was minor compared to the explosive occurrence early in the month. On 8 April, after describing the Army Day festivities, Alspaugh added in his letter home, "Some boys from Camden got in a fight down in Juarez with the police. Three of the boys were shot and one was hurt pretty badly. Now nobody from this regiment can go down to Mexico. We are guarding the bridge to keep the soldiers from the regiment out of Mexico."[24] The men involved in the incident were Harry McGuire, J. C. Boyd, and Bob Hudson, all from Battery E.[25] Juarez occupied a special place in the 206th consciousness. Few if any of the men really liked the place. "Juarez is just a tourist town," Alspaugh described it to his folks on 10 February. "Everybody is trying to sell you something. . . . Juarez is a very dirty-looking city. People who are not selling trinkets are just sitting around sleeping."[26] Jodie Jones was considerably more trenchant: "They should have tested the atomic bomb on Juarez."[27]

Nevertheless, most of the men went there—it was something different to do. A number attended bullfights, others patronized cabarets, still others bought souvenirs of a foreign culture. One veteran acknowledged that probably the main attraction of Juarez was a "well-managed, clean" brothel "legally operating in the city." Before leaving the premises, a patron had to undergo a prophylactic treatment under the watchful eye of "a very large, buxom Mexican woman."[28]

Plenty of on-base recreation was available—the movies, as mentioned, in the big tent theater, games and all sorts of sports, of which softball was probably the favorite. "Some of the flatlanders from Arkansas decided they would go mountain climbing at Franklin Mountain Range just about our camp," Sergeant Gill remembered. "One of them fell into a ravine and broke a limb. The medics and the AA searchlight spent most of one night getting him out."[29] Kinney, who had been a boxing coach at Arkansas Tech College, started a 206th boxing team.[30]

Some preferred less strenuous off-duty activities. 1st Sgt. Robert D. "Snuff" Garret of Battery B was a member of a quintet that sang at churches, supper clubs, the local Junior League Follies, and similar functions.[31] T. Sgt. W. L. "Mac" McKinistry of the band played the clarinet and saxophone "for troops and post functions."[32]

Lack of cash seriously limited available entertainment in El Paso. A private's pay of twenty-one dollars a month, out of which one paid for laundry, dry cleaning, such essentials as shaving equipment and other toilet necessities, left very little money to toss around. Two enterprising men in D Battery "borrowed money from home and bought cars. They used these as taxis to carry men to and from El Paso," wrote Weese. ". . . Some even made extra money playing softball for teams in town. . . . The First Sergeant of Headquarters Company ran a 'bank' and would lend money on recommendation from other First Sergeants to anyone in the regiment. . . ." at 10 percent interest until payday.[33]

Inevitably, individual experiences of El Paso's hospitality varied. "Soldiers were not welcome in the better parts of civilian life," declared Pfc Lawrence R. Henderson of Battery F. "We were compared to the regular army at Ft. Bliss, which had a bad reputation, and the men of 206th were usually rejected."[34]

On the other hand, M. Sgt. James W. Keeton of Battery D, who spent much of his off-duty time with a great-uncle living in El Paso, remembered that after a write-up in *Life* magazine "several of us were invited to church functions, private homes, and by girls attending the college at El Paso."[35] All in all, the men of the 206th must have made a favorable impression, judging from a letter one El Paso woman wrote later in the year to the Camden *News*: ". . . Having had the happy privilege of knowing the '206' boys I want to say in passing, 'I thank God daily for the Arkansas parents whose sons radiate the God-fearing homes they come from and for the genuine fine type of manhood as manifested in that regiment. I wish it were possible to shake your hands and tell you how we here in El Paso came to appreciate their good morals and clean living as compared with much army life we see today.'"[36]

3

"Who Knows Our Destiny . . . ?"

For three months, beginning in April, First Sergeant Drake was out of direct touch with his battery, having been selected to attend "the Regimental Radio School that had been established to train personnel in the use of field radio stations." Courses included "Morse code, radio maintenance, setting up radio stations in the field and practical use of the radio during field exercises. Another function the radio section performed was establishing radio contact with the aircraft towing targets for 50 cal. and 75 mm firing at various firing ranges located in the desert north of Fort Bliss."[1]

About this time, Sgt. James W. Burke, one of the 206th's "head mechanics," transferred on temporary duty to San Antonio to attend "a mechanic school for trucks and tanks." There he experienced the first incident of the bad luck that would plague him during the next few years: "I stepped on some wet steps and cracked some ribs. I spent my time there with my ribs wrapped."[2]

It was probably during Drake's absence that his Battery A won the prize in an "area beautification contest" covering both the mess hall and the area around the tents.[3] Battery C worked hard on their site but had bad luck. "A relatively small rain . . . washed through the battery area, ruining all of the beautification efforts we had put out fixing things up," 1st Sgt. Bill E. Jones remembered ruefully.[4]

Early in May, Alspaugh was relieved of his duty with the "slow group" of trainees and thankfully returned to his battery. On 22 May he informed his family that he and his buddies had finished small arms training and a boxing tournament was under way. He had sad news to report on 1 June. No fewer than four soldiers—one of them from the 206th—had been killed, not, as might have been expected, on the firing range or in some other strenuous activity, but on the road. "We have had several automobile accidents down here in the last 24 hours," he wrote his family somberly. "2 men were killed yesterday morning bringing the payroll out. The car turned over and crushed one of the soldiers against a brick wall. A boy from this regiment was killed in Pecos, Texas, in a car wreck yesterday. Another soldier was killed in a car wreck about 2 miles from here last night."[5]

This was a bittersweet period for Sergeant Massey. His father had passed away on 7 May, but in June he brought his wife to El Paso where they found a small apartment and "began to enjoy life a little." They attended a bullfight in Juarez; however, Mrs. Massey took no pleasure in seeing the animal killed. Massey was professionally occupied with the continuing training—"very hot in the desert but beautiful."[6]

These exercises were intensive. "It wouldn't be any use to send me any magazines, because I wouldn't have any time to read them in the next 2 weeks," Alspaugh informed his mother. "We get up at 5:00 and are on the range ready to fire at 7:00 A.M. We stay on the range until 5:00 or 6:00 in the evening and by the time we eat supper it is too dark to read and we are usually pretty tired."[7]

Parker had his furlough papers and was counting the days until he could catch a bus for Texarkana for his wedding to Vola who, as planned, had resigned her commission. Then something happened—"a big fight in Juarez" as Parker recalled—involving several men of the 206th. "All leaves were cancelled," he wrote, "and I thought my world had come to an end."

He took his problem to his lieutenant, Mort Cox, who could do nothing about it but buck Parker upstairs to the 2d Battalion commander, Lt. Col. Eugene Hampton, whom Parker knew slightly.

After they had exchanged salutes and greetings, Parker burst out, "Colonel Hampton, I need a favor!"

"Why should I grant you a favor?" countered the colonel disconcertingly. Parker had his answer ready. "When you were a major in Pensacola during the summer of 1937, at Guard Camp, I was a guidon carrier for Battery H. We were about to pass in review at the parade grounds and I whispered to you that you were out of step."

Some officers might not care to be reminded of such an incident, but Parker had not mistaken his man. "I remember you and thank you," he said. "Now what is it you need?" Parker explained the situation, and the colonel promised to get him to the church on time. The solution was a three-day pass plus a weekend pass, end to end. "We made it in time—me and the bus driver," Parker wrote triumphantly. The Flag Day marriage was duly celebrated and almost fifty years later was still going strong.[8]

"There has been a lot of rumors going around camp since we came in," Alspaugh informed his family on 18 June. "The regiment is supposed to meet tomorrow night for something and no one seems to know for sure what's in the air. There have been rumors going around all year that we are going to Bermuda, Hawaii, S. Carolina, Alaska, California, Panama, the Philippines etc., but I never did believe any of them. Everything around here is getting stricter. . . . " The meeting of Alspaugh's battalion brought no elucidation. Instead, "the colonel complimented us on our training so far," Alspaugh wrote on 22 June. "We have had only 24 arrests so far this year in the whole regiment. I think that is a pretty good record inasmuch as there are 1700 men in the regiment. 18 of the arrests were attributed to drinking and the others to AWOL and disorderly conduct."[9]

One of the key dates of modern times was 22 June 1941. Hitler invaded the Soviet Union, altering the entire course of World War II. Did the colonel so much as touch on that subject in his talk with his men that evening? If he did, Alspaugh did not think it worth mentioning. Of more immediate concern to the men at Fort Bliss was the tragedy that struck the 206th two days later. Twenty-one-year-old Perley Mitchell of Cullendale, Arkansas, assigned to Battery E, was accidentally shot and killed at 1614 on 24 June "by one of his pals." This happened during a routine change of guard. "He had been on guard duty during the day and had just gone off duty when the rifle of another member was accidentally discharged."[10]

But life went on. "A milestone indeed" was reached on 29 June when the second batch of selectees—fifty-eight in all—joined the 206th. These new men included "the first Yankee blood" in Battery A, whose historian added, "Many a Yankee recruit has since paid homage to General Robert E. Lee by standing at rigid attention while the southern lads present chirp the refrains of 'Dixie.' Such idiotic horseplay has done much to promote an 'Esprit de corps. . . .' "[11]

Heretofore the men of the 206th had been accustomed to thinking of their regiment as strictly an organization for Arkansans. Over the ensuing months and years more and more new blood would trickle in, until men of many states wore the 206th insignia, and the regiment was no longer exclusively composed of "razorbacks."

At 1800 on 2 July Battery A left Fort Bliss to participate in overnight maneuvers at Camp Beasley, New Mexico. They were in place by 2100.[12] Later in the month the 1st Cavalry Division held large-scale maneuvers. The cavalry was split into two teams, Blue and Red, with five Coast Artillery (AA) units supporting each side. Pfc Edward B. Fitzhugh of Headquarters Battery had a very clear recollection of the aftermath:

> On July 28 Gen. Walter Kruger critiqued the maneuvers to the commanders and their staffs, making the statement that the Regular Army should not be proud of itself by letting the N[ational] G[uard] outshine them. He praised no units, but did give the 206th an honorable mention. My thought was that through his report the next day to the War Department of the result of the maneuver caused the 206th to be selected for the Aleutian assignment.[13]

But the decision had already been made before Kruger's report could have reached Washington. On 28 July orders came in "for overseas duty in some out-of-the-way place in Alaska that few have ever heard of—Dutch Harbor, Unalaska."[14] What is more, the destination had been chosen in a thoroughly illogical manner. For some time, a rumor had been circulating "that there would be a coin toss as to whom would be going where."[15] And that is precisely what happened. Colonel Robertson flipped a coin with the commander of the 200th CA (AA) to determine which unit would go to the Philippines, which to the Aleutians.[16]

Not everyone could believe that this event had taken place. An intelligence officer at Regimental Headquarters, 1st Lt. John T. Meek of Battery E, recalled that their commander informed his staff that the 206th would go to Dutch Harbor and the 200th to the Philippines. He commented that originally the destinations had been the reverse, but "that someone higher up had changed the assignment" for two reasons: 1) the men of the 200th were more accustomed to a hot climate than were the Arkansans and 2) many in the 200th spoke Spanish.

Meek could not conceive that "orders of this magnitude would be left to regimental decision." Moreover, the colonel had made no mention of a coin toss, which the S-2 was sure he would have done had such taken place.[17] This is not necessarily so. The colonel may well have thought it best not to advertise the fact that major troop movements were being arranged in such a cavalier fashion. If so, he was hopelessly optimistic and should have known such a story could not be kept from the men. Almost before the coin dropped, the tale was spreading through camp. The only surprising thing about this story is that so many didn't get the word. Among many of the men, two rationales circulated. "One theory was that an AA regiment was required in Alaska on an expedited basis and that the 206th was the most advanced in their training," Corporal Hargrave wrote. "The other theory was that the 200th was sent to the Philippines because many of them could speak Spanish."[18]

Reactions upon learning of their destination fell roughly into three schools of thought—the disappointed, the pleased, and the indifferent. In the first category was S. Sgt. Charles "Spud" Clark of Battery C, who had "wanted to see the tropics."[19] Cpl. Luster V. Tate of Battery A had never heard of Dutch Harbor and had hoped to go to the Philippines.[20] S. Sgt. Robert M. Proffitt of Battery E "thought this was the worst thing that could happen in a lifetime."[21] A little apprehension mixed with the displeasure. "At the time I understood it was thought that the Japanese were planning to invade the US by way of the Aleutians," Corporal Kinney reminisced. "We all thought probably we were headed for a 'hotbed' and I was leery."[22]

In general, the men of Battery D were somewhat disgruntled because the weather in the Philippines was better than in Alaska. And cynicism raised its head. Some suggested that Colonel Robertson chose the Aleutians "because it would be easier for him to check on his bank in Helena . . . ," remarked Pfc James L. Pack of Battery D.[23]

In anticipation that the 206th would be moving out, Sergeant Massey had arranged for his wife to stay with her sister, then with her uncle in Isola, Mississippi. "We lost the toss, our hearts were heavy with disappointment, but who knows our destiny except the Divine Master?" he wrote in his notes for August 1941.[24]

A small group was pleased, but none of them gave any reason

for preferring Alaska to the Philippines. "I was glad," wrote Col. (then Capt.) Minot B. Dodson laconically. Dodson had been with the 206th since 1933 and was attached to Battery C.[25] Another who was "glad to go to the Aleutians" was 1st Sgt. Oscar H. Jones of Headquarters Battery.[26]

Some did not care particularly one way or another. "At the time it didn't seem to matter much, since we had been inducted for 'only a year,'" according to First Sergeant Weese.[27] Another first sergeant, Bill Jones, echoed this sentiment: "As I remember, no one was all that disappointed at being sent to Alaska because we were still thinking of a year at that time."[28]

Sergeant Parker probably expressed the feelings of many when he wrote, ". . . we figured—what the heck!—wherever they sent us we'll be out in four months. That's when our year's service would be up. . . ."[29] As for First Sergeant Garrett, he "felt like the 206th could handle any situation" in which it might find itself.[30]

Although the education level of most of these men was unusually high, a number had only the sketchiest idea of their destination's location. "Some of [us] had to do a little research to find out where the Aleutians were," recalled T. 4 Joe B. Sisk of Battery C.[31] Drake's first reaction "after learning of being sent to Dutch Harbor was to visit the library and look up the location."[32]

With the advantage of hindsight, it is tempting to chastise the two regimental commanders for determining the immediate fate of their officers and men in such a frivolous, irresponsible manner. As Lieutenant Meek had suggested, such a decision should have been made at a level higher than the regimental level. Furthermore, that higher echelon should have taken many factors into consideration, such as the amount and condition of assigned weaponry, the troops' state of training, the efficiency and leadership qualities of the officers and top NCOs, the needs of the command to which the regiment would be assigned, available housing, and a host of other tactical and logistical considerations.

To understand if not necessarily to exculpate Robertson and his colleague, one must realize that neither one had any idea that the choice of destination involved real danger. Lacking the gift of prophecy, they could not foresee that, as a result of their friendly coin toss, the 200th CA (AA) would suffer horribly and be decimated in the Philippines, while the 206th would emerge from the

Aleutians almost unscathed. To the two officers, the choice was not between life and death, but between two overseas stations, one of which admittedly was considerably more desirable than the other.

Nor were these men too stupid to interpret the signs of the times. They had lots of company in their attitude. Able to read the signposts on the road to Pearl Harbor in the light of Clio's lamp, a member of the postwar generations may well find incomprehensible the attitude of complacency verging on coma prevailing in the United States in regard to the conflict. Few indeed genuinely believed that territory under the Stars and Stripes could truly be in peril of attack. Even committed interventionists, who believed that the United States eventually must join the war if freedom was to survive on earth, held the opinion that such entrance would be on American initiative.

As a visible token of how widespread and at what level this myopia existed, within a month of the coin-toss, the U. S. House of Representatives came within one vote of scuttling the draft. Extension of the act passed with 203 yeas, 202 nays, and 27 not voting.[33]

Overwhelmingly, attention was focused on the war raging in Europe rather than on Japan's drive to conquest in the Pacific. Many Americans took a dim view of Japanese capabilities, and they could not conceive that the small island nation would dare challenge the mighty United States, even though the Philippines, then under the American flag, lay right in Japan's path.

In a choice between the Philippines and the Aleutians at this juncture of the war, the former won hands down. The Philippines' climate, although tropical, was bearable; the climate of the Alaskan islands was unfit for human beings. U. S. posts in the Philippines, especially on Luzon, were long established and considered desirable assignments for the officer or soldier when his inevitable overseas tour rolled around. As for Alaska, even the mainland, as late as 1939 its home defense was in the hands of some three hundred infantrymen at Chilkoot barracks, "plus one antique cannon left by the Russians and now used as a flower-pot!" Work had been under way on various army and navy bases,[34] but no one could expect anything like the facilities available on Luzon. No wonder so many men of the 206th set about preparations for their move with a noticeable lack of enthusiasm.

4

"A Sometimes Difficult Situation"

The men of the 206th did not have long to brood over their circumstances. As could be expected, survivors had mixed recollections of their date of departure from Fort Bliss, ranging from 1 July to September. The actual departure date was 1 August.[1] Before that, however, a certain amount of upheaval took place. For some reason, Robertson "felt that being National Guard units, the 1st Sgts were too 'familiar' with the enlisted men in their batteries," Weese wrote. "So he played musical chairs with all the first sergeants, and I was moved from Russellville and Ark Tech to B Bty from Monticello."[2]

It is possible that these rearrangements were an effort to break up cliques. Pfc James Earl Wilson of Battery H stated that "in pre-mobilization days and during the Ft. Bliss period there was little or no fraternization between the batteries of the 206th." And even within the batteries there were rather clear-cut divisions, which Wilson described in relation to Battery H as follows: "The NCO's belonged to 'the old hands' faction and were, for the most part, persons who were married and family providers. . . . Then there was the high-school-drop-out group known as 'pool-hall sweats.' This group formed the more rowdy and brawling element. There was the high-school student group which formed the more civilized element."[3]

The troops were paid on Thursday 31 July. In an act of faith, Robertson told them that they would be pulling out the next morning, but there would be no restriction on leave. So many of the men went into El Paso for their customary payday night winging. The morning of 1 August justified Robertson's belief in his troops, for "of the 1,700 men and officers not one was missing. Not one."[4] How much of this perfect attendance record was due to character and discipline and how much was due to a burning desire to get out of Fort Bliss is an open question.

The 39th Brigade, the 63d, 202d, 260th, and 206th regiments moved to Washington state to provide AA protection for the defense industries in the Seattle area against a possible Japanese invasion of the West Coast.[5]

The entire 206th traveled as a unit in a troop train some forty cars long, their heavy equipment was loaded on flat cars.[6] One of the first stops was at Albuquerque, where the men "got off the train in 100 plus heat to march with our wool overseas caps and with ties on to 'get some exercise,'" Ballew remembered. "You talk about a bunch of soldiers bitchin'!" he added.[7] Alspaugh wrote to his mother on 2 August as the train clicked off the miles between Tucson and Yuma. "This movement was supposed to have been a secret but it was far from that," he informed her, and added a bit of scuttlebutt: "The colonel is going to get reprimanded by the commanding officer of the 4th Army when he gets to San Francisco."

One wonders how a forty-car train, complete with field pieces on flatbeds, could possibly be kept a secret in an open society. Perhaps Alspaugh meant that their destination rather than their movement should have been concealed, for he continued his letter: "I think we will be stationed on the Aleutian Islands off the coast of Alaska. It will take us 6 days on boat from Tacoma. We will be in Washington for about a month."[8]

A halt at Yuma proved noteworthy for Battery B. "It was about 110 degrees in the shade and most everyone was outside of the cars trying to stay cool," Pfc Sheldon L. Radney described the scene. "A little black and white bulldog came waltzing by and one of our guys picked him up and brought him along all the way to Alaska. That little dog was our mascot and never stopped shivering and was always near a stove."[9]

Bill Jones remembered the contrast in the weather in Arizona— "118 degrees in the shade in Yuma . . . and extremely cold when we crossed the mountain at Flagstaff . . . "[10]

Massey's principal memories were of the Royal Gorge—"a beautiful sight"—and of the Utah salt flats.[11]

There can be no doubt that Alspaugh thoroughly enjoyed the trip. On 4 August he wrote his brother a long, enthusiastic description of the scenery through which the train was passing.

"We left Sacramento at 5:00 this morning and we are still in California. . . . The mountains are covered with trees and other growth. These trees sure did look [good] to me as they are the first real forests I have seen since coming West."[12]

Burke had recovered sufficiently from his accident in San Antonio to make the trip, but he felt isolated. "All my army clothes were packed and I had to ride the train to Tacoma, Washington. I didn't have any shaving gear or anything. The trip took 4 or 5 days. We stopped at Bonneville Dam on the Columbia River and since I had only civilian clothes, I wasn't allowed off the train."[13]

At 2130 on 11 August, the train arrived at Camp Murray, not far from Fort Lewis, both of which are near Tacoma, Washington. "The next few days was spent in unloading the equipment from the train and reloading it aboard the transport."[14]

Alspaugh was charmed with their situation. Washington, he decided, was a beautiful state. He and his buddies were living in tents that the Washington National Guard had used for years, in a forest "with a clear cold lake." He mentioned that the 153d was stationed about a mile and a half from the 206th. He continued regretfully, "We probably won't be here for more than 4 or 5 days. We will then go to Seattle by motor convoy and leave from there. They probably will break up the 206 and we want to be at the same station."[15]

The 153d of which Alspaugh wrote was another Arkansas National Guard Regiment, the 153d Infantry. In its current form, it had been designated by that title on 25 October 1921. In many respects its history had paralleled that of the 206th and would continue to do so.[16]

Alspaugh had been correct—the 206th was split up prior to shipment; indeed, various batteries were divided. Twenty-eight men of Battery H would go to Dutch Harbor, while the main body of the battery would go to Fairbanks on the Alaska mainland to protect Ladd Field. A few would remain at Camp Murray and Fort Lewis for further assignment.

Several sets of brothers were serving in Battery H, and the question arose of how to assign them—together or apart. "We credit Sgt. Lloyd Harp for insisting that brothers stay together," Parker wrote. "So it was agreed that they could stay together if they so chose. My brother, James Parker, went with me along with brothers Bill and Everett Carnes, Hugh and Lamar Grant, Bill and

David Ridgeway. Sam Black went to Dutch Harbor, while his brother, Tom, went to Fairbanks."[17]

"I guess this will be my last day here in the states," Alspaugh informed his mother on 11 August. "We are supposed to leave tomorrow for outpost duty. I believe we will be stationed on an island near Dutch Harbor." He added that Captain Dodson, who had been attending a service school, had returned to duty. "It just tickled us all to get him back."[18]

Meanwhile, bad luck had not yet finished with Burke. One morning, on his way to "the shop," a captain stopped him and asked that Burke drive him to Fort Lewis. "It was urgent, he told me, and we didn't have time to get a 'trip ticket.'" On the way back, they had a wreck. "I ended up with a broken leg, broken arm, broken ribs, and facial lacerations. We had important papers for the 206th, orders for Alaska. I spent 3 months in the hospital recuperating."[19]

The troop carrier *St. Mihiel* began taking the men aboard at 0800 on 11 August, but the ship didn't cast off until 1815. The troops spent the intervening time "in securing everything for the voyage ahead."[20]

Not all the regiment sailed aboard the *St. Mihiel*. Some 500 remained at Fort Lewis. "The rumors were that there was not enough room for all, so Battery D and Battery G and headquarters were among the 500 who stayed behind."[21]

For the overwhelming majority, this was their first trip on a seagoing ship. A few had been on river boats, but probably S. Sgt. Louis Taylor of Battery E spoke for most: "It was my first time to sail on a ship. In fact, it was the first ship I had ever seen, other than [in] the movies."[22]

The *St. Mihiel* did not provide the ideal initiation into the delights of an ocean voyage. The *Queen Mary* she wasn't. She had been a German ship, dating from the turn of the century, and after World War I the United States had taken her over as a part of Germany's war reparations. Most of the men retained distinctly negative memories of the *St. Mihiel*, which Drake summarized as follows:

(1) The ship had just returned from hauling cattle from Australia and the whole ship smelled of a barnyard; (2) workmen were still on the lower decks constructing bunks; (3) all living quarters below

decks were very cramped with 4-5-tiered bunks with little space for walkways; (4) barracks bags were stored under and around the stairwells as no room was available to have the bags near your bunk; (5) the air below decks was generally foul except directly under the air intake. . . .

Because of the conditions below decks, many men slept on deck whenever possible.[23]

Jodie Jones had a more explicit recollection, which he declared was still "one of the more unpleasant memories" of World War II. He agreed with Drake—and many others—that the ship was cramped and uncomfortable:

> There was no place to stay below decks and the crew was constantly hosing down the deck. The sanitary facilities were atrocious. There was a trough on each side of the latrine . . . and salt water was constantly running through it. . . . Imagine having a weak stomach from the motion of the boat and having to use the lower end of the trough with twenty other men using the trough above you. . . .[24]

"Well, it sure was no cruise ship," admitted Staff Sergeant Taylor. "When we went to eat we stood at tables with trays and when the ship would roll the trays would slide along with the roll, and really you didn't know whose tray you were eating from." He added, "It didn't make any difference because they all had the same thing on them, unless someone threw up on the table. . . ."[25]

Some, while conceding that the living was uncomfortable, took it in stride. ". . . I had anticipated close quarters as being one of the things that just had to be and made the best of it," reflected T. 4 Joe Sisk. "It wasn't an unbearable situation."[26]

Accommodations for top NCOs were somewhat better. "The ship was rather crowded," remembered Staff Sergeant Garrett, "but those of us (first three-graders) who had staterooms under the poop deck with 3 or 4 to a stateroom were rather comfortable. We had plenty of food and sandwiches were available at all times."[27]

If one took the Battery K history at face value, the trip was a breeze. According to that document, the men amused themselves, "besides the routine G.I. chores," by attending movies on the afterdeck, by skeet shooting, or by "just promenading about the ship enjoying the popular recordings being played over the ship's public address system. . . . Calm seas prevailed throughout the whole trip."[28] Drake stated that "the crossing was rather calm with sunny weather most of the time." But they did experience "rain squalls and sometimes rather heavy seas."[29]

It may have been a fairly smooth trip, as voyages in the north Pacific go, but it would have been difficult to convince those of the Arkansas landlubbers who were honest enough to admit they were seasick. According to Sgt. Harry K. Dougherty of Battery A, "Many people were seasick before we even got out of Puget Sound."[30]

T. 5 Lawrence G. Eheman of Battery F took little part in on-board socializing. The poker stakes were too high for him, and in any case he was too ill to do anything.[31] Asked about his pastimes, Pfc Wayne L. Lindley of Battery C replied laconically, "Throwing up."[32]

"I remember that we had to pass the garbage discharge just before going into the mess hall, and the smell didn't do anything to help those who were either seasick or had queasy stomachs," reflected Bill Jones. He added, "I remember a fellow by the name of Hubbard that I found standing by the rail looking terrible. I asked him what the trouble was and he said that he was seasick, lovesick and homesick."[33]

Cpl. Thomas P. O'Neal of Battery A made no bones about his condition. The five-day trip "seemed like a month" to him. "I thought I was going to die from seasickness . . . I believe if I had remained at sea another week I would have been buried at sea."[34]

Throughout the short voyage, many of the men pulled the same types of duties they would have been assigned if ashore—guard, cleaning details, KP, and CQ. Cpl. Thomas Quimby was the clerk of Battery E and maintained records as well as typing orders and correspondence.[35] Proffitt and Sisk helped out in the ship's bakery.[36]

None of these chores were onerous. In fact, Ballew listed his duties as "to eat three times a day."[37] So the men had plenty of time to indulge in such recreation as the ship offered. Skeet shooting was popular, and the ship held a contest with a fifty-dollar war bond as first prize, a twenty-five-dollar bond for second.[38] At night movies were shown on deck, and always drew a good audience. Others had less-conventional fun. T. Sgt. George B. Faulhaber of the Medical Battery occasionally would make his way down into the hold "where beer was stowed as freight, and liberate a few cases."[39] Some, like Corporal Hargrave, liked to watch the whales and porpoises.[40]

"Poker/dice games were always in progress, day and night," Drake reported. "Although it was illegal to gamble, the officers turned a deaf ear to the actions since it appeared to help morale in a sometimes difficult situation." He got into an occasional crap game, but wasn't well versed in card play, so preferred to watch the others.[41] In the main, stakes were low, anything over twenty-five cents being the exception.[42] Sgt. William S. Newton of Battery F had the heady experience of drawing "five aces in a five-cent limit game."[43]

"After the ship had been at sea for a couple of days, and the ship completely aired out, probably the most popular pastime when not on duty was 'sack time,'" Drake stated. The men kept more or less in touch with doings aboard the *St. Mihiel* and in the outside world by means of the daily newspaper the radio crew printed. This included "miles traveled, weather reports, items copied from radio news broadcasts, newsworthy items submitted by members of the Regiment and other items that would be of interest."[44]

While the *St. Mihiel* plowed its way to Dutch Harbor, the men of the 206th left behind in Washington state settled down to what on the whole was a pleasant period in their military service. They lived in tents until December. The only noteworthy military event that Pfc 5 Paul D. Beasley of Battery H recalled was the receipt of a 268 radar unit to replace their searchlight.[45]

According to Pfc Pack, these months were "fun, for there were so many things to do." Initially, their pride and joy was the regimental softball team. This had been organized at Fort Bliss, where it had qualified for the El Paso city tournament. However, the tournament began on 28 July, and with shipping out scheduled for 1 August, the 206th team had to bow out.

The unit put together another softball team and entered a tournament held in Seattle, where the teams were to be composed of military and naval personnel. The 206th entered the finals to face a group that had won forty-eight out of fifty games during the regular season. To the delight of the Arkansas men, their team came out on top.[46]

When the softball was season over, the 206th organized a football team, the Arkansas Travelers. Most of its members had been athletes at Arkansas Tech. Under their coach, Capt. H. F. Winters, the Travelers routed all comers. The *Arkansas Gazette* reported proudly that the 206th team amassed 279 points, allowing only one touchdown to be scored against them. Plans were made for the Travelers to meet the Moffett Field Flyers from California, the only other undefeated team on the Pacific Coast, for the championship of the National Military League. No other teams in the entire country could match the records of the Travelers and the Flyers. This battle of the giants was scheduled for mid-December,[47] and no doubt the sports-minded members of the 206th's Washington contingent looked forward to the contest as the most exciting event of that month.

As mentioned, a further splintering occurred, which James Wilson described: "On August 6th, 1941, while at Camp Murray, Washington, about 30 Battery 'H' personnel were transferred to Batteries 'E' and 'G' and we got some men from Battery 'E'. This was to augment troops of a .50 cal. MG unit with a 37 mm AW Gun Battery to make us a 'Cold Weather Test' contingent to depart for Fairbanks, Alaska." According to Wilson, "This amalgamation caused some hard feelings and loyalties to original units apparently prevailed."[48]

Cpl. Lewis W. Allen was a member of Battery H when it split with Battery E, so that H's "37 mm outfit would have a .50 cal. machine gun." He, too, sensed that this split caused a certain alienation: "Most of the unit feels that [the] Fairbanks unit is sort of an outcast of the 206th in Dutch Harbor."[49]

In preparation for their move, the Fairbanks contingent received three 37 mm AA guns, six .50 cal. machine guns, 140 M1 rifles and one .22 cal. rifle. The total ammunition supply was 60,000 rounds of .22 cal. long cartridges.[50] So whatever soldier inherited the .22 rifle had enough bullets to keep him busy for the duration, but one wonders how the men equipped with the other weapons were supposed to practice using them, let alone help defend Ladd Field and the Fairbanks area.

This group left from Seattle on 29 August, aboard *St. Mihiel*. Conditions were still cramped and crowded, although, as Campbell remembered, "Everyone had some place to sleep and the food was adequate."[51] Seasickness, however, was still a problem. Some of the cooks were too ill to prepare meals. S. Sgt. Gaines E. Parker went to the galley to help out. He found that someone had left a porthole open, and the floor "was awash with pots and pans floating in water."[52]

S. Sgt. Leonard S. Brown, the battery clerk, rushed to a port-hole to be sick, and scored a direct hit on a sailor who unluckily chose that moment to look out the porthole immediately under Brown's. Brown fled to the other side of the ship, as far from the scene as he could get.[53]

They disembarked at Seward and boarded a train for Fairbanks, awed by the "beautiful, breathtaking" scenery through which they passed. At Fairbanks, they were quartered in an aircraft hangar pending completion of their living quarters, which were not ready until the next spring.[54]

Well before the Fairbanks group left Washington, however, the main body of the 206th had reached Dutch Harbor and had formed their first impressions of what would be their home for—they expected—the next few months.

5

"Is this Alaska?"

For many years, the consensus has been that when on 30 March 1867 Secretary of State William H. Seward signed the Treaty of Cession whereby the Tsar of Russia sold Alaska to the United States for some seven million dollars, he had finalized the best real-estate deal since the Louisiana Purchase. At the time, however, many believed him foolish to the point of being insane.

A number of the 206th soldiers crowding the rails for their first sight of the Aleutians would have endorsed that judgment heartily. Drake's initial impression was: "'My God, what are we doing here?' Nothing but barren rock covered by some type of moss (which we later learned to be tundra) and no trees."[1]

"It must be the back side of the world," thought Staff Sergeant Taylor—an opinion he never changed.[2]

"God! Where in the world have they sent me?" O'Neal asked himself with dismay. "Is this Alaska?"[3]

Sgt. Forrest N. Laubach of Battery A had a similar reaction: "My God! What is this place?"[4]

"Bleak" was a favorite adjective to express the initial view. So were "uninviting," "desolate," and "lonely." Many remarked on the absence of trees. "We thought we were at the end of the world," recollected 1st Sgt. Haskell J. Cathey of Battery B.[5] "They can give this place to the birds," decided T. 5 Eheman in disgust.[6] In brief, as Pfc Lindley remarked dryly, "The travel brochures had overrated it."[7]

Some held modified opinions. "It looked terrible," Sgt. E. F. "Bebe" Paulus admitted, "but I was so sick it looked good to me."[8] And Sergeant Beverburg conceded, "The green-colored mountains looked good after El Paso in August. . . ."[9]

Proffitt reflected stoically that this was to be his home, "and we're here for a purpose." He made a policy of making the best of it, no matter where fate placed him.[10]

Nevertheless, a number of the soldiers succumbed immediately to the austere Arctic scenery. "It was the most beautiful, unspoiled place I ever saw," stated Jodie Jones.[11] "When we arrived at D[utch] H[arbor] . . . I was impressed by how beautiful the scenery looked," Bill Jones remembered. "I was reminded of how I had heard Ireland described as being the Emerald Isle."[12] "Beautiful in late August," recalled 2d Lt. Alvin L. Beverburg of Battery A. "Flowers were in bloom on the mountains."[13]

The Aleutian weather was on its best behavior when the *St. Mihiel* reached Dutch Harbor at noon on 16 August 1941. The sun shone brightly as the men began landing at 1530.[14] Pfc Henderson noticed with some surprise, "All the workers were wearing rain gear on a very fine day. We found out why, because we had to walk about two miles to our barracks during this time, and we were rained on three times. We had to get out our raincoats."[15]

An inauspicious incident sped them on their way. "When we docked there was a soldier standing on the dock crying like a baby," wrote Jodie Jones. "Of course we laughed at him and his return was that when we had been there as long as he had, we would be crazy too."[16]

Battery B of the 250th Coast Artillery, to which this soldier probably belonged, had not been in the Aleutians long, but long enough for some of them to develop a fine case of self-pity, as exemplified by the following poem:

An Alaskan Soldier's Lament

Up on a wind swept mountain,
And what a hell of a spot,
Rattling a hell of a snow storm,
In a land that time forgot.

Into the bush with a rifle,
Down in the ditch with a pick,
Doing the work of prisoners,
And too damned tired to kick,

Up with the Eskimos and whalers,
Up where a man gets blue,
On top of a dismal mountain,
Five thousand miles from you.

At night when the wind is howling,
It's more than a man can stand,
Hell no! We're not convicts,
We're defenders of our land.

We are only living for tomorrow,
In hopes of seeing our gals,
Hoping that if we ever return,
They're not married to our pals.

We are soldiers in the regular army,
Earning our meager pay,
Guarding the Wall Street millions,
For only a buck a day.

No one seems to know we are living,
We wonder, Do they give a damn?
Back home we are soon forgotten,
We have been loaned to Uncle Sam.[17]

It was well that the 206th arrived in summer, because thus they had the opportunity to become gradually acclimated. Not that any of the men from the "lower forty-eight" ever became truly reconciled to their surroundings, although some accepted them as inevitable, and a few claimed the weather wasn't all that much worse than it was in Arkansas.

Actually, it would be difficult to compare the climate of the Aleutians to that of any place else on earth. Certainly it differed markedly from that of mainland Alaska, where the thermometer can drop to 70 degrees below zero in winter and rise to surprising heights in summer. Strictly in terms of degrees Fahrenheit, the Aleutians were seldom very cold. Average temperatures range in winter from 28 degrees to 47 degrees. On the other hand, the islands never really warmed up in summer; the mercury hovers on the average between 34 degrees and 52 degrees. During the brief summer, when the first elements of the 206th arrived, the hills displayed a tapestry of green grass and small but colorful flowers.

What made the archipelago almost unbearable to strangers were the eternal, vicious wind, fog, and rain. In an average year, some form of precipitation falls 200 out of the 365 days. Situated as they are between the icy Bering Sea and the Pacific, which even in these northern latitudes is warmed by the Kuroshio and North Pacific Currents, the islands are natural prey to heavy mists and abrupt, violent changes of weather.

Extending for about 1,400 miles in length and 20 to 60 miles in width, the archipelago is composed of 279 islands, some still unnamed. These are divided into 8 main sections from west to east—Near Islands, Rat Islands, Delarof Islands, Andreanof Islands, Islands of the Four Mountains, Fox Islands, Krenitzen Group, and Unimak Island. The Sanak and Shumagin Islands are off the Alaskan Peninsula. Some 46 undersea volcanoes are still active, and of these at least 26 have erupted since records began being kept in 1760. The most active is Akutan Peak on Akutan Island.[18] The place has an oddly unfinished look. Steam from the volcanoes mixes with the ubiquitous mist; frequent earthquakes carve and recarve the topography; small islets lift their heads timidly out of the roaring seas only to sink again.[19]

This part of the world first came to the notice of Europeans in 1728 when Vitus Bering, a Dane sailing under the Russian flag, discovered the strait separating Asia from North America that now bears his name. He made another voyage in 1741, with two ships. Bering was in *St. Peter* and Alexei Chirikov was in *St. Paul.* Storms separated the two vessels. After sailing along the southern coast of Alaska, Chirikov returned home, reaching Petropavlosk on 8 October 1741. Meanwhile, on 16 July, Bering had reached the Alaskan mainland. Staying only long enough to claim the land for the Tsar, he turned homeward. But the luck that had favored Chirikov deserted Bering. *St. Peter* was wrecked on one of the Komandorski Islands. Bering and many of his crew were suffering from scurvy. At the age of sixty—a ripe old age in the eighteenth century—Bering could not throw off the disease and perished. However, it was summer, the island provided animals, fresh water, and vegetation, so enough men regained their health to build a small boat, and, the next summer, they reached Kamchatka, taking with them a cargo of magnificent furs.[20]

That started the "Fur Rush" that over the next century almost drove the fur-bearing animals to extinction and decimated the native population, although Catherine the Great, who came to the throne on 9 July 1760, charged the fur hunters to neither molest nor cheat the Aleuts. In fact, the empress took such an interest in the Aleutians that for a time they were known as "Catherine's Archipelago."[21]

Needless to say, many of the fur traders paid no attention to their empress's instructions. They were after the rich furs for which there was such a demand in China as well as in Russia. If the natives would sell or trade furs, well and good; if not, these traders were quite prepared to murder, pillage, and rape for them.[22] In contrast, others adopted the Aleut way of life, married Aleut women, and established families. To this day, many citizens of the Aleutians have Russian names and follow the Russian Orthodox faith.

Dutch Harbor is located on the tiny island of Amaknak in Unalaska Bay. Unalaska belongs to the Fox Islands. Their discoverer was Stepan Glotov, in command of the ship *Julian*. On 1 September 1759, he anchored his ship at Umnak Island and passed the winter there. For some time all went well. The Aleuts received him and his men peacefully, and, as Glotov forbade his crew to indulge in rape and kidnaping, relations were cordial for the first three years of Glotov's stay, and he accumulated an enormous cargo of furs.

This pleasant state of affairs did not last long. During the winter of 1763–64, Aleuts destroyed four Russian ships at Umnak, Unalaska, and Unimak, and killed over 160 fur traders. For a little while it must have seemed that the Fox Island Aleuts had taken back their homeland. But soon one Ivan Solov'iev descended upon them with his men and conquered the Aleuts with such grim efficiency that he has gone down in Alaskan history as Solov'iev the Destroyer. The jury is still out on this man's case. Did he take a savage delight in bloodshed, or was he simply a colonial official doing his duty as he saw it in putting down a native uprising? Some evidence exists that the latter possibility is nearer the truth. Apparently he spoke some Aleut, and he wrote accounts of the Aleut lifestyle. Then, too, Glotov, who hitherto on the whole had conducted himself well toward the Aleuts, joined Solov'iev in his punitive measures. In any case, whatever his motives, Solov'iev had re-established Russian supremacy in the Fox Islands. And during his final voyage to the Aleutians, he established the first permanent settlement on Unalaska. The exact date is unknown, except that it fell between 24 July 1772 when Solov'iev's ship entered the harbor, and 21 May 1775, when he left for Kamchatka.[23]

Within the next decade, the Russian government in St. Petersburg realized that some form of discipline had to be imposed upon the fur traders, who were hitherto so many laws unto themselves. In 1799 Tsar Paul established the Russian-American Company, granting it virtual independence provided it "promoted discovery, commerce and agriculture in the name of the Tsar." This was a step toward civilization, and had the climate and terrain been more hospitable, the history of the Aleutians might have followed the course set by the United States and Canada, where the fur hunters were followed by tillers of the soil and herders of farm animals, then by the towns and cities. But all the Aleutians had to offer were furs and fish, and the Aleutians were so far at the back of beyond that frequently the Russian-American Company was cut off from sources of supply for long periods, once for over five years.

Meanwhile, English and American companies began trading with the Russian trappers, who were glad to do so, for thus they could obtain the necessary supplies to carry them over until the next Russian ship arrived—if it ever did. Moreover, the fur crop was almost exhausted. By the mid-1800s, the furbearing animals had been hunted to near extinction, and the costs of maintaining the Russian presence in Alaska far outweighed the dwindling profits.[24]

Of course, not all the Russians came to the Aleutians to profit and pillage. No story of this region would be complete without at least a mention of Ioann Veniaminov, a Russian Orthodox priest who came to Unalaska in 1824 at the age of twenty-seven. Fully expecting to spend the rest of his life there, he brought his family and settled down. He and the Aleuts took to each other immediately. He found the natives "a gentle, honorable, generous people." For their part, the Aleuts recognized pure gold when they saw it, and they enthusiastically helped their priest build first a house, then a school, and finally the Church of the Holy Ascension. As they worked, Veniaminov taught his helpers "carpentry, metal working, brick construction, and other skills."

At the school he founded, the priest instructed the boys in

trades as well as the "three R's" and religion. His wife helped teach the girl pupils and gave them special instruction in housework.

Veniaminov was more than a priest. He was a scientist who kept meticulous records of "winds, tides, thermometric and barometric readings." He was a gifted linguist, having learned the Aleut language and having given them an alphabet. With the Aleut chief Ivan Pank'ov, he wrote a number of religious books in Aleut.

After ten years, Veniaminov was transferred to Sitka and in 1838 returned to St. Petersburg. The next year his wife died, and one year later he took orders as a monk priest under the name Innokentii. In 1841 he returned to Alaska as Bishop. After many fruitful years in that capacity, he became head of the Russian Orthodox Church. Eleven years later he died, 82 years old and blind. To the last, he loved "to speak about his Aleuts."[25]

This noble man of God was still active when the Tsar's government realized that it had seriously overextended the Empire, and with great good sense it decided to unload Alaska while it could. St. Petersburg preferred to sell to the United States—a young country of uncertain destiny that for generations would pose no threat—rather than see Russian America gobbled up by the British Empire, which seemed determined to swallow everything in sight.[26]

The Civil War was under way when St. Petersburg first approached Washington with the offer to sell, and Lincoln and Seward were wholly preoccupied with preserving the Union. Not until 30 March 1867 was the agreement signed by Seward and Russian Ambassador Edouard de Stoeckl.[27] Another nine months went by before a skeptical Congress appropriated the necessary $7.2 million—less than two cents an acre—to transfer "Seward's Ice Box" to the United States.[28]

It would be pleasant to record that under the American flag the Aleuts' lot improved immediately. Unfortunately, the reverse was true. Just as they had been under the Russians, the natives were the workforce of the new fur companies, but they could not rise to management or governmental positions. For many years the fur companies had conducted programs for select Aleuts from which they could take their place in the community leadership; these had been closed. To the dismayed Aleuts it seemed that the United States was bent on "eradicating every vestige of Russian and Aleut culture from the Aleut life."[29]

Possibly, in the manner of colonials throughout history, individual educators might have conceived it to be their duty to try to retool the natives to the domestic model. However, the official attitude of the United States was less one of misguided zeal than of total indifference. The secretary of War remarked, "The Territory from a military point of view has no resources." The army stationed one battalion at Sitka to cover the whole vast territory.[30]

These soldiers had no formal duties, and the twin enemies of all outposts—boredom and loneliness—set in. There is considerable wisdom in the old saying that "Satan finds work for idle hands to do." Many of the soldiers began to manufacture liquor or sell it to the natives. When the news of this situation reached Washington, it triggered a whopping scandal. The army's dragging its feet in this matter forced it to pull out of Alaska in 1876. For two years, Alaska had no government and no source of law and order. Despite a few rather ineffectual laws enacted by Congress, real control was not established until the Organic Act of 1884 formally made Alaska a territory of the United States.[31]

The discovery of gold was both the making of and almost the ruin of Alaska. Within a year of the discovery of gold in the Klondike region in 1898, over $15 million in the precious metal had been shipped to the lower United States—twice the sum Seward had paid for the whole territory.[32] As might be expected, none of this wealth was plowed back into Alaska. For a year, the worst type of "robber barons" had free rein in exploiting the region. In 1899, Congress passed criminal codes to protect the natives and prospectors from the flocks of human vultures attracted by the scent of gold.[33] Far from incidentally, this legislation enabled Washington to impose taxes and thus obtain some of the revenue. Other resources, such as copper, silver, and coal were discovered. At last, during Woodrow Wilson's administration, "conservation of resources and natural preservation of Alaska became the national policy."

It was almost too late for the natives. The number of Aleuts in the archipelago when the Russians came has been estimated at over twenty-five thousand. When they left, fewer than four thousand Aleuts remained. Other Eskimo and Indian communities suffered proportionately. The problem was not deliberate extermination, but the diseases the white man brought. The natives had never been exposed to such plagues as measles, smallpox, and tuberculosis, hence they had no natural immunity to these diseases. In the interior, whole tribes died. It was the sad story of the American Indian all over again. In only one respect were the Alaskan natives more fortunate—at least they weren't herded into reservations.[34]

In the meantime, by serving as a supply base for the gold rush, a measure of prosperity had come to Dutch Harbor. The area boasted hotels, a dance hall, and several bars. The legend persists that Jack London plotted his novel, *The Sea Wolf*, while staying at Dutch Harbor, although his journals do not record any visit to Unalaska. The basis of Unalaska's economy was fox farming, but the Great Depression knocked the bottom out of the fox fur market.[35]

The army had returned to Alaska with the gold rush, establishing some dozen garrisons. Five were still there at the end of World War I. By 1924, all but Chilkoot Barracks had been abandoned.[36]

The years between World Wars were lean ones for the United States armed forces. The earlier conflict had not resulted, as many optimists and idealists had hoped, in a forward movement for mankind worth the sacrifices. Cynicism toward the military, plus the conviction that the money could be better spent elsewhere, made prying military appropriations out of Congress a difficult task indeed. And Alaska was very low on the priority list. A few small ripples disturbed the placid waters. In 1934–35 the navy and the Hydrographic Force, working out of Kiska, surveyed some of the Aleutian islands, in the course of which they spotted Japanese ships engaged in obvious mapmaking operations. And that omnipresent gadfly, Brig. Gen. Billy Mitchell, warned the House Military Affairs Committee that Alaska was the "key point in the whole Pacific."

Actually, the United States could not have done much about the defense of the Aleutians even had they so desired, because the U.S.-Japanese Treaty of Limitation of Naval Armament pledged Washington to install no defense posts in the Aleutians until 1936. When that year rolled around, Alaska's nonvoting delegate introduced a bill calling for nineteen million dollars for air bases in Alaska. Congress was supremely uninterested. "Why should anyone want Alaska?" asked one congressman.

With the outbreak of World War II in Europe, the United States decided to establish a defense triangle in the Pacific—Alaska, Hawaii, Panama—under the basic war plan, Orange. Alaska's share was eight hundred men of the 4th Infantry to form the Alaska

Defense Force, and four million dollars, which even in those days was a paltry sum for defense installations. Not until the Hitler-Stalin pact of 1940 did Congress authorize $350 million for Alaska's defense.[37]

"Defense" was the key word. "American defense in the Pacific is chiefly a problem of preventing Japan—the only other great naval power in that area—from acquiring bases on the eastern side of the ocean," observed A. Randle Elliott in *Foreign Policy Reports*. The army was constructing major air bases at Fairbanks and Anchorage, the navy three—at Woman Bay, on Kodiak Island, Sitka, and Chernofski Bay, on Unalaska. "Unalaska is the farthest Alaskan outpost foreseen at present . . . Unalaska Harbor, including Dutch Harbor, is the only site in all the Aleutian Islands which could serve as a base for surface craft and submarines without considerable development, and is now being improved for both types of vessels."[38]

Some disputed the defensive strategy, believing that, in the event of war, the Aleutians would provide a perfect means of reaching the heart of the Japanese Empire. On paper this looked like a fine plan, but it took no account of geographical realities. As the army air force historians, Craven and Cate, wrote with commendable restraint, "But an all-out invasion—or even a sustained air attack—along this route in either direction would have involved difficulties incommensurate with the strategic gains." The distances involved were enormous, the area was not self-supporting, and the weather discouraged naval operations.[39]

So, when the 206th reached Dutch Harbor, the idea was not to invade Japan via the Aleutians, but to keep the Japanese from gaining a foothold, lest they establish naval bases from which to raid the North Pacific and air bases that might threaten the United States' West Coast cities. This task might have proven formidable, if Japan had made a determined thrust in that direction, for in August 1941 Alaska's defenses were far from ready.

6

"Officially Named Fort Mears"

When *St. Mihiel* discharged her cargo of men on 16 August 1941, both the Naval Air Station and Fort Mears were so new they had not been officially dedicated. Work had been in progress on the naval bases at Sitka and Kodiak since late 1939, but not until 1 June 1940 was a supplemental contract issued to survey Amaknak Island and the Chernofski area of Unalaska with a view to extending the Sitka-Kodiak contract.

The navy had a number of objections to Amaknak. True, Dutch Harbor offered an excellent deep-water anchorage, but it had many drawbacks. The bottom "was too deep and soft for practical finger pier construction, while the turning basin was somewhat too small." The harbor was too restricted to allow seaplanes to land and take off. Moreover, the island's mountainous terrain offered no suitable site for a fighter aircraft base; the harbor's aerial protection would have to be situated elsewhere.

Nevertheless, the navy did select Amaknak. Dutch Harbor might not be perfect, but it was usable, and the navy already had set aside land for Radio and Aerology stations. Then, too, establishing a base further along the Aleutian chain might appear threatening in the eyes of the ever-sensitive Japanese.[1]

So the Dutch Harbor area was added to the Sitka-Kodiak construction contract, and by 29 August 1940, fifty-nine workers were on their way as an advance party. The company under contract for these huge projects was a co-venture of the Siems Spokane Company, the Puget Sound Bridge and Dredging Company of Seattle, and the Johnson Drake and Piper Company of Minneapolis. This organization was usually referred to for brevity as Siems-Drake.

Many prospective areas of disagreement between the army and navy were smoothed out by the Joint Planning Board. Until army strength was sufficient, the marines would provide interim protection. And whenever practicable, the services would share facilities such as the hospital, power plant, and recreation centers. At Dutch Harbor, Army Garrison No. 1 was to be located on flat land on Margaret Bay, adjacent to the Dutch Harbor parcel. The navy did not want to lose this site and recommended that the army build on another some distance away. The army objected; the proposed location was so far away it would preclude shared use of facilities as the Joint Planning Board had stipulated. At last, in November 1940, the navy withdrew its objections.[2]

Meanwhile, the Siems-Drake advance party threw up a bunkhouse at Unalaska village and began work on a marine barracks to house 125 men. This was completed on 5 October 1940, just in time to accommodate the advance detachment of marines, consisting of 4 marine officers and 101 enlisted men, together with one navy officer and 14 enlisted men. On 14 October they landed at the Dutch Harbor dock, where their commander, Maj. A. Cockrell, USMC, awaited them. Except for supplies and the barracks, there wasn't much to protect, so half the men stood guard while the rest trained in the nearby hills.[3]

Siems-Drake's labor force was expanding rapidly, and to provide housing three old passenger ships—*Northwestern*, *City of Victoria*, and *Yale*—were purchased as barracks ships for use at Dutch Harbor, Sitka, and Kodiak respectively. Rescued from the scrappers, *Northwestern* reached Dutch Harbor in October 1940. "She could accommodate 280 workers, parts, supplies and provide power for its 200 kw, 2,300 volt General Electric steam turbo-generators to the project site."

Twice she had to be moved from the dock and anchored in the harbor to ride out storms. After an unusually severe beating in December 1940, the decision was made to beach her permanently.

Personnel problems plagued Siems-Drake, especially at Dutch Harbor, which was considered the least desirable of the three sites. Many of those recruited stayed only long enough to catch the next ship back to the states. Among some of those who remained, both morale and productivity were low. Some, of course, were solid workmen giving a day's work for a day's pay.[4]

The 206th shared the Dutch Harbor area with the Siems-Drake workers for approximately a year and developed a mixed bag of opinions. Ballew saw "lots of them. They gambled a bit and drank a lot."[5] Sisk was among those who noted the workers' problems. "Although they made good money, they hated the weather and would be glad to get out. . . . They were common, everyday, construction guys that, while some worked hard, others didn't." In his opinion, "the men were not pushed hard" because the jobs were cost-plus.[6]

Cpl. Virgil L. Clodi of Headquarters Battery observed somewhat severely that the Siems-Drake men were always coming or going back to the states. They "[w]ere overpaid for the work they did, always on a coffee break."[7]

To Alspaugh, a man inclined to look on the sunny side, "They seemed to be pleasant people doing a job. Of course," he added, "there was some sentiment expressed in the difference in the pay scale, civilian vs. military."[8] Massey, too, found these men agreeable: "All were friendly. They talked about their homes and family same as we did."[9]

Lieutenant Beverburg had good cause to regard them kindly: "I went to see several on different occasions to get (beg, borrow or steal) material that was not available in army supply at the time. These were good Americans that would cooperate if possible."[10]

What was then called "Army Garrison No. 1" at Margaret Bay was built to standard army quartermaster plans. Similar designs were in use throughout the states, so that the soldier moving from one station to another might experience an eerie sense of *déjà vu*. Neat rows of two-story frame barracks with single-story orderly rooms, day rooms, and mess halls—when you had seen one you had seen them all. Nothing changed but the surrounding scenery.

The buildings at Margaret Bay had certain modifications such as arctic storm entrances and the blackout shutters ordered for both army and navy structures. Lt. Gen. John L. DeWitt, commanding the Western Defense Command, of which Alaska was a part, headed a team to inspect Army Garrison No. 1. As a result of this team's recommendations, interior walls were installed as well as drying rooms with clothes lines and hot air heaters.

In addition to twenty-eight barracks, the camp included a 270-bed hospital, mess halls, a chapel, a PX and the usual recreation-type buildings.

By 1 May 1941 the first increment arrived—an advance party of three officers and five enlisted men. Within a week, *St. Mihiel* arrived with Battery B, 250th Coast Artillery, a searchlight platoon, some quartermaster and medical corps personnel. This signaled the transition from marine to army defense, and on her return trip *St. Mihiel* took back to the states Major Cockrell and eighty-four marines. As the army quarters were not yet finished, the incoming soldiers moved into the newly vacated marine barracks. The remaining marine contigent—now designated Marine Barracks, Naval Air Station—guarded the naval area while the army took over coastal defense and the Margaret Bay area. On 21 August Cmdr. W. N. Updegraff, USN, assumed command of the Naval Air Station, which was commissioned on 1 September 1941.[11]

In the weeks after their arrival, the 206th settled into a daily routine. Men of Battery A were soon scouting the surrounding areas of Amaknak and Unalaska Islands for suitable searchlight positions. Certain batteries, including A, were required to provide manpower and equipment for Post duties. They contributed trucks and drivers to transport POL (petroleum, oil, and lubricants), other supplies, and personnel "for work at the various warehouses and supply depot." Further, manpower was required around the clock in off-loading supplies and equipment from ships berthed at the dock. Because of this schedule, mess halls remained open twenty-four hours a day. "About one-third of the battery strength was required to fulfill the ship unloading and Port details on a continuing basis."

Twelve searchlight units and three SCR 268 radar units were assigned to Battery A. These units the men "assembled and tested at various locations on Amaknak and Unalaska Islands. The transmitters were found to be defective on two units due to corrosion from sea water; however, the remaining radar unit was found to be in relatively good condition." Later they set this up on Hill 200 overlooking Dutch Harbor.[12]

Alspaugh's letters home provide a running commentary on events, although naturally he wrote mostly of personal matters. The scenery was still new and delightful to him. "We have a beautiful camp here," he wrote on 2 September. "It is surrounded on 3 sides by water. The mountains are covered with moss and thick-growing grass and flowers. Sometimes the vegetation on the slopes of the mountains are waist deep, but it is usually about ankle deep."

He had a hint of what was to come in the shape of "a lot of new winter clothes. I now have 3 raincoats, 2 pr of wool-lined gloves, 3 pr of shoes, 1 pr of overshoes, 1 pr of leather boots, 1 mackinaw, 1 parka, and more clothing than I could possibly mention. It is all durable, warm and waterproof."

Captain Dodson was now commanding the battery. "He sure is a fine fellow and he knows what he should about our equipment." Alspaugh added, "We had a dedication ceremony today. This camp was officially named Fort Mears."[13]

The camp was named in honor of Col. Frederick Mears, a member of the Alaska Engineering Commission (AEC), in charge of constructing the Alaska Railroad. Mears supervised the railroad from Ship Creek, to Anchorage, and on to Fairbanks. From 1918 to 1919 he took leave from AEC to serve in France. He returned a colonel, becoming chairman and chief engineer of AEC.[14]

On 9 September Alspaugh wrote home in an optimistic vein. "I don't believe we will be stationed here over 5 or 6 months unless we get in the war." He was sufficiently interested in his surroundings to be reading a book about the Aleutians—Bernard Hubbard's *Cradle of the Storms*, and he bragged gently about his outfit: "Our conduct on the trip here was remarkably good. B Btry boys never have been in any trouble since the induction."[15]

Five days later he explained that he couldn't send pictures. They were censored when developed, and the censoring board kept most of them. Despite this censorship, there was no real attempt to conceal the 206th's whereabouts. As yet they had no APO number—Alspaugh's letters were openly postmarked "Ft Mears, Dutch Harbor, Alaska."

The men had been having some trouble getting the guns emplaced on the nearby mountains. But Alspaugh didn't dwell on it. Instead, he launched into another enthusiastic description of Amaknak:

> This sure is a pretty spot. There is a bay at the front of the barracks and another one about 400 yards away at the back of the barracks. There is a small mountain on the west side of the barracks about 300 yards from here and a pretty large mountain on the northeastern side of this barracks . . . about a mile away.
>
> There is some of the blackest dirt I ever saw up here. It sure is

rich. There are flowers about the size and color of larkspur growing all over the mountains. . . .

As for recreation, they went to the movies some four nights a week, explored, read, played cards or dominoes. "We also usually go down to see the freighters coming in and going. . . ."[16]

It probably was around this time that Drake and Frank "Pete" White, sightseeing in Unalaska one Sunday, noticed several Aleuts entering the Russian Orthodox Church. White suggested that they visit it. Being unfamiliar with the Russian Orthodox service, they were surprised to find no pews or any other furniture. All the worshipers were standing.

Shortly, "an elderly Aleutian Indian" noticed the strangers, and hospitably brought up two folding chairs, placing them directly under a heavy iron chandelier. He motioned that the visitors were welcome to sit down. Thus made to feel like guests instead of like interlopers, they stayed until the end of the service. Occasionally, perhaps with dim recollections of *The Phantom of the Opera*, they glanced up nervously at the massive chandelier.[17]

The soldiers had very little contact with the Aleuts. They had been officially warned away from the native women. "We were told in formal lectures by officers that 75% of the native women had pneumonia* and 75% had a venereal disease," recalled Weese. "That meant a lot of them had both."[18] Some found the natives unprepossessing—"dirty" and "very primitive." Others were more favorably disposed. To Quimby they seemed "very calm and placid."[19] Several soldiers, like T. 4 Patrick and Pfc Radney, noted that the Aleuts were both shy and friendly.[20]

At least one soldier, Pfc Abell, had ongoing contact with an Aleut who "had several cases of shotgun shells in his shack for hunting. He supplied my hunting partner, Cpl. Herbert Galloway, and me with ammunition as long as we needed it for hunting Siberian geese, which were plentiful during certain seasons. We borrowed guns from the recreation department."[21]

Some of their own race were curiosities to the Arkansans. "Before we came here we got 8 men from the 260th CA from

* tuberculosis

Washington, D.C.," Alspaugh informed his mother on 18 September, "They are all in this barracks and they sure talk funny . . . but they are all good-natured and hard workers."

Still under the spell of the natural beauty, he wrote, "Mother, I wish you could see the rainbows here." Moving into a minor key, he added, "We haven't been paid since August 1st but I don't need any money here." The first hint of a real problem appeared in this letter: "Of course you will find some people who don't like the discipline and regulations but they must be enforced just as laws are. I can assure you that all the officers are not A-1. We have some in this battery that are not worth much but our captain is sure a fine captain."[22]

Toward the end of September or early October, Fort Mears received a contingent of seventeen army nurses.[23] They were promptly whisked to the hospital area with armed guards to protect their barracks.[24] Thereafter the enlisted men saw the nurses only when sick enough to go to the hospital or when receiving shots. Sometimes they caught a fleeting glimpse of a nurse in the PX. These women were commissioned officers, and, as Parker could have reminded his fellow soldiers, dating commissioned officers was taboo.

"Occasionally a couple of army/navy nurses would come out to Captains Bay to investigate an abandoned gold mine," remembered Cpl. James D. "Chief" Costley of Battery A. He added rather pathetically, "We would invite them for coffee and save the mugs that had lipstick as that reassured us that there were still females in the area."[25]

Of course, the nurses could socialize with their fellow officers. At least one officer of the 206th—Maj. Henry A. Oehrig—found his future wife among the nurses.[26]

Those who sought sex as opposed to romance or companionship took advantage of what Capt. David M. Wall of Headquarters Battery termed "a 'cat' house for civilian workers—Siems-Drake."[27] This establishment was inhabited by "3 or 4 ladies of the evening living on a small island that was accessible by boat . . ."[28] These women were "available if you could spend fifty cents for a boat ride to 'Pecker Point,' a small island a few hundred yards out in the bay near the beached passenger ship."[29]

"It's been told that on any given night boats would be lined up waiting their turn. The place was called Pecker Point," reminisced Private Davis. "I never went," he added emphatically.[30]

"Many men visited the island and the prostitutes until it caused a big problem because [of] so many men," wrote Pfc Henderson. "The men would ride boats over to [the] island during the night and private boats took so many over and did not leave time to bring them back. So the next day the small island would be loaded with AWOL men."[31]

The brothel was soon closed and its inhabitants sent away. But the name "Pecker Point" clung to the forlorn little island long after the reason for the nomenclature was just a memory.

7

"Early On in Our Story"

B y the second week in October, the Aleutian climate had begun
to show its teeth. "We have had a touch of rough weather the
past three days," Alspaugh wrote his mother. "The wind sure has
been blowing. It blew some squad tents off a hill near here." By the
twenty-first, the weather was turning cold, with some snow. The
men had taken pneumonia and tetanus shots.[1]

At this point the weather was not so much a hardship as it was
bizarre. In most parts of the world, fog and high winds are mutually
exclusive; they can co-exist happily in the Aleutians. Such paradoxes
were commonplace. Captain Wall remembered an instance "when
there was a rainbow, sleet coming down, and 75 mile winds within a
100-yard area."[2]

"I have seen it snow, sleet, rain and have the sun shine before
noon," recalled Garrett. "The fog would come down Mt. Ballyhoo
like a blanket."[3] T. 4 Troy E. Burris of Battery D confirmed the
erratic nature of the weather. "Quite often there would be fog,
sleet, snow or rain falling within a 15-minute period."[4]

"I remember that a storm, right out of the Bering Sea from the
north on October 14–16, 1941, caused everything that was movable
to be tied down," wrote Pfc Fitzhugh. "Thirty-foot waves from the
bay crashed on the shore and the high winds blew the water
through the ends of the barracks. . . ." The orderly room and the
First Sergeants' quarters located on that end had to be vacated. "It
was said that the wind gauge blew off the navy's weather station at
120 mph so they never knew just how strong the wind really was."[5]

Then there was the notorious williwaw, a form of squall
peculiar to near-polar regions, such as the Strait of Magellan
and the Aleutians. Its fierceness was only exceeded by its total

unpredictability. It could change direction so abruptly and frequently that it could seem to be blowing from every point of the
compass simultaneously, not to mention up and down. The williwaw "blew so hard we had to lean forward to walk down the hill,"
Ballew remarked graphically.[6] Then it would cease so abruptly that
the struggling soldier fell flat on his face.[7] These winds were not
only uncomfortable but dangerous. Sgt. Oliver C. Raney of Battery
F remembered that williwaws "caused sea water to attack the guns
at 50 feet in the air on [the] hill." He added, "I tied myself to [the]
gun on several occasions."[8] "The fog would get so thick you could
reach out and grab a handful," wrote Private Davis. ". . . the williwaws . . . would blow away anything not fastened down."[9]

In brief, the impossibility of predicting the weather, not only
for the next day but for the next hour, made the Aleutians a meteorologist's nightmare. In that area, weather conditions were to prove
much more destructive enemies than the Japanese.

The 206th passed a minor milestone in October with the loss of
their men over twenty-eight years of age. These were returned to
state control.[10] And on 25 October Amaknak had a distinguished visitor. "Major General Buckner, Commander of the Alaskan Defense
Force, arrived here yesterday from the mainland for an inspection of
the island," Alspaugh told his family. "We had a layout inspection, an
inspection in ranks, and an inspection of the gun position."[11]

This was before the expansion of the armed forces, with the
consequent proliferation of rank, had gotten fully under way, and a
real, live major general was a distinct rarity. One can readily picture
the frantic cleaning of quarters, policing of the area, the polishing
of equipment and weapons that Buckner's visit involved.

Even in the matter of chain of command, the United States had
shortchanged Alaska. The Philippines, Hawaii, and the Panama
Canal Zone had independent army departments and naval districts
with direct access to Washington. Alaska, whose area exceeded by
more than fourfold the entire square mileage of the other three
combined, played second fiddle. In mid-1941 the army established
the Alaskan Defense Command under Brig. Gen. Simon Bolivar
Buckner under the Western Defense Command, located at San
Francisco's Presidio with Lt. Gen. John C. DeWitt in command. So
Buckner, charged with defense of the largest single slice of U. S.
territory outside the lower forty-eight, could not go straight to the

War Department for his needs; he had to channel through DeWitt. Even with the best of good will on all sides, this process was, at best, time consuming. In turn, the navy had created the Alaskan Sector under the 13th Naval District, located at Seattle. Capt. Ralph C. Parker commanded the Alaskan Sector from his head-quarters/flagship, the gunboat *Charleston*. He also had three small patrol craft converted from fishing vessels. Such was the "Alaskan Navy."[12] One of the best-known individuals in the entire Aleutian chain was Carl "Squeaky" Anderson, who in 1941 was captain of the Port at Dutch Harbor. Squeaky had this opinion of these ships: "They would sink if they got rammed by a barnacle."[13]

Buckner proved to be an able and conscientious commander, but in one respect it is doubtful if he was the ideal choice to send to Alaska, where he would be faced with races other than his own. Possibly it was only natural that the son of a Confederate general should have some racial hang-ups, but Buckner overdid it. He would refuse to assign any regular army personnel to work with the territorial guard, which had many Eskimo members. And he strongly opposed the assignment of black troops to Alaska, on the extraordinary rationale that many blacks would probably "remain and settle [in Alaska] after the war, with the natural result that they would interbreed with the Indians and Eskimos and produce an astonishingly objectionable race of mongrels which would be a problem here from now on."[14]

Although no one could reasonably deny that the Aleutians' weather hampered naval operations, Buckner waxed sarcastic about the navy, writing that "the naval officer had an instinctive dread of Alaskan waters, feeling that they were a jumping-off place between Scylla and Charybdis and inhabited by a ferocious monster that was forever breathing fogs and coughing up 'williwaws' that would blow the unfortunate mariner into uncharted rocks and forever destroy his chances of becoming an admiral."[15]

Obviously, the Alaskan commander was something of a charac-ter. The same day as the general's inspection, a slight contretemps occurred, as Alspaugh informed his home folks: "Last night a sol-dier out of the 37th Infantry, who was drunk, stumbled through the barracks and knocked 25 records off a table and broke them all." Phonograph records were prized, because the men could not depend upon the radio. "Radio reception here is bad. They are always running generators and electrical tools here and it messes up the reception," Alspaugh explained. "We can get pretty fair reception between 8:00 o'clock and 10:00 at night." The stations went off the air at 2200.[16]

Relations between the 206th and the 37th were at best a sort of armed truce, especially in this prewar period. There were what Captain Beverburg called delicately "occasional differences of opinion." He added, "Some was 'Pride One Units,' another was the old story—regular army vs. national guard."[17] Pfc Fitzhugh recalled "a few fist fights with the 37th early on in our story . . ."[18] Massey observed, "Infantry units were always in bad humor so our boys had little use for them."[19]

Joe Sisk retained a vivid recollection of a rather serious confrontation:

> There was a lot of rivalry between the artillery and the infantry, especially when we had beer in the PX at D[utch] H[arbor]. I remember one big gang fight where lots of guards were called in to separate them, and did, but the infantry was on one side of the guards and artillery on the other and each side were throwing rocks at the other. There were some shots fired, but nobody was hurt except maybe some guards by flying rocks . . . bitterness of everyone's plight was the cause. It seems to me that the guys from Arkansas held up better under the adverse conditions than did the guys from other parts.[20]

Sgt. Russell R. Haden of Battery A remarked bluntly, "The 37th Inf[antry] tried to bully us the way they had intimidated the CA unit (155 mm) on Ballyhoo. It didn't work so we came to respect each other."[21]

The "unit on Ballyhoo" was the 250th Coast Artillery, and their relations with the 206th could have been better. "They had been there a few months before us," remarked Sisk, "and had already developed a certain amount of bitterness toward their plight, and it seemed they were bitter at us also. In short, we didn't care for them and they for us."[22]

The 206th felt some resentment toward the marines, who "lived in a real nice barracks with shower and all the good stuff. They were only guards for duty of guarding the dock, the power plant and such," wrote Sisk. "We were envious of their not-so-harsh duties and these things irked us badly."[23]

All told, the 206th got along best with the navy personnel, who "helped by closing their eyes to our use of much of their construction material," according to Lt. Col. Voris O. Callaway of Battery F.[24] Fitzhugh agreed that the navy "was especially good to make friends with as one could acquire things which the army needed but couldn't get."[25] After hostilities began, Col. Walton L. Hogan of Battery F "flew on patrol flights as a volunteer machine gunner since the navy was short of gunners."[26]

The navy also cooperated in the important area of maintaining contact with the home folks. Otis R. Holmes of Company A, 151st Engineers, had been a Ham radio operator before joining the army. One day he met a sailor who was a radio operator at navy headquarters. This man "had a 'Ham shack' (amateur radio station)." So they teamed up. "Mail call being what it was—by ship about once a week or so—we sent and received free radiograms each night to a blind Ham in Oregon, who relayed them to other Hams in the states to be delivered, and sent replies to us, which I would carry to Ft. Mears Post Headquarters each night on my way back to the barracks."[27]

The 206th had one particular use for the navy. "We bought torpedo juice from a navy warehouse at $75 a gallon," explained Sergeant Haden. "Some warrant officers made out on that deal. . . . Nobody had $75. We all pitched in and made up the price."[28]

Early on the regiment had discovered the dubious pleasures of torpedo juice. This was the alcohol used in propelling torpedoes, and it definitely was never intended for human consumption. But some enterprising soul discovered that, cut at a ratio of five to one, it was drinkable, if one were that desperate, and many were. Even at five-to-one "it was a potent drink. I preferred to cut it about 7 to one," stated Drake. "Although I drank the mixture, the taste was not to my liking."[29] Nor was it to the taste of Staff Sergeant Buzzan, who "never touched the stuff but once." Once was enough![30]

Corporal Kinney was amazed at the lengths to which men would go for intoxicating drink:

> Alcohol of any kind was like possessing gold. If you happened to acquire some, you would have no trouble selling it for an extremely

high price. However, it would probably be stolen first before you even thought of selling it. It wasn't even possible to even keep shaving lotion on hand without its being stolen. I have even heard tales that some jerks would try straining out the poisonous ingredients of torpedo juice between slices of bread and drinking it. Boy, they must have been real thirsty for any kind of alcohol![31]

Corporal Clodi recalled that some enlisted men who drank the stuff died.[32] Drake, too, remembered that in the winter of 1941 a rumor circulated "that two men of the 37th Infantry had died as a result of drinking 'torpedo juice' full strength. One of the men had managed to obtain some of the alcohol and returned to his post located in one of the passes on Unalaska Island. Later, as a result of no response from their position, they were found frozen. The medical examination of the two men showed their brains had been completely pickled as a result of the 120-proof alcohol."[33]

Another potent form of home brew was that Corporal Costley called "a mixture they called Raisin Jack that would curl your toenails."[34] According to Sergeant Paulus, "Some of the cooks made Raisin Jack of canned peaches and pineapple and baker's yeast."[35]

These heroic measures were not really necessary in the prewar period, because the PX served beer, and there was a liquor store on Unalaska. "Alcohol was not of much interest" to Jodie Jones, and some of the scenes at the PX disgusted him, not only because of the drunkenness but also because to him the situation demonstrated lack of proper leadership. "A man with a red hatband [artillery] could get in trouble in the PX because the blue hatbands [infantry] thought the beer bar was their turf. I could never understand a base commander allowing a situation like that to exist," he stated. "With men lying on the floor it looked more like a pig pen than a PX."[36]

Those who wanted something other than beer went to Blackie's Bar over on Unalaska. This institution seemed to be trying to live up to the image of everybody's idea of a frontier bar, "just like Robert Service would have told it," in the words of Sgt. Aubrey T. Albright of Battery A,[37] with one notable exception—there were no dancing girls. Blackie himself was surnamed Floyd and was said to be a brother of Pretty Boy Floyd, a notorious gangster of Prohibition days.

"The only time I was in Blackie's Bar was in September 1941," related Fitzhugh. "A friend of mine and I went to have a drink. Blackie himself waited on us." He questioned Fitzhugh's age, but when his friend verified that this particular Pfc was "almost 22, . . . all was well."[38]

Descriptions of Blackie's Bar were quite similar. Drake's is typical and well detailed:

> Blackie's Bar was located in a wooden shack near the center of Unalaska. A long wooden bar ran the entire length of the structure while two entrances, front and rear, were used in gaining entrance into the bar area. Several wooden tables and chairs were placed along the wall and to the rear, leaving a space in the center of the room. The bar was rather bare of furnishings, while three or four shelves containing some bottles were behind the bar. The bar was managed by an individual who was an uncle to one of the men of the Battery. Whiskey was sold for one dollar a shot (one ounce) and one could not remain at the bar to consume the whiskey. One had to line up outside, file thru the main entrance, walk to the bar, pay the one dollar, take one shot glass filled with whiskey, drink it and exit the bar thru the rear door and then run like hell to get back in line and wait for another shot of whiskey. The line was always long and during the winter it was cold standing in line for another go at the bar.[39]

Sergeant Newton remarked that the men tended to drink more in the Aleutians than they had stateside, and Pfc Henderson estimated that the rate of consumption was "four times the stateside."[40]

Of course, the men didn't have to depend on liquor for relaxation. Fort Mears offered many opportunities for healthy off-duty activities, both indoors and out. They spent more time inside than they would have had the weather been more favorable. Poker and card games were the favorite indoor occupations. "Some of the games were for pretty high stakes," wrote Private Davis. He added quizzically, "I especially liked to play when Lt. Lennon was in the game. Felt good to win an officer's money." In addition, they "played an awful lot of bridge and had bridge tournaments."[41]

Reading was a close second in popularity. Books were available, and some recalled reading favorite roughly contemporary novels like *The Robe*, *For Whom the Bell Tolls*, and *Gone with the Wind*. Others preferred nonfiction, while T. Sgt. Frank Leeder of Battery A read "anything I could get my hands on."[42]

"The PX was pretty well stocked" with popular magazines, according to Jodie Jones.[43] "They would be old, but we looked at them," added Fox Conway.[44] *Life*, *Time*, *Look*, and *Reader's Digest* were prime favorites.

A number of men received their home-town newspapers, and such titles as the *Arkansas Gazette*, Atkins *Chronicle*, Smackover *Journal*, and Jonesboro *Daily Tribune* provided a touch of nostalgia. "Since B Battery was a pretty close-knit unit, any hometown paper was widely read," said Sergeant Beverburg,[45] and no doubt this was true of all batteries.

A few of the more farsighted took advantage of opportunities to improve themselves. Massey studied every army manual he could get and "attended every school session given at Fort Mears."[46] Among other things, Corporal Hargrave "took a course in trigonometry taught by one of the 206th officers."[47] Burris took correspondence courses from the University of Arkansas that would total thirty hours, which put him a full year ahead of his contemporaries when the war ended.[48]

As with every other outfit, overseas or zone of the interior, far and away the favorite reading matter was letters from home. Especially in these autumn months of 1941, delivery was maddeningly irregular. "Mail was cherished more than food—perhaps because it was so long coming," recalled Private Davis. "Thirty days from Ark[ansas] to D[utch] H[arbor] was not uncommon. No such thing as airmail since the only planes that ever landed in the early days were PBYs."[49]

"I saw men go without evening meal to open mail and write letters to get more mail," related Clodi. "You can't begin to realize how important mail and a letter from home is in a situation like this. It ranks right up there with food and shelter. Some men wouldn't get any letters at mail call and I have seen them cry. Others would let them read their letters. Very heartbreaking! In a situation like this, you really find out who your friends are."[50]

Fishing was just about everyone's favorite outdoor sport. It so happened that the 206th arrived in time to witness the annual salmon spawning. Weese told the story most vividly: "About one week after we landed at D[utch] H[arbor] in 1941 some of our men found a fresh water stream about fifteen feet wide and four to five feet deep where large salmon had come in from the ocean to spawn.

The salmon were so thick in the stream and so placid during the spawning process that the men just waded in the stream, and I picked out the largest ones to bring back to the mess hall. We enjoyed fresh fish for a good while."[51]

The men speared salmon with their bayonets; Ballew and a group of his friends bagged enough for their entire battery.[52]

Religious services were available, of course. Oddly enough, five of the men who participated in this study stated they attended weekly, an an equal number never went. Most attended occasionally. It is important to remember that during their Aleutian experience the men of the 206th were not stationed together at a single, well-established post, as they had been at Fort Bliss, with access to an attractive chapel and a full range of chaplain services. Instead, many of these men were scattered through various outposts, often isolated for days and weeks at a time. As Haskell Cathey remarked, "A chaplain would come to our outpost at different times and hold services, but not on a regular basis."[53] Weese remembered that services were available "at least two times per month somewhere in the regiment—usually at Headquarters Battery." After the move to Hog Island,* a chaplain visited the men about once a month.[54]

On his outpost, "Slats" Massey, although not yet ordained, "had a short service every Sunday and read the Bible two or three times a week on Position 6 for those that wanted to take part." Beasley always participated.[55]

Ballew only attended church "a little bit," but observed that the "Catholics went regularly." He added that after the Japanese attack on Dutch Harbor in June 1942 attendance picked up considerably.[56] The medics had their own chaplain, so Technician James O. Barron went "every Sunday if I could."[57] Fitzhugh, a committed Episcopalian, attended regularly after the Regimental Headquarters reached Dutch Harbor early in 1942, bringing an Episcopal chaplain. "Our commander would have no other denomination, although he himself was a Presbyterian," explained Fitzhugh. "In fact, I was acolyte for our chaplain."[58]

Considering the difficulty involved in churchgoing, and that these young men, little more than boys, were removed from the

---

* See chapter 24.

influence of family and community, it is remarkable that so many made the effort to keep in touch with the wellsprings of their faiths.

The atmosphere at Fort Mears was conducive to fads. "Everyone here is growing mustaches now that can," Alspaugh told his family on 16 November. "I have about a three weeks growth on my upper lip now but it can't exactly be called a mustache yet as it is heavy in places and thin in others. I am going to continue cultivating my growth though and hope for the best."[59]

Six days later, by a humorous coincidence, three recruits, the first since the 206th reached Alaska, joined Battery A. One of them was Pvt. Forrest "Frosty" Karst, who was immediately assigned to be the battery's barber.[60]

8

"Still Just a Big Adventure"

In some respects, the men of Battery H at Ladd Field were having experiences quite similar to those of their fellows at Fort Mears; in other respects, the situations were quite different. For one thing, nearby Fairbanks was a well-established town, and by comparison with Dutch Harbor it was virtually a metropolis. "Mainland Alaska was no different from Stateside in that there were towns to go to on pass," wrote Pfc Wilson. "Women were there to be seen but not many associated with troops and the competition for those who did was keen to say the least."[1]

Nevertheless, the hospitality of the Fairbanks citizens was a bright spot in the memory of all who served there. Richard Cawthron found them like "homefolks." They invited the soldiers to dinner and there were plenty of girls to date. "I would like to live here in civilian life," he wrote home.[2] Sergeant Brown agreed that the people were "so nice," although he entertained a dark suspicion that "a large percentage were 'wanted' in the States."[3]

A good bit of drinking went on, but it seemed to have lacked the desperate, frenetic quality of the drinking at Fort Mears, and evidently was confined to liquids intended for human consumption. "I was never an alcoholic, but living in close proximity with the many Btry 'H' men who lived for barroom brawls some of it gradually wore off on me," conceded Wilson. "It was available at any time one was on pass in town and the cost was like everything else in Alaska—inflated."[4]

Brown admitted that he drank more than he should. "If I had stayed up there I would have been an alcoholic." Apparently it was a joyless exercise—he drank to assuage his homesickness and especially his loneliness for his wife. Despite the pleasantness of their

62 STILL JUST A BIG ADVENTURE

surroundings, homesickness was rife. Brown remembered that one of the unit's phonograph records was a popular song of the day—"Goodbye, Dear, I'll Be Back in a Year." "One homesick guy walked up and broke it in a hundred pieces."[5]

It did not take Battery H long to discover the whereabouts of Fairbanks' houses of prostitution. On one occasion, a number of men were standing in line in front of one such institution when the chaplain passed by. He stopped and remarked, "Boys, I don't approve of this place, but since you're here, be comfortable!" With that, he distributed copies of *Yank* magazine down the line. Poker and craps were popular on base. "One fellow in the outfit cleaned up," Brown stated. "Bought a farm and team of mules for his parents."[6]

Of course, less controversial amusements were available. Wilson's favorite pastime was going to the movies. Refreshing his memory of some of the titles, he observed that "most were 'bombs' and I couldn't be PAID to sit through one of them today." He read a number of novels, and had access to Hot Springs newspapers. Although he did not subscribe, others did, and made them available to their buddies. He had no radio, but one was "generally . . . around somewhere." He enjoyed the Fairbanks station which "had a good repertory of popular and classical—not quite the fare of the average 206th trooper!" Mail was "fairly regular," and he remembered no problem in receiving letters from home.[7]

Perhaps a few of the sorts of delays that plagued the 206th men at Fort Mears might have done Battery H no harm. Brown, who subscribed to the Hot Springs *New Era*, began writing a series of articles about the day-to-day life of the home town boys. "The mothers liked it, and wrote me how they appreciated the articles as their sons wouldn't write."

Camping was popular, and during these expeditions the men would stay in "sourdough" huts. They meticulously obeyed the "law of the land"—to fill the woodbox and leave food staples "for the next guy." Men with an interest in arts and crafts found a beautiful outlet in the many mastodon tusks dug up locally, and they carved the ancient ivory into bracelets and other articles.[8]

At this time, and well into the spring of 1942, Battery H's housing was distinctly unusual, the entire outfit being located in Ladd Field's main aircraft hangar. "Bunks and lockers were arrayed in long lines extending the length of the building," Wilson described the arrangement. "Our mess hall was in the same hangar (without partitions) and our orderly room as at one end as well as supply room. Although entirely lacking in any kind of privacy, the quarters were very adequate and, most important—warm!"[9]

The unit was attached to the air corps for rations and administration. The arctic clothing issued was excellent. As Brown said, "Any time you are attached to the Air Corps, you get the best."[10] The issue included parkas with muskrat-trimmed hoods, sheepskin-lined mackinaws, heavy socks, mittens, fur caps, "felt high-topped shoes to wear inside of rubber overshoes (shoe paks)." During subzero conditions, interior guards wore sealskin pants. Wilson added, "The Army Air Corps people at Ladd Field offered to issue leather flight jackets to all of Battery 'H' enlisted men but our battery commander vetoed the idea on the grounds that the E.M. [enlisted men] would look too much like the Btry. 'H' officers who did have the jackets."[11]

That didn't sound very much like Capt. Richard L. Craigo, whom Brown considered "the greatest." He explained, "That man would loan you money out of his own pocket when you were in town broke. Covered for them when they got in trouble—a prince of a captain." Brown added, "We were blessed with wonderful officers. It was when we were attached that we had trouble."

One "trouble" was a certain captain who, when officer of the day, had the habit of throwing rocks to see if the men on guard duty were alert. After this happened a few times, one guard promised fervently, "I'll fix him!" So the next time the OD pulled his rock-throwing stunt, the guard answered with rifle shots. "Boy, the handkerchief came up fast! 'It's just Captain B_____, Captain B_____, Captain B_____!' That stopped that monkey business."[12]

Such annoyances were passing events, but Battery H had an ongoing problem, a serious one for service personnel. "Our cooks couldn't cook!" declared Wilson bitterly. "What they cooked they burned (including cocoa). We had a lot of goat stew and gristly hamburger meat. Cooks were, in general, a sorry lot and we dreaded serving under them when assigned to mess-hall duty (K.P.)" He added, "Cooked chicken would often show remains of feathers and sometimes be found half raw or partially spoiled." He summed up devastatingly, "I would rate the food and those who prepared it sort of on a level as that served on a Roman galley in ancient times."[13]

One GI—unidentified by name, unit, and location other than Alaska—suffered from food, among other complaints, and obviously felt under no obligation to put a good face on matters. He expressed himself in a letter that was a classic of its kind:

"We lie around in bed every morning until five o'clock, this of course gives us plenty of time to get washed, dressed, make your bunk, etc. by 5:10. At 5:15 we stand outside and shiver while some ?**!?&;**? blows a bugle. . . ." Then breakfast "of an unidentified liquid and a choice of white or rye bread." After that, "we just sit around and scrub the toilets, mop the floors, wash the windows, and pick up match stems, cigarette butts, and sticks within 50 yards of the barracks." Then calisthentics in "six inches of mud." They went on hikes to the mountains wearing "light packs." He explained, "Carrying my light pack, I weigh 253 pounds, so you can see how easy it is to romp and play in the mountains." He ended his letter, "I've got to mush to the mess hall. We're having hominy tonight. OH, BOY!"[14]

At this time, Battery H's official duties were mostly confined to guard. "The only hazard was roving bears looking for food," recalled Gaines Parker.[15]

Inevitably, someone captured two bears, a male and a female, and the battery adopted them. One night a sentry heard a noise near the hangar, saw what he thought was one of the pets, and prodded it toward the cages. He was surprised when it growled at him. Then he saw that Josephine and Bruno were safely in their cages, and he "realized he was prodding a wild bear and let out a yell that echoed throughout all Alaska . . ." The wild bear got away.[16]

Other men from Arkansas were stationed in Alaska, members of the 153d Infantry. These units were located at Fort Raymond, Seward. That port had a special economic and strategic importance, yet army troops weren't garrisoned there until the summer of 1941: ". . . Seward was the critical and most important supply funnel into mainland Alaska. Here was the only ocean terminal of the Alaska Railroad. Over Seward's docks poured vital cargoes destined for Anchorage and Fairbanks. . . . On the eve of World War II, the Alaska heartland, therefore, was almost totally dependent on the Seward sea-railroad connection."

Troops at Fort Raymond were "housed in a tent city at the

north edge of town while base construction was under way." As of November 1941, most soldiers were still in these tents.[17]

Cpl. Ralph I. Gardner of the 153d's Company L wrote to his home-town newspaper, giving a bit of local color. Alaskan prices appalled him. By today's standards, even in the lower forty-eight, the examples he cited are absurdly cheap, but this was 1941, and fifteen cent cokes, thirty-five cent hamburgers, seventy-five cent haircuts, fifty cent shaves, and fifty-five cents for either a "show ticket" or a slice of pie with a glass of milk, were considerably above average. However, Corporal Gardner was fair. He recognized that wages in Alaska were proportionately high. "A day's wage of $15 or $20 dollars here isn't anything." And Seward had its advantages: "This place is pretty good at that. . . . You should see the full moon shining with all its splendor on the tops of these snow-capped mountains."[18]

Around mid-November, Fort Mears received an influx of 206th troops from the states. This contingent included the regimental band.[19] They sailed aboard the *U.S.S. Grant*, a small troopship carrying some eight hundred men.[20] McKinistry remembered *Grant* as being "very cramped below decks with bunks at or below water level. We were eaten up by bedbugs from the bunks and all the mattresses were thrown overboard. We evacuated the holds and had to stay in the aisleways."[21]

Weese had more favorable memories, although he conceded conditions were crowded. However, en route "all of the NCOs (sergeant and above) had staterooms and ate in the ship's dining room. As I remember," he added, "the trip did not seem uncomfortable and for most men it was still just a big adventure because the thought of war was still very remote in our young minds."

As on the *St. Mihiel*, seasickness was rife. Some of Weese's men "got sick before the ship left the dock." Weese kept busy with the usual duties of a first sergeant—"morning report, sick report, assigning KP and guard, inspecting living quarters." And he "tried to keep everyone busy, so ship-cleaning details took a lot of extra time as well as helping in the ship's galley and standing 'watch' with the Navy personnel." What free time the men had was occupied in playing poker for low stakes, "sleeping. . . , writing letters, bull sessions, cleaning rifles, and watching the sea gulls."

Memories were vague as to their first stop on Alaskan soil. Weese thought it was Seward or Ketchikan. Whichever, the men were more than ready "to set foot on solid ground and most of them went to a cafe for solid food."[22]

McKinistry thought that *Grant* touched at Ketchikan, but didn't recall that anyone left the ship. Nor did anyone disembark at Sitka. "We got off the ship at Seward for exercise and [I] remember seeing a Sears-Roebuck mail order house (a very small building) where there was a native Alaskan woman (Eskimo, I presume) in charge." *Grant* stopped at Kodiak, then on to Dutch Harbor after a voyage of some ten days.[23]

Among those arriving on the *Grant* was Burke, recently released from the hospital in Seattle. "At this time I was still having problems with my leg after the accident," he wrote. "Because of this, I was put on flash phone duty." He vividly recalled one night when "a whale got caught in the submarine net. The whole island was put on alert. Everybody had to leave their quarters and get in foxholes."[24]

A soldier at Fort Mears wrote to the Camden, Arkansas, newspaper that the men were happy to see the band. He also observed, "We have excellent food."[25] Compared with Wilson's jaundiced view of the meals at Fairbanks, those meals served to the 206th in the Aleutians were indeed excellent. Considering the fact that it was traditional, almost obligatory, for GIs to gripe about the chow, comments on the subject were surprisingly favorable. These ran the gamut from a grudging "fair" to "good" and "very good." Of course, much of the basic material was canned, frozen or powdered, and took a bit of getting used to.

"We learned to tolerate and even enjoy powdered potatoes, milk, eggs," reported Sgt. Gill.[26] "I was introduced to powdered eggs, powdered milk, Spam, and others," recalled Sergeant Beverburg. "I found that after the cooks learned how to prepare these things, they were fit to eat and drink."[27] Oscar Jones remembered that they "ate a lot of Spam." And he made military history by declaring, "I liked it."[28] This in the face of a legend current during World War II that if you wanted a Section VIII discharge, all you had to do was say publicly, "I like Spam!" and your superiors would accommodate you immediately.

Then there was a form of butter prepared for use in cold climates, so that it wouldn't freeze. The trouble was, it wouldn't melt, either, even "if you dropped it on a hot stove top."[29] Decades later, Private Davis observed, "I wish I had some now to fix my roof."[30] But the men brought to their meals the best of all sauces—healthy young appetites—and in general would eat anything that didn't bite back.

During the prewar months, a certain amount of shakedown problems occurred. "On one occasion in the fall of 1941, groceries got short and we had cornflakes and water for breakfast," wrote Jodie Jones. "Other meals may have been reduced somewhat but we took it in stride. This only lasted a few days."[31]

"There were a few months after we first arrived . . . that the food was not good," said Corporal Hargrave. "We had pancakes just about every morning. At noon we either had sauerkraut and wieners or sauerkraut and pork ribs."[32] Pfc Henderson told of an occasion when the food situation caused a nasty flare-up:

> . . . Before Pearl Harbor there was a time we were low on rations. We ate beans and vegetables for breakfast. The men of Battery F went on strike because of food rations. We unloaded the ships and we knew how well the officers were eating so we all refused to fall out one morning until the food grievance was addressed. We did not win the war but we won the battle. Since we unloaded the ships, the first beef stopped by our mess hall. We had . . . eggs, bacon, chicken, and during our stay at Dutch Harbor Battery F was well fed.[33]

Captain Beverburg, too, remembered a snafu during this pre–Pearl Harbor period: "All canned fruit and vegetables were shipped packed in commercial packages, i.e., metal cans with paper wrappers or labels. We moved some of this by small boats to a searchlight position. We knew that rain or seawater would not damage the cans or the contents. However, no one thought about the labels coming off the cans. They did. So the cook's menu for a meal was determined by what was in the cans he opened."[34]

There was general agreement that whether one ate well or poorly depended largely upon the skill and experience of the mess staff, and the 206th was fortunate in that respect. "There were very few times that our meals were not up to par," stated Jodie Jones. "Innovative mess personnel turned out good meals. . . ."[35] T.4 Wiley H. Croom of Battery D said, "Our mess sergeant always saw that we had warm food. . . . One of our cooks could make the best pancakes. . . ."[36]

"Snuff" Garrett, mess sergeant of Battery B, was justifiably proud of his and his colleagues' record. Batteries A and B and Headquarters 1st Battalion shared "a mess hall assigned for two hundred men." At one time they were feeding over eight hundred men three meals a day. What is more, they fed them all on plates, and the KPs had trouble keeping pace with them. "We would get extra food any way we could. We also had some very good cooks. Butchers and bakers worked at night. We thought we did a good job."[37]

His comment about extra food referred to the fact that the mess sergeant's skill as a scrounger was as important as the skill of the cook. "Our mess sergeants were very resourceful," reminisced Albright. "We furnished trucks and drivers to unload all boats and our drivers were more than alert. If fresh meat, etc., was on the boats, we got our share."[38]

Barron of the Medics considered himself fortunate to eat with Battery A, where "the food was real good . . . and the mess sergeant took good care of us."[39] Stout remembered Battery A's mess sergeant well. "The troops in Alaska and the Aleutians were highly favored as to their diet allowance," he said. "We had no gripes about the food. We ate a lot better there than at Fort Bliss. A good mess hall depends on the mess sergeant and the cooks," he emphasized. "We had the best. Our mess sergeant, Ordie Vick, was the only one I knew of that was 'busted' for feeding too well." The colonel at the time, noting the high quality of the mess, suspected Vick of stealing supplies and fired him. "Immediately the good mess went down." Soon thereafter, the colonel reinstated him. "Good food again. The moral is, if you get a good mess sergeant, keep him."[40]

9

"It Really Looks Serious Now"

Just how forcefully the events in the outside world obtruded upon the consciousness of the men of the 206th is difficult to assess. They had the means to keep reasonably abreast through magazines, newspapers, newsreels, radio. Of these, only radio was truly current, and radio reception was not the best. However, in reading the diaries and letters of the period, and in assessing the oral testimony, one has the impression that they were absorbed in their local affairs, and that Washington, D.C., was as remote to them as Lhasa, Tibet. Yet events on the diplomatic front—the long-drawn-out discussions between Secretary of State Cordell Hull and Japanese Ambassador Kichisaburo Nomura—as well as the Far Eastern military events would soon have a direct effect upon the 206th, indeed upon every living person under the American and Japanese flags.

On 27 November a warning message went from the War Department to the Western Defense Command:

> Negotiations with Japan appear to be terminated to all practical purposes with only the barest possibilities that the Japanese Government might come back and offer to continue. Japanese future action unpredictable but hostile action possible at any moment. If hostilities cannot repeat cannot be avoided the United States desires that Japan commit the first overt act. This policy should not repeat not be construed as restricting you to a course of action that might jeopardize your defense. Prior to hostile Japanese action you are directed to undertake such reconnaissance and other measures as you deem necessary but these measures should be carried out so as not repeat not to alarm the civil population or disclose intent. Report measures taken. A separate message is being sent to G-2 Ninth Corps Area re subversive activities in United States. Should hostilities occur

you will carry out the tasks assigned in rainbow five* so far as they pertain to Japan. Limit dissemination of this highly secret information to minimum essential officers. MARSHALL.[1]

With minor changes to meet the local situations, this same message went also to the commanders in Hawaii, the Philippines, and the Canal Zone.

The next day, the chief of Naval Operations relayed the message for action to the commanders of the Pacific Northern Naval Coastal Frontier and his Southern counterpart.[2]

DeWitt immediately paraphrased the War Department message to his subordinate commands, including the Alaska Defense Command. He outlined to Washington the measures he had taken:

> All harbor entrance control posts continuously manned. One gun battery each harbor defense continuously alerted. Protection against sabotage and other subversive activities intensified. Six infy battalions and necessary motor transportation alerted so as to be instantly available to CG NCA to carry out his missions under Rainbow Five. Constant contact being maintained with corps area and naval district commanders and full cooperation assured. PCF, sector and subsector plans Rainbow Five practically completed and necessary reconnaissance being made to carry out duty and one company furnished to CG NCA for internment aliens at Angel Island.

He reminded his superiors that he had already recommended that WPL 52 be "extended to include Pacific coast and Japanese vessels" and had outlined "steps taken by me in preparation therefore." He strongly urged that he be authorized to direct "Air Forces as well as other Army forces" involved in the execution of WPL 52 "or the preparatory stage of Rainbow Five." He ended with a touch of asperity: "Should hostilities occur this command now ready to carry out tasks assigned in Rainbow Five so far as they pertain to Japan except for woeful shortage of ammunition and pursuit and bombardment planes which should be made available without delay."[3]

On 28 November, the G-2 at Seward received and decoded the warning: "The Fort Raymond commander reacted swiftly. He

---

* The basic war plan.

ordered additional troop deployments around Seward's port facilities and along the north shoreline of Resurrection Bay. He also ordered a blackout of the entire area." These actions fueled a number of rumors, but there was no panic.[4]

Unknown to the defenders of the Aleutians, during this period the area had been under observation by one of Japan's sharpest submarine captains, Cmdr. Minoru Yokota of the *I-26*. He left Japan on 19 November, proceeding on the surface until some six hundred miles from the archipelago. Thenceforth he surfaced only at night. Near Attu, he scouted Kiska on or about 26 November. He sailed from Kiska to Adak in a heavy thunderstorm. As he moved from the outer Aleutians to Dutch Harbor, he decided that the Americans were ill prepared.

He scouted Dutch Harbor on the morning of 29 November. He did not sail into the anchorage itself, but did move in to the point where he could see men moving about on shore. Leaving the area that afternoon, he doubled back westward to Amutka Passage between the Fox Islands and the Andreanofs. He guided *I-26* through the passage on 30 November, and once more he headed eastward, this time to take up his assigned position for the Pearl Harbor attack.[5]

Some in the 206th knew about the alert. Dodson recorded in his diary on 29 November: "Orders issued to man all sections 24 hours. Shoot all Japanese planes and boats. It really looks serious now."[6] Alspaugh wrote his mother on 3 December: "We are now keeping a constant vigilance for any enemy attack. We are manning our positions 24 hours a day. . . ."[7] On the other hand, around 1 December many checked in some of their equipment "since our year was about up . . ."[8]

In one respect the men were better prepared to face a crisis than if it had arisen earlier. They had come to the Aleutians equipped with the 1903 Springfield rifles. In November 1941 they received M-1 rifles and carbines.[9] Just how well qualified the men were to do any damage with these weapons is another matter. "Firing of personal weapons was totally inadequate in the Aleutians or elsewhere," declared Stout. "What is the use of giving a man a weapon when he's not trained to hit anything with it?"[10]

The only such training Paulus remembered was "taking a M-1 rifle apart and putting it back together blindfolded." He never did figure out the reason for this exercise.[11] Weese recalled having "to attend endless classes where the officers taught using manuals printed around World War I. An example was how to fieldstrip, clean and maintain a Springfield rifle. We all had M-1s."[12] "We had not fired the M-1 rifles we had at the time of Pearl Harbor," wrote Hargrave. "On that afternoon we were taken to a place where we could fire them a few rounds of 'familiarization' firing."[13]

Radney stated that they "trained daily, field stripping and cleaning the 50 cal. water-cooled machine gun, but did no actual firing until after the June raids."[14]

Many agreed that their training was adequate per se, and that the officers and NCOs did their best with what was available. However, much of the equipment was outdated. "This is ridiculous," fumed McKinistry, "and I think the US military command in the states should have been made more aware of this."[15]

In some cases, the problem was a combination of inexperienced personnel, primitive equipment, and local conditions. Of course, they had received training in their basic antiaircraft weapons at Fort Bliss and before, so training in the Aleutians was a matter of follow-up and practice. Some considered this adequate. "All we were there for was to fire our 3" guns," said Paulus, "and that's what they trained us for."[16]

"All of my training was on the 3" AA guns," wrote Private Davis. "We mostly just kept in good practice with dummy shells." He added with some pride, "Blackie Bolton and I held the record for the most dummy shells run through a gun in thirty minutes. I think about fifty a minute. I was the relayer and Blackie was the gunner."[17]

Others, though, questioned the effectiveness of both the training and the guns. "Training in the Aleutians was very inadequate," declared Weese. "Our job was to shoot down Jap planes and we never had any practice. We practiced a lot of things, but never the thing we were sent there to do." He explained, "Our units were constantly practicing on the 3" AA guns with dummy ammo. However, when the Japs came our guns had never been fired at a moving target. This included summer camps at Pensacola, FL in 1939 and in Minnesota in 1940. As I was to learn later . . . , the antiquated equipment and ammunition we had in the Aleutians couldn't have shot down a plane if it had been standing still."[18]

Hargrave did not think they received sufficient practice "in firing the 37mm guns, especially those who would have had to replace the gunners if the gunners became disabled."[19] T. 5 Everette C. Carnes of Battery H stated bluntly, "The training was not adequate because there was no one with experience to train us."[20]

Late in 1941, Battery A received "an early type radar device."[21] Many had kind words for the radar and claimed it was useful, especially after war had come to the Aleutians, and it was used to track planes. Nevertheless, "bugs" soon developed. In the first place, no one knew much about it. "Radar training was very poor," averred Costley, "as when we received them we had no qualified personnel. It was a hit-and-miss type situation—field manual and practical experience."[22]

"They sent us radars and no one knew how to set them up and operate them," Stout wrote.[23] "We had very little training about radar," agreed Sisk. "About all we learned before coming back stateside was a basic operation of the contraption."[24]

Nor were these "contraptions" the sensitive, sophisticated equipment into which radar eventually evolved. "The radar units were so crude they were probably a waste of time," said Jodie Jones, "but . . . they were state of the art for the time."[25] And Garrett conceded, "The radar was crude, but it was the best we had there."[26]

The peculiar weather and terrain added to the woes of the radar personnel. It did not work at the two outposts O'Neal helped construct, "and the antennas could not take the high winds."[27] "The areas in which we operated were poor for radar coverage," Alspaugh explained. "We were surrounded by mountains containing mineral deposits and this made searching and tracking difficult." He added, "Our radar equipment was some of the first produced and became obsolete early in the war."[28]

Worse, it proved disappointing as an AA aide. "We knew that we could have fired the guns at anything in their range and hit most water-borne slow-moving targets," wrote Sergeant Beverburg. "But because of its wobble tracking, no good rate could be sensed for computing lead, therefore it would have been very unusual to be able to hit aircraft in flight."[29] The radar units were a bitter disappointment to Capt. James A. Langley of Headquarters Battery: "Radar units (SCR 268) of which we had only one was absolutely worthless—I got my butt chewed out by Col. Robertson frequently because he thought it was only a matter of training," he stated, "but this set (pre-model T) was electrically and mechanically completely unusable for AA fire. I took great pleasure in taking a W[ar] D[epartment] circular to the colonel where 268s were of no value except early warning on flat coastal areas."[30]

Nor did searchlights live up to expectations, although some were loyal to them. "At that time searchlights were an integral part of defense against planes," said Jodie Jones. "Not only did they show a target for the guns to shoot at, but when a plane was caught by the light the pilot was blinded and possibly disoriented."[31] Dodson observed crisply, "Searchlights were useful and a wonderful morale factor."[32] In that respect, the searchlights occasionally served as a homing device. Alspaugh thought they may have "aided aircraft which were lost or off course in some instances."[33] "The only time they were of use was when a PBY was lost or late from a patrol," wrote Haden. "We would shine the lights vertically at night to give the flyboys something to home on."[34] Proffitt agreed that over the long haul, "The powerful illumination of the searchlights saved a lot of pilots as they were used in heavy fog for navy PBYs trying to land."[35]

Others, such as 1st Sgt. John A. Thomason, Jr., of Battery G, believed that the lights were of indirect use, providing experience that was valuable in the European Theater later in the war.[36] Some, for example, Sergeant Beverburg, believed that while the lights themselves were of little value, their outposts filled a need, ". . . having men at the outlying sites reporting that they were still there and not captured was of some value and comfort."[37]

The general opinion, however, was that operating searchlights in the Aleutians was a waste of time. Their awesome 800 million candlepower could no more penetrate the Aleutian fog than it could have shone through solid concrete. "They were useless in the fog and low-lying clouds," remarked Stout. "They would more likely guide the enemy to us!"[38] The major reason for having searchlights was to spot enemy aircraft at night, and many Dutch Harbor veterans agreed that nobody in his senses would launch a night air attack in that area. As Costley observed, ". . . any commander would be foolish to send aircraft of that vintage into the air in that area after dark."[39] Burris, too, thought the lights "a waste of time and money. The weather was so bad that you could only fly in the daytime, so we really had no use for them."[40] "Without some form of electronically controlled guidance system, there was no way possible to keep a light on target," explained Weese. "If the guns couldn't see the target, there was no way to fire. So the whole operation was useless at night."[41]

To sum up, the 206th men were on the alert, were willing and courageous, but ill equipped to face a major crisis. The same could be said of their airborne colleagues. The army air force had a mere 2,200 officers and men stationed in Alaska as December 1941 opened. Units had begun arriving in February 1941, on 29 May were consolidated into Air Field Forces of the Alaska Defense Command, and on 17 October this organization was redesignated Air Force, ADC, with chain of command through ADC to Western Defense Command to War Department.[42]

In the case of overseas bases accessible by air from the continental United States, the army's policy was to hold the local air strength to the minimum deemed essential to meet emergencies, on the rather naïve assumption that reinforcements could be rushed to the spot. Buckner, DeWitt, and Lt. Col. Everett S. Davis, the air force commander, urgently requested that more air strength be permanently stationed in Alaska. They pointed out that even if air reinforcements could reach Alaska in time to be of use, their crews would be "unfamiliar with the Alaskan terrain and flying conditions, and the resulting loss of life and equipment might be prohibitive." Headquarters AAF was sympathetic and promised help as soon as aircraft were available. But, while plans were under way to enlarge the Air Force, ADC, the fact remained: As of the first week of December, "the aircraft strength in Alaska still consisted of twelve B-18As and twenty P-36s. . . . The air force of the Alaska Defense Command was, in fact, the only overseas air force which did not possess a single up-to-date plane prior to the outbreak of hostilities."[43]

In fact, joint army-navy plans postulated that defense of Alaska "was essentially a function of the navy, supported by air and ground forces at those points where coastal installations required protection from air raid." Prewar strategy was to center Alaskan defense in the Seward-Anchorage area, while the navy bases at Kodiak and Dutch Harbor would be the hub of the navy's control of the North Pacific.

Realizing that the latter anchorage would require protection from the air, the AAF wanted to construct an airfield on Umnak

Island. Some naval authorities objected on the ground that Umnak had no adequate harbor, and "construction of the base would put an increased strain on sea communications. . . ." But the hundreds of miles that the Umnak base would add to the bombers' range were cogent arguments. Nevertheless, the navy insisted that the proposal be put to the Joint Board. That organization flashed the green light on 26 November—just one day before the War Department's warning.[44]

Noted naval analyst Fletcher Pratt etched in acid his opinion of matters in Alaska at this stage:

> The actual situation on the day of Pearl Harbor was this: At Sitka the antique liner *City of Baltimore* housed a thousand workers, who were making a good job last as long as possible while they set up facilities for two squadrons of seaplanes. At Kodiak the derelict *Yale* housed a similar party who had run the price of red-eye up to $5.50 a quart in town; at Dutch Harbor (Unalaska) there was another game on the old *Northwestern*. . . . The Anchorage base had its runway, with a single squadron of dowager B18 bombers and a squadron of the P36 fighters that had been hot stuff eight years before.[45]

This period of watchful waiting climaxed with a bang at Seward on 6 December, ironically in a manner not in the least related to the crisis for which Alaska's defenders had been preparing. What the press termed "the most disastrous fire in the history of Alaska" devastated the business section of Seward and left hundreds homeless. The Arkansas men stationed there were among the most active fire fighters. They "rolled out of bed in the early morning . . . , faced a howling gale and fought fire during the remainder of the night with the water freezing and coating their clothing with ice." In the morning they were relieved to eat and change clothes, but soon returned to the scene. Some manned hose; some removed people from the path of the fire, saving what valuables they could; others stood guard to keep people out of the danger zone. The army donated clothes, bedding, and helped feed the refugees. The only way to stop the fire was by dynamiting buildings in its path. Damage was estimated at $1,000,000—a stunning amount in 1941.[46] Dreadful as the fire was, the events of 7 December soon relegated it to the inside pages.

10

"This Is It!"

S taff Sergeant Proffitt was on guard duty at the E-1 gun position overlooking Dutch Harbor and the *Northwestern* on 7 December 1941. At about 1000, he was surprised to see "the company of Marines . . . march by his position, in full battle dress and heading in the direction of Mt. Ballyhoo." He didn't learn of the Japanese attack on Pearl Harbor until some two hours later, but, in view of the marine exercise, assumed that the navy "had the information of the attack before 1000 hours that morning."[1]

Since it was Sunday, Drake slept in, rose about 0800, and sauntered over to the mess hall an hour or so later. The men chatted about the football game due to be broadcast from the West Coast at 1100 Dutch Harbor time. Drake and some of his buddies were back in the barracks listening to the game when the announcer interrupted with the news of Pearl Harbor, stating that "the attack had caused heavy damage to the naval ships and installations . . ." The men listened incredulously; this must be a hoax!

But "within minutes, the siren sounded at Post Headquarters and an officers' call went out to all US Army units to assemble at Post Headquarters. 1st Sgt. Vernon Nash assembled all available NCOs and instructed the men of the Battery to remain in their barracks to await further instructions." At about 1300, Captain Schiebner briefed the NCOs on the attack, stating "that all military units at Fort Mears and Dutch Harbor had been placed on alert and combat status. Also, the entire island would revert to blackout status during the hours of darkness."[2]

That morning Cpl. Robert L. Walkup, Sr., of Battery D was admitted to the Fort Mears hospital with the mumps. Evidently there had been a minor epidemic of this distressing disease, because he found himself one of sixty-five suffering from the same complaint. They had taken sidearms and ammunition with them to the hospital. They "heard the news on the radio . . ."[3]

Sisk was also in the hospital, recovering from the flu. "I asked to get out of that hospital so I could go back to my gun position and have a fighting chance. My request was promptly granted." He felt quite pessimistic. Considering the personnel and equipment available, "things didn't look good for our side."[4]

Another hospital patient was Alspaugh, who had contracted pneumonia at his gun emplacement. As he had just been admitted on 6 December, there could be no question of release.[5] Under the circumstances, he had been unable to mail the letter to his mother he had begun on 3 December and now made an addition dated 7 December: "It looks like it has come. We are on a constant alert now. Our gun positions are manned at all times. We haven't heard much from Pearl Harbor but it is enough to start a war. . . ."[6]

Corporal Tate "was playing knock poker with some of the fellows. We were all sitting in our underwear when Staff Sergeant Dick Kaufman, acting first sergeant, blew his whistle and hollered, 'Fall out, you SOBs! The Japs have bombed Pearl Harbor!'"[7]

Staff Sergeant Taylor didn't get the word until that night. He had just been issued an M-1 rifle, a type he had never seen before. "I had placed old newspapers on the floor of my bunk in the barracks to put the parts of my rifle on in order to clean it," he related. "Our 'top kick' came to the back door of the barracks screaming, 'Turn out the lights! The Japs just hit Pearl Harbor!' Well, here I am down on the floor with a brand new rifle all apart and no lights. Anyway, I got that rifle cleaned and put back together in record time."[8]

Another who got the news late was O'Neal, then a corporal in charge of a squad constructing a forward observation post. As he remarked later, during 1941 "it seemed like everything required some sort of a hole in the ground. We dug little holes, big holes, and holes in between the little and big." So on 7 December, as he later wrote, "We were building this position when Japan made the attack on Pearl Harbor and it was the morning of December 8, 1941, before we knew of the attack. As usual the radio was not working. . . . On December 8, 1941, an officer and a squad of men were sent around the beach to our position to warn that we might be attacked at any time." O'Neal and his men "went into high gear working to complete construction of the outpost." A number of foxholes surrounded the complex. "Most of us felt at the time that the fox holes would serve as our graves as we were in a forward position that could not be held against an attack on land. Our feelings were to take as many Japanese with us as we could when the time came. . . ."[9]

The men of the 206th shared to the fullest the general American reactions of shock, anger, and incredulity. Sergeant Laubach was stunned, and he couldn't believe what he heard on the radio. He was only eighteen years old, and this was the first time he "ever experienced anything of this magnitude."[10]

Weese "had just turned 20 years old, knew very little about the world situation or the war in Europe . . ." He couldn't believe that the United States "could be so vulnerable and ill-prepared—after all, we had been raised to believe the US was the greatest country in the world and as such was indestructible. It never entered my mind that we could lose the war and thought it would only be a short while before the war was all over. As I said, we had very little news and had no idea how badly crippled our navy was." He emphasized, however, that for at least a week the 206th had been on a red alert. "When the word came, the only surprise was that it was Pearl Harbor instead of Dutch Harbor."[11]

Pfc Fitzhugh experienced a solemn sense that this was war, and he and his buddies would see action, "that we were at a point in the history of the US where we would play a role in it."[12] Jodie Jones wasn't certain what this would mean for the 206th. "I knew it wasn't far to the Kurile Islands, but as an average American, I didn't think they could hold their own against us for very long." That being the case, "Let's get on with it and get it over."[13] Pfc Devoe H. Cowell of Battery F shared this initial sense of optimism. He thought, "about like everyone else—that the Japs would be whipped in a month or so."[14]

Sgt. James M. Massey, who had been released from active duty earlier in the year to help settle his father's estate, was promptly recalled to active duty in his old unit. "People say we can whip the Japs in 6 months, but I doubt it," he noted. "The country in a turmoil."[15] In addition to these generalized sentiments, Pearl Harbor forced two exceedingly unpalatable circumstances upon the 206th's collective consciousness. First, the expectation of returning to Arkansas in January had been sunk deeper than the waters of Pearl Harbor. In the words of the official diary, "Gone was the sadly mistaken impression that they were in for a year."[16]

Callaway's initial reaction was, "Here goes my college education." Instead, he was stuck with "an extended tour in an undesirable country."[17] Henderson, too, was "very disappointed" at the interruption of his career plans. He had wanted "to return to college at Russellville," then go on to the University of Arkansas. Now he and his comrades faced "a long war" and a "cold campaign."[18] Sergeant Beverburg "was told not to expect reinforcements or replacements." He added, "It didn't take much of a genius to figure out that the one year of Federal service limitation was out of sight."[19]

Of even more immediate concern was the almost unanimous fear and expectation that Dutch Harbor would be next on the Japanese hit list. Sergeant Gill's thoughts "ran the entire gamut of possibilities. The Japanese were on the attack—why not the Aleutians, too?" He didn't look forward to fighting, either on the ground or in the air.[20] This was not cowardice; it was a realistic assessment of their ability to engage a determined, well-equipped enemy.

Pearl Harbor shocked Fox Conway. He knew the 206th didn't have very many men, and it had very little equipment to fight with, so he wondered what would happen next.[21] O'Neal's initial thought was that he had no ammunition for his rifle, and asked himself, "When do we get ammunition?" He added, "When things finally soaked in, I felt we would be the next target, and with no navy to protect us and knowing what we had I felt we would be attacked and overrun."[22]

S. Sgt. Clifford C. Caldwell was "bewildered, scared, angry." He anticipated "continued air attacks with invasion to come."[23]

Many years later, Raney observed in a newspaper interview that "a lot of the men at Dutch Harbor were convinced that the Japanese would attack the United States from the north and that the 206th Coast Artillery already had been written off as expendable by the American command." He added, "Some of us buried our personal effects and valuables in tin cans and vowed not to be taken alive. I fully expected to be buried at Dutch Harbor."[24]

Captain Wall felt a surge of increased interest in their mission, "realizing that this was not a maneuver but real war." He expected "a similar attack at any time. Communication between army and navy was nil." [25] Walkup believed that he and his comrades "must be ready to fight. We probably would be attacked by sea, air, and troops coming off landing barges." [26] Garrett reflected gloomily, "At the time, we had only enough ammunition to fire the 3" guns for two minutes rapid fire." [27]

Sgt. Cleo J. Eason of Battery F felt some anxiety because "it was thought that the Japanese would attack U.S. by way of Alaska." [28] Taylor admitted to being "scared as hell," nevertheless, "At the time I didn't think the Japs were crazy enough to want a place like that. Later I got my mind changed. I never did think the Japs could take us," he emphasized. "Even though we had our backs to the wall, there was no place to go, we were there already." He produced a touch of youthful gasconade: "Those Japs had never been in a fight with a bunch of guys from Arkansas," an exercise he described as "like punching a bear in the butt. He will turn around and kill you." [29] T. Sgt. Alfred F. Nichols of Battery B delved below the surface, reflecting, "Someone was asleep at the wheel in Hawaii since we had been notified by G-2 that Hawaii or DH would be attacked." [30] Technically, this was incorrect. The War Department had warned only: "Japanese future action unpredictable but hostile action possible at any moment."* Nevertheless, Nichols raised a valid point: Dutch Harbor had been on the alert; why hadn't Pearl Harbor? This reflection was what stunned Lt. Otis E. Hays, Jr., who was Fort Raymond's intelligence officer, with additional duty as public relations officer. When the word of Pearl Harbor reached Seward, Hays "felt numb and confused." He explained why: "When we heard that neither Hawaii nor the Philippines had been on war alert, I could not understand why. After all, they had received the same warning message that I had decoded 10 days earlier." [31] Many years, investigations, books, articles, and studies later, no definitive, single answer satisfactory to everyone has ever been forthcoming. [32]

"We were awakened by our Commanding Officer, Richard L. Craigo, . . . the Sunday morning of the attack," recalled Sergeant

---

* See chapter 9.

Campbell. "He informed us of the attack and instructed us to prepare ourselves as an attack on our installation (Ladd Field) was probable."[33] Wilson was "'thunderstruck' to say the least. This was 'war' and I would be a part of it. I wondered what would develop for us next besides not being demobilized in early 1942."[34]

Out in the wilderness, not too far from Fairbanks, a beaver trapper's homemade battery radio brought him the news of Pearl Harbor. Many native Alaskans detested the Japanese for reasons unconnected with the war. They had had too many fishing boats rammed, nets slashed, and salmon catches hijacked, too many fox pelts stolen to have any cause to love the Japanese. The trapper saw a chance to do his bit. He knew that a hundred drums of aviation gas stood out in the open near an emergency runway. So he rounded up a number of Indians and with their help moved the drums into the woods, buried them in snow, and camouflaged the site with spruce branches. The canny trapper dragged boughs behind him as he snowshoed home, to erase his tracks. Next, he hitched up his dog team and mushed to Fairbanks. At Ladd Field he found an Army official, and matter-of-factly told that somewhat dazed officer, "Thought I'd better tell you where I hid your gas, in case you might want to find it again."[35]

The men of the 206th back in the lower forty-eight experienced much the same sensations as animated their colleagues in Alaska, lacking only the fear of immediate, personal danger. According to Sergeant Haden, they "had more or less expected war." Still, the actuality delivered a punch: "What the hell!! This is it! Pearl Harbor? Where's Pearl Harbor?"[36] Sgt. James Ryals of Battery G "didn't know where Pearl Harbor was," either. This he did know: ". . . it wasn't good news."[37]

"We were completely flabbergasted," wrote Costley. "Guys of our age at that time were not familiar or paid that much attention to world politics. Consequently, it came as quite a shock."[38]

Patrick "was about to get released from the army on a hardship case," and the news of Pearl Harbor plunged him into depression. "I knew that I would not get to go home. I don't think I ever thought about the heartbreaks and hardships that were to come."[39] Maj. Pat M. Kee of Battery D knew he could bid farewell to his basketball scholarship at Louisiana State University. "This meant war."[40]

Possibly the most disconcerting experience was that of Sgt. James M. Simmons of Battery A. His discharge had been signed and was waiting for him to pick up. But there seemed to be no hurry, so he waited to see a football game between the 206th and, to the best of his recollection, the 41st Division. As a result, instead of having his discharge in hand and being well on his way to Little Rock, he was still in camp when the Japanese struck Pearl Harbor. "Upon the news of the bombing, my discharge was torn up right before my eyes," he related.[41]

Pearl Harbor had an immediate, abrupt effect upon these men. "We moved out that afternoon for Boeing Field near Seattle," said Burris. "We set our guns up around the field."[42] So sudden was the move that Corporal Kinney, who had been washing his clothes, "had to dump them wringer-wet" into his duffel bag.[43] While dressing that morning, all Keeton could think was, "Well, here it is, what lies ahead?" He soon found out, for his unit "immediately left Fort Lewis on reconnaissance to Boeing Aircraft plant to emplace our guns for defense.

"After getting over the shock of the PH attack and emplacing our guns at Boeing," Keeton went on, "we continued practicing for the football game with Moffit Field, CA, for the Pacific coast championship. . . . The game was to be played at the University of Washington stadium and was a sellout." But the men were in for a sharp disappointment and another if minor grudge against the Japanese. "Gen. DeWitt issued a statement that 40,000 troops could not be assembled at one location." He canceled the game and sent the California men back to their station. Within about a week, the stateside 206th men had been issued M-1 rifles, and many were on the verge of leaving for the Aleutians.[44]

Meanwhile, the Fairbanks contingent was having weapons troubles. Capt. John T. Meek's platoon was equipped with .50 cal. machine guns. "When the Japs bombed PH we had no ammunition, and the air corps sent a plane to Anchorage and brought us one case of ammunition."[45]

"About 1 week after Pearl Harbor," reminisced Sergeant Campbell, "I was able to locate some practice ammo for our 37 mm AA guns." This, too, was delivered by aircraft. "As soon as we received the ammo, Capt. Craigo scheduled a practice session with our new 37 mm guns (which we had never fired.) To our surprise, the recoil mech[anism] would not work. The guns had to be thawed and anti-freeze installed in place of the oil."[46] One suspects that at this time the job of supply sergeant in Alaska would have ranked high on any list of the army's most frustrating occupations.

The events at Pearl Harbor brought to Lieutenant Hays at Seward a task that he frankly dreaded. That evening he received a telephone call from Alaska Defense Command Headquarters at Fort Richardson, ordering him to detain the proprietor of the local laundry, Harry Kawabe. Kawabe and his wife Tomo lived over the shop.[47] Kawabe was much more than the owner of a laundry. He had come to Alaska in 1908 and had lived in Seward since 1916. After purchasing his steam laundry, he branched out in many directions. His interests included "a fur store, gift shop, gold-mining operation, and investment firm."[48]

In his account, Hays made no mention of Kawabe's many business connections, and possibly he was unaware of them. Thus his distress at having to arrest Kawabe seems not to have been from a disinclination to push around one of Seward's leading citizens, but from a genuine degree of sympathy for a harmless human being caught up in forces beyond the control of either of them.

Kawabe put up no fight and stoically left his home "without a backward glance." Tomo, one hand over her mouth, followed her husband with her eyes. Feeling helpless, Hays said to her, "Don't worry. You'll see him soon." He had no idea whether or not this was the truth, but had to offer some comfort to this woman who was "in an apparent state of shock. . . ."

Anticipating "bigotry and fear" in the wake of Pearl Harbor, Hays arranged for Kawabe to be smuggled to Anchorage in the caboose of a freight train. Nearly forty-eight hours later, Kawabe's laundry workers were sent after him "in like manner," while wives and children went to Anchorage a few weeks later.

This was well before the major transport of Japanese Americans from Alaska to the mainland. After the peace released Kawabe and his fellow internees, he never returned to Alaska except to visit. He established himself in Seattle so well that eventually the city honored his memory by naming him one of its "outstanding minority leaders."[49]

11

"Under Trying Conditions"

The opening of hostilities resulted in a number of drastic changes in the life style of the men in Alaska. One of the first and most annoying was the immediate introduction of censorship. Freedom of speech and writing is a concept so deeply ingrained in the American tradition that the very word "censorship" raises the hackles. No sooner had the news of Pearl Harbor been received than orders were issued that "until further notice, a strict censorship of all mail leaving Dutch Harbor would be in effect, to include photographs and film negatives. This announcement utterly stunned everyone present; however, the men accepted the censorship of mail as a necessary evil. . . ."[1]

This was only partially true. Some indeed accepted the censorship in the same stoical spirit they accepted all their other hardships. Sisk, for one, thought the arrangement fair. "We had instructions about what we should not write about and all you had to do was obey the rules."[2] Croom agreed: "We were aware of what we could write about."[3] And Captain Beverburg quoted the wartime slogan: "Loose lips sink ships."[4]

In contrast, Dodson considered the censorship "excessive and ridiculous."[5] Weese explained, "Mail was not censored when we first arrived at DH since the war hadn't started. So everyone back home knew where we were and all about DH. Censorship was started after the attack on PH but didn't make much sense because we didn't know anything to tell or write about that was censorable. Everyone knew where we were but if we mentioned DH or anything remotely concerning it, the censor would cut it out. Yes," he added resignedly, "it was excessive and, as usual, we had no recourse or no one to complain to, so we griped to each other."[6]

Usually O'Neal took the attitude that although "what they cut out was a little silly," the officers "were just trying to do a good job." But he did get "a little mad one time when they rejected a letter that was written on toilet paper out of a K ration box." It was the only paper O'Neal had at the time.[7] "You could not mention [the] word Dutch or even Harbor, or [the] name of an officer."[8] Moreover, noted Raney, "Any mention of the weather was cut out."[9]

Jodie Jones was reprimanded for mentioning that he saw their dog chasing a fox. He noted, "Letters to men with German names had incoming mail closely censored."[10] After Rybel returned to the states, his family showed him some of his letters. "I couldn't read [them] myself."[11]

"Pictures were the problem," according to Stout. "Our intelligence officer confiscated scenic and local pictures and put them in individual folders. When we returned to the states each person could get his pictures from him."[12] Costley "heard later that our area was the most heavily censored of any theater of operations."[13]

In addition to this generalized belief that the censorship was much too tight and, in fact, was unnecessary, the men had a more personal problem with it, which Gill explained clearly: ". . . I did have a complaint of who was doing the censorship. Company and Regimental officers who knew many of the men, some on a personal basis, were doing the censoring. Even in war time this should never have occurred. The censors should have been people that had no acquaintance in any way whatsoever with the troops whose mail was being censored. This is the type of entrance into one's private life and relationships that should never have been allowed. . . ."[14]

Ryals, too, resented the officers' reading his mail.[15] Kinney noted that "the officers whose duty it was to censor knew too much about personal affairs."[16] At Ladd Field, Brown had the same complaint: "I really didn't like it that our officer did the censoring. He knew my wife well and I resented it, but nothing I could do."[17]

Dislike of the restrictions went much deeper than standard GI griping. Admiral Pratt fulminated that the entire Alaska campaign was conducted

. . . under the veil of a censorship that yielded nothing to those of Germany or China for restrictiveness and sheer stupidity.

A good case of the stupidity is the fact that throughout Alaska territory the people for nearly two years of war never got a magazine or a newspaper from which all reference to Alaska had not been carefully clipped; and that correspondents were not allowed to mention the presence of our troops at Amchitka and Adak till they had been there for six months, with Jap bombers coming over almost daily and telling the world about it all the time in radio broadcasts; and that even private mail was censored. . . . The ridiculous censorship came down hard on the soldiers and still harder on the base workers; a lot of the base workers quit, and the morale of the Alaska Defense Command began to go down as rumor chased rumor and the Japs crowed over the radio.[18]

Next on the agenda was the institution of a blackout. Under the supervision of Battery A's carpenter, T. 5 Joel McDill, work began immediately on blackout panels. McDill had already designed a panel to act as a pattern. Following this design, the men worked steadily, and the entire project was completed on 8 December.[19]

Work stepped up provisioning outposts. Headquarters 1st Battalion had an observation post on top of Mt. Ballyhoo. Three soldiers, rotated frequently, manned this location. Fitzhugh vividly described the action on that memorable day:

> . . . Immediately after our noon meal on Sunday, December 7th, all battery personnel fell in to resupply the observation post, as no one knew what would take place later. We convoyed to the 250th CA (HD) gun positions which were located about two-thirds up the mountain. There the trucks were parked and each person took a case of C rations, a 5-gal. can of water and/or fuel oil, or some presto-logs. We walked the rest of the height to the top of Ballyhoo through snow which was above waist deep. After depositing our loading some of us got the cardboard cartons from C rations, flattened them out and tobogganed down the south slope to the foot of the mountain. We were there waiting for the truck for some time.[20]

In the period after Pearl Harbor, the men were "hard at work increasing their tactical positions and preparing for any eventuality." The Battery K historian added, "Construction crews of all sorts were formed including what the boys like to affectionately refer to as the 'Burma Road of the Aleutians.'"[21]

Just how much affection "the boys" actually had for these

details is highly questionable. There are more pleasant lots in life than working outdoors in an Aleutian winter, struggling through waist-high snow while loaded down with supplies because the motorized equipment had either stalled, had never got started, or could only go just so far. "All of our vehicles were 'vintage' National Guard types, many years old and no 4-wheel drive at all," related Weese. "The men would spend hours each day trying to get just one started and running, and then had no place to go."[22]

Oscar Jones remembered snow so deep that it stalled heavy trucks,[23] and Cathey recalled having "to stake our trucks down with chains" when the wind reached fifty or sixth mph.[24] To reach a searchlight position on an 800-foot hill, steps had to be dug in the side of the slope. Even so, ice and now made climbing up difficult and hazardous. Going down was easier, according to Cpl. Bernard W. Anderson of Battery B—"just sit on the edge and let go. In times of williwaws, everything had to be sandbagged as the gusts would blow away even the heavy items such as tool chests."[25]

At Outpost No. 4 across the bay at the foot of 1,200-foot Mt. Newhall, they had to put a searchlight generator "on a shoulder about 1000 feet up from the beach." The weather during the winter of 1941/42 was "unbelievable," said Haden. "We finally got the equipment in position sometime in April."[26]

The searchlight and radar programs both suffered as a result of the emergency. Providing men for various battery and post details "certainly depleted the available personnel essential in establishing and constructing the various searchlight positions," admitted the Battery A history. "Also, the radar section, consisting of an NCO and ten men, was reduced to four men. In essence, the radar operation was put on the back burner for the time and operated only during times of good weather, which was very seldom."[27] Sergeant Leeder, who was the noncommissioned officer in charge of searchlight electrical maintenance, stated that at times the wind and cold made it impossible to work on electrical equipment.[28] The weather also presented special problems to the men working in telephone communications. They "had a terrible time keeping the phone lines in working order," according to S. Sgt. George W. Cathey of Battery D. These "were mostly laid on the ground and would be blown around and covered with huge snow drifts." Where the lines crossed roads, they were on poles, and "the strong winds caused trouble here also. In addition, the high humidity caused moisture to condense in the switchboard to cause a lot of cross-talk between the lines."[29]

Even the mess hall personnel suffered during the Aleutian winter. "It was so cold that the diesel fuel would congeal and we were not able to cook," reminisced Proffitt.[30]

"One night at midnight I was in charge of a detail of men to unload trucks loaded with wood blocks," wrote Taylor. It was windy, bitter cold, with sleet "cutting us to pieces." Taylor's men "looked as if they were going to freeze and drop in their tracks." Obviously they needed a break, so he ushered them through a nearby door "into a boiler room of some building." After about five minutes, "the door opened and in stepped a captain." Taylor expected to be chewed out, but he explained that they were "trying to keep from freezing to death," and the officer let them stay.[31]

"Many times the wind blew so hard during snow storms that lines were strung from mess hall to barracks to get around," said Weese. Still, he considered himself and his comrades lucky. "B Battery was fortunate during the first winter because our gun positions were on a hill very near the nice barracks and we were allowed to live there," he explained. "Some units were farther out and had it much rougher. We did have one machine gun outpost high on a hill. Their main problem was heat in their dugout. Each man on the trip out had to carry three presto-logs—this was his fuel allowance for a day."[32]

Guard details, strengthened after the declaration of war, presented special problems. Guard duty is boring under the best of circumstances; in the Aleutians it could have been lethal. "Posts were not walked like they were back in the states," noted Garrett. "No matter which direction you faced the snow hit you right in the face. . . . We concentrated on guarding specific things rather than areas."[33] Hargrave, too, remembered the gales interfering with guard duty: "I could look downwind, but if I tried to look into the wind it was like I think it would be putting your face up to the nozzle of a sand-blasting machine."[34]

Soon individual stints of guard duty were shortened, but this proved a mixed blessing, for shorter hours meant pulling the duty more often, and some didn't find the time between shifts long enough for rest and thawing out.[35] Gill remembered "coming off two hours of guard duty with about half inch of ice covering my parka during ice and snow storms."[36]

The next modification was the construction of what O'Neal called a "dugout type guard post with about two feet of the top above the surface. . . . Much like a foxhole with a top on it. We would steal glass from the Navy to put windows in the top area."[37]

Also, some small shelters were constructed, not only as protection from the cold, but because "the wind would blow metal, lumber, etc. and injure people."[38] "When the weather was really bad, we had huts to stand in," said S. Sgt. Doss D. Dale of Battery A. "These huts were constructed with glass so we could see in every direction."[39]

"Guard duty during winter months presented severe problems," Weese stated. "Two men were required for each post, one to keep the fire going inside a small hut and the other to stand guard. Thirty minutes was about all one man would stand watch at a time. Telephone communications were very important and also difficult to maintain. Guards were required to report in every 15 minutes. . . . Presto logs were allowed to be used as fuel for the furtherest outposts but coal was used at the gun positions. It was a real problem just to keep fuel supplied to all the posts."[40]

Obviously the men took their guard duty seriously, because Stout observed, "The inspecting officers were very nervous and cautious in approaching guard areas for fear of being challenged and not hearing it and possibly shot."[41]

For the most part, the men accepted all the inconveniences and discomfort with a good spirit. As Jodie Jones said, "We were well outfitted and young and tough."[42] Bill Jones amplified, "We did what we had to do. Maintain our equipment, serve on guard duty, stand alerts—and there were many of those that proved to be false alarms. The majority of the time it was very boring after we had dug out our gun positions and our quarters."[43]

Rumors abounded, helped along by the Japanese propaganda machine. Pvt. C. O. Pruitt, Jr., wrote home telling his parents not to worry about him, because "his Arkansas National Guard outfit was the best trained he ever saw and really showed their stuff in manning their stations under trying conditions." He added, "We heard a news flash from Japan that they had captured Dutch Harbor and that the Japanese flag was flying over the harbor. Everyone got a laugh over that."[44]

A young army officer at Dutch Harbor wrote to his family on 15 December, assuring them that reports of the Japanese bombing Dutch Harbor were false. "The weather has been bad here all the time, and even a whale couldn't find the place. Last night was the first clear night we have had here, and we were looking for an attack, but it never came. We are constantly on the alert, and guns are manned 24 hours a day."[45]

Among the men, the mustache craze still flourished, according to one of the dispatches Pvt. Elmo Cunningham sent to the *Camden News*. The current fads, he wrote, were pipes, and growing mustaches and sideburns. "Anything goes except one of those Hitler smudges."[46]

The sideburns didn't have a long life. "My mustache is growing quite thick now," Alspaugh notified his family on 18 December. "We are not allowed to grow beards. When we first arrived long sideburns were the rage, along with beards and mustaches, but orders have come out prohibiting sideburns and beards now. . . ."

Radio reception had improved, and the men listened "to Japanese Broadcasting 'shoot the propaganda' in English. Some of their broadcasts are amusing," Alspaugh continued. "They claim the destruction of practically all the Pacific fleet. We have gotten some good laughs from them. . . ."

He explained that the war had "changed things here quite a lot. Most of the men in service here who were married were to get out in January. Now no one is getting out. I had a good chance to get a promotion when these men were discharged, but now there will be no promotion." However, he had one bit of good news: "Everyone in service a year will get a $10 monthly increase in pay. . . ."[47]

On 18 December, the same day that Alspaugh wrote the above letter, a platoon of one officer and eighty-one enlisted men of the 206th left Seattle aboard the troop ship *Chernikoff* "for what turned out to be an eventful 27-day voyage to Dutch Harbor."[48]

In many respects, *Chernikoff* could have been the twin of the *St. Mihiel*. She, too, had been "taken from Germany in World War I."[49] Opinions differed as to whether she had spent the interval between wars as a cattle boat or a fishing vessel. Both Keeton and Leeder insisted that she "had a strong odor of fish."[50] Living quarters were "very cramped and crowded. Sleeping bunks were four high, with fourteen inches between bunks."[51] Sanitary conditions were the main gripe. "The head (latrine) was filthy," Tate remembered. "Vomit everywhere. Deck awash with stopped-up toilets." He admitted to being "very seasick," and that seasickness was "very much a problem."[52]

KP was the principal duty, featuring the time-honored peeling of potatoes. The ship used cold storage eggs which had a spoilage rate of some 25 percent, so each egg had to be broken into a small container to weed out the bad ones. *Chernikoff* had Filipinos for mess hands.[53] Assessments of the food ranged from a sweeping "too many people, poor food, poor crew. Especially poor food," from Cpl. James M. Kimberlin of Battery D[54] to Captain Langley's "good and plentiful." Langley had been "exposed to seasickness conditions but never got seasick." The *Chernikoff*, however, was almost too much for even his cast-iron stomach. "During one period of extremely rough weather" the ship's engineer told him "that new records were set on both 'pitch and toss' instruments and 'roll instruments.'" The first morning of this period, Langley found himself alone in the officers' mess. He gave his order to a KP, "and waited and waited and waited." Finally he went to the galley to see what had happened to his breakfast. He found the mess personnel cooking—of all things—pork chops. The air was heavy with their oily odor, "and all the cooks and KPs were at the garbage cans 'tossing their cookies.'" Langley "felt queasy but a quick trip to the open deck" settled him down.[55]

Poker and dice games were almost nonstop, although Keeton discovered that "the ship's crew were the big gamblers."[56] Nevertheless, Paul Beasley, who at seventeen was the youngest man in the 206th, enjoyed phenomenal luck. He raked in about three thousand dollars. Inasmuch as the base pay of a Pfc was thirty-six dollars per month, this meant that on the *Chernikoff*'s twenty-seven-day cruise he won the equivalent of about eight years' salary.[57]

Instead of proceeding directly to Dutch Harbor, the ship touched at a number of ports. This of course was time consuming, and in addition there was a long delay because the *Chernikoff* waited for her destroyer escort at one location, while the destroyers were awaiting the troop ship at another.[58]

The first stop was for two days at Prince Rupert, British Columbia, where they loaded a locomotive.[59] Then the ship proceeded to Alaska. Despite all the discomforts, many of the men remembered the voyage through the Inland Passage as "beautiful and a pleasure." Their first stop in Alaska was at Ketchikan, where they docked on Christmas Eve.[60] There they debarked a few GIs and unloaded supplies for the townspeople."[61]

Ketchikan itself these newcomers could take or leave alone. It looked "dirty, just what it was, a frontier town."[62] But the people! That was something else again. "After we docked, I think the entire population collected at the dock," recalled Keeton. "After a lot of talk, some left and later returned with fruit and half-pints of liquor, throwing [them] onto the ship shouting 'Merry Christmas!' and 'Good Luck!'"[63]

The *Chernikoff* stopped at Ketchikan only a few hours, then moved on to Seward, where they remained for ten days. Every day they had permission to leave the ship.[64] Kinney "spent hours just taking walks, visiting the old gold mines (caves) and wondering about life there in the very early years."[65] Keeton and some of his buddies "ran into some members of the 153d Infantry from Russellville." They walked the town but "there wasn't much to see except the Red Light District." It looked prosperous but the men didn't sample the merchandise.[66]

To help pass the time, the men formed a basketball team and played the team of the local high school. "Most of our players were college players and had a pretty good lead at half," said Langley. "We decided that since winning meant nothing to us we missed lots of shots and made bad passes, etc. and they beat us, which gave them a real thrill."

The captain had a thrill of another sort when he discovered that "someone left an SCR 268 radar on a side street, and at the time it was top secret."[67]

The delay at Seward was due to the difficulty in unloading the locomotive. "There was no crane large enough to lift the engine off," Caldwell explained, "so engineers laid rails to the side of the ship." The ship's railing had to be removed, then the men "waited for the tide to heave." Eventually the locomotive was maneuvered onto the tracks.[68]

The next few stops before arriving at Dutch Harbor on 13 January were brief and uneventful, broken only by a submarine alert while sailing from Sitka to Kodiak. "We on guard duty were informed to keep a sharp eye out for enemy subs," said Kinney.

"But it would have been very difficult to see one in the dark of night and while the ship's bow would dip into the huge waves of the rough water."[69]

The men had plenty of opportunity to assess the landscape. As with the *St. Mihiel* contingent, impressions varied widely. Burris "did not want any part of it,"[70] while Walkup thought he "had come to the end of the world."[71] In sharp contrast, Trimble found the country beautiful. "I think it changed my life. The trees made one hell of an impression"—so much so that after the war he became a forester.[72]

12

"Snafu!"

If the men at Dutch Harbor needed a reminder that others were much worse off than they, they received it just before Christmas of 1941. Alspaugh described the incident when writing to his mother on 2 January 1942:

> The other day I went to Dutch Harbor with Whalen.* We saw a Dutch freighter there. It sure was a dilapidated-looking ship. The crew was principally Chinese. I have never seen such a motley-looking crew. There were kids on the boat that looked to be about 15 years old. Most of the crew, however, was older than this. The crew was poorly clothed and fed. They didn't have anything on except cotton clothing and that was badly worn. Many of the men wore sandals on their feet while others had worn-out low quartered shoes on. Almost all the crew shivered while on deck. Some civilians and soldiers threw candy and cigarettes on the deck of the ship and there was a wild scramble by the crew. I sure felt sorry for them. They sure must have envied our warm clothing.[1]

Ballew remembered that the Chinese "fought over candy like dogs," and exchanged it for Chinese money and "pictures of naked women."[2] According to Quimby, this ship had been at sea on 7 December, had been cut off her route and had been evading Japanese ships. "Their provisions were exhausted so they made port at Dutch Harbor. We had dinner with one of the officers and provisions [were] given."[3]

This undoubtedly was the same vessel which Harold R. White

---

* Full name unknown. Whalen is mentioned several times in the Alspaugh diary and letters.

of Camden described. White happened to be returning to the states for aviation cadet training and was detailed to guard two Japanese prisoners. "The two Japanese were officers on board a Dutch freighter when the United States declared war on Japan. . . ." When the freighter got the word, it "immediately changed its course and brought the Japs to Dutch Harbor." On the way homeward with the prisoners, White took due note of the obvious hostility of the troopship's Filipino crew members. "I don't think I would have had my job long if the Filipinos could have managed a short visit with the Japs."[4]

Soon after this ship docked, the 206th men enjoyed what Alspaugh termed "a nice Christmas, considering the circumstances." Few of these men were consistent churchgoers, but many, including Alspaugh and Whalen, slogged through eight inches of snow to attend morning services. The mess hall personnel had gone all out to make this, the 206th's first wartime Christmas, a memorable one. The result was "one of the best meals I have eaten in the army," as Alspaugh wrote home. "We had turkey with all the trimmings."[5]

Meanwhile, at least three troopships were en route to Alaska with other members of the 206th. Corporal Clodi was aboard the *Lackinaw*. The ship was "very crowded, dirty, had just returned from the Aleutians with a load of evacuated civilians and was never cleaned up." These civilians probably were the military dependents evacuated shortly after Pearl Harbor.

Clodi wasn't a gambler, so he didn't join in the poker sessions. In any case, the sea was too rough to permit much activity. The activities that remained were mainly "reading, talking to bunk-mates, and heaving your guts out." Clodi was so seasick he was excused from duty, but he "was in the minority."

The *Lackinaw* made a fairly rapid trip, spending only two to four hours each at Ketchikan, Kodiak, Seward, and Sitka to unload cargo. The passengers stayed aboard at all stops. Clodi's first impressions of Alaska weren't flattering: "Pretty barren, desolate, what a place to fight a war!"[6]

The *Merriam L. Thompson* departed from Seattle on 17 December. Among the passengers was Troy Burris. He pulled guard duty and spent most of his free time reading. Many of his fellow passengers "were seasick and had to stay in their bunks with a bucket tied to the head of their bed," but Burris didn't succumb.

After leaving Seward, the ship pulled into "a bay in the Alaska chain" to await a convoy. "We had been there two days when an American destroyer pulled into the entrance to the bay and began firing over our ship," wrote Burris. "At that time we did not have the American flag up." They remedied this omission on the double."[7]

The last of the three ships to reach Dutch Harbor was the first of them to leave the states. The *M. S. Dellwood* departed from San Diego on 15 December. Warrant Officer Pedersen remembered the ship as being "not crowded and quite comfortable." The usual gambling went on: "A few fellows were real card sharks and seemed to have a lot of money." Others "did some reading and writing and a lot of talking about Alaska . . ."

Security measures were quite strict. "We were concerned about submarines and had many tight blackouts and no smoking on decks. We followed the inside passage as much as possible and had no close calls."

The *Dellwood* reached Ketchikan on 10 January, Pedersen's twenty-third birthday. He telephoned his sister who lived there, and she came to the dock to see him, although he couldn't leave the ship. Two days later, the troopship touched at Juneau late in the evening to disembark a man with appendicitis. About a week later, they stopped at Woman Bay, the naval base at Kodiak. There Pedersen met "several civilian friends" from his home town. One pitch-dark night he took a taxi into Kodiak to visit a bar, passing through two blackout doors into "a real lit-up happy bar."

When the *Dellwood* reached Dutch Harbor on 29 January 1942, the area was enjoying one of its good days. Snow was everywhere underfoot, but the sun was shining, and there stood the 206th band to welcome the newcomers with rousing music. "What a beautiful sight!"[8]

At least three Arkansas men began diaries on 1 January 1942— Alspaugh of the 206th, Lt. Robert H. "Buck" Miller, and Cpl. Willie Stubbs, both of Company F, 153d Infantry. John Bowen of the 206th also kept a diary, commencing 24 January.

Characteristically, Alspaugh had something pleasant to record in his diary and to report home: On 2 January, he had seen his first lunar rainbow.[9] It was a fairly routine month for him. He pulled guard and unloading duty, attended church and the movies, and spent as much time as possible in the barracks because he had picked up a nasty cough and feared a recurrence of pneumonia. He had a birthday on 13 January: "I never thought I would see my 21st birthday in Alaska." He made friends with "Blackout," one of the "regular" cats. "We have had him since the outbreak of hostilities. He is the most active cat I have ever seen."

Alspaugh had one unpleasant experience. He was "accused, tried and convicted of leaving a loaded rifle on post," despite the fact that the rifle had been picked up before he went on post. Alspaugh was unable to get that fact through the captain's head, so he drew some extra duties. And he said farewell to a good friend and ex-tentmate, Pfc Elmo Cunningham, who had secured an appointment to West Point.[10] No doubt Cunningham's hometown newspaper would miss his lively tidbits of news.

The most important event of January, from the strategic viewpoint, was that the projected base at Umnak finally began to show signs of life. When authorized on 26 November 1941, it had been with the proviso that "previously approved projects in presumably more vital areas" would take precedence. But Pearl Harbor changed that.

For security purposes in the Umnak project, the Alaska Defense Command operated under the name of "Blair Packing Company," and the necessary logistical equipment was crated and shipped as cannery equipment. The first troops for Umnak, the 807th Engineers (Aviation) had reached the area on 17 January, but, as Umnak boasted no harbor, the troops had to land at Chernofski on Unalaska, and then they had to be ferried to Umnak piecemeal in barges. At the end of a month, half the men were still at Chernofski. Meanwhile, near the end of January, the army learned that three million square feet of pierced steel planking (PSP) could be shipped immediately, so they decided to abandon the original plans for paved runways.[11]

Among the troops earmarked for Umnak was Company F of Arkansas's 153d Infantry, then at Camp Murray. Lt. Robert H. "Buck" Miller was pleased with his assignment; he had always wanted to visit Alaska. He commenced a diary of the sort that is a historian's dream—detailed, accurate, articulate, and witty. Moreover, Miller was a talented cartoon artist and embellished his narrative with many humorous sketches. He had the immediate job of "directing the packing and crating of the company impedimenta which virtually totaled some 25 tons, not including the personal effects of the men. For example," he wrote, "we took 6 months' supply of food, 650,000 rifle-cleaning patches, 7000 bars of soap, 22,000 cans of field rations. . . ."[12] Cpl. Willie Stubbs spent the first five days making and packing boxes in preparation for the move. His diary was much less detailed than Miller's, but gives the picture from the enlisted angle and serves as a valuable check on his lieutenant's story.[13]

On 3 January the platoon drew some Arctic clothing and had the inevitable shots. "My arm feels like hell," wrote Miller, "—two typhoid shots, tetanus and smallpox injections, Wassermann test and blood type make it pretty sore. Coupled with this cold I feel generally about like a wounded skunk."[14]

After several maddening delays, the men boarded the St. Mihiel and she upped anchor. "Shortly before noon we were underway on our voyage to somewhere," noted Stubbs on 11 January. "Everyone seemed to be in good spirits and trying to see everything that took place." By the next day, seasickness began to set in. "1st Sgt. George Paszdarah said that he didn't care if the ship sunk."[15]

Miller expressed sympathy for the men "packed in like sardines." At the same time, "there are four officers in this phone booth-sized stateroom and we can't even turn around." Oddly enough, he found the food better than he had been eating on the mainland. Blackout was "a ghostly experience." The portholes had been painted over, "and inside lights go out when the outside doors are opened. Like a refrigerator."[16]

During the night of 13 January, the St. Mihiel struck bottom "and almost threw some of the boys out of bed . . . ," but no harm was done. Miller paid tribute to the ship's pilot. "Understand we have an Alaskan pilot aboard who has sailed these waters since '97. He draws $50 a day and is worth it as we sailed without lights through places where it seems you can put your arms out and touch land." Then he added a touch of humor: "Lt. Gus Phillip of H platoon wrote three girls in Arkansas and asked if they would marry him—two of them accepted. And he took off for the frozen north!"

After a brief stop at Ketchikan,[17] St. Mihiel proceeded to a position "just out of Icy Straits" where she was to pick up a convoy, then go on that same afternoon. One munitions ship had already arrived.

That night Miller, who labeled himself a "nature lover,"

engaged in a religious discussion with Lieutenants Cohen and Kister, who presented the Jewish and Christian views respectively. Naturally, the talk centered on religious principles in relation to their duty as soldiers. "Then, of course, there is the question of whether humanity deserved the blood we spill for it; and just what is humanity anyway, and why are we humans here in the first place." At this point, Miller decided the waters were too deep to navigate safely. "We can't afford to delve into those illogical and unanswerable questions now, because if we did we'd soon be nutty as a fruit cake and a total flop as soldiers. From now on my philosophy is to be happy when conditions are good, and to be as satisfied as possible when they aren't good."[18]

This admirable design for living was sorely tried over the next few days, with *St. Mihiel* "somewhere off the coast of Alaska at anchor, not knowing where we are or where we are going—like a Democrat." Among other reasons for the delay, they were waiting for the *David Branch*, "reportedly hung up on a reef a day behind us." *Branch* had aboard all the platoon's vehicles and most of the other equipment, so her fate was a very serious matter for the combat troops.

The next day, Miller and his buddies "heard about the plane crash that killed Carole Lombard. Tough!"[19] Miss Lombard, one of Hollywood's best light comediennes, married to superstar Clark Gable, had plunged most effectively into selling war bonds, so her death caused widespread sadness.

At night, a primal, impenetrable blackness descended. "The boys on submarine guard couldn't see one if it was in their lap," wrote Stubbs.[20] And Miller declared, "It was so black last night that you could have used a black cat for a flashlight."

At last, at 1800 on 21 January, *St. Mihiel* began to move again, in company with the destroyer *Hatfield* and the coast guard cutter *Atalanta*. *Branch* was still "hung up," and Miller worried over how he and his men could manage without the equipment she carried.[21]

Two PBYs and two patrol boats escorted *St. Mihiel* into Dutch Harbor on the morning of 25 January. There was bad news: they were to pick up tents, Sibley stoves, and other necessities and go on to Umnak. "The *Branch* was hurt so bad off Prince Rupert she was abandoned and the cargo taken off of her."[22]

Some of the 206th men came down to the dock to greet the

newcomers. Stubbs saw several old schoolmates from his hometown, Atkins. The next day the troops went ashore, and on the 28th Stubbs looked up a few more of his cronies from Atkins.[23]

For John Bowen, Wednesday 28 January was notable for two reasons. "An attack was expected today by the officials but in weather like this we are safe though. These fake alarms are getting old and the men don't like it." Likewise, the men didn't like some of their officers. "A 'group' talked to Captain Hutch about our officers and we expect a change soon."[24]

The alert was the least of Miller's worries on 28 January. The plan had been that the 153d men would remain at Fort Mears until the quartermaster troops and civilians had built temporary quarters for them at Umnak, which would probably be ten days to two weeks. Miller looked forward "to clean clothes and a bed again." This sensible arrangement didn't last long. Instead of unloading *St. Mihiel* while she was docked, the ship "ran out in the bay and began transferring cargo to the *North Coast*." Miller explained, "When we are unloaded, the *North Coast* will sail ¼ mile to the dock and unload, we will warehouse it until we go, then load and unload it again for Umnak." They "worked all night in a driving snowstorm," and at 0500 Miller tumbled into bed for a sleep of all of two hours, after eighteen straight hours on duty. He was thoroughly exasperated. "I have ceased to wonder at the magnificent mistakes and bulbous blunders of those above us—such stuff as this beat the British at Norway." Worse was to come the next day: "We are moving again (God give me a pup tent to call my own!) back to the *Mihiel* and RELOADING everything we just took off!" (Miller's capitals.)[25]

Early in the morning of the 30th, the *St. Mihiel* left for Chernofski, reaching port at 1400. Miller was still fuming:

> It is a damn shame to make stevedores out of good combat troops and make them do the same work over and over again. Actually, when we left we had only a few more tons of cargo aboard than we did when we got here last Sunday morning. In other words, we wasted the manpower for 5 days and accomplished nothing. Now we must unload at this Bay, set up a temporary camp and then set out for Otter Point, 11 miles away in barges for our permanent camp. Snafu!

Among those on board *St. Mihiel* were a group from the 206th.[26] These men had been informed they were going to Umnak for fourteen days and were issued extra clothing. "The reason for going was to furnish beach protection for the 802nd aircraft engineers. . . ." At Chernofski, "we went over the side with about eight-foot waves," recalled Proffitt. "When the wave brought the forty-foot boat close to gang, you jumped. I thought I broke my leg but didn't." The temperature dropped to approximately fifteen degrees, and Proffitt could hear men "from other outfits" crying out, "I'm freezing, please help me!" Some men at Chernofski had been transferred from the *David Branch*. "They had two blankets and no food prepared for them." The 206th detachment had a fine breakfast featuring scrambled eggs, ham, oatmeal, and milk. The stranded men tried to join in, but the 206th lieutenant had to refuse them—there was not food enough for all. So the refugees wistfully stood near the garbage cans, asking for what remained in the 206th's mess kits.

After breakfast, the men broke camp and with their equipment boarded a power barge to Pistol Point on Umnak (later Fort Glenn). They carried food for twenty-one days, "the best they had on Dutch Harbor." Upon landing, they set up machine guns on the beachfront, and put up sleeping and cooking tents.

Every gun pit dug turned up at least one skeleton. The men were astounded at the size of these ancient Aleuts. Proffitt was a large man, but the disinterred jawbones fitted easily over his.

The engineers began to unload the barges with an air winch. "We had to carry all water from a lake in the foothills in five-gallon cans." The anticipated time on Umnak would stretch to eighty-seven days. "We ran out of meat. . . . We had only hominy and sauerkraut at quartermaster." When C rations were unloaded on the beach, guards had to be posted "to stop the soldiers from stealing them."[27]

The men at Dutch Harbor had a little snafu of their own, which Bowen recorded with a touch of enjoyment. The infantry held a practice maneuver at midnight on 31 January. Dodson and those on his position hadn't been informed, "so when the first shots were fired we just knew the Japs were on us. We had plenty of excitement for a little while. These false 'alerts' are hard on the nerves and everyone is on edge. . . . A good joke on us just the same." Bowen added, "The Dutch boat with the Chinese crew is still here unloading the cargo of coal. The two Jap officers were sent to the states for the duration. . . ."[28]

All told, January 1942 had been a notable one for the Arkansas men in the Aleutians, and a fairly typical example of how things worked—or didn't work—as America went to war.

13

"This Country Gets You"

February 1942 started with a touch of the unusual. "Russian ship docked today. Supposed to have been chased into nearest port by Jap sub," noted Bowen.[1] Alspaugh recorded that one of the rumors making the rounds was that "the Russian ship is manned by women." Alspaugh's comment on this was, "Ho-Hum." He had the day off on 2 February and went to the harbor to watch the vessels. "The old Dutch ship and a Russian ship were tied up out by the spithead."[2] He did not mention it, but this ship did have "a partial crew of women,"[3] although not the full complement at which rumor had hinted.

Thenceforth an occasional Soviet freighter or submarine stopped at Dutch Harbor. Caldwell saw some Russians in the PX "going nuts over candy and ice cream."[4] The submarines' officers were allowed ashore, utilized bachelor officers' quarters facilities and patronized the navy officers' club.[5] Impressions of the Russians varied. Some of the Arkansas men found them aloof, others found them quite friendly. Once Ballew went aboard a Soviet ship with Lieutenant Nesmith. "They were spooky and would not have much to do with us." Nesmith showed his .45 to one of the ship's officers and gestured that he would like to see the officer's sidearm, but he would not take it out of its holster.[6]

The submariners seemed somewhat more laid back. Not only Major Oehrig but also his wife were among the guests permitted aboard.[7] The 206th's band "played a welcome to a Russian sub and swapped cigarettes with the sailors and officers."[8] Anderson "visited with Russian submarine sailors at times trading cigarettes etc. They seemed friendly enough."[9] Sisk received what amounted to a guided tour of one undersea craft. An English-speaking Russian showed him around. "His attitude was indifferent but not unfriendly." The two swapped cigarettes, and Sisk decided he got the worst of the deal. "Theirs were black and very strong. Too much for me!" Nor was he impressed with the boat. "The entire ship stank and to me looked outdated." Later he had the chance to go aboard a U. S. submarine, "and ours was neat and clean in comparison."[10]

Such outside contacts were welcome breaks in the daily routine. This boredom probably helps account for a weird manifestation that took place that first winter, although Weese charged it up to their immaturity. For some reason, ". . . word got around that being circumcised was the 'in' thing, so before long we had so many people in the hospital for circumcisions that a limit was placed on the number each unit could have in the hospital at one time for this purpose," Weese recalled. "The hospital care was good and that was one place females were in plain view . . ."[11] Why any medical officer would authorize or agree to perform minor surgery for which there was no medical necessity is anybody's guess.

Many men kept busy digging as the gun position crews moved underground. After the alert of 26 November, half of Alspaugh's unit "was sent to maintain and fire the guns which were on a hill near the barracks." At that time they slept in tents. "Before the outbreak we had dug holes with jackhammers near our gun position," Alspaugh explained. "We were unable to get lumber to finish the dugouts until hostilities occurred. At that time Siems-Drake generously supplied us with lumber. The dugouts were very crowded. Our hole had metal beds stacked four high."[12] Cowell remembered stealing wood from the navy to construct their underground huts.[13]

Some of these shelters were simple—what T. Cpl. Tony Junevitch of Battery F described as "Hole in the ground with roof cover made of wood and covered with sod."[14] Others were quite elaborate. "We dug large holes in the ground with pick and shovels and built rooms for each gun position," said Eheman. "Plus building for ammunition storage, rest room, guard house, and all were covered with dirt with tunnels to each room. However, the guard stuck up about a foot above the ground with glass all round so we could see anything that came up the hill to our position." He added, "These buildings were of wood, constructed with boards and 2 x 4 and 2 x 6 plywood or anything we could find, beg, or steal."[15]

Some remembered these underground quarters as acceptable,

the assessments ranging from "comfortable" to "not too bad." However, there was a problem. "We stayed in underground bunkers with rats . . . ," noted Sgt. Leo L. New of Headquarters Battery.[16] "Rats were a real problem," admitted Sgt. Jean D. Thatcher of Battery F.[17] "Dugouts with wooden structures were very good for winter weather, but not suitable because of rats and other animals," observed Keeton.[18]

Many survivors claimed to have had no trouble with rats, but others had horrendous stories to tell. Rats dug into Costley's position on Hill 200. "Guys coming back from the movies would carry clubs and flashlights. Rat killing was one form of entertainment."[19] "We were living in underground quarters with six or seven men to the unit. The rats would come out as soon as the lights were out. . . ." wrote Ryals. One landed on his face and chest; he threw it against the wall. Shooting them was impossible at such close quarters, so the men made slingshots. "Our plan of attack was for several guys to shine flashlights and others to shoot rocks. Well, this wasn't such a good idea since we almost killed each other with rocks flying all over the place. . . . We finally stopped up their entry holes enough to keep most of them out, and we also used traps."[20]

Sisk was frankly afraid of these night visitors. One woke him up by gnawing on his shoes as he stretched out on his bunk. The rat "ran up my body and across my face, making a squeaking sound," wrote Sisk. "Another time soon after that, one woke me up by chewing on my rifle sling and the stock of the rifle. They were hungry and were after the oil" used to grease shoes and guns.[21] The men were told that "these rats came off Russian, Chinese, or even American ships in prior years."[22]

The rat situation became so bad that eventually all their natural predators were protected. The shooting of eagles, hawks, owls, and foxes was strictly prohibited, and many sanitation measures were in effect. By 1943 a dozen terriers had been requisitioned to join the anti-rat campaign.[23]

On 6 February, Bowen recorded in his dairy, "Finished covering the dugout with rocks and dirt today. It is quite comfortable inside."[24] Over on the Alaskan mainland, the 206th men at Fairbanks had also moved certain installations, such as gun positions, underground.[25] Rats were no problem in that location,[26] but the weather, so much colder than at Dutch Harbor, posed special complications. "Vehicles had to be left running during winter," wrote Gaines Parker. "If driving for any length of time, we had to put burning candles on [the] dashboard to be able to see. Heaters weren't efficient enough to keep windshields clear of frost."[27]

There were compensations for those who could appreciate them. One night when the men were asleep in the hangar, "some guy came in and said, 'Boys, come here quick!'" Brown and his companions "rushed out, and the sky was lit up with the aurora borealis." It was "the most beautiful thing" Brown had ever seen. "There we were, standing in our Long Johns freezing to death, witnessing something these old Arkansas boys had never seen. You just cannot describe it . . . and to think Uncle Sam paid for my seeing it . . . !"[28]

Back at Dutch Harbor, on 5 February, "one of the prettiest days of the year," some of the men were busy improving the capability of the 3" guns. "Boy, I sure did work today!" Alspaugh informed his diary. "We changed our ammunition. We are now using a mechanical time fuse on our projectiles. I changed the fuse setter today."[29] Bowen noted two days later, "Old 3" ammunition changed for the new *high explosive* which is much more efficient and has mechanical in place of powder train fuses" (Bowen's italics).

He added, "Place is getting on some of the boys' nerves. Fights are frequent and trouble is expected in some form."[30] This same psychological problem arose in even more virulent form at Ladd Field. "The isolation and loneliness that was also part and parcel of Alaska Mainland duty began to get to the troops as cabin-fever became more prevalent," wrote Wilson. "Drunken brawls became more violent and a few of the members got into serious trouble clashing with the denizens of Fairbanks. . . . The brawlers lived for confrontation and it was their fondest hope that someone on the receiving end of their caustic remarks would take offense and offer to do combat."[31] Wilson gave them a wide berth. "I was not a brawler and had no intention of incurring serious bodily harm at the hands of some of the drunken barbarians who were members of H-206."[32]

At all levels there was a certain amount of war jitters coupled with an attitude of possibly justified defeatism. "There is a possibility of enemy aircraft carriers in these waters," noted Alspaugh on 6 February.[33] Bowen remarked on the tenth, "On the 'alert' twenty-four hours a day. In case of a serious attack, the people have little hopes of holding out. Officers and men both wonder why more help is not sent to all outposts *now*" (Bowen's italics).[34] The same attitude seemed to prevail at Ladd Field, where Brown declared, "All the Japs had to do was land at Seward and [they] could have had the mainland."[35]

One unlikely manifestation of this apprehension went into effect. As Bowen recorded on 22 February, "It is rumored that Sundays are going to be changed to Wednesday to lessen the possibility of a surprise attack." Sure enough, the calendar was changed accordingly.[36] Many remembered this adjustment, which they attributed to the fact that the Japanese had attacked Pearl Harbor on a Sunday. It made little practical difference to the men. The calendar was the least of their worries. "Most of the time we worked seven days a week and were on duty most of the time anyway," explained O'Neal.[37] A number of survivors pointed out the ironic circumstance that when the Japanese did attack Dutch Harbor, it was on a Wednesday—"GI Sunday."

In view of the number and variety of tensions in the air, it is not too surprising that some men broke under the strain. "A sentinel in the 37th Infantry shot himself last night," Alspaugh noted on 19 February, and two days later added, "There were two more suicides in the 37h Infantry last night. One soldier broke his neck by jumping from the bed. Another took poison."[38]

The man who broke his neck did so by a strange means: "There was an odd 'fad' that went around," related Sisk. "A man would get up on the top bunk and put his head through the hoop that formed the foot or head of the bed and turn a flip. This thing happened quite a lot, as I understand, and I never heard of an unsuccessful attempt."[39]

Cpl. Frederick H. Raymond of Battery G remembered a pathetic case: "Once, on payday, a young enlisted man, after receiving his pay, went to every man in the hut paying any debt he might have owed. He then gave one of the sergeants money to send back to his home, went to stand guard duty, and promptly shot himself."[40]

"We had only one suicide in our battery," Thomason wrote, "a boy from Minnesota—a quiet boy and a good soldier. Had a bad effect on the men in his gun section, especially his section sergeant."[41]

Some took place in Kinney's battery. "I recall one soldier sticking an M-1 rifle barrel into his mouth and pulling the trigger.

Another suicide occurred when a soldier stuck his head inside the railing of an army bunkbed and turned a flip. . . ."[42] There were some questionable cases. "I saw four bodies being removed from a furnace room in one of the barracks at Ft. Mears," said Sergeant Beverburg. "Our officers said that this could have been suicide or accidental from inhaling carbontetrachloride used in cleaning weapons."[43]

At least one case in the 37th Infantry left a grim question mark behind: "An infantry captain who was extremely disliked by the men—real tough on courts-martial, etc.—was found dead under a Jeep which was still running when the body found," related Captain Langley. "No evidence of any kind. His neck was broken and no sign of struggle, and apparently nothing was ever found to indicate cause. General opinion was that no one looked too hard."[44]

Henry Swanson, a resident of Unalaska with an encyclopedic knowledge of the Aleutian Islands, their people, and the surrounding waters, remarked in retrospect, "Well, I guess some of the group stationed here went crazy with boredom." Swanson was operating an outpost tender with an all-GI crew of young men from the 37th Infantry. He explained that there were about three hundred men at Morris Cove. "It was new then. They were just in tents. Well, I guess one of them went crazy. Another man shot him. I went over there in the middle of the night to pick up the shooter."[45]

Of course, the overwhelming majority toughed it out, went about their jobs, and even managed to enjoy themselves. The Alspaugh diary gives a picture of one such man, probably typical of hundreds. He pulled guard and whatever duties were assigned with good nature. In his off-duty time he enjoyed his radio and went often to the movies, meticulously listing the titles, which give the impression that someone had sent every "bomb" in circulation to these entertainment-hungry men. In mid-February he began a course in electricity and radio, run by "civilians working for Westinghouse." He plunged into this enthusiastically, and for the next month spent much time studying, working out problems, and at the library.[46]

Bowen's diary for the period reveals a rather reflective mind. "Singapore and the Philippines are in a bad way and are expected to be lost before long. Men here are only mildly disturbed . . . ," he recorded on 10 February. Five days later he noted the arrival of a number of Siems-Drake men. "Labor is scarce so all civilians here have been made exempt from the draft." Two days later he commented on the rumor that Captain Hutchison might be transferred. "We will all hate to see him go. . . . It seems that Batry. 'B' has the highest I. Q. in the Regiment." The twenty-first found him in a caustic mood. "A submarine refueling base is being built near the Sheep Ranch. A little of everything *is being built* but not much has been finished yet" (Bowen's italics). He ended the month on a somber note: "Sgt. Bates of the 151st Engineers was buried yesterday afternoon in the Cemetery back of Unalaska—a cold, wet bed for a good man."[47]*

Meanwhile, the Arkansas men of the 153d Infantry had finally moved to Umnak, not before a frustrating week at Chernofski. On 1 February Lieutenant Miller brought his platoon ashore, pitched shelter tents, then unloaded items from the *St. Mihiel.* Chernofski left Miller bereft of speech: "Had I the wit of Irvin Cobb, the rhetoric of Edgar Allen Poe, the descriptive prowess of Fenimore Cooper and command of all the words in the dictionary I still could not portray for you conditions at Chernofski. . . . The wind blows almost constantly and seems to resent our being here. . . . The beach where we work is a sea of mud from the antics of a couple of caterpillars and the pissant activities of 400 men. . . . " He ended in venomous capitals, "IF THE JAPS TAKE THIS COUNTRY, IT'LL SERVE THEM BLOODY WELL RIGHT!"[48]

Willie Stubbs recorded on 3 February, "Some of the boys swiped some canned goods."[49] One man was caught, and Miller was unhappy because he had to sentence him to eight extra hours' work for stealing a can of peaches. Miller knew that others were doing the same—"in other words, I sentenced him, not for stealing but for getting caught at it."

He was fiercely proud of his men: "Weary, dirty, red-eyed soldiers of the 153rd—doing everything save what they are supposed to do—a fighting force wallowing in mud and slime at stevedoring—yet one is singing 'Happy Days' while carrying two bags of flour thru knee-deep gumbo."[50]

---

* This sergeant died a natural death from a burst blood vessel.

On 7 February the men had an early and somewhat exotic breakfast of hominy and apricots, then boarded ship for Umnak. "Sure was a hungry bunch on the ship," wrote Stubbs. "They finally fed us before we got off."[51] Miller and Lt. Tex Laidlaw led this contingent. The former was exceedingly uneasy about Umnak's prospects: "This is a hard place to defend. Many beachheads and little protective features on the terrain except rolling knolls. . . . The Japs are smart enough to know we are here and weakly manning this big island—we are living on borrowed time, sho 'nuff. . . ."

Almost immediately they ran out of fuel. Miller had to set his men to salvaging driftwood and was understandably exasperated when a barge arrived with all of two sacks of coal "and nothing else but prefabricated houses for civilian workers.

"About half our 15-day rations disappeared the night we unloaded the barge in the dark, desperately trying to salvage her cargo before the surf beat us to pieces. . . ."[52]

Stubbs's diary indicates that Miller did what he could to ease the situation, giving Stubbs permission to build a tent floor for his squad. By dark they had moved in. "This beats sleeping on the ground." On another occasion, Stubbs and his squad were digging foxholes in the rain. "When Lt. Miller told us we could go to camp as soon as we had our hole finished, we got them dug in a hurry."[53]

Proud as he was of his men, Miller recognized their limitations and wished he had a few veteran regulars available: ". . . these kids are all right but they have no age, no experience, no practical training—in fact, they try hard but are almost helpless—we need some 40-year-olds in the outfit. This gang couldn't even dig satisfactory fox-holes without me standing right by. . . . We have constructed a 16-hole Chic Sale which is undoubtedly the finest of its kind in Alaska."

Personnel problems arose that were more serious than "liberating" a can of peaches. One soldier gave away all his ammunition, announcing that he was a conscientious objector. "I think he's lazy and had a talk with him." The dentist "chopped off his trigger finger in a footlocker." Miller was on a board that investigated whether this occurrence was intentional or an accident, and he had his suspicions. Another man fought imaginary Japanese "at dinner, in his sleep, and while brushing his teeth. This country gets you if you don't keep busy."[54] In fact, as time went on, the suicide problem reached Umnak. "Mail call was when it reached its peak," recalled Proffitt. "Bed roll suicide was very prevalent on Umnak, especially [among] New York boys." He remembered that one morning a sergeant woke up to find one of his men cleaning his gun. "What are you going to do, kill yourself?" asked the sergeant banteringly.

"Yes," was the brief reply.

Still not taking the incident seriously, the sergeant countered, "Wake me up when you're ready." Thirty minutes later the man shot himself.[55]

14

"We Plowed On"

During the early months of 1941, more troops reached Dutch Harbor. Aboard the *U.S.S. McKinley*, which left Washington state in February, was Pvt. Edgar L. Nixon. It was seasick time again. Nixon did not succumb, and as a result he spent considerable duty time cleaning up after those who did. He had quite a bit of the ship to himself, because almost everyone stayed in bed.

The *McKinley* had no encounter with the Japanese, but it did run into a serious storm: "We tried to pull into a cove and drop anchor but the chain broke and we lost our anchor and we were set adrift. Seems we had engine trouble. During a lull in the storm, a cruiser came along side and gave us a spare anchor, but that night that chain broke and we lost that one. We got the engines fixed and we plowed on through the stormy sea."

After about a week they reached the first Alaskan port—Juneau, Nixon thought, but wasn't sure. He polished off his initial impression of Alaska in one word—"Wilderness."[1] Another troop ship, the *North Coast*, left Seattle on 26 February.[2] According to Ryals, interest in poker, other card games, and "just sightseeing" was high until the ship entered the Gulf of Alaska.[3] After that, "most of the men [were] too sick to play poker or even do duty," Thomason recalled. "The Alaska Gulf is a very rough place." He was not ill, but admitted this was only because his duties as First Sergeant kept him fully occupied.[4]

Like *McKinley*, the *North Coast* had no contact with the Japanese. "The enemy was the ocean," said Ryals. "It was all we could do to just ride."[5]

Among the passengers was James Massey, back in his old outfit, although he had requested transfer to the air force. "After leaving

Juneau, the ocean was in an uproar," he wrote. ". . . I never saw so many sick people, nearly all aboard was nauseated, some wanted to die. . . . I was never sick, I kept busy, was all over the ship. I even took over the cooking galley for several days. . . . As we neared our destination, the wind began howling and screaming defiance at anyone that entered these waters."[6]

The arrival of the *North Coast*, which with the *Yukon* docked at Dutch Harbor on 8 March, aroused special interest, for among the approximately one thousand new arrivals were "many of the old men who had been relieved."[7] Alspaugh "went down to the docks at Dutch Harbor and Unalaska to see some of the boys who came back."[8]

The *North Coast* did not respond to the harbor defense's challenge quickly enough and took a shot across her bow—not a very cordial welcome. Moreover, the first glimpse of his destination filled Massey with dismay: ". . . what a site, mountainous, snow-covered saw-toothed peaks, how cold and desolate-looking! I asked myself what in the world would any country want with such a place."

The men were hustled off the ship to get them to their locations before nightfall at about 1500. Massey's section was a gun position at the foot of Mt. Ballyhoo. The next day, they were "really socked in, wind howling, blinding snow swirling . . ."[9]

Massey covered the experiences of himself and his men for the month of March in one entry, which gives a graphic if somewhat jaundiced picture typical of the time and place:

> Guards had to be changed every 15 minutes, that's about all a man could endure. I don't know why we had guards out, they couldn't see or hear a damn thing, even if it was upon them. . . . We had to exercise the weapons every hour. Two men would take a board, place it over the muzzle, and force the barrel back several times in recoil. What a hell of a place, what a life we had! . . .
>
> Work began as did training, weather or no weather we had to get used to it. Gun drills, target practice and plenty of it. Infantry tactics up and down the mountain sides, rifle practice, roll in the snow, dig foxholes and trenches, survival tactics was vital to the soldiers here.[10]

Such old-timers as Bowen and Alspaugh were so acclimated that their diaries had little to say about conditions beyond an occasional laconic note. Bowen observed that the hospital had been placed "under a diphtheria quarantine" on 1 March.[11] Alspaugh remarked on the fourth, "We are on another twenty-four hour alert now." On the tenth he noted a Russian ship in harbor—"a pretty clean-looking vessel."

Both men recorded the arrival of Joe E. Brown. "He ate in our mess hall at dinner today. He is giving performances at the Post Theater every night," Alspaugh amplified.[12]

The men appreciated all the entertainers who visited them in their remote area, but the wide-mouthed comedian was their far-out-front favorite. "Joe E. Brown . . . went to each unit and just talked to the guys," reminisced Major Kee. "I was walking across the Unalaska river and met him on the bridge. We talked a while and I invited him to come to my bunk and have supper with us. He did and we had a ball. He was a very wonderful fellow."[13]

"A prince of a man," agreed McKinistry.[14] Costley called him "tremendous."[15] A surprising number of men remembered not only seeing his show but meeting him personally. He "visited with us in the barracks," said Garrett. "He also gave us a 35mm movie projector (portable) to use in our regiment. He was an interesting person to talk with."[16]

Of those who visited the troops in the Aleutians, some were top figures in their profession, whose names still evoke instant recognition. Many men of the 206th remembered Errol Flynn. The swashbuckling star drew mixed reviews. Fitzhugh liked his show, but when he spoke with Flynn briefly, Fitzhugh found him "a very self-centered man."[17] In contrast, McKinistry called Flynn "a nice fellow and good sport."[18]

A surprising few mentioned the legendary Bob Hope.[19] A number of others remembered Edgar Bergen and his sassy dummy, Charlie McCarthy.[20] Captain Wall had a rather disconcerting experience. One afternoon he strolled out of the theater where he had been watching a movie starring Bing Crosby and Marjorie Reynolds. Just outside, "this good-looking girl was sitting in a jeep. She asked me if I could show her the way to the navy club." Wall did a double take. "The girl in the jeep was Marjorie Reynolds."[21]

Not all the visitors were movie folks. The sports-minded recalled a group of baseball players headed by Stan Musial.[22] Sgt. Charles D. Robertson rather vaguely spoke of a violinist who played classical music and "Turkey in the Straw."[23] This was probably the great Yehudi Menuhin, who visited the Aleutians rather late in the 206th's tour.

In 1942, however, routine and echoes of far-off combat closed in soon enough. Alspaugh recorded on 14 March, "I hear they had a big naval battle off Java today."[24] This may have been delayed news. Several engagements took place off Java between 25 February and 2 March.[25]

Two days after Alspaugh's notation, one of the 206th's men suffered a serious accident. Pvt. Millard Bowden of Battery D, "a good man," was operating a caterpillar bulldozer at D position on the side of Mt. Ballyhoo when he lost control of it. Realizing that it was going off the mountain, he jumped off, but one of the tracks caught his left hand and arm. After "sliding thirty feet in the snow and ice," the cat fell off a cliff. Bowden had to have his left arm amputated to the elbow.[26] This was the sort of nasty accident calculated to stick in the men's minds. Granted the local conditions, it could have happened to almost anyone.

The influx of new men caused some crowding. "We have 882 men eating three meals a day in our one mess hall now," Bowen told his diary, "which is far too many."[27] Military training and building continued apace. On 17 March Alspaugh stood the "first real rank inspection since the war," and three days later participated in "a practice alert and an hour's bayonet instruction . . ." On the twenty-eighth, he spent the day on the hill, "in charge of a road-building detail. We are rebuilding the road to our position," he explained. "It is a good thing, too, because our old road was just mud and mire."[28]

Bowen had a sharp and somewhat critical eye for military preparations. "There are four PBY planes here now instead of two," he observed. "None of us can understand why we don't have a few more planes of any kind than we do. Any kind is better than none at all." He added on the nineteenth: "New ammunition dumps are being built all over the island. Twenty-five new ones are under construction now. Some piles of 30 C. rifle ammo. is on the ground covered with tents for lack of a better place. There must be enough powder here to destroy the entire island." The next day he wrote, "Many steel huts and tents are already built and ready for occupa-

tion. When we first came up there wasn't even a path to the mountains. Now there is a road up to a camp as large as the main part of
Dutch Harbor."[29]

The "steel huts" to which he referred were the Quonset huts—
originally called Icelandic huts—which became such a ubiquitous
feature of the military landscape. Battery D on Gobbler's Knob
received the first of these buildings. "The floor came in sections,"
Captain Langley remembered. ". . . The front end was made of pre-
fab sections with a conventional door. The rear was similar except
this door was a two-piece door so that either the top or bottom
could be opened or closed independently."[30]

Pedersen's hut on Ballyhoo boasted an oil stove, sheets, and
electric lights. It was partially underground, and during the winter
"completely under snow with a tunnel entrance of twenty feet. It
was very warm and comfortable during the worst weather."[31]
Campbell remembered his hut as some thirty feet long by twelve
feet wide and eight feet high "at the top center." At first they had
only candles for light; later electricity was installed.[32] Ballew
remembered that the "snow on Mt. Ballyhoo got so deep we skied
over one hut. . . ."[33] These buildings were placed close to the unit's
equipment. "Gun crews could run out the door and jumped on the
gun. . . . These huts were precut so that a crew with little construction experience could put one up in a day or so."[34]

Keeton described his adventures in obtaining electricity for
Battery D's huts. He had recently been promoted to master
sergeant, with duties as first sergeant and battery fire sergeant, i.e.,
range sergeant.

> Our supply sergeant and assistant supply sergeant one day asked if
> the radar generator would furnish enough power to have at least one
> light in each hut. I told him it would, but we have the problem of
> wire, fixtures, and gasoline for the generator. Early one morning I
> walked out of my hut for the orderly room when I noticed a large
> roll of electrical underground cable. I immediately assigned a crew to
> bury the cable. The Battery commander asked me what the men
> were doing. I told him that Sergeant Caldwell and Corporal Horne
> requisitioned some wire and we were installing electrical lights. His
> only comment was, "Are you running wire to my hut?" The lights
> were a great morale builder. Sergeant Caldwell and Corporal Horne

had a hell of a time convincing the gasoline supply dump we needed all the gasoline to run the generator.[35]

If the spirits of any old-time Aleuts happened to be hovering over their homeland, they must have enjoyed a laugh over these huts, for the arrangements were remarkably like their traditional homes, called barabaras: the framework was of driftwood and whale ribs, covered with turf or sod, and partially buried to a depth of three or four feet. There was a small window of glass or translucent seal gut. "The door was placed to the leeward of the prevailing winds and led into a little hall, like a storm porch." These dwellings were described as dry, clean, warm, and comfortable.[36] In fact, they were not unlike Battery D Quonset huts.

For the Arkansas men on Umnak, March began with a "37-hour williwaw" that dumped snow and sleet, tore some tents in half, and blew down others.

A new commander, Colonel Hallowell, took over the 153d and the Otter Point garrison. On 4 March he visited the troops and ate at their mess hall.[37] To Miller he remarked that he looked for a Japanese attack by spring. That was good news for Miller, who was getting restive and would "hate to go thru the war without firing a shot." He had a realistic if somewhat cynical view of their mission, and evidently had begun to moderate his earlier pessimism:

> We are to do a job here when the bombers come—they need bases to protect naval establishments at Dutch Harbor, the fighter planes will protect the bombers, anti-aircraft will protect the fighters, 50-cal guns will protect the anti-aircraft, 30-cal guns protect the 50s and Private Dogface, USA, will protect the 30-calibres. The foot slogger with his rifle is still the most important man in the Army. We'll keep the Japs out and if some land is to be gained we'll do it and hold it.[38]

On 7 March, Stubbs noted in his diary, "We are becoming more civilized every day."[39] Miller agreed with this assessment, so much so that he instituted a training schedule to keep the men busy. "We are no longer struggling to keep alive, we eat well, sleep long and keep warm—with minor discomforts." But he was still aggrieved at the 153d's passive role: "Troops outfitted like we are—hard, well-trained, should be sent to smash someone instead of passively waiting for someone to come smash us—Hell, if we'd take the offensive we'd have them whipped even tho we might suffer early losses. . . ."

Among his activities, Miller started a newspaper, using broadcasts from the states for material. These were typed up and distributed to the men. One burden was off his shoulders—the investigation of the dentist was over and had found in his favor—"but none of us think he did it accidentally—in the absence of any absolute evidence, however, we had to find him innocent.—Fooey, now I and my children probably, will have to pay for his disability . . ."[40]

During this period the enlisted men continued to haul wood up from the beach, unload barges, hike, train with bayonets and gas masks, and attend classes on various weapons. "Every man in the Co. has to learn the functions of each weapon in the Co. Rifle, machine gun, mortar, pistol and automatic rifle," explained Stubbs.[41]

For Stubbs, and probably for all his buddies, the prime event of the first half of March was the opening of a small canteen. It carried only candy, magazines, and toilet articles, with candy bars rationed six to a customer. "We all filled up on candy for the first time in six months," recorded Stubbs. "Had to stand in line for about an hour to get into the canteen." By the next day, the ration had been cut to three bars per man per day.

On 10 March, "We got the good news tonight that we would have no more hikes in inclement weather."[42] This was because another williwaw had descended upon them and blew for thirty-six hours. Miller marked the occasion with a truly classic description of a williwaw:

> Can you imagine men out on a great barren, walking against a 65-mph wind that rips the grass out by its roots; that blows marble-sized chunks of snow horizontally without dropping them; a wind of fits and starts, of gust and gusto, that drives your words back into your teeth before you can utter them, that freezes your breath on your parka and on your beard—that ices your eyelashes shut and frosts your cheeks—a wind that rips a tent from side to side in 10 minutes and drives sleet right thru a piece of 26-oz canvas. . . . When you've seen that, brother, you've been out in a Williwaw![43]

A mild scare took place on the nineteenth when around 1500 "two vessels were sighted about 15 miles from shore and would not return the signal. Thinking they may be enemy ships, we were given the command to prepare for battle and stand by." These ships turned out to be two American power barges.[44]

Of more immediate interest was the fact that on 22 March the men received their first pay since 31 December, "and nowhere to spend it" after a rush on the quartermaster for cigarettes.[45] Then, as Miller remarked, "The great poker tournament is on . . . $35,000 and no place to spend it except over the gaming table. . . ." He added, "Our regimental staff arrived t'other day and are they a panic—oh, well, we can't all be tough. . . ."[46]

From this point until the end of the month, all efforts and most thoughts concentrated on finishing the Umnak runway at Otter Point. "We unloaded a barge of steel runway material tonight," Stubbs recorded on 22 March. "They started putting down the runway today. The 2nd platoon unloaded 65 tons of steel tonight. (We carried the steel on our backs across the deep sand on the shore and up a hill and loaded it onto a trailer that was pulled by a caterpillar to the runway site.)" From then on, life was one steel-laden barge after another at the approximate rate of one every eighteen hours.[47]

All of which irritated Miller who believed his men were doing most of the work. "First runway must be down by April 1 and E Co. is working nite and day laying it—What in hell are the engineers and civilians doing? What would they do w/o infantry?" He admitted, however, "That's pretty fancy runway steel, tho'—easy to lay. . . ."

Plans called for an impressive permanent post on Umnak—"if the Japs give us six months to finish they will never take it. But they won't, of course . . ."

On 28 March Generals Buckner, ADC commander, and Colladay, in command at Ft. Mears, touched down on the runway—the first plane to land there. Miller wasn't impressed, noting that the VIPs "blew in today, spent an hour inspecting and flew back to the tea tables at Dutch Harbor." He added bitterly, "Runway of portable interlocking steel sheets is now our task—we [are] working night and day to have it down by Apr 1. . . . Our mission is to defend this airbase, but by God we've got to build it first! Oh, you wouldn't believe the tangled mess this hell-hole is in. . . ."[48]

Nevertheless, for all the griping and snafus, all concerned had reason to be proud of the runway at Otter Point. Working in fright-ful conditions and on impossible terrain, the army had constructed a workable runway. It was far from ideal. In the words of Admiral Morison, "This airstrip was so unstable that fighter planes bounded thirty feet into the air on impact. Aviators said it was like landing on an inner-spring mattress, and every bomber that landed gave the field a sort of permanent wave."[49] But it was usable, and would play its part in the action to come in the not too distant future.

15

"A Dangerous Game"

April 1942 opened with a bit of good news for two of Alspaugh's buddies: they had been selected for Officer Candidate School (OCS). "They were sure excited and it didn't take them long to get packed and ready to go."[1]

That same day, Bowen recorded, "'B' is moving into the steel huts at the foot of the hill today and tomorrow, which will be more convenient for all of us."[2] Alspaugh agreed with this assessment. Battery B moved into the new quarters on 4 April, which made everything "a lot more convenient." The next day, Easter, he added, "I like the nearness of the mess hall and huts to the position. . . . We have a much finer mess hall than we had previously. Our food is better, too."[3]

Keeton recalled that G-2 having indicated that the Japanese were going to attack Dutch Harbor, an alert was called for Easter morning during a severe storm. As Keeton climbed the steps to his gun emplacement, the wind tore off his helmet. "Needless to say this alert was unnecessary and very miserable."[4] Neither Bowen nor Alspaugh mentioned this alert, so it may have been confined to Keeton's Battery D. Bowen had remarked on 2 April, however, "There is a general belief that the island will be attacked before the 15th of the month." Bowen doubted the rumor, but wouldn't have been surprised at anything.[5]

The sixth brought their "worst spring storm" with "quite a bit of snowfall and plenty of wind and sleet." It blew down a number of communications lines, and Alspaugh and some of his men spent most of the next day restoring them.[6] Bowen wrote with ill-concealed satisfaction "Colonels Robinson* and Hargis came up on

---

* Probably Robertson.

the hill this afternoon and the wind blew Robinson down flat two times in as many minutes."[7]

In Battery G, Massey was settling in, although he still disliked the place. He complained that there was no recreation and the mail was slow. "Most of the men played cards or checkers." Massey spent his evenings studying gunnery and air-sea navigation. "Some Navy ships limp in for repair, others came in for refueling," he noted. "Most are weather-beaten, some shot down. . . . What a change we have made from the hot, sultry desert of Texas to the sudden cold, sharp wild winds of this horrible place!"[8]

For Stubbs on Umnak, this first week of April included routine work unloading barges. The third was enlivened by "wieners for dinner. Stephens ate 18 of them before they were gone." On the fourth, Miller informed Stubbs that he and his buddies would have to give up their wooden tent floors; they were needed for a mess hall. "Here we go back onto the ground." They spent Easter moving the tents "to make a kitchen and mess hall combined. We live right beside the kitchen now."[9]

Miller had a proud moment on 1 April when a large transport plane landed on the runway, and the runway "held up the big ship—Okay, Infantry, chalk up another tally!" But this was his last cheerful thought for many days. He was in a fever of fury and dismay because the mission had been changed: "We have just learned that War Dept. has disapproved further progress on this westward expansion—the drive from the north is off—we no longer have any impetus—everyone has lost his spark—we've given up. . . . We took all this grief in the hope that we might be the advance guard heading for Japan through Russia. We worked overtime . . . we sweated—we cried—we went hungry, wet and sick—and now, now it's been taken from us."[10]

In retrospect, it is difficult to believe that a man of Miller's intelligence could have accepted the notion that the United States would invade Japan from the Aleutians, let alone built up his hopes and expectations on such a shaky foundation. The Washington decision represented a concession to reality. In no way could the Aleutians have supported an expeditionary force of the size necessary for an effective attack on the Japanese home islands. As for using Russian territory, the USSR had not declared war on Japan and would not do so until the Japanese were thoroughly beaten. Few events were less likely than Stalin's permitting the Americans to use his Far Eastern territory in a way sure to bring the Russians into the Pacific War at this stage.

What really hurt Miller was the reflection that he seemed unlikely to have a crack at the enemy. "The bigwigs have cut down our garrison, reduced our appropriations, reduced our importance (and our potence) to that of a bladeless knife without a handle, and are planning a drive from the south. God be with MacArthur! I wish to hell I were. . . ." He did not relish the prospect of telling his three nephews that he fought the war "from a tattered tent on Umnak Island." He thought the 153d might "hold out for weeks against the best the Japs could throw at us. . . . But why should the Jap waste men and materiel on us when a few submarines operating in the Inside Passage could cut off half of Alaska from its supply and starve us in 30 days and/or freeze us in 36 hours!"

Easter found him still so down he did not feel like going to church. The next day was Army Day, and Colonel Hallowell did not help matters by making a speech extolling "how tough" were America's fighting men of old. "God Almighty—so we're not tough! . . . At that, I guess he's right. The nation is so soft it doesn't know how to fight any more. These boys are tough, but nobody will let them even get drunk—let alone mix it up with friend Jap."

In a mood to lash out at anybody, he made a few choice comments about the British in India. "Did you ever see any nation make such a mess of its wars, its politics and its general misbehavior. . . ."[11]

That evening Miller and Stubbs were scheduled to go to the quartermaster to accept a prisoner—their first among eight hundred men. However, a snowstorm blew up, so fierce that they could not erect a tent for the man. The next day the quartermaster brought the prisoner to Miller. "He went batty the other day and wanted to fight a duel with his First Sergeant," noted Miller. Stubbs was surprised to see that the prisoner was a boy from Nashville, Tennessee, whom he had met on the ship coming to Alaska.[12]

The tragic news coming in from the Philippines penetrated the consciousness of the men of the 206th as nothing had since Pearl Harbor. Wrote Alspaugh on 9 April: "Well, we suffered our greatest defeat today in the Philippines. It was pretty bad and probably could have been avoided. We kind of won a moral victory however for holding off such a superior force for so damn long. I guess the

Japs found out what kind of fighters they have run up against. Tough luck, 200 C.A."[13]

Bowen remarked, "Philippine Islands are as good as gone. 'F' Btry of the 200th CA was wiped out to the last man." He added two days later, "Boys are discouraged by the loss of the Philippines. I think it is the boys we were with being killed that hurt the most. Some of the boys are just beginning to realize that this is a dangerous game."[14]

Early in April, 1st Lt. Vernon Nielsen came to Battery A from Battery F as, among other duties, officer in charge of the Radar Section. With his arrival, "meetings were held relative to the disposition of the radar position located on Amaknak Island overlooking Dutch Harbor." Don Drake pointed out that this was not a favorable location "to detect water targets to the north due to the heavy daily activity in the Iliuliuk Bay area. . . ." Also, the oscilloscopes recorded false blips "caused by the radar signals being reflected from the surrounding mountains." This problem had been experienced at other locations tested. Nielsen decided they should travel to Nikolski, Umnak Island, to reconnoiter. On 15 April, he and Drake went to Umnak aboard a small tugboat.[15]

This little expedition is worth recounting because it was probably typical of many such reconnaissances. Their mission was "to survey the extreme end of Umnak Island; to chart topographic features of the island; to determine the locations to best serve as a radar site . . . , and to ascertain the best shore locations where barges could be beached to off-load equipment and supplies."

The tentative site was twenty miles south of Nikolski, which at the time had a population of around ninety Aleuts. Due to the elements, the trip took three days. Nielsen and Drake arrived at Fort Glenn on the morning of Easter Sunday, 19 April 1942. While lying off shore, they "witnessed the first aircraft, a C-47 transport, land on the recently completed steel-matting runway." In mid-morning the men pushed on, entering Nikolski Bay at about 1700, after a smooth trip. There they experienced trouble when the hawser line became fouled in the tugboat's propeller. A coast guard cutter had to clear out to avoid a possible collision.[16]

High waves prevented their landing at Nikolski, so Nielsen and Drake were sent ashore with all their equipment in a small dinghy.

"In addition to wearing their arctic clothing and shoepacs, each was carrying an M-1 rifle, a bandolier of ammunition, a sleeping bag, a case of C rations, maps and other items. . . ." Thus burdened, it took them an hour to cover the approximate half mile from the landing point to Nikolski.

There they contacted a small detachment from the 206th's Headquarters Battery, who had arrived earlier on an unrelated assignment. Nielsen and Drake were billeted in an Aleut house. Late that afternoon, Nielsen visited the overseer of a large sheep ranch, who offered the loan of two horses and pack saddles. These Nielsen accepted gratefully; neither he nor Drake had looked forward to a twenty-mile hike, loaded down as they were.[17]

The next morning, they had breakfast with the rancher's family, enjoying their first fresh eggs and fresh milk since August 1941. The rancher offered them the use of a "small line shack" with a corral for the horses near their destination. They had reason to be thankful for this unexpected shelter, for in the course of their survey activities they were battered by one-hundred-mile-an-hour winds that pitted their goggles with blowing sand and skinned Nielsen's nose, since he had failed to secure the nose flap of his parka. On the ninth day, they had completed their mission and had hitchhiked a trip back to Dutch Harbor in a small freighter.[18]

Some nineteen days after they returned, it was decided to relocate the radar site from Dutch Harbor to Morris Cove, "across Unalaska Bay from Mt. Ballyhoo." Work would not begin until May.[19]

About this same time, mid-April, the army established its Harbor Craft Detachment to ferry men from Dutch Harbor to the various outposts. Drake called this service an "enormous morale factor." It enabled men from the outposts visiting Fort Mears to return to their positions in the minimum time "without having to hike the shorelines carrying provisions." The navy's large harbor boats handled the resupply of these outposts with food and other necessities.[20]

Another event took place in April that had no direct connection with the fighting men, but which was a part of Alaskan history, indeed of all American history. Early in April, General Buckner declared Alaska a military area and ordered all "persons of Japanese blood" to report to the nearest army post by 20 April for transportation to the continental United States. Army transports took them in four groups late in April and early May. Evacuation began on 25 April. While most hated to leave, some feared that if they stayed they might find themselves blamed for every "mysterious fire" or other "act of treason" that took place. This fear was probably well founded, for anti-Japanese feeling was running high, so much so that Filipinos wore "red, white and blue identification buttons bearing the word Philippines."

Many of the two-hundred-plus evacuees worried about the property they left behind, which was considerable. Ralph J. Moore, the project director at Minidoka, Idaho, discovered that forty families had left behind assets totaling over two million dollars—a very tidy fortune by 1942's standards. He was astonished to find that most of the evacuees had been important personages in their communities, and they all "seemed to be comparatively well off."

To anticipate, even when American citizens of Japanese ancestry were permitted to return to their homes, those from Alaska ran into extra complications. Although Alaska was a territory of the United States, for all intents and purposes it was treated as a foreign country, and the Alaska Japanese had to get a State Department "Permit to Depart." Other paperwork came into play, and the red tape was horrendous. It was many months before they finally reached home.[21]

There is no indication that this shameful roundup of Americans whose ancestors happened to come from Japan touched the Arkansas men in Alaska, and probably they did not know if it at the time. For the enlisted diarists, routine shut down again, punctuated with events favorable and unfavorable. Alspaugh was confined to quarters for several days with "a chest cold and a slight fever." Soon he was out and around again, helping to build an addition to the dugout. "We are having a hard time securing lumber. We are using Quonset Hut crates." The news of the Doolittle raid on Tokyo on 17 April thrilled him. "Boy, we sure are tickled! It sure was heartening news for us."[22]

Oddly enough, neither Stubbs nor Miller mentioned this event that gave such a lift to American morale in the darkest days of the Pacific War. Stubbs was caught up in an exhausting routine of long hikes, digging foxholes, standing inspections, training, and, of course, unloading barges, often at unholy hours. On 11 April, he went to bed at 2100 and was routed out an hour later for barge detail, working until 0415. Two days later, he rose at 0230 and unloaded until 0815. This work could be dangerous as well as tiring. "Graves got a leg broken while we were on a barge detail this afternoon," Stubbs wrote on 16 April. In his world, events worth recording were a distribution of candy bar rations, letters from home, a carton of cigarettes, a softball game. So far, the fighting was too remote to mention.[23]

Miller was somewhat ashamed of his griping in the last few entries, because he had been "really driving and happy as a lark" until recently. "The loss of pressure upon us coupled with indecision, evasiveness, . . . on the part of so many has grounded us," he explained. "We can't help it—one captain (staff) is so scared he wears a pistol everywhere, to bed I believe, and gets up to put his clothes on every time there is a suspicious noise at night." Miller reflected that pistols would be of little use if the Japanese attacked the island some night. "It boils down, I believe, to the commander who says we gotta be tough and the next day bawls hell out of our officers' mess force for not *heating* our china before placing it on the table—Gawdamighty!" (Miller's italics).

A thousand additional troops, including the remainder of the 2d Battery of the 153d reached Umnak aboard the *Grant* on 23 April Rough seas prevented their landing and they sailed back to Dutch Harbor to be outfitted for Alaskan weather. All told, the twenty-third was a notable day. "Civilians all quit . . . —350 of 'em."[24]

A man from Company E, with his companions on a mission in the mountains, became lost in the storm. His own company searched all night fruitlessly, and in the morning Company F took over. At about 1700 they found him "still on his wobbly pins," much to everyone's astonishment. He was still alive after having been lost in the snow for a full night and day. He had walked "all around Idak Cape all night (40 miles), wading in the sea and following beach . . ." He was picked up some three miles from camp "out on his feet—lucky to be alive."[25]

The new men finally reached Umnak and debarked late on the twenty-fifth. "Our camp is three times as large as it was last night," Stubbs wrote the next day. ". . . The boys that brought whiskey with them from the States are selling it at $10 a pint and $16 for a quart."[26]

Considering some of the price gouging on alcohol that took place during the Aleutian years, this was something of a bargain. Sgt. Frank Snellgrove of Battery C remembered the going price as $20 a fifth.[27] Major Kee recalled that it could go much higher. "When a ship would come in, some guys would get some from the crew for $75 a fifth."[28]

On 18 April Alspaugh noted an addition to their lives. "We have a radio station on the island now. It is not a very strong station but they give us some good recordings."[29] Pack recalled that this station broadcast music by such favorites of the day as Glenn Miller and Tommy Dorsey.[30] Radio reception from other locations varied from poor to surprisingly good. Laubach "listened to Hot Springs, Arkansas radio station—KTHS—in the barracks and guard shack."[31] Sergeant Beverburg "erected radio antennas so we could receive news from the rest of the world— . . . San Francisco, Australia, and Hawaii, navy channels and Press Wireless."[32]

"The supply clerk had a radio in our hut," wrote Caldwell. "We were able to get all the armed services radio programs. Duffy's Tavern—Harry James—Hit Parade—Jack Benny—Fred Allen and sometimes Tokyo Rose."[33] In fact, this Japanese offering was by far the best remembered, one might almost say the favorite program. Transmission must have been powerful, for even small radios picked her up. The Japanese might have been gratified to know how many GIs in the Aleutians tuned in, and almost certainly would have been chagrined to learn how much of their star's message sailed in one ear and out the other. It was almost as if these young minds came equipped with filters enabling them to accept the entertainment value and reject the propaganda. As Abell remarked, they "frequently listened to Tokyo Rose in Japan, mostly for laughs."[34]

According to Alspaugh's diary, the latter part of April was marked by misadventures of one sort or another. The popular Captain Hutchinson transferred out on the twenty-second, and Alspaugh went down to the Ballyhoo docks to see him off. "This outfit lost a capable officer when they lost him," Alspaugh wrote regretfully. "I could go through hell and high water with a commander like him."

The next day, after an alert at 0400, "a little artillery practice" and "a little infantry drill," Alspaugh noted without comment, "The navy pumped 18,000 gallons of gasoline into the bay by mistake today." On the morning of 24 April, Sergeant Beverburg "got hit in the head with a shovel . . ."[35]

That same morning a major accident occurred, to which Massey was a horrified witness: "I watched two PBYs roll down the ramp for takeoff. One started his run from the ramp straight towards the spit, too short a distance for a loaded plane. . . . As he neared the spit he tried to bounce over it but pancaked on the rocks and split open and exploded. The depth charges under the wings jarred loose and rolled free. I only saw two people get out of the gun blisters. A harbor patrol boat sped to the rescue, but no one could do anything."[36]

The other PBY was unharmed. Casualty reports varied. Bowen wrote that three of the crew were killed instantly. "Remaining four suffered from shock but not seriously injured."[37] Alspaugh believed that there were "four casualties and four more seriously injured."[38]

All deaths of those serving in wartime are tragic, but special bitterness clings to accidental deaths under such circumstances. Those on active duty more or less budget for possible death in combat, and the families can have at least the thin comfort of feeling that their loved one's death had a meaning and purpose. But accidents are never really expected, the deaths involved seem pointless, and there is always the nagging suspicion that they might have been avoided if only someone had been paying attention. For those at Dutch Harbor, this particular accident was a reminder that war, even far from the fighting front, was indeed "a dangerous game."

16

"Tomorrow May Bring Untold Things"

Bowen's initial entry for May revealed a disturbing situation: "Colonel Robertson is having a private dugout built for himself. Many are in doubt as to just where he will be and what his duties are in case of an attack. He has long since lost popularity in the Regiment among both men and officers."[1]

Bowen was a good soldier, not given to exaggeration, so one must assume that these views were widespread, not just one man's opinion. While it was reasonable enough that Robertson should want "a private dugout" for himself and, one certainly hopes, for his staff, there should be no ambiguity about the whereabouts and duties of a regimental commander under combat conditions. He should be in his field headquarters and his job is to command—to lead and inspire, to make the often heartbreaking decisions, to accept responsibility for what goes wrong, to spend as much time as possible with his troops. The Old Man may be a prince or a stinker, but he will be *there*, the living symbol and rallying point of his regiment.

Over on Ballyhoo, Massey was having a few lessons in the art of command, for no officer was assigned to his section. "I have a good section," he wrote, "the men keep busy, grumble a lot but that's natural under such conditions. I believe in being stern with my men, good to them, but demand respect. . . ." He added with satisfaction, "I have the full respect and confidence of our battery commander." His men aroused him to mingled exasperation and pride: "Lord, what a crew to put up with! They curse, bitch and drink anything with alcohol in it from shoe polish to torpedo juice, but they still like to get together and sing hymns. Dependable? Without a doubt. I wouldn't trade them for nobody's damn section. . . . I have found out as long as the men are busy they get along. Many get to brooding, quite a few suicides on the island. I surely don't want that to happen in my section."[2]

A general air of uneasiness set in early in May. On the fifth, Alspaugh stood a stiff inspection "on personal appearance, equipment and ordnance." He added, "We are going to have lots of work for the next few weeks. We have to dig a dugout immediately."[3] That same day, Bowen gave a reason for all this activity: "Corregidor fell today, so all guard posts were doubled in anticipation of an attack. G-2 says Jap troops are being withdrawn from India and other southern parts and are expected to attempt an invasion of the Aleutian Islands. Enemy sub was sighted near here early this A.M., but no shots were fired."[4]

The loss of the Philippines had a very special meaning for the men of the 206th. Massey and his section "sat up listening to Tokyo Rose read names of soldiers killed or captured and call the name of the unit they were in. Many of them were in the 200th AA. This was the unit that won the coin toss. We feel, however, it will only be a little time before our fate may be the same. . . ."[5]

A direct touch of war came their way on 7 May. "One of the submarines came in from patrol duty today with the periscope shot away and two of the tail plates buckled in," Bowen reported. "They had to stay under water for 42 hours so the batteries ran down and they were hardly able to make port. They were near enough to Tokyo to see the radio tower in the city."[6]

On Umnak, Stubbs took "an intelligence test" as a preliminary to applying for OCS.[7] Quite a few of those stationed in the Aleutians took this action. One suspects that they were impelled less by a burning desire to become officers than because it offered an honorable way to escape the Aleutians. Indeed, Alspaugh, who was also making the effort, admitted as much on 10 May when he finished his physical examination and turned in his papers. "I don't think I will ever get a chance to leave here but it doesn't hurt to try."[8]

Meanwhile, Stubbs was promoted to sergeant on the third.[9] The subject of promotions was a sore one with Miller. He had been fairly confident that he would make first lieutenant. Since coming to Alaska, he had been second in command of F Company. Whenever the commander, Capt. Frank Ingram, had to be absent, he left Miller in charge. However, the one promotion allotted went to Lt. Neil N.

"Snippy" Snyder. Had almost anyone else been selected, Miller probably would have taken it in stride, but Snyder happened to be Miller's particular *bête noir.*

"Snip has gone plumb to hell since we've been here—surly, morose, sarcastic, uncooperative and nasty . . . but Snip has more service than I and is of the 153rd hierarchy while I am a Reserve Officer." On one occasion, Snyder called one of Miller's men an s.o.b., whereupon Miller "threatened to spank him—he apologized publicly . . ."

To Miller's credit, he returned to this entry a year later with a generous amendment: "Snip has changed so much in the last year that I'm going to rescind all of the above. The kid is actually likable and who knows but what it was my fault as much as his that we didn't get along."[10]

Stubbs made one of his usual laconic entries about barge detail on 7 May. Sgt. Jack Corn "got tight last night. When he came in we thought we were having an attack by the enemy." Stubbs had never seen Corn in that condition before, so the incident was worth recording.[11]

Such entries as Stubbs's about the unloading process give the impression that all of this was routine. But in a little history of their part in the Aleutian campaign, Miller wrote a description of barge detail worth repeating in part as a tribute to these men stuck with such jobs for months on end:

> The "harbor" on Umnak . . . fronted on one of the wildest stretches of water in the Aleutians—the 11-mile Umnak pass between the Bering and the Pacific. With every tide change this pass became a mill race. . . .
>
> When a barge came in, the power boat would aim it for the beach and cut it loose. The surf would beach it, usually sideways, and the men on the beach would loop a couple of lines around the king posts and anchor it to deadmen, or sometimes to an engineering caterpillar. A couple of two-by-twelves would be run up the front of the barge and the ant lines of infantry guys would start unloading on the double. . . . When the tide was running full, the surf pulled the barges in and out, tearing down temporary unloading platforms hastily built, snapping five-inch lines like string and more than once coming close to mashing a jumping, dodging, swearing Arkansas doughboy.

The barges came in at night or at daybreak and it made no difference: a runner came a mile from the beach and woke a platoon leader and he took his men and went to unload it, come williwaw, blizzard or high water. When it was unloaded he crawled back to the tent area and into his sleeping bay, and prayed there wouldn't be another for at least four hours.[12]

Miller was in a fret these early days of May because it seemed to him that they had been spinning their wheels—they had kept busy but nothing had been done toward finishing the base. "We have not been authorized to construct any field fortifications yet—one foxhole we have and no more," he complained. "While we've been doing basic training for the past two months we could have done a lot of digging—but the old man wants to wait until our permanent stuff gets here—and what if the Japs come before the concrete does?"[13]

One moderately bright spot illuminated these early May days. "I heard about the naval battle in the Coral Sea that is raging today," recorded Alspaugh on 9 May. "It must be some engagement. From all indications it looks like we are going to emerge victorious in the battle."[14]

Actually, this important engagement was more in the nature of a standoff. The United States lost *Lexington*, a destroyer, and an oiler, with *Yorktown* heavily damaged. Japan lost the light carrier *Shoho*, one destroyer, and several minecraft, with *Shokaku* badly damaged. Hence, Japan could claim the tactical victory and most emphatically did so. However, the Japanese strategic objective was the capture and occupation of Port Moresby, which the Coral Sea battle made impossible. Thus, the United States scored the strategic victory.[15] In any case, at this stage of the Pacific War, any good news was exceedingly welcome.

That spring, one of Roosevelt's trouble-shooters, Cmdr. Paul F. Foster, was on an inspection tour of certain naval bases to assess their defense readiness. On 15 May he reached Dutch Harbor, where he found plenty to make him unhappy.

First and foremost, no fighter aircraft were nearer than Fort Glenn on Umnak. He recommended "the construction of a small fighter strip utilizing a catapult and arresting gear." This was done, but not until too late to be of use when the Japanese struck.

Foster also discovered that although the army's 37mm and 3" guns had been emplaced for nearly a year, the crews had never fired at targets. The army countered "that ammunition was in short supply and that target sleeves had been requisitioned but not received." Moreover, the Aircraft Warning System was inadequate, as was the army radio network between Amaknak Island and the outposts at Cold Bay on Amak Island and Fort Glenn. Power was insufficient to insure that messages would reach their destinations.

Fuel tanks were exposed and uncamouflaged, except for those next to the navy barracks. What is more, only roughly half of the buildings had paint camouflage. The clustered wooden barracks and station hospital presented a potential disaster area. Not only the fuel supply but ammunition magazines were vulnerable, having been constructed "in open areas without revetments or other shields." Nor did the air arm escape criticism. There was no coordination of army and navy flight schedules, resulting in many airborne planes being unidentified. Foster concluded that the bases "were in a state of infancy and not ready to be adequately defended." Construction had received the major effort at the expense of training and camouflage.[16]

To all of which the men of the 206th would have uttered a fervent "Amen." A certain amount of vulnerability is inherent in any military installation, but in hindsight it is difficult to justify some of these vulnerabilities. For example, it is all very well to save ammunition, but no one can learn to shoot straight with any weapon, from sidearms to AA gun, without practice. He may know theoretically how and when to squeeze the trigger, which button to push, which handle to crank, even how to take his weapon apart while blindfolded, but these things are no substitute for target practice.

As for camouflage, in this treeless land the only natural concealment was the earth itself, and one could not bury an entire fort, naval base, and outlying posts. Artificial camouflage measures, such as nets and paint, should have ranked high on the list of priorities for the Aleutians.

The shortcomings in relation to ammunition and camouflage might have been the fault of the upper echelon, which assigned priorities, but there was no excuse for the failure to coordinate flight schedules. In wartime, any unidentified aircraft should be considered hostile and promptly treated as such. The defenders of the airspace should not have to pause to ask themselves, "Is it one of ours?"

In one respect, Dutch Harbor was operating in traditional style. "Talk about paperwork! I mean papers!" snorted Henry Swanson, who possessed in full measure the rugged individualist's scorn for red tape. "I'd get an order to go somewhere and I'd get three copies. Here would come a messenger and give me three sheets of paper all the same ordering me to do this. He'd keep three other copies at the office and three copies went to Washington, D.C. There was a dozen copies of each paper. I'd be lying at the dock and they would want something down at Morris Cove or over in Humpy Cove. There'd be twelve copies made of that request."[17]

Swanson also had problems with army officers who, although wanting to do the right thing, had no notion of what was involved in moving equipment by sea. On one occasion, he was sent to Chernofski where a scow loaded with "brand new trucks and cars" awaited a tow. Swanson's little ship was not equipped for towing; moreover, the cargo had not been lashed down. Swanson explained to the army captain in charge the need for this action, and the latter complied. But the only towing equipment available was some small cable.

About midnight, a boat arrived at Chernofski, bringing orders that Swanson was to leave immediately with the load of trucks and cars. Resignedly, he sent word up channels that he would obey orders, but was going to lose the scow, which he did when a gale blew up.[18]

During mid-May, three officers and forty-five men of the 153d helped search for a PBY from Dutch Harbor that had been missing since the ninth. They left Umnak on 12 May and searched Unalaska thoroughly but fruitlessly. There was no trace of either the patrol plane or its seven crew members, nor had any radio signal been received. The search party returned to Umnak on the fifteenth.[19]

The second half of May could be summed up in the words "rumors and alerts." Miller's history remarked, "Rumors, fantastic rumors, scary rumors, swept the island like fire in the tundra, only to die down in a few days until someone thought of another."[20] Bowen and Alspaugh noted alerts on the fifteenth and sixteenth respectively, occasioned by a reported sighting of enemy planes.[21] Bowen added on 17 May, "Rumors are flying thick and fast and the entire post is working overtime in preparing for the supposed attack. The trench all around our hill is dug, sandbagged and boarded up. The hill has been issued 70,000 more rounds of 30 caliber ammunition to bring the total extra to 280,000 rounds besides the 30 and 3 inch. 'B' Btry is ready for any emergency." He and his men spent most of the next day "getting everything ready for the attack if it does come. . . . Hauled extra fuel to the gun positions and started setting up the field kitchen."[22]

Miller was slightly contemptuous of all this activity. "Poor DH, they black out at the least excuse. What a bunch of old maids!" But Umnak was just as busy and just as rumor-ridden. On the nineteenth, "every gun on the island was fired from dawn till dark in an emergency training program. You see," Miller explained, "many men had not fired their weapons and it is about time to learn, hey! . . . One of the 155s burst during firing—heh! Drag $50,000 worth of machinery up here and blow it up when the first shot is fired."

The previous week had seen two alerts on Umnak, because "HQ is all spooked up about a huge attack on Glenn and Mears very soon. . . . At any rate, the attack is expected momentarily until June 15 when the fog sets in on the Aleutians and makes aerial work impossible which would allow for a sea-borne invasion."[23]

The Arkansas men in the Aleutians were having one break— they were enjoying "some wonderful spring weather," at times hot enough for sunburn, and the vegetation was turning green. While grateful for the pleasant weather, the men were more happy about the upgrading of their defenses. On 22 May, three B-18s landed at Umnak to become part of the island's air protection, which would soon include interceptors. By the end of the month, the island had twelve P-40s and nine bombers "on 24-hour patrol." And on Amaknak, seven PBYs arrived from Kodiak, bringing the strength up to nine.[24]

Of special interest was the arrival at Dutch Harbor of the light cruiser *Nashville* on 24 May. A number of the 206th men, including Bowen and Alspaugh, visited the ship. Her personnel welcomed them and showed them all over the cruiser. Alspaugh paid particular attention to the gun turrets.[25]

Nashville was part of the Main Body of Task Force Eight (later designated North Pacific Fleet), organized as recently as 21 May under the command of RADM Robert A. "Fuzzy" Theobald. The

Main Body, TG 8.6, would consist of the heavy cruisers *Indianapolis* and *Louisville*, the light cruisers *Nashville*, *St. Louis*, and *Honolulu*, plus four destroyers. Theobald also had an Air Search Group, a Surface Search Group, a Destroyer Striking Group, and a number of miscellaneous craft. Being in overall area command, Theobald could call upon the Army Air Striking Group under Brig. Gen. William O. Butler. So far this naval force was not physically in being. The vessels were scattered throughout the Pacific, and Theobald himself did not reach Alaska until 27 May, when he arrived at Kodiak. In fact, TF 8 did not get together until after the Japanese had struck Dutch Harbor.[26]

On 26 May, Alspaugh relaxed sufficiently to go to the movies. The powers-that-be had sent a good one for a change—the comedy-fantasy *Here Comes Mr. Jordan*.[27] It would be the last real relaxation in many days.

"I'd better bring this book up to date tonight, for tomorrow may bring untold things," Miller recorded. "A naval force of 3 carriers, 16 cruisers, destroyers and transports is massed in a position from which they are capable of striking the Aleuts . . . Tomorrow is Sunday and Japan's Navy Day—a logical time for the treacherous bastards to strike. We have WD warning to expect an attack tomorrow and are reveilling at 4 A.M. to meet it."[28]

As far as figures were concerned, this was excellent intelligence. Japan's Northern Area Force, under VADM Boshiro Hosogaya, consisted of two light carriers, one seaplane carrier, two heavy cruisers, two light cruisers, one auxiliary cruiser, eleven destroyers and four transports, plus service vessels. But as yet they were not in a position to strike the Aleutians. Of the massive Midway-Alaska forces, first to leave Japan was RADM Kakuji Kakuta's Second Carrier Striking Force; it departed at noon on 26 May Japan time. The rest of Hosogaya's fleet sortied two days later.[29]

By a combination of skill, hard work, and a few bits of good luck, U. S. intelligence had pieced together a fairly comprehensive, although not perfect, picture of Japan's intentions and strength. So Admiral Chester W. Nimitz, commander-in-chief, Pacific Fleet, was quite sure that the Aleutian campaign was a sideshow designed to distract attention from the main thrust at Midway and to lure American naval strength northward away from the principal theater.

Naturally, for the men in the Aleutians, the battle in which they would engage was the big one, never mind what was going on elsewhere. Whatever happened, they could not complain that they had not been warned. "G-2 expects an air attack between the 31st and the 2nd, and a ground attack between the 2nd and 4th," Bowen wrote on 30 May. "It is rumored that the Jap Navy has been sighted and we know that one of our subs left yesterday and did not return. . . . All guards have been doubled on our gun position. . . . In any eventuality we are ready for the worst."[30]

17

"It's the Damn Japs!"

To say that the defenders of Alaska expected the Japanese to strike the Aleutians is putting it mildly. From the highest to the lowest on the military totem pole, officers and men anticipated enemy action.

On Umnak, Miller was suffering from a fever, and the doctor ordered him to bed; however, from the "high command" came orders on 1 June to "sleep in clothes and remain alert all night."[1] Stubbs and his men also were "going to sleep with our clothes on for a few nights now. Expecting something to happen."[2]

Dutch Harbor was equally if not more on the *qui vive*. According to Raney, warning came in May of a large Japanese force headed for Dutch Harbor. "The word was that there were 65,000 Japanese troops on board. We figured our goose was cooked."[3] "We are expecting an alert early in the morning since there are only two more days in this period of expected attack," recorded Bowen on the second. "Captain Love is sure they will be here soon. G-2 has sent out many warnings so we are as ready as it is possible to get. This period of waiting and expecting is wearing on all the men's nerves."[4]

Aboard the transport *U.S.S. President Fillmore*, steaming into Dutch Harbor on the evening of 2 June, Keith Gilbert noted approvingly, "The island was on the alert." He knew this because the "captain didn't identify his ship properly," and *Fillmore* "received a shot over the bow . . . The gun crew on Ballyhoo fired the shot—so they were on the ball . . ."[5]

Pfc Dennis P. Abell was assigned to a supply detail "housed in a small warehouse located in the personnel barracks area of Ft. Mears." To the south was a hill with a 206th 3" AA gun battery.

Eastward lay the personnel barracks; beyond them were "several fairly large supply warehouses." Northward, just beyond the enlisted men's barracks, were officers' quarters, then "an office complex housed in quonset huts tucked up against the base of the hills."

About 2200 on 2 June, a phone call informed Abell and his co-workers that the *Fillmore* had just arrived in port. Aboard were several officers assigned to the 206th. Would a supply detail set up bunks for the new officers? So the whole group, under Sgt. Jerry Silas, loaded the necessary equipment and hauled it to the officers' quarters to set up the beds.

This done, most of the detail returned to quarters, while Abell and one or two others stayed to make up the beds. Working in a room "next to one occupied by a resident officer," Abell overheard him explaining the situation to some of the newly arrived officers. "He told them that we were expecting a Japanese air raid the next morning and possibly a land forces invasion within the next few days," Abell wrote. "I knew that a Japanese Task Force was in the general area of the Aleutians because of periodic intelligence briefings, but that an attack was imminent was a shocking surprise to me."

He hurried back to the living quarters, routed his comrades out of bed, and told them what he had overheard. None of them "had any idea that an attack was expected on the following morning." They decided to fill their backpacks, "go up into the hills and spend the night in the bunkers." After packing, however, they had second thoughts, and decided to stay in the barracks. They placed their packs, guns, ammunition, and other necessities beside their beds and retired, most of them "fully clothed except for boots."[6]

According to Pvt. Edward Shapiro of Chicago, a passenger aboard *Fillmore*, "The whole island turned out to see us dock our ship. . . . The band was there and played all sorts of gay* music. When we turned in that night aboard ship we weren't too concerned about a bombing. We knew one might come at any time. But it seemed remote." This despite the fact that *Fillmore* was loaded with explosives.[7]

It was not in the least remote to Massey, a responsible type who took his duties very seriously indeed. He noted:

---

* In 1942 "gay" meant "cheerful."

Intelligence reports the Japs have a task force headed this way. . . .
Our Headquarters estimates they will outnumber us 6 to 1. . . . We
are ready, weapons in good shape, plenty of ammunition and spare
rations. . . . I left the 37 mm cannon cocked with ammo on the trap,
took gun cover off and laid it across gun, tied it down with bow-
knots so gun can be easily and quickly put in action. I doubled my
guards, had everyone sleep in clothes. . . .

I lay thinking long in the night. I realized we were in a hot spot.
We were almost on top of that damn hangar, jammed against the
mountainside. . . . A bomb storage is on the edge of the airfield.
Damn! What a location, nothing camouflaged, why couldn't we be
further up the hill? Another of our battery sections was also in a hot
spot. They had three large gas and oil tanks a short distance from
them, no camouflage. I said a little prayer.[8]

Sgt. Aubrey T. Albright, assigned to F-2 Battery, recalled that
this position "had been on alert since 2 June for many hours with
full gun crews in the pit." F-2 was located on Hill 200, overlooking
the POL dock and the oil tanks. Around 2200, WO Russell
Newman, who had just left the Regimental Headquarters
Command Post, visited F-2 that night. He told the men to maintain
the alert the next morning, "advising that intelligence had been
received that a Japanese Task Force had been located and an attack
was imminent." Newman, who had been Albright's gun sergeant
before his promotion, had a special word for his former colleague:
"Albright, be in the saddle of that gun in the morning. They will be
here." Albright "took him at his word."[9]

Even the local civilians had been well briefed. For several days,
Mayor John W. Fletcher of Unalaska had been aware "of the
approach of a portion of the Jap fleet." He explained, "This information was given in order that I could check up on the preparations
necessary for civilian defense of Unalaska." At the request of the
military, he had ordered "all liquor establishments" closed three
days before. Then on the night of 2 June he learned "that a Jap carrier was within 400 miles of Unalaska Island."[10]

"We had expected an alert for weeks," remembered Mrs. James
Parsons. "The bars had been closed. Everyone had built an air raid
shelter in his yard. For weeks I kept a suitcase packed with essentials for myself and the children. Before we had our shelter, we
would run into the hills when practice alerts were sounded."[11]

Admiral Theobald of Task Force 8 shared the belief that the Japanese planned to attack Dutch Harbor, Cold Bay, and Umnak from the air, then send in ground forces to take over. On 28 May, Nimitz informed him correctly that the occupation forces were scheduled for Attu and Kiska. Theobald couldn't believe it. What would the Japanese, or anyone else, want with those dismal little islands? This must be a trick. So he decided to trust his own judgment rather than his chief's. He not only kept his task force in eastern Aleutian waters, he persuaded General Butler to send more than half his aircraft to Cold Bay and Otter Point. Then Theobald set out to rendezvous with his force some four hundred miles south of Kodiak.[12]

Theobald has been criticized for this action, but in the long run it may be counted one of several strokes of luck that blessed the Americans during the vast Midway-Aleutians battle. An encounter with Hosogaya's fleet could have been disastrous. While the Northern Area Force and Task Force 8 were fairly well matched in surface fighting craft, Theobald had no air cover. Hosogaya had two light carriers, their aircraft manned by skilled, experienced pilots. Neither Attu nor Kiska was worth the loss of even one U.S. cruiser, not to speak of hundreds of American casualties.

Nor was Theobald alone in his estimate of the situation. As we have seen, the defenders of Alaska fully expected a Japanese attempt to capture Dutch Harbor. What is more, it was widely believed that Japan intended to invade the North American continent, using the Aleutians as stepping stones. This illusion persisted long after the Japanese had actually taken Attu and Kiska.

"Little short of a miracle kept the Japs out of Alaska last June," intoned an article in the *Reader's Digest* issue of March 1943. "They were not aiming at the Aleutian Islands; they were heading straight for the North American mainland.

"'And but for the grace of God,' as one staff officer of Alaska's Defense Command soberly put it, 'they'd have come right through. By now they'd be running Alaska from the governor's house in Juneau.'"[13]

For their part, the Japanese believed that the Americans might well invade the home islands by way of the Aleutians, and in the latter part of May they sent several submarines to check out the Western Islands, Dutch Harbor, Kodiak, and even Seattle for possible concentrations of shipping.[14]

Hence the 206th and other units in the Aleutians were awaiting an enemy landing at Dutch Harbor, which did not happen, and were not adequately prepared for landings on Attu and Kiska, which did.

Some accounts give the impression that everyone on Amaknak was ready and waiting that early morning of 3 June. An order had been issued for a maximum alert from 30 May through 4 June. All leaves were canceled, ammunition was issued, "Dutch Harbor went on full alert with around-the-clock aircraft patrols. . . . All movies were canceled, and the large mess halls were replaced by dispersed field kitchens." The men slept at their outlying positions. "Reveille was moved up to 0300 with battle stations manned from 0430 to 0600. . . . " If no attack had come by 0600, the troops resumed their usual work day.

"Since an invasion was considered a possibility, manned defenses were established at invasion beaches." Both army and navy antiaircraft guns "were on the alert for enemy planes . . ."[15] At 0225 a flash message went out: "Be especially watchful between now and daybreak. By order of Colonel Robertson."[16]

With all the advance discussions, all the alerts and drills, how to account for the fact that almost half of the veterans who participated in this study claimed they had no warning of the attack of 3 June? Perhaps it is a question of semantics; i.e., they were in a general state of alertness, but received no direct warning of imminent attack until the Japanese flew in.

There are also indications that the "Cry Wolf" syndrome was part of the problem. "We were told three months, 30 days, and were told 24 hours before that an attack was imminent," wrote Bill Jones, "but had been on so many alerts and had heard so many rumors that no one believed the Japs were coming."[17] Cowell declared that "from lookouts and radio we had been told days before that a Jap fleet was headed our way. No one believed it."[18] "It may sound odd that we should have been caught asleep in bed at the time the attack came. We learned the hard way, because we had many alerts before—that is, practice alerts. We became indifferent to the danger ahead," admitted Mayor Fletcher. "In one sense we had depended on getting a 'flash' message from the amateur Alaska aircraft warning system. However, our particular frequency was extremely noisy that night."[19]

Thanks to the fog, Admiral Kakuta's carriers had eluded the

U.S. search planes and had reached the designated launching point, some 165 miles south of Dutch Harbor, around 0250. Fog delayed takeoff until 0318. At this point, good fortune bestowed a further favor upon the Americans. The fog prevented the flights from *Ryujo* and *Junyo* from joining the forces as planned.[20]

Moreover, a Catalina from PatWing 4, piloted by Lt. j.g. Jean Cusick, came in sight. *Junyo*'s Zeros broke off to deal with the hapless PBY, shooting it down before Cusick could get off a radio message. Copilot Lt. j.g. Whylie M. Hunt and two crew members, gunner Carl Creamer and mechanic Joseph R. Brown, survived the crash, were picked up by the Japanese, and sat out the rest of the war in a POW camp.

They had served their country better than they knew. Because of this encounter, plus the low ceiling, the *Ryujo* and *Junyo* flights lost contact; the latter could not locate Dutch Harbor and had to turn back to the carrier. Thus the initial stroke would come from only *Ryujo*'s seventeen aircraft, and the Americans were spared much additional damage and many casualties.[21]

The seaplane tender *Gillis*, moored alongside the Ballyhoo dock, is generally credited with the first detection of the incoming aircraft. Her radar operator picked up unidentified signals at 0537, and ten minutes later the vessel went to General Quarters. It was too late to sortie, so she commenced fire at 0548. The coast guard cutter *Onondaga* likewise opened fire. This encounter resulted in no hits or casualties.[22]

In the initial shock, six of *Fillmore*'s crew members promptly jumped overboard. But this troop ship, in harbor less than a day, fought well. Each time an alert sounded, she pulled away from shore and backed into the bay, firing as she went. Her crew had a special worry—the load of ammunition still on board. "One well-placed bomb or torpedo and we'd have been blown to kingdom come, and so would a lot of the island," said Shapiro. He added, however, that the aim of the Japanese was "lousy." But Valentine Dotolo, a waiter aboard *Fillmore*, paid tribute to their skill: "Several times I didn't think they'd pull out of their dives on time. . . . We watched our anti-aircraft bullets hit a plane until it climbed out of range and still they didn't go down. Anybody that says those Japs aren't aviators should have seen some of those boys. They really know how to fly."[23]

Zeros caught the mail PBY, just taking off for Kodiak. Her pilot, Lt. J. E. Litsey, managed to make a crash stop near Ballyhoo spit. Litsey survived, but a passenger did not, and an injured crew member drowned trying to reach the beach.[24]

Gilbert's first thought when he woke to the noise was that the army must be practicing. Then the reflection flashed through his head: ". . . the Army doesn't waste that much ammo on practice!" He had slept in his clothes, so only needed to put on shoes, grab his helmet and rifle, and head for the hills. "As I left the hut a Zero buzzed by spraying lead in front of me—then I knew this was for real!"[25]

The men of the 206th learned of the attack in various ways. Many were asleep, among them Sisk, who was in his bunk "having a bout with the flu and cutting a wisdom tooth." He recalled, "I came up quick and got on the gun in my long-handled underwear and unlaced boots. I must have looked terrible for my baptism into combat."[26]

Pvt. John Davis, like Sisk a member of C Battery, was also asleep, and he awoke to a doubly memorable occasion—it was his twenty-second birthday. He ran outside to see what was happening. One of his comrades, Blackie Bolton, was outside. "Blackie, what the hell is going on?" Davis asked. And Blackie replied, "It's the damn Japs!" With no further ado, they seized helmets and guns and hurried down the spithead to their gun position.[27]

The 3" guns of B Battery awoke Fitzhugh of Headquarters Battery in his barracks across the road from regimental headquarters. "I quickly dressed as if I would never return to that barracks," he remembered, "and with my field wear made it to my foxhole." He had just time to take shelter when a bomb exploded about ten feet away, between Fitzhugh's foxhole and that of his friend T. Sgt. John Harp. "After the confusion was over we looked at each other in disbelief, as each thought the other would have been killed."[28]

Euell "Big" Smith had been released from the Army Guard House for only a matter of minutes when he woke Dick Ballew at Battery C, shouting, "The Japs are overhead and everybody better get moving out of the barracks!" Most of Battery C's men were already out on the spithead jutting into the bay, manning the three AA guns. Those in the barracks "were mostly truck drivers, cooks, mail clerks, etc." They watched briefly "as the Japs flew over in groups of three planes. The men then rushed in to dress and 'get cracking.'"

Ballew jumped into his jeep, "intent on picking up Lt. Niesmith to go to the harbor for his job of dispersing the Army tugs and shipping in the harbor." The other soldiers scrambled into other vehicles, principally a two-and-a-half-ton truck driven by "Willie Boy" Wiles, to go to their combat stations."[29]

Ryals's platoon of G Battery was located near a new hangar being built next to the airfield. They had been on the alert earlier that morning but had returned to quarters. Ryals was stretched out on a top bunk, still wearing his combat gear, "helmet, gun belt and all." His lieutenant occupied the lower bunk. When the alarm came, the two men collided as they scrambled for the door.[30]

Appropriately enough, Staff Sergeant Taylor woke when one of his E Battery comrades, called "Rooster" because he was thin and had a very long neck, burst in the back door of the barracks, screaming, "The Japs are here!" Taylor "fell out of bed," dressed, grabbed his rifle, and headed for the truck he had waiting just outside. As soon as the men piled in, he headed the truck for the nearest gun position, which was on Suicide Hill. Several Japanese planes shot at them on the way but failed to hit. At the hill, everyone surged out, loaded their rifles and made for the gun position. "Before I reached the top of the hill," said Taylor, "that truck was hit with a bomb and not with us anymore."[31]

Some men were up and on duty. Junevitch and his gun crew had no warning of the first attack. They had just left their placement to go to breakfast when "the bombs started falling . . . a truck came along, so I hopped on and headed for the gun position in the hills." Junevitch added, "I thought the Japs were going to take over."[32]

S. Sgt. Wyre T. Mitchell of A Battery "was fixing breakfast when a truck driver named Betsy Simmon came in" and asked him, "Have you seen all the Jap planes out there?" Mitchell stated, "Betsy got up the 206th and I got up the 37th Infantry and everyone headed for the mountain. . . ."[33]

Pack had been on the midnight shift and was on his way to wake up their relief when one of the men said, "Look at those planes!" Recalled Pack, "I took one look and knew what they were, for we did hours of plane identification. So I turned back and woke my range people and the gunner woke all the gun people."[34]

Bill Jones was in his bunk when he heard the first bombs fall. It flashed through his mind "that if it was a full-scale attack we were in for it because there simply were not enough troops to withstand an attack by land, sea and air." But his instinct as a gun sergeant took over—"to get my crew out to the gun position and do what we had been trained to do—that was to shoot back . . ."[35]

Pedersen's searchlight division of A Battery was located at Affirm #11, on top of Ballyhoo. "Some of us had cleaned our rifles the night before," he said. "Some were still apart in the morning. Mine was at ready."[36]

At Platoon No. 1 of F Battery, "on the harbor side of Ft. Mears facing the sea and Mt. Ballyhoo," Henderson had arisen at 0230, being on KP that morning. "I was ready to go on duty when I heard gunfire outside," he recalled. "At first I thought the engineers were doing some blasting but when the second shot went off I knew what to do." He awoke his comrades, ran to the gun where only a guard was in place, "loaded the gun and operated it until the others got there."[37]

The words of Sergeant Snellgrove of C Battery may well sum up the first minutes of action on 3 June: ". . . we had no warning whatever on the first attack and most of us were asleep and were awakened by the bombs dropping and things of this nature and all of us hurriedly went out to the guns and started firing at the Japanese planes.[38]

The picture that emerges from these fragments of memory is clear. The men of the 206th were surprised, but they were prepared. Some were frankly and naturally frightened, but there was no panic, no confusion. Each man knew exactly where he was supposed to go and what to do when he got there. Their quick, efficient reaction reflected great credit upon the officers and noncoms who had indoctrinated and trained them and upon the men themselves.

A view of Fort Mears on Amaknak Island. Photo by Bill Tracy, courtesy of Paul Beasley.

Downtown Kodiak, Alaska. Photo courtesy of Michael P. Bouchette.

The small village of Unalaska. Photo courtesy of Larry Obsitnik.

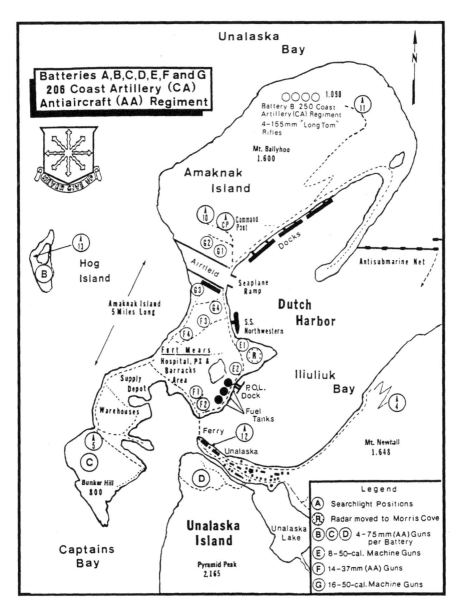

Map showing positions of the batteries of the 206th Coast Artillery
Antiaircraft Regiment on Amaknak Island. Map courtesy of Dennis P. Abell.

The remains of the converted passenger ship *Northwestern* after she was struck during the Japanese attack on Dutch Harbor, 3–4 June 1942.

Lawrence "Larry" Obsitnik at the Mt. Newhall A-4 base camp. The east, lower portion of Amaknak Island is shown in the background. A portion of the village of Unalaska can be seen to the left. Photo courtesy of Larry Obsitnik.

An SCR 268 radar unit in operating position overlooking Iliuliuk Bay. Mt. Newhall is in the background. The unit was installed in December 1941 and was moved to Morris Cove in May 1942. Photo courtesy of Donnel J. Drake.

A work crew moving a tent and frame from the Morris Cove beach area to the top of Hill 300, the location of the radar unit. *L. to r.*: Cornelius Carrico, Edward Sauter (on hood), Eli Santos (driver), Clifford Lamb, Donnel Drake, Jack Cheatwood, and Samuel Schmitt. Photo courtesy of Larry Obsitnik.

A portion of the supply area, warehouse, and barracks on Amaknak Island. Mt. Ballyhoo is in the background. Photo courtesy of Larry Obsitnik.

→

The Aleutian Islands in 1942, showing the route of the Japanese air attack, 3–4 June, and the distance from Dutch Harbor to Fort Glenn on Umnak Island and the distance from Fort Randall located at Cold Bay, Unimak Island. Map prepared by Donnel J. Drake.

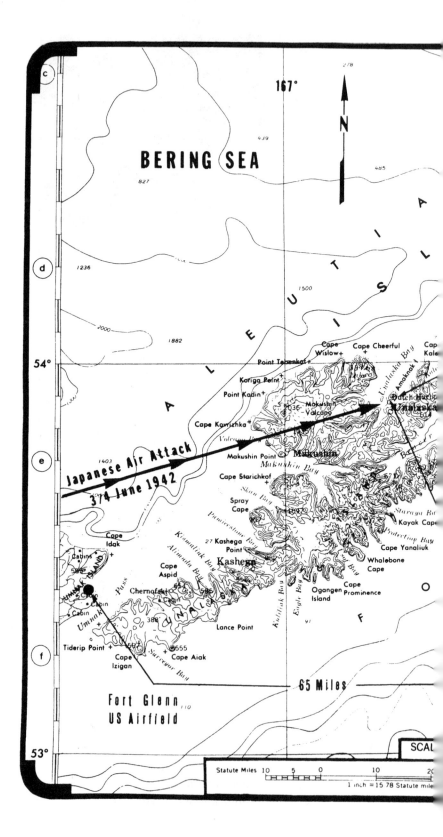

BERING SEA

167°

N

Japanese Air Attack
3-4 June 1942

ALEUTIAN ISLANDS

Cape Wislow+
Cape Cheerful
Cape Kale
Point Tebenkat+
Kariga Point+
Point Kadin+
Makushin Volcano
Unalaska Bay
Amaknak
Dutch Harbor
Unalaska
Cape Kowizhka+
Makushin Point
Makushin
Makushin Bay
Cape Starichkof
Skan Bay
Spray Cape
Pumicestone Bay
Staraya Bay
Kayak Cape
Protection Bay
Cape Idak
Kismaliuk Bay
Kashega Point
27 Kashega
Atnuada Bay
Kashega
Cape Yanaliuk
Whalebone Cape
Cape Aspid
Chernofski
UNALASKA
Kashiuk Bay
Eagle Bay
Ogangen Island
Cape Prominence
O
Cabins
UMNAK ISLAND
Cabin
Cabin
Pass
Umnak
Lance Point
Tiderip Point +
Cape Izigan
Surveyor Bay
Cape Aiak
F

65 Miles

Fort Glenn
US Airfield

54°

53°

c
d
e
f

165°

Eickelberg
Peak
1094
Ethel Caldera

Cape Sarichef

Pogromni
Volcano

Faris Peak   Westdahl Peak

Sennett
Point

165

U N I M A K   Bay

US Airfield Fort Randall, Cold Bay

180 Miles

ALEUTIAN   ISLANDS   NATIONAL

P A S S

un Head   Billings Head

810

Akun Bay

un Bay   AKUN ISLAND

Akutan

Avatanak Strait

Rootok   ALEUTIAN IS   Avatanak
Island   NWR   Island

Ugamak
Island

Aiktak Island

Ugamak Strait

Tigalda
Island

E N I T Z I N   I S L A N D S

106

S

I

S

L

A

N

D

S

1737

108

2798

3894

PACIFIC OCEAN

3831

00

50   60   70 Milles terrestres

e = 15 78 Milles terrestres

Japanese bombs fall harmlessly into the waters of Dutch Harbor, probably during the 4 June 1942 raid. The Spit and Mt. Newhall are in the background. Photo courtesy of Larry Obsitnik.

Warehouses destroyed by fire as a result of the Japanese air attack on 4 June 1942 on Amaknak Island. Photo courtesy of Larry Obsitnik.

Only the foundation remained of this warehouse as a result of the Japanese air attack. Photo courtesy of Larry Obsitnik.

A view of the hospital in Unalaska, bombed 4 June 1942. Photo courtesy of Henry A. Oehrig.

A U.S. Army truck destroyed by bomb fragments during the Japanese bomb raid on the warehouse area of Amaknak Island. Photo courtesy of Larry Obsitnik.

A Japanese airplane shot down over Dutch Harbor. Photo courtesy of Michael P. Bouchette.

18

"Friendly Planes, Hell!"

As is so often the case in combat, several individuals were convinced that theirs was the unit that fired first at the enemy. Of course, it is possible that there were several "firsts," for locations were spread over Amaknak.

Massey claimed the honor for his group from Battery G. "I was jolted awake by one of my men, Hal Duncan, 'Here they come, boys! Up, boys, up!' Everyone hit their positions." According to Massey, no other gun crew was out. He continued: "I could hear the whine of the plane engines somewhere. . . . I shoved the ammo clip loading the 37. Just then a flash came around the west side of Ballyhoo Mt.—A Jap Zero bearing down on the Navy's runway target, and I remember saying to the gunner, 'Shoot, damn it, shoot!' and the gun belched deadly projectives at the enemy. . . . The Zero banked over sharply to get out of range. No one else firing; we were the first."[1]

Cathey of Battery B likewise claimed that ". . . our guns were first to open fire." He wondered "how many more bombers and fighters would come" and if landing forces would follow. In any case, "We were in the midst of the news."[2] Bowen, too, gave Battery B credit: "We were waked at 6:00 by the guns firing. 'B' was the first Btry to fire. We went on the hills, half-dressed and manned the guns and filled the trenches."[3]

A truly bizarre incident complicated the initial reaction, so strange that one might be tempted to dismiss it as legend were it not so well remembered. Garrett of Battery B, who was in his hut when the firing started, declared, "Sergeant Gruner's gun was the first to open fire. Then they received orders by phone 'to cease firing, that they were friendly planes.' At about that time a bomb exploded nearby. 'Friendly planes don't drop bombs,' remarked Bruner grimly. 'Fire that gun!'"⁴

"The first shot fired in DH at the Japanese was ordered by Lt. James Everett Johnson. . . . ," reported Captain Langley. Johnson was OD for Battery D at the time, and in charge of an alert crew "manning guns and fire control equipment." The heightfinder observer spotted the approaching aircraft and believed they were Japanese. Using the heightfinder in turn, Johnson verified. The gong alert was slow, so Johnson "pointed one 3" gun toward planes and fired a round jarring all other men out of bed." Langley hastened to join the gunners. "While we were firing, the telephone line to our range section rang. Col. Robertson ordered us to cease fire, that planes were our navy planes. I told him their planes had red stars on them and we kept on firing."⁵

Croom had a slightly different version. He was on duty with Battery D on Gobler's Knob when word came by phone that "planes were over Mt. Neuhall." The gun crew took position; Croom pulled the lanyard, firing "the first shot that shook the bay out of their bunks." He continued, "Lt. Johnson came out of the command post yelling, 'Cease fire, friendly planes!' Doc Stanford, leaning on the gun admiring the planes, said 'What beautiful planes! What we need is more of them.' Then the planes started laying bombs and Doc said, 'Friendly planes, hell!'"⁶

A similar case of mistaken identity occurred at Unalaska village. Mayor Fletcher and his wife awoke to the sound of AA fire. Looking out the window, Fletcher saw "at least three Jap Zero fighters." At first they thought these aircraft were American. "Hot dog!" exclaimed Mrs. Fletcher. "Here comes one of our fighters!" Then they saw the Rising Sun emblem and headed for their basement.⁷

"I had just finished dressing when I heard one of our guns fire a round," reminisced Keeton of Battery D. "This was the first round fired by any unit. The round was fired by Troy Burris and 'Doc' Stanford. . . . Initially we were told not to fire, but by the time I climbed the steps to our guns Jap Zeros were all over us."⁸

Burris confirmed the impression "that this was the first round fired at Dutch Harbor." He added, "These rounds were fired prior to the bombs being dropped. In fact, we received orders to cease firing, that we were firing at friendly planes." The men accordingly stopped, but "a few seconds later all hell broke loose over at Fort

Mears" and firing recommenced. Burris later declared that he "could see approximately 60–70 planes." This was about twice as many aircraft as *Ryujo's* entire complement, but in the heat of battle such mistakes are natural.[9]

"While we were in the process of shooting at the Jap Zeros," said Snellgrove, "on the radio hookup a message came over, 'These are friendly planes. Cease firing.' We paid no attention whatever to this command since we knew they were not friendly. . . ."[10]

At Cathey's location, a voice kept coming in on the phone hook-up, saying, "Friendly planes!" The lieutenant on duty snatched the phone and barked, "Friendly planes, hell! Come over here where we are and see!"[11]

Parker remembered the call saying "Do not fire! These are friendly planes!" A man named Joe Randell, located in the height-finder section of Battery B, shouted back over the hookup, "Friendly, hell! I can see the big red spot on the planes!"[12]

A parenthetical note timed 0555 in the log of flash messages gives a rationale of sorts for this extraordinary order: "(Our gun crews, which were alerted and ready for action, opened fire on four bombers which flew the length of the island in formation, dropping no bombs, and reporting on our radio frequency that they were friendly.)"[13] Nonetheless, the cease-fire order argues a high degree of naïveté under the circumstances, plus a low degree of skill in aircraft recognition on someone's part.

Fitzhugh of Headquarters Battery blamed the navy: "When our unit's radar and heightfinders picked up the Jap planes, the navy, who were in charge of the overall operation would not permit firing our hot line. But after the planes made a pass without bombing in order to photograph and started their second run with bomb bay doors open, George Love, the BC of Battery B saw the red sun. He disregarded the navy's 'no firing' and commenced firing the 3" guns. These were the shots that awakened me."[14]

O'Neal had recently transferred from his forward observation post to another location, east of Unalaska village "near the end of the valley." Strolling to the door of the dugout "to see if the cook was up," O'Neal barely escaped a spray of machine-gun bullets.

The Japanese plane dipped so low he could see the pilot, who appeared to be smiling. O'Neal fired his rifle, but doubted if he hit the target. He routed out his men, grabbed a steel helmet and a bandolier of ammunition, and headed for his foxhole. As he ran, he heard the 206th's guns roar into action. "I sank down in the fox hole and got as much of me under the old World War I steel helmet as possible. I could hear the chunks of steel shrapnel hitting the tundra all around the hole. . . ."[15]

Opposition to the Japanese on 3 June was confined to the ground defenders. The army air unit at Cold Bay received word of the attack, but it was over for the day before the P-40s could cover the distance to Dutch Harbor. The newly arrived fighters at Fort Glenn remained grounded because the underground low-power radio receiver on Umnak did not pick up the message. At that time, communications between Amaknak and Umnak left much to be desired. The service was a temporary arrangement, pending the laying of a secure ocean cable. The cable was finally laid in July, which of course did nothing for Dutch Harbor on 3 June.[16] Meanwhile *Ryujo*'s aircraft had things almost entirely their own way.

Accounts of the action are naturally somewhat confusing; everyone concerned was much too busy to note times and take notes. Still, from eyewitness accounts a fairly clear picture emerges. Gill, whose Battery B position was "on a large hill at the end of the main village area" of Dutch Harbor, had a good view: "I recall seeing a couple of Zero fighters coming down toward our position; however, they ended up strafing the row of buildings just below our position . . . ," he explained. "The high altitude bombers made some direct hits on barracks in the main area. This caught many troops still in the building and this is where the principal casualties occurred. . . ."[17]

Despite the earlier fog, the Japanese found the weather over Dutch Harbor calm, with good visibility, thus having unusually favorable conditions under which to place their bombs. By a tragic irony, most of the casualties to which Gill referred were troops who had arrived aboard *Fillmore* only the previous day. They had not been told to come to the shelters at 0430. Four high-level bombers, codenamed "Kates," were the first to bomb Fort Mears. The first two missiles fell into Unalaska Bay, but the third and fourth struck Barracks 864 and 866, catching the new troops just as they were "leaving the barracks and into formation." Seventeen men of the 37th Infantry and eight from the 151st Combat Engineers were killed, and another twenty-five were wounded.[18]

"The worst tragedy was in the small fort . . . ," Massey wrote.

"An officer of the Engineer Company fell his men in ranks to march them to their foxholes. A bomb hit in their midst, killing around twenty-five men. Their barracks burned to the ground as did two of their trucks."[19] "Main target was the warehouses at the foot of our hill," Bowen recorded. "Two warehouses and the Engineer Barracks were demolished."[20]

The Fletchers had a good view of the action because, while they took refuge in their basement, they did not immediately close the cellar doors. They saw "four very large bombers" headed northwest. "Then, a moment later from the southwest approaching Dutch Harbor, came three more. . . . Two warehouses were struck and one barracks.

"There were some casualties, most of which definitely could have been avoided if the men had remembered to be flat on the ground. In the confusion of running for shelter, they forgot the lessons taught them."

AA fire was bursting "above, below and all around the bombers." Fletcher was astounded at the "enormous size" of the Japanese aircraft. Among the things they destroyed was a myth: "The results definitely proved that there is nothing wrong with Japanese eyesight," remarked Fletcher. "At the point they struck, the land is very narrow. At the height they were flying their marksmanship had to be good to hit anything on land."[21]

Nurse Martha Tutiakoff was on duty at the Native hospital in Unalaska village when the Japanese struck. The first sound of aircraft engines she mistook for the mail plane taking off, but when she looked out the window she "saw planes coming down from all directions." After hearing gunfire, she gave the alarm. Thirteen patients were in the hospital at that time, all but three suffering from minor ailments. In accordance with plans, Nurse Tutiakoff and her colleagues hustled the patients into the cement basement.[22]

A linguist visiting Unalaska did not let the raid interfere with his ruling passion. As Mrs. Anfesia Shapsnikoff hurried toward a bomb shelter, "the linguist scurried along beside her with his notebook and pencil trying to record the subtle variations of sounds in the Aleut language. Over and over she would repeat combinations of sound while he frantically, and not very successfully, repeated them!"[23]

Massey was certain his gun crew downed a Zero that "came

flashing around the airstrip." As Massey "swung his gun around by the gunner's seat," the tracer bullets seemed to have a "good lead" on the fighter's nose. Wrote Massey, "The Zero pulled up, banked slightly to his right showing his belly to us. We made a hit, the plane continued to climb, rolling over on its back at about 800 feet. It arched down and went nose first into the water between Ballyhoo and Summers Bay." He added with satisfaction, "That is one damn Jap that is through; he never knew what hit him." An army doctor, a captain, at the base of Ballyhoo, saw this encounter. Later he told Massey that he had written an account of it, and Massey's gun crew "would get credit for the kill."[24]

Henderson's position "began firing at Zeros attacking us at very low altitude. They were strafing us in groups of two." The AA men held their fire until the Zeros were almost overhead, and Henderson was sure they scored some hits. "We fired until our gun jammed."[25]

Raney, however, doubted the effectiveness of his comrades' fire. He observed that the Zeros flew so low that the AA was useless, because the guns "couldn't be depressed to an angle lower than 15 degrees. . . ."[26]

Massey took measures to get extra mileage out of his weapon. "The gun manual said a 37 mm could only fire 120 rounds steady and then lock up. . . . There was a carbon ring seated in the tube transmission, when it gets hot, it expands and locks the tapering tube in recoil." Massey cut this ring out. "The C.O. was amazed at the number of rounds we fired; some guns locked," added Massey. "Later all carbon rings were cut out of the weapons."[27]

F-2 position of Battery A's 75mm guns "first began firing at the high-flying Japanese bombers approaching the island and shortly every gun on the island began firing at the planes. The first salvo of bombs hit the Fort Mears area and shortly bombs began falling all over Amaknak Island." The battery history recorded proudly, "All men of F-2 performed their duties in an exceptional manner, a little scared perhaps, but all remained at their positions."[28]

The sound of AA firing from the hills awakened Abell and his Headquarters Battery comrades. They scrambled out of bed, donned boots, backpacks, and gun belts. "Just as the first person reached the door to exit the building, the bombs started exploding all around us," Abell recorded. "We all fell to the floor and remained there until the bombs stopped falling." The adjacent barracks was hit and engulfed in flame, killing several men.

A soldier Abell didn't know was standing just outside their building, apparently in shock. Abell checked on him and noticed that a pocket of his ammunition belt had been blown out. "Probably a piece of shrapnel had struck his belt a glancing blow and one or more of the 30-06 rounds in that pocket had exploded." Examination proved the wound to be superficial, so the man decided to go to a nearby foxhole and wait for the medics. Abell left him there and hurried "to the office complex at the north end of Fort Mears. . . . On the way, along the beach road," he wrote, "I passed by a truck that had been riddled with shrapnel. Nearby were two men, both dead." A fragmentation bomb had landed nearby. "The men had apparently stopped the truck, got out and were running for cover when the bomb hit. No doubt they were killed instantly."[29]

This was indeed the case. Willie Boy Wiles had stopped his truck when the bombs began falling. Ballew in his jeep shot past the truck, then hit the brakes, but a bomb struck nearby and threw him out of the jeep. "I scrambled up and 'two-stepped' the barbed wire laid near the edge of the beach. Looking for safety, I ran by and ducked under a 20-caliber machine gun dug in the bank. No cover. So I crouched and watched the bombs fall in the bay and one just above hit an engineers' barrack and, as the lumber and dust mushroomed up, I thought, 'the world's coming to an end!'"

Soon, however, the noise stopped and Ballew climbed up the bank. There he saw Morris "Mousie" Brooks "jumping around, his arm dangling, fingers missing." Two men were dead, one "a bugler named Collier," the other Willie Boy. Ballew was "in shock," but recognizing that he could no nothing there, he returned to his jeep. As "all four tires were flat and holes were in the hood," he took his rifle and teamed up with Big Smith, "trotting down the road toward the spithead." As they walked along, suddenly Ballew realized that he had been wounded in his right hip, and, giving Smith his rifle, he headed for a nearby Quonset hut used as a first aid station. There a good friend, Merle Thompson from Paragould, Arkansas, "slapped on a huge bandage with plenty of methiolate." The wound, although painful, was not serious, and Ballew considered himself lucky.[30]

The men at Morris Cove were well positioned to watch the

attack on Dutch Harbor, but they were too far off to participate actively. The duty lookout alerted them that AA firing was coming from the direction of Dutch Harbor. "All men grabbed their rifles and helmets and ran to their defensive positions along the beach." Soon they could see high-flying aircraft over Dutch Harbor, "and columns of black smoke . . . rising from the area of the fuel tanks located on the southeastern end of Amaknak Island." They phoned the Battery Command Post that all was well at Morris Cove, and were told to relocate "the defensive positions from the beach area and the radar unit to Hill 300."[31]

The first Japanese aircraft that Hargrave of Battery F saw "were over the mountains beyond Unalaska. Shortly we saw other formations which seemed to be all around us." Hargrave and Jesse Wright manned one of the two 37mm guns at their position, Wright as a gunner and Hargrave operating "the horizontal tracking mechanism." They tracked a plane, but as yet did not identify it. Then one of the 3" gun crews recognized the aircraft as Japanese and fired. Wright and Hargrave followed suit, but by that time the target had flown out of range.

Hargrave turned over his seat to the man assigned to it. After that, he didn't remember his actions for the rest of the day, "except watch the Jap bombers come over and drop their bombs, and watch things blow up and burn."[32]

One can sense Hargrave's frustration, a feeling shared in several quarters, among them Parker's unit. Parker "could see our men getting scared, restless, and seemingly helpless. I yelled to Cpl. Hugh Grant, 'Get out the blue-nosed ammo for our 37mm guns.'" Parker had fired about two clips when a call came in over their telephone, "WHO IS THE FOOL THAT WAS FIRING AT THE BOMBERS? DON'T YOU KNOW THEY ARE COMPLETELY OUT OF RANGE?" Parker identified himself, and soon several officers "charged up the hill demanding an explanation. Parker replied, "Sir, the men were scared and they felt helpless. I thought by firing some of our solid-head projectiles we had used for practice, it might help us feel like we were doing something to help the cause." At that, the officers turned and slowly walked away, leaving Parker "quite relieved."[33]

Alspaugh's Battery B gun position fired at about four groups of aircraft and the battery "was credited with getting three of the four planes that were shot down." He added, "The planes broke up into flights of three and four. They came in from all directions and different heights. The noise of our AA defense and the bombing was terrific. . . . While we fired at high planes Zero fighters came in low and fast trying their damnedest to strafe us."

Alspaugh admitted, "I guess we all had a little buck fever. I was scared quite a bit and everybody else seemed to be, but we did pretty good with our firing."[34]

Not everyone could rise above fear to perform his duties. On Massey's position one lieutenant "was scared to death, we couldn't pry him out of a foxhole."[35]

Nixon of Battery H lost all respect for his gun sergeant. "About the time we would get a plane in our sights, he would yell, 'Take cover!'" observed Nixon disgustedly. "And yet we were never bombed or strafed. It could have been disastrous."[36]

But such incidents were the very rare exceptions. The vast majority of the Arkansas men, and their comrades from other states and organizations, behaved in an exemplary manner and did their best with the means at hand.

19

"The Waiting Is Torment"

After the Japanese had inflicted the damage already described, another three bombers concentrated on the Naval Radio Station. Of the six bombs dropped, three hit the ground, inflicting no damage. Another struck the corner of a brick apartment house, "broke out windows and severed a transmitting antenna." The fourth missile destroyed a Quonset hut; the fifth cost the life of George P. Deal, a Siems-Drake worker, when it hit a shelter trench.[1]

It is not certain whether the bombers at Power House Hill were aiming at the Radio Reception Station's antenna or at camouflaged fuel tanks. In either case, they hit no installations but did kill several men. At a fire station, shrapnel killed a sailor standing outside and injured another standing inside the shelter. A third man, who in accordance with instructions remained seated in the shelter, was uninjured. An army cargo truck took a hit that killed the driver. Marine Pvt. Andy Corbin died when a bomb struck and collapsed his trench position. Later Power House Hill was called Suicide Hill because of these losses.[2]

The Japanese lost two aircraft in the raid of 3 June. *Gillis* claimed the kills, but, as we have seen, several others did likewise, so just who downed them is anybody's guess. The Japanese later described the AA fire as "powerful," but when they departed, approximately an hour after they arrived, it was because they had dropped all their bombs, not because they had been driven off.[3]

They headed north, then turned southwest, passing over Makushin Bay. There one of the pilots spotted five of Theobald's destroyers and radioed the news to the 2d Mobile Force. Kakuta decided they were worth attacking. At about 0900 he launched twenty-four aircraft, including two reconnaissance seaplanes, one each from the heavy cruisers *Maya* and *Takao*. By this time, however, the fog had shut down again. Not only could the Japanese see no destroyers, they could not even find Makushin Bay.[4]

Two hours later, veteran Aleutian seaman Henry Swanson brought his Outpost Patrol Boat into Makushin Bay. With a working party of about twenty-nine GIs, he had left Dutch Harbor at 0500 under orders to "go to Makushin and either destroy or bring in the Bristol Bay fishing boats that were stored there at the time."

When he stopped alongside the first destroyer in line, someone informed him of the Dutch Harbor raid. Swanson was incredulous. "Hell, no," he protested. "I just came from there. There's no damn Japs there!" He was soon convinced, and he and his men spent the rest of the day and part of the next preparing the boats to be towed back to Dutch Harbor.[5]

In retiring, the two Japanese reconnaissance aircraft had the misfortune to fly over Umnak. Two P-40 pilots on patrol, Lts. John B. Murphy and Jacob W. Dixon, spotted the intruders, pulled out of patrol formation, and pounced. They shot down one plane, which fell into Umnak Pass, and damaged the other so badly it crashed near its home cruiser. The pilot was rescued.[6]

Miller's account of this incident, written on 10 June, reveals how rapidly a story can blow up out of proportion: "Lt. Murphy June 3 came out of a cloud bank right on top of a Jap bomber—both were surprised as hell. Murphy recovered first. The Jap never recovered. Murphy fired 2 short bursts and the Jap hit the water in sight of camp."

Murphy had not shot down a bomber, but a catapult-launched E8N, the type the Americans codenamed "Dave." This aircraft was quite slow, and a P-40 in good hands was more than a match for it. This is not to downgrade Murphy's and Dixon's presence of mind and professional skill. As for the Japanese reconnaissance pilots, no doubt they were, in Miller's words, "surprised as hell," because the Japanese as yet had no idea that Umnak boasted an airstrip.[7]

By the time Miller wrote his article, "The Aleutian Islands Campaign," he had matters straightened out and produced an accurate account in his somewhat flamboyant literary style. There was no rain "for a change" that morning, the men as usual were digging trenches. Everything was calm, when "down through the clouds comes a strange biplane with spots on its wings. Photo Charlie, and he smacks square into Umnak Pass and meets his ancestors with his snoot full of icy Bering Sea water. His buddy got away. The P-40s came home and turned in a report of ammunition expenditures—24 rounds.

"That was all," Miller added. But it was enough to cause a frenzy of activity. Weapons were cleaned, ammunition was issued. "Each company had its sector of beach to defend, with a ration dump nearby. . . ."

Sgt. Alva "Red" Parker, an F Company squad leader, asked Miller if he could leave his sleeping bag behind when they went out that night. "Gees, Red, you're gonna need your sack," Miller demurred, "it still gets cold night." The sergeant protested that it was too heavy. Suddenly suspicious, the lieutenant opened the pack, and discovered that Parker had taken everything out but one mess kit, one spoon, one can of C rations, and had filled up the pack with 349 rounds of ammunition instead of the usual 48 rounds.[8]

Except that they were no longer being shot at, the men on Amaknak were almost as busy after the raid as during it. Even before the last Japanese aircraft had winged away, a "military patrol" visited Mayor Fletcher to inform him "that all women and children should proceed to the main highway in the middle of the town, where they would be picked up by truck and taken to the valley for better protection." Using his own car, Fletcher aided in this evacuation that included the hospital patients as well as the women and children. He had high praise for the military in charge of the move. "The soldiers were positively swell in their assistance to all the civilians," he said. "They were cheerful, and this helped a great deal in holding up the morale of the people. They did everything to make the sick, women and children comfortable. They also brought hot coffee and other things."

Fletcher likewise paid a somewhat qualified compliment to the enemy: "The Japs showed either great courage in coming so close, or they have absolutely no regard for their lives, whatsoever."[9]

While the attack was still on, Abell and some officers had decided that foxholes would be safer than Quonset huts. A bomb exploding nearby kept them rooted to the spot. After the raid was over, they went out to see what had taken place. "One bomb had scored a direct hit on one of the foxholes to which we had intended to go. . . ." Another had struck an officers' barracks, one end of which housed the Officers' Club. "The side of the club where the liquor storeroom was located was blown away, leaving a pile of broken cases of alcoholic beverages." The inevitable happened. Before guards could be posted, some of Abell's colleagues "took advantage of the situation, and were able to get away with some choice bourbon and scotch. It was quite a treat," he explained, "because at that time the only hard liquor available to enlisted personnel was in a civilian liquor store in the town of Unalaska nearby, reached only by barge, and it was very expensive."[10]

At Morris Cove, the men spent the rest of the day moving to their new positions and digging foxholes. This was because the Japanese were expected to attempt a ground assault, in which case the Morris Cove area might be a beachhead. By 2100 the men had completed their new defensive positions, then waited all night and into early 4 June anticipating an attack. "Morale was high among the men and camaraderie was excellent."

The men at F-2, as at all the 37mm gun positions, kept busy cleaning their weapons and strengthening their positions with more sandbags. At all Battery F positions, field kitchens were set up.[11]

Parker of Battery C was taking no chances, and he arranged his own personal defense measure. When the all-clear sounded, he ran to his hut and dug out the little Bible the congregation of the Grand Avenue Methodist Church in Hot Springs had given him "for protection over my heart." He doubted, however, if anyone got any sleep that night.[12]

The barracks assigned to Battery G "was hit and wrecked," recorded Massey. "Our guidon was riddle with shrapnel. Not many stayed in the barracks; it was used when crews had a chance to come in from their positions and take a shower."

Massey sent his truck driver to Fort Mears as part of a clean-up detail. "The rest went about quietly cleaning up empty brass, getting more ammo, loading in clips and checking over the gun."

Whether from a sense of immediacy or from dramatic instinct, Massey shifted to the historical present: "We look for an invasion or naval bombardment tonight. . . . Everyone quiet, tense, talking in low tones, the waiting is torment. Our Battery C.O. visits us, I tell him about our targets and the Zero we hit.

"The fire from the oil tank has the island lit up like a torch all night. Some men sleep from sheer exhaustion, some wide awake . . ."[13]

O'Neal agreed that this was a period of great tension: ". . . we all knew that was only the first attack and there would be more to follow. I know I felt they would be back and next time it would not only be with aircraft but with ground troops. If they came with ground forces I felt that they would have the force to do the job and our goose would be cooked. There was little doubt in most of our minds that we would be out-numbered, out-gunned and it had been proven that day they had control of the air." Soon an officer phoned for O'Neal to report to Unalaska Village with as many men as they could spare "to help move some of our heavy guns to new positions."[14]

After the raid, someone "decided that a gun position on the spithead was not such a good idea, so we moved up on Mt. Ballyhoo that evening and night . . . ," recalled Sisk of Battery C.[15] Davis stated that they had the help of the Seabees in this move. But as the Seabees did not arrive until July, Davis probably meant the Siems-Drake men. In any case, "They were a great bunch of guys and we never could have had our battery in position and ready for the slant-eyes by 4 o'clock the next afternoon if not for their help."[16]

Through the rest of the day and night, Battery D moved from Gobbler's Knob to Unalaska, establishing positions between the village of Unalaska and the water's edge at "the entrance to the bay east of Ballyhoo."[17] They took the precaution of leaving dummy guns behind, driving long telephone poles into the vacated pits. Evidently this measure did deceive the Japanese, for they dropped "a string of bombs" on these empty positions the next day.[18]

Keeton remembered the move well:

> In anticipation of attempted landing our battery was reinforced by one 37mm battery. I had accompanied the guns and fire control equipment to this new position. The respective section chiefs and crews were frantically working to get the guns emplaced. I was assisting orienting and synchronizing the fire control instruments (M-4 Director) with the guns when I was approached by several civilians. They identified themselves as employees from the Siems-Drake

company. They asked if they could help us in any way. I answered, "Yes, you certainly can! We desperately need sand bags and it is not long till daylight." One asked, "How many?" I remember specifically saying to them, "Bring them until I say stop." They did. By daylight we had sand bags on site and shortly after daylight we had equipment and crews protected.

He could not sufficiently praise the Siems-Drake people, "their compassion and willingness to help their fellow man . . ."[19]

Sandbags were urgently needed because dirt had proved to be an unsatisfactory filler. "Shortly after the first raid the Battery Officers began to check out the dirt bags we had stacked around the gun positions," wrote Burris. "They found that a 30-cal bullet would pass through the dirt bags and still do a great deal of damage. This information told us that we needed to use sand bags instead of dirt bags."[20]

Croom recalled that one truck operator handling the bags from the Siems-Drake plant "decided he had enough and was going to quit. One soldier loaded his rifle and told him to work or else."[21]

Mayor Fletcher allowed Battery D's telephone unit to occupy his house. They used his sleeping quarters, and the mayor left them "some soft drinks and some liquor."[22]

A heartbreaking task remained to be done. Capt. Guy D. McCoy, the regimental supply officer, said to some of his men, "Let's go pick up the dead." This was one of the duties of supply personnel. "The first man we came to," said Fitzhugh, "was a man he had recruited and had made his battery bugler. He cried."[23] This was Pfc Allen C. "Cop" Collier. "He had a reputation as a musician and traveled over the country with a stock company for several years."[24]

Abell was a member of this detail. He recalled that they first picked up the two dead men Abell had seen near a bombed truck. "They were located in front of a barracks. We went into the barracks, took mattresses off of two beds and used the springs for bearers. One at a time we placed the men on the makeshift bearers, carried them into the barracks, placed them on beds and covered them with blankets. The captain recorded the names from their dogtags and reported them to the appropriate authorities. One of the men was from the captain's own battery. His last name was Collier. . . ."[25]

As mentioned, the second body was that of Pvt. James R. "Willie Boy" Wiles of Jonesboro, Arkansas, a truck driver.[26]

Another 206th casualty of 3 June was Sgt. Hugh B. Timberlake of B Battery*—"a fine person well liked by everyone." He was running to the Post Office, his duty post in case of attack, "when strafing Zeros' fire killed him."[27] Among those wounded was Pfc Millard J. "Red Nose" Smith. His wound was not serious—Massey believed "a rock hit him, not shrapnel."[28] Another who was fortunate enough to escape with a minor wound was Pvt. Elmer H. Brents, who was in a foxhole with another soldier and a sailor when a bomb struck some sixteen feet away. "It tore a crater right in front of the foxhole," he told the press later. "I and one of the others were struck by a shower of dirt. The third man was lifted out of the foxhole."[29] Brent had escaped with a broken ear drum.[30]

Cpl. Bruce B. Richardson and Pfc Robert J. Milam, manning a gun together, "were hurled 30 feet through the air when a bomb exploded nearby." The concussion knocked all their teeth out. "It hit about five feet behind us," said Milam. "I think we were lucky to come out with only our teeth missing."[31]

Captain McCoy and his detail drove around the Fort Mears area until they were sure that all the dead and wounded had been accounted for. During their search they could see the results of the raid. "In addition to several barracks damaged by fragmentation bombs or completely destroyed by fire, two or three large supply warehouses were burned to the ground." These warehouses still had several tons of Christmas packages destined "to bases further down the Aleutian chain and points north. Obviously, at that time shipping space was at a premium and Christmas packages were very low on the priority list," said Abell. "They were destroyed along with the rest of the contents of the warehouses."

At first "things were more or less in a state of disarray and confusion." But as the day wore on, "things began to fall in place. Units regrouped and returned to normal routine." The supply detail collected their belongings "and proceeded to the hills to spend the next few days with our Regimental Headquarters Battery." The quarters there could not accommodate everyone; some had to use

---

* General Order No. 10, 8 July 1942, containing awards, some posthumous, listed Timberlake as assigned to Hq and Hq Det; however, both Weese and Albright identified him as belonging to Battery B.

pup tents. Abell and Pfc Leonard Barker shared a tent. "We kept dry and slept very comfortably."[32]

Meanwhile, the navy was searching for the Japanese carriers. Sometime on the afternoon of 3 June, Lt. (j.g.) Lucius D. Campbell's PBY made a radar contact with "four large enemy ships." As he closed to within twenty-five miles of the sighting, a Japanese aircraft attacked, riddling the PBY with .30 caliber bullets. This fire wounded one crewman badly and inflicted considerable damage to the radio, rudder control, gasoline tanks, and an aileron. Then the Japanese delivered a cannon shot that blasted half of the forward starboard strut.

Somehow Campbell managed to elude his attacker in the clouds and continued to scout the Japanese ships until he had to break off, his fuel having dwindled to a half-hour's supply. The gasoline failed some twenty-four kilometers south of Scotch Gap. Campbell made a dead-stick landing on the sea, and with everyone but the wounded man pitching in, kept the PBY afloat. They got the radio working long enough to repeat the "initial contact report" and to advise that the PBY was down and badly damaged; however, the radio conked out again before the radioman could furnish the plane's position. Unfortunately, the report was garbled, and the situation was not understood until the PBY's crew was rescued on 6 June.[33]

Flash messages of the post-attack period show much activity on and over Dutch Harbor, plus some evidence of very natural nervousness. "A-10 reports water target at 28,000 yds."; "Enemy has attacked PBY south of here"; "Six unidentified planes flying Northwest of Captains Bay from Navy"; "Air attack expected at Dutch Harbor"; "Expect another air raid on Dutch Harbor soon. Be ready."; "Planes coming over Ft. Glenn right now."

These flashes all occurred in the late morning. The evening hours reported only routine activity until Colonel Robertson issued a message at 2035: "All positions must be occupied until relieved. Relief crews should get as much sleep as possible. All positions be on the alert for ground attack throughout the night. Everyone must be up by daylight. Be especially watchful for both high and hedge-hopping dive bombers should we have another air attack. Well pleased with work today."

A parenthetical note on the record of flash messages made a

realistic comment: "(Nothing came of expected air raid. . . . Men not on gun positions or on guard trying to get some sleep in their 'fox-holes' to be ready for an air or land attack. It will be hard to get plenty of rest as we only have 5 1/2 hours of darkness.)"

After that, flashes dwindled to two concerning an unidentified submarine before 3 June passed into history.[34] It had been, in Taylor's words, "one long scary day."[35]

20

"Like a Big Bunch of Mosquitos"

The fourth of June began with a message dispatched "by order of Colonel Robertson": "Be especially alert for small water craft and landing parties from now until dawn."[1]

The warning was probably redundant. The veterans who participated in this project were unanimous that on 4 June, in contrast to the previous day, everyone anticipated a second attack and was prepared for it. "Second day we were alert and ready," stated Pedersen.[2] Costley remembered that "we had the guard wake us at 0400 so that we could be as ready as possible."[3] "We were ready to use all weapons on anything in range," averred Callaway.[4]

None of this would have been necessary had matters proceeded according to the Japanese plan. No second attack on Dutch Harbor was scheduled. Having fueled the Mobile Force's destroyers, Kakuta had headed for Adak under orders to soften it up for invasion. Daybreak, however, found his ships in a fog so dense that they had to slow to a crawl, and the meteorologist assured Kakuta that the weather to the west would be even worse. He added that at Dutch Harbor visibility should be good. Therefore, Kakuta decided to forget Adak and play a return engagement at Dutch Harbor, where results of the previous day's raid had been disappointing.[5]

As early as 0845, Lt. (j.g.) Marshall C. Freerks, piloting a PBY from PatWing 4, had spotted Kakuta's carriers some 270 kilometers southwest of Umnak. He sent in a business-like report, including a description of the Mobile Force plus "weather, visibility and sea conditions." Freerks had been patrolling all night, and his aircraft was low on fuel, so he was ordered back to Umnak. Before returning, Freerks tried to bomb a carrier, but AA fire frustrated his attempt.[6]

Two other PBYs, piloted respectively by Lt. Charles E. Perkins and Lt. (j.g.) Gene Stockstill, were dispatched to maintain contact with the enemy force. After losing it temporarily, Perkins found the quarry again and reported its course and speed. The mission took him two hours, and his fuel was running low, so he, like Freerks, attempted a torpedo attack before breaking off contact. He, too, suffered AA damage, even worse than Freerks's: one engine was knocked out. Although the plane was almost out of control, Perkins managed to coax it to Dutch Harbor.[7]

This was probably the PBY that Parker remembered coming in, flashing what at first his men thought was an S.O.S. Then "a voice came in saying, 'It's not S.O.S., it's JAPS.'" The badly shot-up aircraft started to sink, and some of the 206th men helped rescue its crew.[8]

Stockstill, whose plane had remained on the scene to tail Kakuta's carriers, was never heard from and had to be presumed lost.[9]

Meanwhile, Freerks' report had triggered army air force action. Capt. E. O. Meals, from the 77th Bomber Squadron on Umnak, led a flight of five B-26s to the Japanese position. Although the bombers reached the specified location and searched for about an hour, they could not find the enemy, since heavy fog had set in. They had to return to base at 1355 without having glimpsed their targets.

Next, another five B-26s took up the search, setting out from Cold Bay under Col. William O. Eareckson. Oddly enough, the only member of this group who sighted the Japanese was Capt. George Thornbrough, whose bomber had become separated from the others. He drew a clear bead on *Ryujo*, released a torpedo, and by all the laws of probability should have been able to report "Scratch one carrier." However, American torpedoes of the time had a distressing habit of either missing their target or failing to explode, and this attempt was no exception. Thornbrough's torpedo struck *Ryujo*, but failed to detonate. Bitterly disappointed, the pilot disregarded his orders to wait for the other aircraft at Umnak. Instead, he returned to Cold Bay, where he rearmed, this time with five-hundred pound AP bombs, and returned to try his luck again. On this occasion he could not find the Japanese and had to return to Cold Harbor. Most unfortunately, Cold Harbor was socked in, and attempts to guide him home failed. About two weeks later, his bomber was found to the east of Fort Randall, crashed with no survivors.

That afternoon, five B-17s and an LB-30 from Cold Bay, under Captain Dunlop of the 36th Squadron, took off from Cold Bay to resume the search, with no success. This flight lasted from 1545 to 2145, during which time Kakuta had reached and bombed Dutch Harbor and was well into retirement.[10]

The flash report record reveals a pattern of PBYs coming and going, and a few false alarms.[11] At each of the latter, the men at Ballew's position "would run and climb the ridges on Mount Ballyhoo." After several such incidents, Ballew informed Sgt. Damon Mathis that he was "through climbing," because his wound was bleeding. "Finally, the fellows had a hole scooped out at the base of Ballyhoo and we all piled in there. . . ."[12] At 0950 all concerned were informed that Battery E of the 250th Coast Artillery at Sumner Bay and Morris Cove would fire four trial shots "in the next 30 or 45 minutes." Practice firing by the 37mm Infantry beach guns was scheduled for some time between 1600 and 1700. "Danger zone—Town of Unalaska across Illuliuk Bay toward Mt. Coxcomb." And Battery D of the 206th would be firing .50 cal. machine guns at 1630. "Danger area—Mt. Newhall area."[13]

The heavy fog that hampered the search aircraft was equally troublesome to Kakuta. After vainly waiting for it to lift, he characteristically decided to go ahead with the operation. Kakuta was not the cautious type, but he was not a fool, and he permitted only his finest pilots to take off under these conditions where the Aleutian weather could well prove more deadly than American planes or AA guns. At 1600 he launched a single wave from *Ryujo* and *Junyo*, consisting of eleven dive bombers, six high-level bombers, and fifteen fighters.[14]

Dutch Harbor began to pick them up as early as 1740: "A formation of planes now approaching Fisherman's Pt. Azi, 120°. Disappeared behind clouds." Three minutes later: "Several planes heard in Southeast at A-8 position." And three minutes after that: "Eleven bombers headed for Dutch Harbor from Fisherman's Point. Watch for three flights."[15]

The luck that seems to favor the bold had smiled upon Kakuta, and at Dutch Harbor his fliers found the fair weather his meteorologist had predicted.

Wrote Drake, ". . . at about 1800 hours, 4 June 1942, the island became deathly quiet. The silence was broken by the wail of sirens."[16] A number of men remembered the sound of "Moaning Minnie" calling them to arms.[17]

First and foremost, the men of the 206th remembered the Zeros. Indeed, one has the impression that they viewed the bombers with a curious impersonality, as if they were a force of nature or mechanical monsters with little to do with human beings. But the Zeros, skimming so low that the pilots' faces were clearly recognizable, put the war on a man-to-man basis. Here was the enemy, almost close enough to touch. The men on the ground hated the Zeros and took them on savagely, even when it was obviously futile. Zeros "relentlessly strafed" the hill on which Abell and his men were located, "as well as other areas." One came so close that Abell could see the pilot. He fired a clip at each passing fighter.[18]

Looking out from the spithead, Parker and his men could see "the Japs . . . coming at us like a big bunch of mosquitos." Placing his hand on the Bible resting over his heart, Parker silently uttered what was probably the most deeply felt prayer of his life to that date: "Dear God, please help me not to be scared, especially in front of my men!"

One of the younger men admitted, "Sarge, I'm scared. What can I do?"

"I'm scared, too," replied Parker. "Fire your rifle at them or pick up a rock and throw it at those Japs."

This was sound psychology. Action, however futile, would steady the nerves.

At that moment a plane scattered the gun crew by strafing. "Now I was really mad," declared Parker. He took over the gunner's seat. "By getting on the gun it helped my fear subside," he added, "and the more I fired the better I felt."

Finally, Parker and Cpl. Don Pipkin hit a Zero in its tail. "That's the way, Sarge!" yelled his crew. However, the shell went through the tail and apparently did no damage, because the Zero banked and headed directly for the gun site. "I said to myself that this was it," Parker wrote. "Several things flashed into my mind— maybe dying is not all that bad." Nevertheless, he was by no means eager to find out. "So," he related, "I again placed my hand on my Bible and asked the Lord if He would help me and my crew one more time. Then I slammed my foot on the trigger pedal and started firing away. And lo and behold, the Jap fighter plane banked again and headed out to sea."

Parker stroked his Bible and offered up a prayer of thanks, less for his life than for having been permitted to prove to himself and his men that he was "just as tough as the enemy."[19]

Three Zeros made "a strafing run at about 200 feet over the ferry between Unalaska and Amaknak Island." Then they climbed and flew over Ugadaga Pass to the south. At one point these aircraft flew so near the F-2 position that the men could see one pilot grinning "like skunks eating saw briers." The Zeros flew by so fast "the gun crews had no time to be scared," wrote Drake; "afterwards, seeing the damage done by the strafing planes, all were glad to be alive."

The 37mm guns were made to track manually a target flying at about 110 to 150 mph. As Drake and his men estimated the speed of the Zeros at 200 mph, the gun crew's fire was about 150 to 300 yards behind the planes. One disgusted gunner declared he could have done better with a 1903 Springfield rifle.[20]

Indeed, O'Neal was sure that his men of Battery A had scored a hit: ". . . a Zero broke through the pass and began firing directly at our position. Every man opened up with a rifle. . . ." They continued firing as long as the plane was in range. Then the Zero's pilot made the mistake of returning, thus presenting an easy target. "As he banked over toward the end of the valley black smoke began pouring from the engine and the engine began sputtering and missing."[21]

One Battery A position caused a scare when an enemy plane, smoking, came low over the site. Mistaking the smoke for gas, a sergeant ordered the men to put on their gas masks. The word spread, and a flash message went out at 1758: "F-2 reports possible GAS. PUT ON GAS MASKS." Pvt. D. D. Baker had a chew of tobacco in his mouth when he clapped on his mask, then was afraid to take off the mask long enough to get rid of the chew. He paid for his prudence with a very upset stomach.[22]

Battery C had a close encounter with a Zero that "came up the side of Ballyhoo. He wasn't more than thirty feet off the ground," related Davis. "I think he was as surprised as we were." Evidently this particular fighter did no damage to C's position.[23]

The Japanese caught the first platoon of Battery F in an uncomfortable position. This platoon had been ordered to reposition "on a mountain over Ft. Mears after the first raid." Although they worked all night, 4 June found them stuck on the side of the mountain. Despite bulldozers, trucks, winches, and other equipment, the platoon could not reach the top of the mountain. So "we just sat our gun on rough terrain on the side," said Henderson. "While some of our men were gone on a mission to work on completing our task," he went on, "we were raided by Zeros first and then dive bombers. Since our gun was not dug in and level, we shot all over the place but were not effective. The Zeros came in so low I caught myself shooting between the 3" guns of D Battery and had to elevate the barrel in order to keep from shooting our own people."[24]

"During the dive bombing the Zero fighters strafed nearly all gun positions but we had no casualties," Bowen recorded in his diary. "One plane charged our hill and we gave him hell with 50s and 30s while 3" men covered up. The ceiling was low but had risen a little during the attack. A boy at the foot of the hill got his pants shot full of holes but was not hit. Our hut was shot full of holes and two beds were hit. The orderly room was also hit badly." Bowen believed his outfit had shot down three planes, but was bitter because they had "*no air support*" (Bowen's italics). He added, "Battery B was given credit for two of the planes, one of which we got by rifle fire while he was strafing. We could easily see the pilot he was so close and a perfect target but flying fast."[25]

Alspaugh also recorded the strafing attack on Battery B: "On our second attack an enemy fighter attempted to strafe our hill but machine gun and rifle fire was so great he had to turn. He strafed our huts at the foot of the hill and put a 20mm H.E. shell through the hut next to mine. It tore a hole about 18 inches in diameter through the Quonset Hut. There were some holes in our hut." He remarked that he "had been praying for aerial support," but so far there had been none.[26]

The entire crew of Burris's Battery D gun was in place when the Japanese struck. "I pulled my field jacket off and pitched it on the sand bags," he remembered. A Zero came in "just over the power lines" headed directly for this gun position. "We ceased firing and everyone moved over near the sand bags or got under the gun platform or laid by the outriggers. I could see two spots of fire coming out of each wing." Burris counted four machine guns in the wings and a 20mm cannon in the nose. The latter "would not fire as fast as the machine guns." Apparently this Zero did no damage; at least, Burris did not mention any.[27]

Sergeant Raney of Battery F was sure that with more effective guns they "would have knocked down several Zeros as they were as low as 75 feet at times, even lower on occasion. I thought of throwing rocks," he added. "One pilot had his canopy rolled back and was looking around. I hold the sergeant in the same foxhole, 'My God, he's wearing a World War I helmet!'"[28]

Massey of Battery G kept copious notes of the action in which his men participated. "The Zeros and Vals were all over us, diving, bombing, strafing," he wrote. "One Zero peeled over in a dive to bomb the hangar, I quickly put the crew on it and opened up. The barrel let go, it struck its target center, wrecking three PBYs under it. Debris crashed down all over us."

As the Zero pulled out of its dive, it sprayed bullets over Massey's position, "tearing up the turf. I spun the gun around," continued Massey, "and the gunman opened fire, the Zero seemed to falter as a puff of light smoke came from it. It peeled off to its right and leveled off just above the water of the harbor and headed out toward the Bering Sea 'Hell-bent for leather,' skimming the surface."

Next, three Zeros "came tearing across the Navy landing strip . . ." Massey was sure his men hit one of them. Then "they pulled up sharply back away from us toward Ft. Mears." At this point the AA gun jammed. Massey ordered the gunner to rout the men out of their foxholes and start firing their rifles, which they had with them in the foxholes, in anticipation of a land attack. "How those boys moved, scrambling like a covey of quails!"

In his anxiety to get the AA gun working, Massey tore loose some fingernails. "I was drenched with sweat: it only takes five pounds of pressure to detonate one of these projectiles," he explained. "I don't know why it didn't explode . . . the barrel was red hot." The gunner jumped out of his foxhole and dashed for the shell "as it skidded down from the gun and tossed it into a pit."

For a while everything was quiet; "the Zeros had withdrawn. I could see them grouping south of Ft. Myers. The big guns began to open on them."[29]

For all the terrifying strafing, the Zeros inflicted comparatively little damage to the land installations. The lack of U.S. air support over Dutch Harbor, of which Bowen and Alspaugh complained, gave the Zeros no opportunity to display their expertise in their primary role—aerial combat. Nevertheless, the Zeros took a toll of the patrolling PBYs. Out of a total strength of twenty, only fourteen remained flyable, while "pilots and crews were at the limit of their endurance . . ."[30]

21

"They Sure Did Some Damage"

While the action by and against the Zeros was going on, the dive bombers—code-named Vals—were dumping on their assigned targets, beginning with fuel tanks. This suggested that someone in the Japanese navy had taken to heart one of the errors at Pearl Harbor—failure to target the vital yet vulnerable tank farm. Here at Dutch Harbor, they gave the U.S. fuel supply a priority position. One of the first bombs, however, damaged a nonstrategic building and quite possibly was released prematurely.

This missile scored a near miss at the hospital in Unalaska. "Actually it did not land on the hospital but at the side," explained ward attendant Martha Tutiakoff. "It was a terrific explosion. It tore out the whole end of the building and destroyed the nurses' quarters and all their belongings. It twisted and shattered the rest of the building, making it unfit for use. There was no fire."

Happily, no one was injured. The hospital had received a warning in time to move the patients to safety in dugouts. Head Nurse Margaret Quinn and the janitor were removing supplies from the basement storeroom when the bomb dropped. Neither was hurt, but they lost no time in scurrying to the dugouts.[1]

"A devastating but spectacular sight was the dive bombers making their bombing runs," wrote Abell. "The bombs were so large it made the planes appear to have double fuselages. When they dived in and dropped their bombs it appeared as if the fuselage split in half—the bottom half being the bomb. They scored direct hits on huge petroleum storage tanks with the ensuing spectacular explosions and fires."[2]

The Vals went into 30° to 40° dives to bomb the fuel-tank farm. Unknowingly, the Japanese had chosen an auspicious time. Only 3 days earlier, the tanker *Brazos* had filled 4 oil tanks with 6,666 bar-rels each. The dive bombers destroyed all 4. They also hit and set afire a 15,102-barrel steel diesel tank. They punctured a smaller diesel tank of 2,800-barrel capacity; however, it did not catch fire.[3]

"One bomber made his dive over the F-2 position, scoring a direct hit on the oil tank nearby," recorded the Battery A history. "The oil tank ruptured, blew sky high and burned fiercely, emitting billowy black smoke."[4] Damage had been quite heavy, but not as bad as that rolling black smoke made it appear. To observers at a little distance, it looked like the entire tank farm had gone up.[5]

"It burned for about three days," declared Proffitt. "Oil was burning on top of the water out fifty feet." Proffitt also had a closer encounter with a Val: "Battery F on the second raid had a 37mm gun by the power plant, 100 feet from my foxhole. The Jap dive bomber was about thirty feet over my head when he released his bomb. I could see him grinning. He got a direct hit on the gun pit and blew the gun out of the pit. Also covered two of our men in their foxholes with dirt and sand. The boys jumped out of their fox-hole and we covered them, saving their lives."[6]

Following their attack on the tank farm, the Vals turned their attention to the ships in harbor. *Gillis* fired its 3" gun, but the tar-gets were out of range. Two Japanese bombed and strafed *Fillmore*, which replied with such heavy 37mm fire that the Vals turned away from the transport and concentrated on *Gillis*. The latter opened up with all her AA guns and "reported an unconfirmed hit."[7]

Having been unsuccessful with *Fillmore* and *Gillis*, the dive bombers concentrated on *Northwestern*. They released two missiles against the beached vessel, one of which missed her, ripping off a piece of the Dutch Harbor dock. The other scored a direct hit on *Northwestern's* forward port section. "They set the *Northwestern* on fire and it burned, killing one million rats," Proffitt claimed.

As a bonus for the Japanese, flames from the barracks ship blew across to the nearby issue warehouse which burned to the ground, together with the hardware and spare parts stored therein.[8]

Except for the human victims of the attack, *Northwestern* was the loss that aroused nostalgic regret, especially in the Alaskans. She had been built in 1889, under the name *Orizaba*, and she plied between New York and Cuba. Then the Northwestern Steamship Company brought her for use in the Alaska trade. For twenty-five years, under the Alaska Steamship Company, she had been a well-loved feature of Alaskan waters. Legend had it that she had struck every rock in the Inland Passage, "but they couldn't keep a good ship down."

Wrote the Seattle *Post-Intelligencer*, "The echoes of her whistle rocked back from the hills and you thought 'Good old *Northwestern*—bringing news from the states, bringing mail, bringing a can of fresh peaches.'"[9]

It is possible that, misled by her size, the Japanese believed they had struck pay dirt. That evening, to the exasperated amusement of the men on Amaknak, Tokyo Rose came on the air boasting "that the Japanese bombers destroyed a warship at the Dutch Harbor pier."[10]

Massey watched as a Val "started a bomb run on the hangar. . . ." It was much slower than the Zeros, and Massey's gun crew was "right on it. It pulled out without dropping its bomb. . . . He was right on Mt. Ballyhoo, he let his bombs go to lighten his weight, he seemed to be hit, almost stalled out, but made it over the mountaintop out of sight."[11]

Alspaugh paid a professional's tribute to the dive bombers: "The pilots sure were deadly. They hit some of our oil storage tanks and they burned for over a day. They also hit the hangar, the *Northwestern* and the radio station. They sure did some damage in this attack. We fired continuously but with little effect as the sky was overcast. The planes came through the clouds, picked their targets and let loose." Rather optimistically, he believed four or five planes had been shot down, although he noted, "Our azimuth seemed to be short."[12] Bowen agreed with Alspaugh's assessment of the enemy. "The Japs have good planes and their dive bombing was almost perfect."[13]

The high-level technique of the Kates did not permit the precise bombing of which the dive bombers were capable. On the other hand, when their heavy bombs found a target, they could be devastating. Thus these bombers missed such enormous objectives as the fuel tanks on Power House Hill and the ammunition magazines on the side of Mt. Ballyhoo, but struck two AA gun positions, one army 37mm, one navy 20mm. The latter site was at the junction of Ballyhoo and Ammunition Road. This strike killed three men—Lt. (j.g.) Kenneth Greiner, S2c Robert Loucks, and RM2c David Strong.[14]

The bombing of the army position was probably the incident witnessed by Sergeant Robertson of Battery F. "We had a Quonset hut underground very near the gun positions," he recalled. "Had dug a trench some eight or nine feet deep from the hut to an ammunition dump and to the gun positions. Ammunition dump was also underground. A bomb exploded in the trench. The two men in the dump were killed." These were Pvts. Charles M. Hill and Ambrose D. Regalia, both of San Francisco.[15]

Having struck out at the tank farm, the Kates moved on to the seaplane base where they bombed the steel seaplane hangar. "One bomb penetrated the roof of the hangar creating a fifteen-meter hole and further damaged a PBY hit the previous day." Five bombs fell harmlessly into the harbor at Ballyhoo spit.[16]

Massey and his men of Battery G were in the thick of this action, and he kept detailed notes. "I heard a low droning sound and saw three Kate bombers approaching from the west," he recorded. "They were coming right over us, not a big gun fired at them." Massey's unit opened fire, although they realized the bombers were much too high to be viable targets. They dropped their bombs, and Massey gave the order to take cover.

"They were after the warehouse, hangar, airfield, and bomb storage," he went on. "I stepped down in the doorway of our dugout. Claps of thunder erupted across the hillside and several sharp jolts as the bombs hit, then a tremendous blast rocked the place. Glass from our skylight (2'x4') splintered in a million pieces."

The concussion forced the lid off their new gun tube box and slammed it against the top of the dugout. A board six feet long, eight inches wide, and an inch thick split in two, one half hitting Massey across the back. In addition, although Massey did not notice this at the time, a "large bottle of oxblood shoe polish one of the boys had left on the shelf exploded and covered the back of my right leg from the knee down."

His gun position wasn't hit, "but a Navy 20mm position twenty-five yards down the slope from us took a bomb direct. Three sailors killed. . . . The 6 x 7 ammo dump they had buried was thrown down the hill. Some of my men rushed down, stood staring." Massey ordered them back to the gun, and "one man to the aid station at the foot of the hill, but the medic was already running toward us." At that moment one of the men exclaimed, "My Lord, Sergeant, you're bleeding!" Having felt nothing, Massey checked himself out, and discovered the shoe polish, which had left his leg a gory-looking mess.

"One bomb hit higher on Ballyhoo, uncovering one end of a fox-hole a soldier occupied, a piece of shrapnel about the size of a marble went through the center of his helmet into his brain. He was completely paralyzed, died about an hour later. . . . All became quiet after the three bombers faded away, not a shot fired at them except ours. . . ."[17]

Their missiles exhausted, the Japanese aircraft headed back to their carriers. According to plan, *Junyo*'s pilots rendezvoused over the westernmost point of Unalaska. They could scarcely have chosen a worse spot, for it put them in easy range of the fighters stationed at Umnak, and indeed the Otter Point airfield was plainly visible to the hovering Japanese. This was their first knowledge of that installation.[18]

The phlegmatic Stubbs polished off his account of the ensuing action in two sentences: "Had another plane fight here. We had two planes shot down and shot down two of theirs."[19]

Otter Point was aware of the fighting at Amaknak. By 1830 "news of the plastering of Dutch Harbor had reached us, and the Jap fleet was fairly well located about 60 miles abeam of Umnak," wrote Miller in his article. Lt. C. D. "Tex" Laidlaw, the G-2, phoned to report, "The carrier is 60 miles away. We expect to have an alert within an hour."

Miller knew that Dutch Harbor had "nothing to put up against the Zekes. Our tiny force of Warhawks stays home for we have a base to protect. If Umnak gets one bomb on it to smash that tiny runway, there is no airfield in the Aleutians anymore."[20] Miller was on a ridge watching "when P40s dip-boomed the runway to sound the alarm . . . I saw two planes shot down and one damaged," he noted in his dairy, "and can't yet identify them in my mind although I know now they must have been Japs. It is impossible to watch a dogfight and see all that goes on." He added a truly astounding statement: "I did spot a flight of 4 German ME109s of Jap color just before they were intercepted and could positively identify them for intelligence."[21]

In the early months of the war, many believed that Japan and Germany were working hand in glove, that Hitler was furnishing the Japanese with aircraft and even pilots.

"Again there is a cloud cover with maybe 1500 feet of clear space under it," wrote Miller. ". . . Down over the locks comes a Zero chasing a P40, with another Warhawk chasing him, all three going like a sailor's pay, and not 100 feet off the water . . ." The Zero was the faster and was giving the P40 a hard time, but a second Warhawk dove in and sent the Zero "pulling up into the clouds with his motor smoking."[22]

"Lt. 'Lucky' McIntyre shot down a Zero and was in turn attacked and shot down," Miller recorded in his diary. "He hit on his belly on Unalaska Island in full view. . . ." Later McIntyre declared that he heard the Japanese pilot say over his radio in perfect English, "You're dead, you bastard!" McIntyre lived up to his nickname. His fighter skidded several hundred yards and flipped over. McIntyre emerged with nothing worse than a black eye, and he calmly sat down to await the crash boat.[23]

Lt. John Cape was not so fortunate. He was credited with bagging the one Zero shot down at Umnak, but a second Zero sent him to his death. "He was reported the best flyer in the squadron and the toughest man they could have lost," according to Miller. Later Otter Point was renamed Cape Air Force Base in his memory.[24]

Meanwhile, two bombers, piloted respectively by Lt. Thomas F. Mansfield and Capt. Jack L. Marks, took off from Cold Bay somewhat later than the Dunlop flight and spotted the Second Mobile Force. Marks took his aircraft up into the overcast and sent down five bombs blindly but hopefully. In contrast, Mansfield took his bomber to minimum altitude and aimed at the cruiser *Takao*. The bomb missed its target; Japanese AA did not. They shot down Mansfield's plane and picked up the lone survivor.[25]

Marks reached Umnak where he reported the location of the enemy ships. According to Miller, Marks's plane had been quite badly damaged, an AA shell having hit the nose, and twenty-seven machine gun holes were in the fuselage. The shell had struck the bombardier, who, Miller observed, "will live minus his right eye and jaw."

Five B-26s under Captain Meals set out from Umnak for the location Marks had pinpointed. Three of these planes found Kakuta's carriers. The bombers launched two torpedoes and believed they had hit a cruiser for certain and perhaps a carrier.

Actually the Japanese ships came, attacked, and left with no damage on either 3 or 4 June.[26]

Kakuta had more important matters to worry about than American land-based bombers, which were proving as ineffectual against ships in Alaskan waters as they had been earlier in the day off Midway. At about 1600, while his planes were still aloft, he received two disquieting messages from *Yamato*, the Combined Fleet flagship. The first ordered him to rendezvous with VADM Chuichi Nagumo's First Mobile Force. Kakuta was too intelligent not to read between the lines. The First Mobile Force, under the formidable Nagumo, had with it four of Japan's best carriers—*Akagi*, *Kaga*, *Soryu*, and *Hiryu*—manned by combat veterans of Pearl Harbor and the Indian Ocean. Something must have gone very wrong indeed at Midway if Commander-in-Chief Admiral Isoroku Yamamoto needed Kakuta's two modest light carriers.

Hard on the heels of this shocker came confirmation—a second message that "temporarily postponed" the invasions of both Midway and the western Aleutians. So Kakuta turned prows southward and was still underway when Yamamoto changed his mind and radioed the Northern Area Force that the latter project would go on as originally planned. Kakuta did not get the word until the next day, by which time his Second Mobile Force was over halfway to the designated rendezvous point with Nagumo. Obviously, having taken a beating at Midway, the Combined Fleet was determined to salvage something from the wreckage.[27]

22

"We Calmed Down Some"

The defenders of Dutch Harbor couldn't believe that the Japanese had finished with them, so the remaining hours of 4 June and much of the next day were spent in preparing for another attack and almost certainly an invasion. "We were told at approximately 2300 hours on June 4, 1942, that the Japanese were making a ground invasion of Dutch Harbor," Burris remembered. "We were marched out toward the beach and told to get on our stomach and crawl on toward the beach. We expected to meet the Japanese any time and we knew at that point that we had ammunition for only about fifteen minutes of firing. It was sad, we thought we would be wiped out any time."[1]

Sergeant Harp of Headquarters Battery declared stoutly that the 206th "would have given them one heck of a fight had any Japs landed."[2] Others shared Burris's pessimism. Pedersen believed that "if the Japanese would have followed up with more attacks and landing they could have taken the harbor. I don't believe we had enough ammo, AA guns, or navy ships to stop them."[3]

"They asked for volunteers to go down to the barracks area to help man a pill box on the beach," said McKinistry. "I volunteered but don't ask me why!"[4] According to Massey, everyone at his gun position was "keyed up," and he "had to send one man to the medics for a shot to quiet him down." Massey himself required treatment for his injured hands.[5]

With four hours of daylight remaining on 4 June, the Morris Cove men of Battery A enjoyed a warm meal and settled down to await the Japanese invasion expected to come the next day. Drake decided to use these remaining hours to see if he couldn't "rectify the false image situation which had plagued the radar operations for so long." They moved the antenna unit to a "flat shelf near the edge of the cliff overlooking Unalaska Bay," so that the crest of Hill 300 screened it from the surrounding mountains. They made the move very cautiously, tried out the new position—and "all the oscilloscopes showed crystal-clear images." Now water targets "could be detected some twenty-two miles into the Bering Sea with an azimuth sweep of about 68°."[6]

After the attack, Keeton of Battery D checked the sandbags the Siems-Drake people had filled, and he was more grateful than ever to his civilian colleagues. "The sand bags were shot up so badly the sand was pouring out of them. There is no way to evaluate the injuries and lives saved by this aid and work from the personnel of Siems-Drake." That very evening, the battery clerk informed Keeton that orders had come in, directing him to board the next ship for the mainland and to report to OCS at Camp Davis, North Carolina. He left on 8 June and after graduation was once more assigned to Alaska.[7]

"After the second raid, about 9:00 P.M. that night, they told us to be prepared to abandon the island during the night, going into the foothills of Unalaska Island," Proffitt recalled.[8]

A certain amount of this moving around took place. Parker of Battery C remembered that the AA guns were "moved to top of mountain during the night."[9] And Cathey of Battery D wrote, "After the raids occurred, our unit moved to the top of the big mountain (Ballyhoo)."[10] In contrast, M.Sgt. Clarence F. Williamson's unit of Battery D "was moved to lower ground around the hospital."[11] The medics made no immediate changes, but later repositioned the aid station.[12]

"After we calmed down some and cleaned our gun, we were told to keep full gun crews on all guns 24 hours and we did," wrote Albright. "We had field kitchens moved to the gun positions and from then on for several weeks guns were manned at all times."[13]

Burris's unit of Battery D moved their guns from the mountain to the beach,[14] whereas Ryals's unit of Battery G "moved up the mountain, two or three thousand yards . . ."[15]

Sleep was interrupted several times during the early morning hours of 5 June. Colonel Robertson issued a directive sometime before 0230: "Be prepared and watchful during the night for seaborne attack. Be prepared for early morning air attack." Then at

0344 came: "ALERT—all gun positions!!!"[16] Henderson of Battery F was deep in sleep. "I was so tired . . . I could not be awakened, even though I could hear the men trying to get me up."[17]

Another "FULL ALERT!!!" sounded later in the morning, but all aircraft sighted proved to be friendly, so the welcome ALL CLEAR was signaled, adding, "Eat breakfast and be on the alert as planes expected to return."[18]

Following the attacks, some marines and army field-grade officers stopped by Hargrave's platoon of Battery F "and said in effect that they though we were doing a good job and to keep up the good work." But the powers that be could not leave well-enough alone. "Later a letter came down criticizing the AA units for a criminal waste of ammunition."[19] Nor was the criticism confined to Battery F. Quimby of Battery E remembered, "The commanding general issued an order next day restricting firing of small weapons, decrying the 'criminal waste of ammunition by small arms.'"[20]

Despite this downer, the men of the 206th had no cause for dissatisfaction as far as their conduct was concerned. Some admitted candidly to fear, as would any honest man under the circumstances. "We were really scared," declared Henderson. "I believe that because we were kept in the dark as to what to expect, we were not prepared for battle—not prepared psychologically."[21] "We were all scared and feared for our lives," said Eheman.[22]

Ballew noted a sudden if temporary tendency to seek the protection of Higher Authority: ". . . we had full trucks for awhile when the trucks carried our fellows to church on Sunday."[23]

"We were scared to death," Ryals conceded, "but I think we did our job as best we could." He added, "On the second or third afternoon, after the raids, we were still on alert and watching the sky. Suddenly, voices from other positions announced planes approaching. We got ready to fire and when they came in sight they were our own P40s. The prettiest sight I ever saw!"[24]

The record reveals clearly, however, that nobody panicked, and most performed their assigned duties coolly and briskly. Effectiveness was another matter. There was considerable dissatisfaction with results, which most attributed to the poor quality of weapons and ammunition. "Our guns were useless as tits on a boar hog," was

Albright's graphic evaluation. "I could have done better with my Springfield when the Zeros were strafing our position. Our 50 cal. machine guns were worn out and 3" guns were noise makers."[25]

Raney attributed the trouble to a "stupid mistake" on the part of "the original planners" of the move to Dutch Harbor. "Each platoon was supposed to have one or two HD-cooled 50 cal. AA guns," he explained. "They were given to H Battery and all sent to Fairbanks."[26]

"Both the 37mm guns and the 3" AA guns with the old powder train fuse were obsolete against the target the Japs threw at us during the raids," stated Oehrig. "We should have had 40 mm guns and 90 mm guns."[27]

According to Proffitt, all the ammunition was of World War I vintage. "Time, humidity, hard knocks, caused it not to fire, jamming all machines continuously. . . ."[28]

"There wasn't a great deal that we could do except shoot at the planes with rifles," admitted Cathey.[29] A minority view came from Barron of the medics, who thought "that every man on the island was doing his duty to protect the island and had good equipment to do it with."[30]

Henderson believed that he had learned valuable tactical lessons: "Each unit needs to defend a particular sector; stick to a game plan; be sure your men get plenty of rest; test your equipment for all flaws by actually firing it as in battle."[31]

The Americans on Amaknak lost forty-three men in the raid—one each of the marines and Siems-Drake, eight navy, and thirty-three army.[32] "That's a good many men," Alspaugh commented in his dairy, "But it is comparatively light the way we are crowded on the island."[33] In addition, American losses in aircraft pilots and crewmen reached twenty-five.

At Dutch Harbor, the wounded amounted to approximately the same as the total killed.[34] It is possible that this number represented the minimum, because those who did not report their wounds could not be counted. For instance, one of the men in Battery D, a Private Pappus from Chicago, received a superficial wound. "We tried to get him to go to the aid station, but he would not go," said Burris. This surprised all his buddies, because Pappus "hated the Army and could not wait to get out." If he had reported for treatment, "he would have received the Purple Heart and this would have been good for five points when time for his discharge rolled around."[35]

The wounded were treated at the naval station dispensary. There the five civilian nurses employed by Siems-Drake—Mary Kain, Margaret Jaklan, Fern Tellifron, Veronica Janastych, and Lucille DeWell—helped the navy personnel in caring for these men. The next day the patients were en route to Seattle aboard *Fillmore*.

In addition to the dead and wounded, Amaknak had lost four fuel tanks with their contents, a 20mm gun, four warehouses, and two army barracks. The steel seaplane hangar had sustained minor damage, *Northwestern* major damage. The most serious material loss was a radar set stored in an army warehouse, scheduled for installation at Cape Winslow. To replace it, a set had to be diverted from the South Pacific.

None of which had any lasting effect on operations at Dutch Harbor. The lost oil and supplies were replaced in short order. Even *Northwestern* became useful again. Fire and damage control saved her steam and power plants. Within a week, her boilers were generating electric power for the naval station.[36]

The historians Craven and Cate have observed, "On the side of the enemy, it is probable that he achieved about all he had hoped for; losses were light, no damage had been incurred in any of the attacks, and the way was open for landing on the outer Aleutians."[37] On the other hand, one could argue that the whole operation was an exercise in futility. The Japanese had inflicted personnel losses, but not enough to alter the balance of power or even materially to affect the local mission. Damage to installations and stores had been temporary, and no major warships had been in harbor where Kakuta's aircraft might have damaged or sunk them. As for the way to the outer islands, it was Theobald, not Kakuta, who opened it by setting his judgment against that of Nimitz in moving his ships eastward.

Certainly the Dutch Harbor venture did nothing to further the Japanese cause at Midway. On the contrary, it drained ships, aircraft, and men away from the major theater, where the presence of *Ryujo* and *Junyo*, with their skilled pilots, just might have made a considerable difference in the ultimate result. For the Americans had been badly outnumbered and victory had been little less than a miracle.[38]

At Dutch Harbor, aircraft losses had been almost even. For the Americans, Patwing 4 lost four PBYs, the Eleventh Air Force two B-26s, two P-40s, one B-17, and one LB-30. Japanese losses totaled nine, one of which cost the Japanese more dearly than they knew for some time.[39]

On the way back to their carriers, several Zeros saw a PBY over Beaver Inlet on Unalaska, and promptly attacked. The PBY's defensive fire seemed ineffective, so all but one, possibly two, of the Zeros continued toward their mother ships. One of the fighters that remained behind was piloted by twenty-year-old Tadayoshi Koga, assigned to *Ryujo*. It is believed that he lingered to continue the attack on the reconnaissance aircraft. At 1743, observers at Fisherman's Point saw the PBY crash in flames at Beaver Inlet, near Egg Island. These same—or other—observers saw some of the seven-man crew board a raft and paddle toward shore. They watched in horror as a Zero machine-gunned the men in the raft.

The hapless PBY was No. 42-P-4, piloted by Ens. Albert Mitchell of VP-42. This aircraft seemed destined for trouble. Mitchell had patrolled the whole night of 3 June with his engines coughing from contaminated gasoline. Rust and sea water had mixed with the fuel the PBY took aboard from a seaplane tender. Returning to Cold Bay, he had the non-self-sealing tank thoroughly cleaned and filled with clean gasoline. The aircraft, however, also had a self-sealing tank, and this one could not be cleaned with the facilities at hand. So Mitchell's commanding officer, Lt. Cmdr. James S. Russell, ordered Mitchell to fly to Kodiak where better facilities were available and not to return without both tanks clean. But instead of correcting the discrepancy, the wing commander at Kodiak, Capt. Leslie E. Gehres, directed Mitchell to deliver some wing operations orders to Cold Bay and Dutch Harbor.

Unhappy that the problem had not been corrected, Russell warned Mitchell to check with Dutch Harbor before he entered its air space, and sure enough, Dutch Harbor warned him off because the second attack was under way. Russell could only surmise that Mitchell sought refuge in Beaver Inlet because he could not rely on his still-contaminated fuel supply, and there was shot down.[40]

Following the encounter, Koga noted gasoline spraying from his plane. So he radioed his flight leader, Lt. Minoru Kobayashi, that he did not have sufficient fuel to make it back to *Ryujo*. Then he headed for Akutan Island, which the Japanese had designated as an emergency landing site. There a rescue submarine would eventually pick up any downed flier. Any American airman stationed in Alaska would have recognized that smooth, inviting stretch as tundra and, if he absolutely had to land, would have tried it wheels up. Koga, however, was unfamiliar with the terrain; he landed wheels down, the Zero turned over, and Koga was killed instantly.

Upon reaching *Ryujo*, Kobayashi reported that the Zero had apparently been badly damaged and the pilot either killed or seriously wounded. "Since the island surface seems to be tundra," he advised, "it would be difficult to remove the wreckage."[41]

So there it remained for over a month, until a PBY from VP-41, stationed at Dutch Harbor, was blown off course. Passing over Akutan on the way home, its crew spotted the Zero. Lt. William N. Thies, the PBY's pilot, was excited over the find and after some argument persuaded his squadron commander, Cmdr. Paul Foley, Jr., to let him head a salvage party. They found the Zero, with Koga still strapped in, his head under water. This party did not have sufficient equipment to salvage the plane, so they removed Koga's body, his gear, and the 20mm guns from the wings. "We were rather surprised at the details of the plane, for it was well built," wrote Thies's co-pilot, Ens. Robert R. Larson. "We could see but one bullet hole in it, in the vicinity of the oil cooler." After it was salvaged, however, other bullet holes were found, both top and bottom. "Bullets from above and below is evidence of an aerial engagement," declared Russell. Therefore, some question remains as to whether Koga fell victim to Mitchell's PBY.[42]

Many men of the 206th saw the Zero when it was brought to Dutch Harbor for shipment to the United States mainland, and some believed their units should be credited with downing it. Raney of Battery F "saw the plane hit but thought it was spraying gas on the barracks area." It was "obviously hit by small-arms fire."[43]

"I believe Battery G or Battery H were the ones who put a hole in one of the gas tanks," Pack of Battery D remarked, "for it was a 50 cal. machine gun that hit it." He added, "I saw the plane when they brought it in. . . . The plane was in good shape, only a hole in the fuel tank . . ."[44] Beverburg of Battery B was even more specific. "I am convinced that one of the 30 cal. bullets that I fired through my M-1 rifle was what ruptured its oil line and caused it to go down."[45]

Why was the discovery of one Zero so important? The Japanese had been flying this type of fighter for approximately two years, and several had been shot down at Pearl Harbor. The latter, however, had been too badly smashed to give the Americans a clear picture of them, and the reports of the Zero's prowess verged upon science fiction, at the time. Some of the accounts were exaggerated, but most were true. For example, in a five-month period in 1940, twenty-two Zero missions of 153 sorties resulted in 58 Chinese planes shot down with 101 destroyed on the ground. Not a single Zero was hit.

In addition to being able to outmaneuver anything in the air, the Zero had an astounding range. In this respect, much credit must go to the skilled, dedicated fighter pilots who knew how to coax the last inch of range and ounce of gasoline out of their aircraft. Of course, the Zero wasn't perfect—the Japanese had skimped on safety features, and as a result it was highly vulnerable; that is, if the enemy could catch it.[46]

So the salvaging of a Zero with only minor damage was a major slice of luck. Taken first to San Diego, then to the Anacostia Naval Air Station, the fighter received exhaustive testing and analysis. While no new U.S. aircraft were developed as a result, the information gained was so important that the authors of *Zero!* believed that the capture of the Akutan Zero "did much to hasten our final defeat."[47]

One incident in relation to the Akutan Zero annoyed Burris exceedingly. He saw a picture in a stateside magazine "showing the plane with a U.S. Marine guarding the plane. The heading stated that the marines had shot it down in the Aleutians. I knew this was not true," Burris emphasized. There were few marines at Dutch Harbor, "and their duties were to guard the installation. They had only 55 cal. pistols."[48]

Another example of the exuberance of the U.S. Marines' highly efficient public-relations machine caused considerable bitterness in the 206th. Wrote Alspaugh, "After the raids, while Mears and the naval installations were aflame, some marines were photographed in our trenches. These photos were later used in the states showing the marines defending the Aleutians. To my knowledge," he continued, "the only marines at Dutch Harbor at that time was a small contingent used as guard personnel at the naval base."[49]

Sisk took this incident very much to heart. "But the worst part came after the two air raids occurred," he related, "when we saw in our very popular magazine (on front cover) pictures of these marines in trenches with combat clothes and dirty faces resting during a lull in the action. . . . [Everything] the article mentioned was tied in with these guys, even the Zero fighter that was downed. They were only a company . . . and got all the credit! We, the 206th, were the only antiaircraft at Dutch Harbor and it was only natural for us to be resentful toward the marines and *Yank* magazine for programming and having these men pose for that picture."

Sisk figured this ploy was "a scare tactic intended to put fear in the Japanese and make people back home think everything was under control." How could the civilians fear for the Aleutians with the marines in position? "I should mention," Sisk went on, "that in those days everybody was supposed to shiver and quake when marines were mentioned."

Sisk added generously, "The marines were a very tough and well-trained branch of the military, and they proved it everywhere in the Pacific. I don't mean to take anything away from them. These things I mentioned were not to downgrade the marines, for this was the isolated case of only a few men who were only doing what they were told to do . . ."

Nevertheless, the incident rankled. "GIs everywhere read the magazine and swallowed the whole untruth," Sisk pointed out. Even worse, with all mail censored, the men of the 206th could not correct the story and assure their home folks that they, too, had been among those present.[50]

23

"The Japs Are Here!"

The Japanese invasion of the two islands, Kiska and Attu, immediately following the attack on Dutch Harbor, was marked by serious miscalculation on both sides. On 5 June, a patrol plane sent in a report that two large carriers, two heavy cruisers, and three destroyers were in the Bering Sea, headed for Dutch Harbor. Every available plane was dispatched to the scene, without result.[1] Whatever the patrol crew saw, it wasn't a Japanese task force.

Among the search aircraft were six B-17s, which picked up radar contacts that resembled the enemy ships. They dropped their bombs. Swinging down to see what damage they had inflicted, to their chagrin they found that they had been trying to sink the Pribilof Islands.[2]

Another case of mistaken identity took place that same day. Some fifteen thousand yards off Dutch Harbor lay a Russian merchant ship, flying the Japanese flag. A few days earlier a Japanese submarine had fired across her bow, and the Russians prudently hoisted the Rising Sun. Dutch Harbor was aware of the visitor's identity, but the pilots of several P-38s of the 54th Fighter Squadron, en route to their new station at Umnak, were not. They spotted the ship and strafed it heavily. Fortunately no one was killed, but eight sailors were injured. "Later we sent out a ship to pick up the men and put them in our hospital," Bowen recorded in his diary, adding worriedly, "We all hope it will not cause trouble with Russia." The Soviet merchantman went on her way on 8 June, leaving the wounded men at Dutch Harbor.[3]

The Japanese made the most significant errors, however. No military operation, by its very nature, can be truly comical, but the invasion of Attu and Kiska came perilously close. Estimating that

Attu, outermost of the Aleutian chain, supported "a wireless station, observatory and garrison unit of unknown strength," the Japanese sent against the island the Adak-Attu Occupation Force, under the very able RADM Sentaro Omori. From his flagship, the light cruiser *Abukuma*, Omori commanded four destroyers, the transports *Magane Maru* and *Kinugasa Maru*, with the "Northern Sea" Army Detachment from Hokkaido aboard. This detachment comprised 1,200 men under Major M. Hozumi. In addition, Omori had the seaplane carrier *Kimikawa Maru* and her six float planes, her escort destroyer *Shokaze*, and some small minesweepers.[4]

Actually, the United States had no military installations on Attu, and its entire population consisted of forty-one people—thirty-nine Aleut Indians, of whom fifteen were children, and a sixty-year-old teacher, Charles Foster Jones, and his wife, Etta.[5]

As for Kiska, the Japanese estimated that two or three hundred marines were stationed there and sent against it the Kiska Occupation Force under Capt. Takeji Ono. His command consisted of the light cruisers *Kiso* and *Tama*, the auxiliary cruiser *Asahu Maru*, three destroyers, three subchasers and several minesweepers, with the transports *Hakusan Maru* and *Tamagawa Maru*. The former carried the 550 men of the Maizuru Special Landing Force under Lt. Cmdr. N. Mukai; the latter transported 700 labor troops with construction equipment.[6]

All this power would face the might of the United States on Kiska—ten unarmed men and their mascot, a dog of uncertain ancestry, named Explosion. This little group operated a weather station.[7]

Kiska took the first assault at 0120 6 June. The little band of Americans were not totally unprepared. The chief of the weather team, AG1/c William C. House, had gathered from his radio traffic that no one knew for sure just when and where the Japanese would strike following the Dutch Harbor raids. He was responsible for his station, so he took what precautions he could. He put his men to caching emergency supplies, to be available in case the Japanese landed and drove him and his crew into the canyons beyond their camp. On Kiska there was no question of preparing firearms and ammunition; the group had no means of defense. So they went to sleep, having done what little they could.[8]

Yet House could not have really believed the Japanese would

strike Kiska, for when AG2c Walter M. Winfrey woke him up screaming, "Attack! Attack!" House's reaction was: "Go back to sleep—you're having a bad dream." However, Winfrey displayed convincing evidence that he wasn't dreaming—a bullet had hit him in the leg. RdM 3/c M. L. Courtney caught a slug in his hand. House ordered his men to run and take cover. He and AG2/c J. L. Turner stayed in the cabin to burn the code book, somehow evading the bullets that continued to crash into the cabin, destroying the transmitter.[9]

Later Winfrey explained that the sand dunes had delayed the Japanese long enough to permit them to finish their task. The men split up. Winfrey was one of a group of four that set out for Vega Bay. They found the Japanese had been there first: the cabin had been burned, the cache of supplies destroyed. In fact, the invaders had soon discovered and staked out the buried material.

The invaders captured two men immediately, but made no effort to find the others. They knew it was only a question of time before the fugitives turned themselves in.[10] There are wilderness areas under the American flag where a reasonably healthy person with a smattering of woodlore and survival techniques could live, if not well, at least adequately, for long periods. Kiska is not one such area. Gradually the Americans surrendered. Winfrey's group held out for some ten days. The little dog, Explosion, accompanied them and helped them catch fox which they stewed for food. But Winfrey's wound was showing signs of infection, so they gave up. These Kiska prisoners were much more fortunate than many of their comrades elsewhere in the Pacific War. Their captors treated them like human beings and fellow soldiers. In a hurriedly erected tent, a surgeon removed the bullet from Winfrey's leg.[11]

Meanwhile, House had almost immediately become separated from the others. "I lay on the ground and seemed to hear footsteps closing in," he remembered. "And then I realized it was my heartbeat." He was wearing only light clothing, but fortunately had on his rubber-bottomed shoepacs. He wrapped himself in gray blankets and settled down on some gray rocks high on a ridge. Thus camouflaged, he watched the Japanese land. Close to daylight, he moved to the northeast coast and hid in a cave in a ravine. There he kept warm and dry by spreading dry grasses under and over his blankets. For food he ate, "the inner parts of young rush" and of "cow parsnip." For protein he gulped down worms he found in a stream. By such means House held out until 28 July—an amazing feat of endurance.

At first he expected the Japanese would leave after having destroyed the weather station—the only object of even remote military value on the island. All he would have to do was evade capture until they left. When it became apparent that the invaders were digging in, his hopes took another direction: Surely the Americans would soon come and chase off the enemy.

It quickly became evident that this was not going to happen in the immediate future, so he had to reassess his position. He had lost eighty pounds; he was cold, eternally hungry, and steadily weakening. At last he surrendered to a Japanese gun crew. He must have been an astounding apparition—little more than a skeleton clad in rags, with a long brown beard. Like his fellows, House was fortunate enough to fall into humane hands. His captors treated him "with courtesy and respect," and plied him with soup, tea, and biscuits. After about three weeks, he had recovered sufficiently to be put to work filling sandbags.

At 5' 11", House was not particularly tall by American standards, but he towered over his captors, who called him "The Giant of Kiska." A friendly pilot drew his portrait and started him on the rudiments of Japanese. Relations were sufficiently cordial that House could ask a bomber pilot, "Maybe you could drop me at Dutch Harbor with a parachute?" The flier grinned, but said that he "couldn't do that."[12]

When the Joneses on Attu spotted a large transport in Chichagof Harbor on 7 June, they were not alarmed. They had received word that soon an American ship would arrive at Attu to evacuate its inhabitants, leaving in their place "a few soldiers or sailors" to operate the radio station and transmit weather reports, as Mr. Jones had been doing.[13]

The ship, of course, was one of Omori's *marus*. He had been some 225 miles southwest of Adak when, early on 5 june, VADM Boshiro Hosogaya, commanding the Northern Area Force, canceled the Adak invasion and ordered Omori to proceed against Attu. After receiving these orders, the admiral headed for Attu. Off Holtz Bay, the Japanese laid mines and reconnoitered the beach—not that they could see much in the heavy fog. Everything looking peaceful; Omori's 1,200 men landed and marched on Chichagof. It was not one of Japan's more efficient operations. As Samuel Eliot Morison remarked, "The main part of the detachment got lost and made Massacre Bay by mistake. Although the Japanese blamed this on poor maps, their performance was lamentable; a few hundred Marines could have thrown them back easily."[14] However, they could manage twenty-four adult Aleuts, fifteen children, and two white middle-aged teachers.

Chichagof was about as remote as a village could be. Occasionally a trader dropped in to restock the tiny store, collecting pelts in exchange. A U.S. Coast Guard cutter touched base even more rarely. That was about all Attu's scant populace saw of the outside world. At one end of town stood a Russian Orthodox Church. No priest was in residence; the island's well-respected chief, Michael Hodikoff, officiated at services. He also ran the store.[15]

The first hint that anything was wrong came when Mrs. Jones heard rifle shots, and a woman burst into the cabin, screaming, "The Japs are here!" Mrs. Jones ran to the window; Japanese were surging toward the village, yelling at the top of their lungs and firing haphazardly. Some Aleuts were injured in this initial rush, but none seriously. These first attackers were "young kids who shot into houses and generally mistreated the Aleuts." The second group comprised older men, most of them officers.[16]

Mr. Jones perished in the invasion. Some mystery remains as to just how he died. According to Mrs. Jones, the Japanese took him away for questioning the next morning and she never saw him alive again. She never learned how he died. Japanese records indicate that he bolted for "his secret hideout in the hills" and was shot down near the edge of town. Some Aleuts insisted that he committed suicide rather than be captured, and that Mrs. Jones also attempted suicide but "recovered under Japanese care." The last may well be true, for Mrs. Jones later stated that she believed she lost her mind temporarily, and the next few days were a virtual blank in her memory.[17] However he died, Mr. Jones was the only American to die in the Kiska-Attu invasions.

If any American citizen of the two islands was more frustrated than any other, that one was Chief Michael Hodikoff. A "keenly intelligent" man, he had been elected chief at the village's annual election for several years and was considered "a most excellent man for the office—capable and just." For a number of years he had been telling anyone who would listen, mostly men for whom he acted as fishing guide, what to expect. "The Japs, they come sometime—they take this place," he predicted to one Allan May. To another visitor, Simeon Oliver, he stated, "We live in fear. . . . They come all the time in their fishing boats—right up to the shore—and look and look and take our fish beside."[18]

One of his most detailed stories told of a Japanese warship that had anchored in the harbor, disgorging a small party of naval officers. Hodikoff was somewhat frightened when they asked to see the chief, but they reassured him. A Japanese prince had died on Attu, they claimed, and they asked permission to erect a cross on the death site. It struck Hodikoff as strange that these men should know the exact spot where the prince was buried, but the request seemed harmless enough, and he assented.

We do not know if he also wondered why Japanese officers should want to place a cross over a presumably Shintoist prince. But his suspicions were further aroused when the visitors selected the highest point on the hill to place their marker. What is more, they snooped around the island and took many measurements. Then they thanked Hodikoff and left. As soon as they had gone, he took a shovel, climbed the hill and dug deeply under the cross. Finding no sign of a body, he removed the cross and at the earliest opportunity turned it over to the U.S. authorities.[19]

Then there had been the occasion in the 1930s when a Japanese warship, with U.S. permission, had dropped off little groups at various points along the Aleutian chain, ostensibly to observe a projected good-will flight. These observers had no equipment but a rowboat and "fishing tackle." Hodikoff thought this was mighty peculiar fishing equipment—just "a long string with a piece of lead on the end."

A rather engaging incident of Japanese familiarity with the area occurred the next year. The U.S. cutter *Northland* was navigating a narrow channel, taking every precaution, "and making at best about four knots an hour," when with "a polite toot . . . a Jap cruiser edged past her, doing some twenty knots."[20]

To anticipate a bit and round off the story of Attu's inhabitants, the Japanese kept a close watch over the Aleuts, allowing them to leave their houses only occasionally and for not more than a few yards. Finally, in September 1942, the Japanese collected them, moved on to Kiska to pick up the weathermen, and took them all to Japan as prisoners. The Aleuts were taken to Otaru on Hokkaido; Mrs. Jones had already been moved to Yokohama in a transport. Later she said, "I have one vivid recollection. After climbing the long stairway of the ship and getting on deck, I noticed myself in a mirror. I was laughing like an hysterical fool. Perched on the back of my head was a blue knit cap. The reflection was enough to shock me back to normalcy, and from then on I remember everything clearly."

She reached Yokohama on 21 June, and soon convinced her captors that she had no military knowledge. A little later she was placed with eighteen Australian nurses from New Guinea. The Japanese treated Mrs. Jones well and called her "Oba-san,"—the aged one—a title of respect. At the war's end she was repatriated.

The Aleuts were not so fortunate, for while the civilians at the camp were decent to them, the army officers were not. Their diet was the scantiest, and they were not permitted to speak either English or Aleut. So perforce they picked up a smattering of Japanese. Their days were spent digging clay for a nearby factory. Only twenty-five of them survived. Among those who perished was Michael Hodikoff.

When the war ended, they hoped to go back to Attu. Uninviting as it might appear to a stranger, to them it was home. Instead, they were resettled on Atka in the Andreanof Islands, about halfway down the Aleutian chain. There the government built new homes for them.[21] Thus the Kiska-Attu campaign may have begun with elements of comic opera, but it ended as a bitter tragedy for the Aleuts.

Meanwhile, the Japanese lost no time in settling down on the two islands, placing AA and harbor guns in position. They really could have saved themselves the trouble. Yamamoto's grand design had postulated the Aleutian stations as the northern anchor of a protective sea shield for the homeland, with Midway the southern anchor. After the Japanese failure at Midway, the whole scheme came apart at the seams, rendering the two islands meaningless to Japan.

Having received no weather reports from Kiska and Attu for several days, the Americans correctly took this radio silence to mean that these islands had been captured. With the twenty-twenty vision of hindsight, one can speculate that the best policy for the Americans to follow would have been to leave the Japanese alone, allowing them to play about harmlessly in the fog and snow.

But emotions, so much more potent than logic, were at work on both sides. The Japanese needed something to help distract attention from Midway, even though that disaster was being kept strictly under wraps. The Japanese people would pride themselves on the fact that their forces had captured American territory in the western hemisphere. As for the Americans, the invasions struck a raw nerve; every attempt must be made to chase off the invaders.[22]

So for many weary months, the Japanese held on grimly and the Americans expended precious time, matériel, and men, on one side to hold, on the other to retake, two forlorn bits of land, the strategic value of which was not worth the sacrifice of a single American or Japanese life.

The Russian Orthodox Church located at Unalaska. Photo courtesy of
Donnel J. Drake.

A typical Quonset hut. Photo courtesy of George W. Cathey.

Martha O'Driscoll and Erroll Flynn visited Amchitka in 1943. Photo courtesy of Cecil L. Gibson.

The comedian Joe E. Brown posed with these soldiers on Dutch Harbor in 1942. Photo courtesy of Dennis P. Abell.

Members of Battery I, 206th Coast Artillery Antiaircraft Regiment at the entrance of the Battery Orderly Room in Unalaska Valley, 1943. *L. to r.:* 1st Sgt. Donnel J. Drake, Sgt. Dewey W. Gartrell, and Cpl. Edward Knudson. Photo courtesy of Donnel J. Drake.

Sgt. Homer Busby inside the Battery I Orderly Room located in Unalaska Valley. Photo courtesy of Donnel J. Drake.

Battery I has a rare beer bust near its gun position in Unalaska in the Spring of 1943. Photo courtesy of Donnel J. Drake.

Members of the Battery F-2, 37mm AA gun crew, located at the base of Mt. Newhall in Unalaska Valley in winter 1943–44. *L. to r.*: Sgt. Aubrey T. Albright, D. A. Cox, and Gertie Lee. Photo courtesy of Aubrey T. Albright.

NCO Jerald F. McKinney of Battery A-ll standing in the entrance to the underground living quarters at the northern end of Mt. Ballyhoo. Photo courtesy of Larry Obsitnik.

Larry Obsitnik and Edgar "Dynamite" Justice at the Mt. Newhall A-4 base camp. Photo courtesy of Larry Obsitnik.

Living quarters of Battery A-2, 206th Coast Artillery Antiaircraft. Since the living quarters, mess hall, and rec hall of A-2 Battery were underground, the men were called "The Mole Hole Gang" by the other members of the battery. *L. to r.*: Donnel J. Drake, Frank "Pete" White, Irving Reichel, Kent Jones (standing), Benjamin Bailey (sitting in rear), Luther Clements (sitting on bunk), Woodrow Trimble, Eli Santos, Clyde Hill (with paper), and Samuel Schmitt. Photo courtesy of Larry Obsitnik.

Battery I, Provisional 90mm (AA) Gun Battery, 206th Coast Artillery (CA) Antiaircraft (AA) Regiment in June 1943. The unit, consisting of five officers and 122 men, was established 18 August 1942, and assigned to Unalaska Valley about two miles south of Unalaska. Photo courtesy of Donnel J. Drake.

The monument dedicated to men who served with the 206th Coast Artillery Antiaircraft. It was designed by Paul D. Beasley.

24

"Settled on Hog Island"

Military installations can be hotbeds of gossip under the best of circumstances, so it may be unnecessary to note that in the first weeks of June 1942, Dutch Harbor swam in scuttlebutt. Quite a selection appears in Bowen's diary. "A big naval battle was fought about 60 miles out, and we could hear the guns," he recorded on 6 June. "We downed 20 Jap planes according to the reports in an air battle. . . . We had several air raid warnings and expected a landing party tonight, but it did not come." He added that it rained on the sixth, and several more warnings sounded. In addition, "the air troops sank their second aircraft carrier and a troop transport here . . . we are expecting an attempt to land troops tonight. But they may not have much left. I think from all reports that we have nearly won the first battle."

On 15 June Bowen claimed that U.S. bombers "made a direct hit on an aircraft carrier, sank a destroyer, and damaged two cruisers . . ."[1]

It is difficult to say how these overblown assessments took root; possibly echoes of the victory at Midway reverberated northward and became transmuted into local action. The Japanese, too, were doing their share of rumor mongering. "Tokyo Rose blowing up their occupation force in the islands," observed Massey. He added savagely, "I sure would like to kill that bitch!"[2] Not a particularly charitable sentiment but very understandable in the circumstances.

The diaries of Bowen and Alspaugh reveal that the men of the 206th took heart from reports of successful American strikes against the invaders. Actually, army aircraft scored a few hits and near misses, but during June experienced many more frustrations. Such remarks as "No effect observed," "abort due to fog," and "bombing mission canceled due to weather" pepper the record.[3]

The navy fared even worse. Its PBYs and their mother ship, *Gillis*, were stationed at Nazan Bay on Adak. On 10 June, Captain Gehres issued a remarkable order: Beginning the next morning, the PBYs were to take on a full bomb load and attack Kiska, keeping these attacks up regardless of weather until either the Japanese abandoned Kiska or until the PBYs ran out of fuel and bombs. This would have been an unreasonable order even for a bomber squadron; for a PBY wing it was murderous. That type of aircraft was a sitting duck for ground fire or fighter planes—slow, inadequately armed and armored, with an inefficient bombsight, exposed fuel tanks, and "all the maneuverability of a hippopotamus." Results were predictable: "Within seventy-two hours, half the PBYs now moored in Nazan Bay would be destroyed," and the surviving crews had nicknamed Kiska "PBY Elimination Center."

What probably saved the remainder was a mistake. Military commanders in Washington misinterpreted a Japanese intercept as meaning Hosogaya was planning a large scale bomber attack on *Gillis*. Nimitz ordered Theobald to call off the PBY raids and move *Gillis* out of Nazan Bay. On 14 June, a PBY stopped at Kanaga, one of the Andreanof Islands, located between Adak and Tanaga. There the crew evacuated the five men of the U.S. Navy weather station. Thereafter, no more American forces remained in the Aleutians west of Umnak.[4]

All of which was of little more than academic interest to the 206th, fully occupied with its own tasks. Drake and his men at Morris Cove were especially busy. On or about 8 June, a tractor-trailer met the supply boat and found that "a reinforced infantry squad from Company A, 37th Infantry Battalion had been assigned to Morris Cove to establish defensive gun positions along the beach. The squad consisted of 15 men equipped with a light 30-caliber machine gun, a BAR and 14 M-1 rifles." The tractor moved them to a location near the radar base camp. The next day, Drake's men and the NCOIC of the squad met "to coordinate defensive positions and fields of fire along the beach area."

Some four days later, navy personnel arrived with "a 20mm gun, equipment necessary to operate the gun and three cases of ammunition." Pete White and Hugh Weatherford were designated gunner and assistant gunner, respectively. The navy instructed them in the operation and maintenance of the weapon. The two gunners selected an area to place the gun. "The position was completed in five days, including sandbagging the parapet and bolting the pedestal mount for the gun to a concrete slab on the floor of the parapet . . . During the ensuing weeks, permission was granted to test fire the guns at bobbing oil drums in the bay. Both gunners soon became quite proficient at firing the weapon."[5]

The radar operators had been having difficulty in distinguishing between such water targets as an oil drum and a submarine periscope and had sent the navy off on a few false alarms. "After that, the radar operators soon became proficient in recognizing the difference between an oil drum and a bona fide water target. Air and ship targets were no problem to recognize, as the images on the oscilloscopes were constant."

For a long time, these radar operators had been "exposed to the elements 24 hours a day, wearing water-repellent clothing for protection." Morris Cove sent for Joel McDill, the battery carpenter, "to determine the feasibility of building an enclosure around the three oscilloscopes on the antenna unit . . ." McDill arrived, took measurements, "and advised that an enclosure could be made without difficulty." Within three days he was back with "the necessary pre-cut lumber." He "completed the entire project in less than six hours without interrupting the radar operation."[6]

In times of dense fog, at night, the searchlight crew would activate the light to help guide pilots of aircraft headed either for Dutch Harbor or Ft. Glenn. "Apparently, however, the fog was too dense for the 800 million candlepower beam of light to penetrate. Finally, the noise of the motors would trail away to the northeast in the direction of the Alaskan Peninsula. Because of the blinding light reflecting from the fog, the searchlight operator had to wear goggles with dark green inserts for eye protection."[7]

One evening during a bull session, the conversation turned to the infantry squad's Quonset hut, equipped only with candles and a gasoline lantern. Someone "casually mentioned it would be nice if electrical lighting could be made available to the infantry squad. The radar generator had the capability of providing electricity for a small town."

The next day, two of Drake's men went to Ft. Mears and returned with enough equipment to provide the infantry with both electricity and telephone service. One day later, "Electrical fixtures were added to those already included in the prefabricated Quonset hut wiring and the hookup was completed. The lookout on Hill 300 was called to have the power cable connected to the generator panel and within minutes the lights went on at the infantry position."[8]

The Morris Cove unit soon settled into a daily routine. Those not on duty engaged in various recreations, including ship-watching, which was very popular. "One such ship for which the men were always looking was the Russian supply ship that would stop at Dutch Harbor to unload lumber and take on fuel. What made the Russian ship so popular was the fact that other than the captain and the first mate, the entire crew was comprised of women."[9]

Many men of Battery B were busy preparing to move to Hog Island, due west of Ballyhoo. The project began almost immediately after the actions at Dutch Harbor, Kiska and Attu. The timing was opportune because, as Bowen noted on 8 June, ". . . due to various causes some of the boys are sick and so nervous they cannot sleep or do much. . . ." Work is fine therapy for psychological problems resulting from tension, as Bowen probably realized when he added, "Capt. Love said tonight that we are going to move to Hog Island tomorrow. That means a lot of work." Batteries C and D had already transferred.[10]

"Sgt. Hooker took a detail of men over to Hog Island to make a temporary camp so we can set up over there," wrote Alspaugh on 10 June. "There are about fifteen men over there from B Btry as well as a group of engineers. They went over in a forty footer."[11]

The move was by no means routine. "Hauled supplies to the Sheep Ranch to go to Hog Island for the men already there," Bowen recorded on the eleventh. "One of our 'Cats' fell off the barge about 50' from the bank and is temporarily lost. . . ." Three days later came a similar incident: "Started to take a CAT to Hog Island today, but the barge sank before we even left shore. We just have too much work that requires good equipment of which we have none. . . ." The next day he added, "Boys at Hog Island have put up five tents, built a small dock and filled a few hundred sand-bags. They like it fine over there which is more than I can say for it here."[12]

For the rest of the month, Alspaugh was on "a detail hauling huts to a barge . . ." These were the Quonset type. "They are pre-fabricated wood and sheet-metal huts packed in boxes weighing anywhere from 750 to 1200 lbs. per box. When constructed the huts are 36' by 16'." Alspaugh was exasperated because his detail experienced "quite a lot of difficulty in getting any cooperation from the Army Harbor Service, so we are having to unload the huts at the docks and then loading them on the boats. It would be much simpler if we could load them from the trucks to the boats as we are doing all of the loading by hand."[13]

Bowen, too, was having his troubles: "Winch cable block broke today while we were loading huts on the barge. . . . Everyone is dog tired but some of the boys still 'goldbrick,' making it harder on all the rest." On Monday 22 June, a bundle of Masonite fell on a man named Greer, injuring his leg. "We need some more equipment to do such heavy work," Bowen wrote. "It's just too much for men to pick up and handle." Greer had a second narrow squeak the next day when he "was caught between the side of one barge and a piece of Masonite and had to jump in the bay to keep from getting killed. The bundles weigh 190 lbs. each. . . ."[14]

Meanwhile, other units on Amaknak were in a frenzy of construction. "They have started clearing buildings for a runway down at the airport now," Alspaugh noted. "They are doing the razing in a very easy manner. They just run a cable around the building and put a winch on the cable. After applying pressure on the cable the building collapses. They then tear the section up and haul it away." Evidently Alspaugh felt only admiration for the efficiency of the demolition.[15] Bowen could praise, but he also saw reason for a little headshaking: "The new steel hangar that is really taking shape and looking good is already being torn down to make room for an airplane runway . . . ," he observed on the nineteenth. "A number of warehouses and barracks are finished in the valley back of 200 hill. They were not even started until after the attack. The new submarine dock is also nearly completed. . . . Lots of new projects have been started which admits that errors in planning [in] the past were made."[16]

Battery B commenced its move on 1 July. "We have torn the sandbags down from around our gun preparatory to moving," noted Alspaugh. "We spent the afternoon casing up ammunition and packing equipment. The whole section has been working earnestly." Marching orders came at 1400 the next day. "Our weapon was hard to get out of position. It rained all day and it was cold." They left

Amaknak at 2200, reaching Hog forty minutes later. "We worked all night unloading the barge. . . . I sure am tired, cold and sleepy."[17]

"One road gave way and nearly cost us a gun," Bowen remembered, "but we straightened it out all right. I was the last man from our Btry to move over since I cleaned the camp with some outside help."

Hog Island may have been an improvement over Amaknak, but it was no earthly paradise. Most of the soil was of "very spongy" volcanic ash. "Consequently we have a lot of trouble keeping the roads open when it is wet. And it is wet all of the time."[18]

Croom recalled some of the 206th's early experiences on Hog:

> The hill called Goblers Knob did not have a road. So with pick and shovel we went to work digging away the side of the hill. we called it the Burma Road. We got a bulldozer to finish to the top of the hill. Later in the late summer we hauled rock—some were four or five feet thick—to fill a lake on the first level of the Goblers Knob. We hauled for a period of two weeks. Filled in with dirt and gravel. This was done so that a building could be built. This would be the mess hall for Battery D. When completed, we also got electricity. They built the building in about a month or so. We also got running water. The mess hall was built in a volcano crater. . . . We built the Quonset huts. One of our men . . . was the foreman and did a fine job . . . [19]

Some of their problems the men imported with them. "After we got settled on Hog Island, they organized as NCO club where beer was available," Jodie Jones recalled. "A man had to be a confirmed drinker to tolerate the green can GI beer. As remote as we were, there were men that borrowed materials from the mess hall and brewed a powerful drink. Even this remoteness could not stop the heavy drinkers from getting drunk."[20]

The beer, however, was a sometime thing. "On Hog we seldom had beer," wrote Weese. "So seldom that one night two of our men broke into our PX supplies and drank all the hair tonic, shaving lotion and other liquid containing alcohol. It sure made them very drunk and very sick. I don't remember the cost of 'green beer' but money had little value there. If you didn't have any you could always borrow from your hut mates."[21]

Before the military took over, Hog Island had been a fox farm. Most of the animals had been removed before the 206th arrived, but a number still remained. As it was summer, they were not in full coat, and Sisk remembered them as "a bedraggled lot. . . . Skinny and always wet from the weather, and looked as disappointed about their plight as we felt about ours."[22]

The men were ordered under pain of court-martial not to harm the foxes in any way. Soon the animals learned that they were in no danger, and "became a real problem. Raiding garbage cans at the mess hall and even making dens to raise their young under some of the huts. In winter when in full coat the fox was beautiful, but under the huts they smelled awful."[23]

"They are as tame as dogs," wrote Bowen, "and stay around the kitchen most of the time."[24] Alspaugh wrote to his mother that the foxes "come up to our living quarters sometimes at night. There have been several instances where the foxes tried to get into our living quarters."[25]

Perhaps because as a first sergeant he was directly involved with his men's living conditions, Weese had particularly sharp recollections of life on Hog Island:

> Hog was one mile long and half a mile wide. The north shore line was mostly beach or rocky coast. It sloped up gradually for a half mile to a height of about 500 feet then dropped off in a sheer cliff down to the sea. Our 3" AA guns and 50 and 30 cal. machine guns were dug in along the slopes. We erected Quonset huts for living quarters and mess and recreation huts. Ten to 13 men shared a hut and these were usually members of our gun crew, motor pool crew, communications crew, or mess hall gang. One hut was used as officers' quarters where one captain and four lieutenants lived. One hut doubled as a Btry orderly room and living quarters for me and two battery clerks. The orderly room was arranged much like an office with desks, file cabinets, tables and chairs and counters to serve the men as they came in for assignments etc.[26]

The men's furniture was made from salvaged materials or lumber. Cots were of steel with cotton mattresses, although a number of the men had air mattresses they had brought from the lower forty-eight. "We had foot lockers and shelves with clothes racks under the shelves. Many men were very ingenious in [devising] tables and cabinets to set beside their cots. 'Pin-ups' were everywhere—Betty Grable was the most popular."

Lighting was no problem for this unit. "Being a 3" gun battery, we carried our own electric generating equipment with us, so all huts were wired for electricity." Heating was less sophisticated, being provided by coal-burning pot-bellied stoves. "Fire was always a danger in the huts," Weese admitted; however, he recalled no serious fires on Hog Island."[27]

The island's isolation was the chief problem. For several weeks there were no facilities for bathing, so the men "had to go across the Bay to clean up." As the navy had not issued a boat, they had to use their own, a dory Bowen and several others had bought and renovated, to get to Amaknak for such purposes as bathing and picking up equipment. "All of our groceries and supplies, laundry, gas, oil, fuel etc. have to be hauled on a barge or a forty-foot launch and there just aren't enough boats to go around to all of the outposts." Several times Bowen had gone over to procure 1500 gallons of gasoline and "had to wait three days for a boat to bring it back." He anticipated that with the advent of winter fuel would "present a major problem."[28]

Occasionally news of the war drifted into the 206th's little backwater. "One of our subs ran on a reef five miles from the Kiska Harbor and the boys had to leave it for the main island where they lived eight days only a few miles from the Japs. One of our PBYs finally found them and brought them here."[29]

This was not exactly factual, but not too far off the beam, as GI rumors go. The submarine S-27, under the command of Lt. H. L. Jukes, was reconnoitering Amchitka Island on 19 June. She had to surface at 2200 to recharge batteries. Lacking either fathometer or radar, she was an easy prey to the fog and the current that sent her onto a reef. The sub listed, a battery leaked chlorine, and the motor room was awash. Jukes's distress call was picked up but not his position. Meanwhile, he had no choice but to abandon ship. A rubber boat carrying crew, food, weapons, and ammunition landed on Amchitka. While not, as rumored, Kiska itself, Amchitka was also one of the Rat Islands, much too close to Kiska for the comfort of a stranded American submarine crew. Luckily enough, the men located several abandoned buildings and managed quite well for a week, when a PBY from Dutch Harbor picked them up.[30]

Jukes remained at Dutch Harbor as commander of the new submarine base. A Naval Construction Battalion, the famous Seabees, who did such a remarkable job throughout the Pacific War, had replaced the Siems-Drake people.[31] The Seabees, whom Sergeant Haden called "good, hard-working guys,"[32] cooperated fully with the army and were prime favorites. "The Navy Seabees . . . at Dutch Harbor gave us help in construction of our tactical positions," stated Captain Wall, "as well as supplying us with material to build them with."[33] In an astonishingly short time, the Seabees had the local submarine base ready to be commissioned on 24 July.[34] U.S. submarines made a few kills in Aleutian waters, but not as many as hoped for—only six for the entire year of 1942.[35]

25

"Unfit for Pigs"

While the 206th was settling down on Hog Island, another and much less well-handled move was under way. Discussions had been going on for some time concerning advisability of evacuating the Aleuts from the islands. Control over Aleutian affairs rested with the Interior Department, three divisions of which were involved. The Office of Indian Affairs (OIA) had charge of education, establishing primary schools, and appointing teachers for the larger settlements. The Fish and Wildlife Service (FWS) was responsible for what was then the very profitable harvest of seals on the Pribilof Islands. The local Aleuts provided the necessary labor, so the FWS also was responsible for the education and welfare of the Pribilof Aleuts. Finally, the Division of Territories and Island Possessions got into the act because the Territorial government of Alaska was under its jurisdiction. It was supposed to coordinate the efforts of the territorial and the various war agencies in regard to both supplying the Territory and evacuation of the Aleutians. The military agencies involved were the navy's Alaska Sector, the North Pacific Force, and the Alaska Defense Command.

Immediately after Pearl Harbor, Buckner had ordered all military dependents in Alaska evacuated. In January, the navy recommended removal of "all white women and children" from Unalaska. The army suggested that Aleut women and children also be evacuated. The Division of Territories forwarded this to Alaska's Governor Ernest Gruening, concurring with the army's suggestion that "the activities of the Army and Navy connected with evacuation be coordinated with the activities of the Governor's office"—a logical enough arrangement.[1]

It requires no expert in governmental administration to see that here were the ingredients of a potential disaster. Too many agencies with too many unrelated responsibilities were involved for this very important issue to receive the attention it deserved. Not until 13 March 1942, when Gruening was in Washington, did the acting governor, E. L. Bartlett, call a meeting to discuss evacuation plans in the event of an attack. No military personnel attended this meeting. The attendees reached several conclusions, one being that a "joint declaration of some kind . . . stating evacuation problems and recommending lines of procedure" should be sent to the army, navy, and governor.

They also decided that Aleut women and children should be moved to Unimak Island and to the Alaskan Peninsula. In this connection, Homer Stockdale, the Indian Service teacher at Unalaska, interviewed the local Aleuts as to their wishes in case relocation became necessary. Naturally, the majority preferred to locate in villages as close to home as possible and with similar geographical features.

Finally, the meeting agreed that evacuation would be a bad idea, even in case of an attack. The Aleuts were accustomed to a highly specialized environment and would not be able to adjust to any other. If left at home to their own devices, they could "take to the hills" and hold out for a long time.[2]

For a considerable period, this seemed to be the consensus. A dissenter was Superintendent Claude Hirst, an OIA official from Juneau, and he later changed his mind. Buckner told Gruening that evacuating the natives would be "pretty close to destroying them; that they now live under conditions suitable to them; and that if they were removed they would be subject to the deterioration of contact with the white man, would likely fall prey to drink and disease, and probably would never get back to their historic habitat." Gruening agreed that "a forced evacuation would . . . involve greater risks to the ultimate welfare of the people than the probable risk if they remain where they are."

Discussions went on through the spring, with letters flying back and forth between the various agencies. In retrospect it is clear that nobody wanted responsibility for a potential no-win situation. The government would be in an equally awkward position if the Aleuts were left in place and decimated in the anticipated warfare or if they were evacuated and all the gloomy predictions of Buckner,

Gruening, and others came to pass. James C. Rettie, counselor of the Alaska Office of the National Resources Planning Board, was sufficiently upset by the lack of proper coordination that on 7 May 1942 he wrote a strong letter to Harold D. Smith, director of the Bureau of the Budget:

> . . . If nothing is done to remedy the administrative paralysis and lack of clearly defined responsibility now prevailing in Alaska and the inadequate preparations to evacuate civilians, the confusion and loss of life which will follow an attack may easily be worse than it was in Hawaii. The record of inaction, delays, interagency squabbles and bickering, and the lack of proper liaison with the armed forces will be terribly ugly. . . . An outraged public opinion in the United States will rightly insist upon a hard-boiled investigation which might easily shake this administration to its very foundations.[3]

But the months were flying by, and, before any suitable relocation spots had been chosen and a reasonable period given the Aleuts to prepare, war had come to the Aleutians. As a result, the authorities acted hastily and in about as ill-considered a manner as they could have devised had they tried.

One motive cited for removing the natives was that relocation was for their own protection, and perhaps some of the officials in fact felt this responsibility. But the main reason seems to have been for the convenience of the armed forces. Supplying the villages would place a burden on the navy. "Working out a coexistence between the tiny Unalaska village and the 10,000 military personnel was a security problem."[4]

To paraphrase Madame Roland, "Ah security! What crimes are committed in thy name!" The locals and the military had been coexisting for months, if not cordially at least amicably. Certainly the Aleuts posed no "security problem." These were loyal American citizens, not likely to collaborate with the Japanese, whom they had hated for years before the war began.

Action began on the morning of 12 June, when *Gillis* received her orders to evacuate Atka and to "apply a scorched-earth policy before leaving." At that time, only Ralph C. Magee, a maintenance man, and his wife, Ruby, a schoolteacher, were taken aboard *Gillis*. Having spotted a Japanese scout plane, the Magees had sent the villagers to their fishing site, some three miles away, in the belief that they might be safer there. The detail of sailors gave the Magees twenty minutes to pack, then set fire to the village, including the church. Only four houses remained. Then *Gillis* departed for Dutch Harbor.

That evening, when most of the Aleuts returned, the *U.S.S. Hulbert** found them and took them aboard. Nineteen more remained until 15 June, when two PBYs took them off. It was all so sudden the evacuees had no chance to collect personal effects. Many boarded ship or plane with no more than the clothes they were wearing. This tragedy would have been unnecessary if the navy had waited to fire the village until all the natives had been accounted for. The Magees had warned them soon after Pearl Harbor that "the Coast Guard or someone" would evacuate them, and they received a further suggestion of evacuation from the Juneau Native Service Office in April. Therefore many had packed a few possessions to take along.

Eventually the Atka Aleuts were housed in an abandoned cannery at Killisnoo Island in Chatham Strait, the passage between Admiralty and Chicagof Islands in southern Alaska.[5]

Next to leave were the Pribilof Islands Aleuts. One indication of the lack of coordination was the fact that the navy's *U.S.S. Oriole* reached St. Paul on 14 June to evacuate, only to learn that the army's *USAT Delarof* would reach St. Paul the next day. The villagers were told to pack, and on 16 June the 294 St. Paul Aleuts and 15 non-Aleut FWS employees embarked aboard *Delarof*. The transport reached St. George the same day. The natives had received their notice to pack on 14 June, which should not have taken them long, as they were permitted only "one suitcase per person and a roll of blankets." *Delarof* took off 183 Aleuts and seven non-Aleut FWS employees, leaving behind only a radio operator on St. Paul.[6]

This account gives the impression that the Pribilof natives had plenty of time to prepare, but that is not how Maryann Krukoff remembered it. The Krukoffs lived on St. George, where she was one of five brothers and five sisters. She was only ten at the time, but she recalled that her family had only about half an hour to get ready to go.[7]

---

* *Aleutian Invasion* gives this name as *Heather*.

Before leaving St. Paul, the island's physician, Dr. Berenberg, packed up "eight sealskin barrels of medical supplies and equipment," as well as the X-ray machine. When *Delarof* docked at Dutch Harbor on 17 June, the army ordered these items turned over to the hospital at Ft. Mears. There was no excuse for this high-handed action. The Pribilof people had no other medical facilities and soon would need them desperately. They were never replaced, nor were the owners compensated.

To make matters worse, the presence of the evacuees was "creating a food shortage" in Unalaska. So on 18 June, the Magees and eighty-one natives from Atka were added to the Pribilof population aboard *Delarof*. This ship had no means of separating the sick from the well, and a nasty grippe-like infection called "ship's cold" raced through the hold. The doctor from St. George seemingly believed that boarding ship absolved him of his Hippocratic oath. He refused to attend the sick, and would not even help with the birth of a baby. He remained aloof when the baby caught bronchial pneumonia and died. Dr. Berenberg and nurse Fredrika Martin tried their best, but, being unable to isolate the infected, they could make little progress.[8]

It is typical of this mismanaged operation that not until 16 June did the authorities settle upon relocation sites, much less make arrangements to make them liveable. One sensible decision was made: Aleuts of the same village should be housed together to retain the community integrity. Finally an agreement was reached to settle the Atkans at Killisnoo where there were "job opportunities in nearby canneries," while the Pribilof people would go to another disused cannery at Funter Bay, also at Chatham Straits. The OIA also secured "abandoned facilities of the Alaska Mining Company" across Funter Bay.[9]

After these two removals, a pause ensued, because Japanese intentions were unclear. Buckner recommended against further evacuations, but RADM Charles S. Freeman commanding the Alaska Sector directed that all natives be evacuated. The evacuees received only a few hours to prepare for the move. This group included Aleuts from Nikolski on Umnak, Akutan village on Akutan Island, and Makushin, Biorka, Chernofski, and Kashega on Unalaska.

Nikolski was the first village evacuated. On 5 July the army and navy took off seventy Aleuts, the non-Aleut OIA teacher and her husband, and the foreman of the Aleutian Livestock Company. The refugees—forty-one from Akutan, eighteen from Biorka, seventy-two from Nikolski, and nine from Makushin, "including one white"—sailed aboard the Alaskan Steamship Company's *S.S. Columbia.*[10]

The "one white" was Pete Olsen, a Norwegian by birth, and it is doubtful if anyone mourned his departure. He had the reputation for having a hair-trigger temper and had done time for assault. He was reputed to mistreat Aleuts, although some considered his stern measures justified in the absence of enough government officials to ensure "law and order." Henry Swanson, who apparently knew every human being in the Aleutians and apparently had total recall, conceded that Olsen "did good for the village but he also did a lot of bad." Swanson believed that Olsen was guilty of murder. "He was the only eyewitness once when several men disappeared."[11]

The turn of the Unalaska village Aleuts came on 19 July, when the *S.S. Alaska* docked at Captain's Bay. All persons of as little as one-eighth native blood had to leave, the only exceptions being those "employed by the civilian contractor or the military . . ." They could stay if they chose, and many did. Some, in fact, flatly refused to go. The officer in charge of the Unalaska evacuation was all for forcing them, but Cmdr. William N. Updegraf, in command of the naval station, refused permission. Thus, of Unalaska's 230 Aleuts, 189 were relocated.[12]

Instructions prior to departure were stringent. Depending upon its size, each family could pack a suitcase and a trunk. If it had no trunk, several suitcases could be used. A family could take only clothing. Every treasured possession had to be left behind, even icons that were priceless antiques from Czarist Russia as well as being of incalculable religious significance. Before the luggage could be locked, MPs went through it to insure compliance. This provision was both cruel and unnecessary. What possible harm could result from allowing these unhappy people the comfort of the family icon, a cherished book, or a child's favorite toy? Perhaps worst of all, they had to leave their pets behind. Only those who have shared their lives with a friendly animal could understand the very real depth of that grief.[13]

Originally the Aleuts went to Wrangell Institute, located six miles south of the city of Wrangell. At the time, this was the boarding school run by the OIA. The newcomers were divided, the men and boys to the dormitory, the women, girls, and children to tents. They ate together in the dining room. All were "examined, deloused, and given all sorts of shots." Eventually the residents of each village were settled in their destined locations—those from Akutan, Biorka, Kashega, Makushin, and Nikolski to Ward Lake, those from Unalaska to Burnett Inlet.[14]

Living conditions came as an intense shock, for these native Americans were not savages. In their Aleutian communities, many lived in comfortable homes with such amenities as electricity and indoor plumbing. So they were understandably resentful at finding themselves herded into locations offering neither schools, hospitals, churches, nor stores, and into housing with no electricity or plumbing, and they were so crowded that many had to sleep on the floor.[15]

Steve Stepetin of St. Paul expressed their sentiments: "The Aleuts wondered if they were the enemy, rather than American citizens, when they arrived. They were told not to leave the bay. Armed guards were posted. Quarters were terrible. People became sick and died from flu, tuberculosis, pneumonia and other diseases. One doctor, who visited the camp, said the Aleuts were kept in conditions which were 'unfit for pigs.'"[16]

Maryann Krukoff described living in what she called "blanket houses"—wooden frame structures with blankets hung to divide them into rooms. "The Aleuts were fed just like pigs practically." Day after day, the meals consisted of corned beef, boiled potatoes, and hot dogs. Young as she was, it was not lost upon Maryann that the few white people present "had fresh vegetables, fresh fruit, and a lot better living conditions."[17]

One refugee, Alexander Petroff, stated, "Right next to the kitchen, where we ate, was a meat locker . . . and next to that a slop chute for the kitchen garbage and people's waste buckets. I saw flies from the slop on the meat. I think that's when people started getting sick." Even the clams some tried to dig were contaminated from the "slop chutes" and from "outhouses perched above the shallows on stilts."

Nor surprisingly, such diseases as that Stepetin mentioned raged through the camps.[18] At Burnett Inlet, every man, woman, and child suffered from boils. A doctor told them that this meant their bodies were "getting used to a new atmosphere."[19]

Conditions of the St. Paul people at Funter Bay seem to have been particularly atrocious. The two dormitories were so crowded that many inhabitants had to sleep in relays. The other buildings were dilapidated beyond possibility of repair. "People fell through the rotten wooden floors. A single toilet on the beach just above the low water mark served ninety percent of the evacuees, whose clothes were laundered on the ground or sidewalks." No cleaning equipment or soap was available. Conditions were little better for the St. George evacuees. Yet one official actually wrote that the situation was "well in hand" and predicted that the Funter Bay camp would "serve as a model for others to be established later."

In October 1942 the Aleut women of St. Paul protested by a formal petition, pathetic in its sincerity. Predictably, "The women were told that under war conditions they could not expect to enjoy the comforts and conditions as they existed on the Pribilof Islands." And the superintendent in charge described what he had done to alleviate conditions. This cannot have been much. A full year later, in the fall of 1943, a group of officials, including Gruening, visited the camp, and the report of Dr. Berneta Block of the Territorial Department of Health could not have been more damning. But conditions did not improve for months.[20]

At that time, few able-bodied men remained in Funter Bay. Some had been drafted; others had returned to the Pribilofs, under compulsion, "to harvest the seal; they were told that if they did not, they would never see their homeland again." That left 281 women and children and 32 older men in camp. A doctor went with the sealers, but none was in camp when an epidemic of measles struck.[21]

The Atka Aleuts had a slightly better life at Killisnoo. The buildings were in bad shape, but cots were available, as were stoves with plenty of driftwood. There was a laundry, but very little water; rainfall became the "major source of supply." One bathtub and three privies served over eighty people. Even the stoves could not stave off the cold of 1942—the bitterest winter in fifty years—and some of the older people died. During the three years at Killisnoo, a doctor paid a four-month visit once, a nurse stayed two weeks. The doctor arbitrarily treated everyone in camp for VD without, according to testimony, checking to see who, if anyone, was infected.

Some of the Atka men took jobs, some were drafted. Once an Aleut was employed, he no longer received free food and clothing, and this was resented.[22]

The large group at Ward Lake was housed in a former camp of the Civilian Conservation Corps, with "nine small cabins and four communal buildings." The good news was that each cabin had a kitchen, a wood-burning stove, and two bunk beds in the bedroom. The Aleuts secured lumber from the Wrangell Institute and built furniture, even housing. The bad news was that the entire village shared an outhouse, a "long open trough without seats . . ." The laundry had two shower stalls and cold water faucets, but for hot water, one had to fill buckets from the cabin's outside faucet, heat it on the stove, then haul it to the laundry.

The only way to Ketchikan, eight miles away, was by taxi, but the only phone to summon one was in the OIA school, "and the teacher would not let the Aleuts use it." Help came in the form of one Eugene Wacker, who drove them to town and back for 35 cents each way, helped them find jobs and took them to and from work. He kept this up for the three years the Aleuts were at Ward Lake, and they were duly grateful. His actions were doubly commendable, for the townspeople feared contact with the Aleuts because of the infectious diseases at the camp. The proprietor of a lunch room asked the Ketchikan Police, Health and Sanitation chairman "whether or not she could refuse their patronage for the reason that they were unsanitary and diseased and thus obnoxious to her regular customers besides requiring an unusual amount of trouble in sterilizing this dishes. . . ."

Disease was indeed a problem. A doctor and nurse had found many ill, but, although they were diagnosed, the Aleuts testified that they were not treated. Twenty died in less than a year, and Ward Lake's death rate was "one of the highest of all the Aleut evacuation camps." Eventually the townspeople became more sympathetic as the circumstances became known.

On the plus side, schooling and jobs were readily available; nevertheless, as anthropologist Gerald Berreman wrote, most Aleuts at Ward Lake were unhappy: "Money, liquor, and movies were hopeless substitutions for the security of old and familiar ways. . . ."[23]

By contrast, the Unalaska Aleuts at Burnett had a somewhat easier lot. The original poor facilities were augmented when the OIA brought in materials sufficient to build a school, a church, and a few more homes. The men began building immediately.

The death toll at Burnett was not as high as at other sites. In part this was thanks to an Aleut midwife who not only delivered babies but treated various illnesses and accidental wounds.[24] Her daughter, Gertrude Svarney, remembered that the Aleuts "got her situated first so she could concentrate on everyone." Many of the accidents occurred as the men learned the hard way the unfamiliar task of cutting wood.

Mrs. Svarney added, "We built our own little church, a Russian church, and had our services there. . . . We also had pets; dogs and cats." Fortunately, when the time came to return, they were able to take these pets with them.

The men went hunting and fishing. There were many animals to watch—bears, porcupines, flying squirrels and frogs, the latter "a new sight for us." Gertrude was only twelve or thirteen years old then, and and principally remembered "the fun stuff." One summer she and her mother worked in a cannery. She made ninety dollars for the summer—"a lot of money then."[25]

Another prominent member of the Burnett community was Martha (Mrs. Kenneth) Newell, a feisty lady who had buried three husbands and was married to her fourth. Known to all Unalaska as "Ma Newell," she was the type who can be a community blessing or a pain in the neck, according to the point of view. Verne Robinson, deputy U.S. marshall at Unalaska, remembered that she would rout him out whenever she saw a problem. "She was a nuisance," he said, "but she was a big help. She was interested in helping people and she had a lot of principle. I had great respect for her."

She was not the sort of person to take conditions at Burnett lying down. On 18 March 1943 she wrote her husband, "If I am able to go back I'll walk the ocean. . . . We're all anxious to go home. . . . The Japs in the States . . . are probably treated better than we are." Writing again on 26 March, she charged him to contact Washington on behalf of the evacuees. "They practically treat us as if we were so dumb, or as aliens. . . ."

Mr. Newell accordingly passed her complaints to Anthony Dimond, Alaska's representative in Congress, who in turn interceded with the superintendent of OIA in Juneau. Dimond wrote warmly of Mrs. Newell, saying he knew her quite well and admired her.[26] Needless to say, the OIA did not accept her criticisms as true. Her complaint was "the first to our knowledge," and officials were sure that "the large majority" of the evacuees were "satisfied with the present conditions." The school teacher at Burnett, Edythe Long, responded angrily, "Mrs. Newell has a firm conviction that the more complaints she registers and the more dissatisfaction and discontent she can arouse among the evacuees here the sooner the Authorities will be obliged to send her back to Unalaska. Her entire being is centered on that one purpose—to go back to her home this spring, and it seems she will go to any lengths even to gross misrepresentation to attain this end. . . ."[27]

It should be stressed that none of this mistreatment of the Aleuts arose out of wanton cruelty or even malice. They had fallen victim to one of the constants of history—the tendency of the Establishment to regard anyone or anything different as *per se* inferior. Add to that tendency too many hands on the helm and galloping inefficiency, plus the sort of paternalism that in itself can be maddening. "The most galling and demeaning feature that many of us recall explicitly," testified Philemon Tutiakoff, "is that those in charge regarded us as incapable . . . of any form of decision making."[28] One senses in the official correspondence a sort of hurt bewilderment that these people could be so ungrateful as to complain of their lot.

Even when conditions were brought to official attention by non-Aleuts, the official reaction seems to have been fear of public opinion rather than concern for the evacuees. This is exemplified by a letter dated 28 October 1943 from Frank W. Hynes, assistant supervisor, to Ward T. Bower, chief of Alaska Fisheries:

> Censorship has kept the press off our necks thus far but this line of defense is weakening rapidly. A few days ago we were advised by one of the physicians who had inspected the camps and aided in emergency work there, that he was preparing a report to the Surgeon General of the U.S. and also to Secretary Ickes and has no intention of "pulling any punches." He warned that it was only a question of time until some publication . . . would get hold of the story and play it up, much to the disadvantage of the service and the Department of the Interior as a whole. He pointed out that the value

of this year's fur seal take from the Pribilofs would nearly equal the original purchase price for Alaska, yet the people who made it possible are being herded into quarters unfit for pigs; denied adequate medical attention; lack of healthful diet and even facilities to keep warm and are virtually prisoners of the Government, though theoretically possessing the status of citizenship. . . .[29]

Some problems were beyond solution short of return to the Aleutians. The climate at the camps was so different from that of the home islands that it was difficult to believe they were in the same Territory. "When it rained down there it rained straight down," reminisced Phil Tutiakoff. "That took some getting used to." The men of the 206th, homesick for the sight of a tree, could never have understood how these alien growths unnerved the Aleuts. They were accustomed to an uncluttered landscape of tundra and mountains; here, everywhere they turned, trees were in the way. For many, the distress amounted to claustrophobia. The trees "gave them a closed-in feeling; they couldn't see anything."[30]

With the recovery of Attu in May of 1943 and Kiska that August, it was obvious that the Japanese threat to Alaska, if it ever existed, had gone. Yet their benevolent-minded pharaohs still would not "let the people go." There was some talk of returning the Pribilof Aleuts in the fall of 1943, but they themselves declined for reasons that have never been determined, although it was certainly too late in the season to avoid drift ice, and supplies were not available on St. Paul and St. George. They returned the following summer.

Homecoming for the other Aleuts was delayed for a year, although the subject came up for discussion as early as April 1944. At that time the commander of the Alaska Sector advised the chief of Naval Operations that in view of the "impracticability" of securing qualified teachers, the difficulty in "supplying the villages and impossibility of prevention of intermingling with military personnel they are not desirous of returning Aleuts to the Aleutian Chain." At first the OIA supported this view, but soon shifted gears when higher officials, Gruening among them, advocated early return. Agreements were worked out and funds appropriated, but no other Aleuts were returned until April of 1945. No reason has yet been forthcoming for the delay.[31]

Among those who did not return alive was the redoubtable Mrs.

Newell. She died of pneumonia in February of 1945. In death as in life, she was controversial. She had asked that she not be buried in southeast Alaska, and her friends had quite a battle with the authorities to allow them to take her body back when they were repatriated to Unalaska. And once there, again they had "to argue with authorities in order to be allowed to off-load the casket and have the burial." But in the end, she had her way.[32]

It would be pleasant to state that the Aleuts returned to pick up the threads of life where they had left them. Unhappily, they found the ultimate insult awaiting them. Many of their homes were uninhabitable and had been thoroughly looted, although the villages had been under MP patrols. A survey taken of thirty-four such homes on Unalaska on 12 January 1944 indicated a shameful condition. Some damage had been the inevitable result of weather and rats. But that was minor:

> Inspection of contents revealed extensive evidence of widespread and wanton destruction of property and vandalism. Contents of closed packing boxes, trunks and cupboards had been ransacked. . . . Dishes, furniture, stoves, radios, phonographs, books, and other items had been broken or damaged. Many items listed on inventories furnished by the occupants of the houses were entirely missing.
>
> It appears that armed forces personnel and civilian alike have been responsible for this vandalism and that it occurred over a period of many months. . . .[33]

GIs had stripped the "surprisingly fine homes" of their plywood lining to line their foxholes. "Glass windows and frames appeared in observation foxholes. . . . Souvenir hunters grabbed choice items."[34] Evidently enlisted men were not the only looters. A range belonging to Sergei Savaroff of Nikolski turned up "at an officers' quarters in Umnak," and his dory had been taken to Chernofski.

As a result of these depredations, many Aleuts had to camp outdoors. Eventually the Unalaskans received army cabanas with which they seemed content enough until the cabanas had to be chained down lest they blow away. On Atka, where the navy had burned down the village, the natives lived for a year in crowded Quonset huts in "conditions worse than the camps."

The Aleuts were never fully recompensed, either by replacement items or with money. Figures cited for the refunds, supplies, and equipment were ridiculously inadequate. Significantly, the commission appointed to investigate the evacuation and relocation of the natives of the Aleutians was "unable to recover any further details of those expenditures, the disposition of claims filed, shipping lists, or other documents to verify or disprove the Aleuts' allegations."[35]

Of course, some losses could never be compensated. No money could pay for heirloom icons and holy lamps, native artifacts, or even the homely *lares* and *penates* sacred to every family everywhere. The ecology itself had suffered enormously. This was before the days of widespread concern for the environment and wildlife. Members of the armed forces and ships' crews killed for sport great numbers of seals, caribou, foxes, and other animals vital to the Aleut economy. The military had filled in herring-spawning lagoons on Unalaska; oil spills almost destroyed "pond and tidal-harvest foods."

The untimely deaths of so many older Aleuts struck at the very foundations of native culture. In the normal course of events, these people would have lived to pass on traditional skills in basketry, clothing, and skin boats. Now few remained to instruct the next generation. All these things added up to disruption of the Aleut way of life, and all North America was the poorer for this loss of cultural diversity.[36]

26

"But Duty Is Duty"

Throughout the summer of 1942, the Aleutian campaign continued on in its indecisive way. Day after day the records spell out the frustration: "Result not obtained"; "return with bombs due to weather"; "bombing mission canceled due to weather."[1]

If anyone could have reversed this trend it would have been Col. William O. Eareckson, who on 1 July 1942 assumed command of the newly activated XI Bomber Command. Eareckson was an intelligent, innovative, and inspirational leader, just as likely to be found on a bombing run as in his office. His citation for the DSC reads in part: "Instead of remaining in comparative safety at his headquarters, he repeatedly took to the air in direct personal attacks against the enemy, and personally filled gaps on numerous flights by acting in every capacity from first pilot to gunner."

He devised new techniques or adapted existing ones. His pilots learned to fly as low as ten feet off the water. His bombers would soar over the peak of Kiska's volcano as a reference point, calculate their distance, make a run, and drop bombs through the fog. Of course, such dead reckoning was not accurate, but it accomplished its purpose, which was to keep the Japanese off balance, and once in a while hit something if only by accident.

Even before activation of the XI Bomber Command, this tactic aroused the wrath of Admiral Theobald, who considered it an unacceptable waste of bombs and ordered blind bombing halted. The net result was that bombing was limited to clear days—possibly one or two a week—and gave the Japanese time to fortify Kiska strongly.[2]

By mid-July Theobald was ready to try his own luck against

Kiska. On 18 July he sortied Kodiak aboard the heavy cruiser *Indianapolis*, taking with him cruisers *Louisville*, *Honolulu*, *St. Louis*, and *Nashville*. By the twenty-second the ships were close to Kiska, but the fog was no kinder to Theobald than to Eareckson. He could not even see the island, much less bombard it. On the twenty-seventh he ordered a supporting strike by army and navy bombers, but they encountered a zero ceiling and turned back when Theobald's ships failed to appear. On 27 July, while retiring, two destroyer-minesweepers crashed into each other, and the destroyer *Monaghan* rammed a third. They could move, but barely, and Theobald had to call off the operation without firing a shot.[3]

Theobald received a wrist-slap from COMNORPACFOR for being at sea instead of in his headquarters. So on 3 August he turned his ships over to Rear Adm. William Ward "Poco" Smith for another try. At Smith's second approach, at 1934 on 7 August, the fog lifted. Under orders to stay well away from shore, Smith ordered six observation planes up to spot, while Eareckson's bombers hit the harbor. However, the SOCs were no match for the new Zero float-fighters—Rufes—and AA fire. One was shot down, another set down near *Indianapolis* with 167 bullet holes, *St. Louis*'s scouts could not find the cruiser and flew on to Umnak. The rest hid in the clouds.

To add insult to injury, the Japanese shore guns began to fire on the American ships—a classic case of mice attacking cats. Furious, Smith threw up such a heavy bombardment he used up his ammunition in seven minutes. He had to retire after inflicting minor damage.

The Japanese were not faring any better. Their aircraft were never an offensive threat after early July when Yamamoto withdrew the carriers and other capital ships from Hosogawa's force. They then had to rely on land-based planes, but of twenty-four fighters moved into Kiska about the same time, only two were operational sixty days later.[4]

None of this would have made very inspiring reading for the American public, and the army and navy cooperated in a policy of censorship as silly as it was ham-handed. Reputable journalists, such as Corey Ford, were sent out of the Aleutians shortly after the attacks on Dutch Harbor. Some tidbits of information did manage to get through. Keith Wheeler of the Chicago *Tribune*, the first correspondent accredited to the Alaska Theater, sent back sympathetic if unrevealing reports. One concerning the Dutch Harbor attack appeared in the *Arkansas Democrat* on 22 July 1942. He remarked, ". . . Dutch Harbor was ready for attack with everything but weather. Weather along the Aleutians is never favorable for anything but getting lost." He added that the Japanese "managed, believe it or not, to hit the only hospital in 500 miles."

Two days later his article gave glimpses of the servicemen in that area: "They lead as brutally hard, cheerless and dangerous a life as a man can. They have pared living down to its essentials—and these do not include baths, clean clothes or beds to sleep in."[5]

But hard facts weren't available. *Time* remarked sourly that the only news from that area came from Radio Tokyo. Alaskans found all references to their Territory snipped out of their newspapers and magazines. Even servicemen assigned to the Aleutians didn't know where they were going until they got there.[6] "We sit on the ground here and listen to news commentators and for the life of us can't match the two—except in place names and they don't even sound like we say them," Lieutenant Miller on Umnak wrote in his diary.[7]

As the authors of this policy should have anticipated, the news blackout backfired, breeding rumors and distrust. Senator A. B. "Happy" Chandler of Kentucky threatened to head an investigating committee to the Aleutians if the censorship wasn't eased up. What is more, the Senate Special Committee to Investigate the National Defense Program—famous as the Truman Committee, so-called because its chairman was Senator Harry S Truman of Missouri—suspected that the horrendous tales of Aleutian weather were part of a coverup to conceal poor leadership.

So off to Alaska flew a select team of senators, headed by Chandler and including Owen Brewster of Maine, Harold Burton of Ohio, and Mon Wallgren of Washington, together with some of their staff inspectors. They arrived on 17 August, which, by a demonical stroke of luck, happened to be a clear day. The senators thus saw the Aleutians as islands of green hills starred with wildflowers, vivid in the pure, clear air. After less than half a day in the archipelago, touching base at Umnak and Dutch Harbor, they returned to Washington, convinced "that reports of adverse weather in the Aleutians were exaggerated and possibly used as an excuse for poor performance." Chandler had statistics worked up to prove to his satisfaction that the North Atlantic was foggier than the Aleutians, and he denied that fog in the latter locale posed "a serious threat to bombers." When word of these extraordinary comments drifted back to the Aleutians, it gave birth to the phrase "senatorial weather" for any sunny day.

One good result came of this junket. Neither Theobald nor Gehres seems to have impressed Chandler favorably. So he recommended that Buckner "be given more authority over the Navy," plus a big increase in air power.[8]

The day after Chandler and his cohorts winged away, the artillery experienced a revision of its table of organization. A third battalion had been added to the 206th, the 250th had been "changed entirely," noted Bowen, "and some of their men are with us. . . ." Battery A was divided into two new batteries, I and K, while many men "and a lot of the best ones, were transferred to the new 'A' Btry which is now a 3" outfit." As part of the reorganization, specialists were changed to technicians, so Bowen became a t. corporal.[9]

The popular Captain Love was transferred to Battery C, much to Alspaugh's disgruntlement. "I can't see why the hell they don't quit changing officers in this regiment," he burst out. "Capt. Love was the best line officer this battery has ever had, and they have had some of the best. The entire battery hates to see Capt. Love leave us at this precarious time."

Captain Dodson replaced him,[10] and one must spare him a pang of retrospective sympathy. The officer who takes over from a very well-liked predecessor always goes through a period when his subordinates silently but definitely put him on trial.

Alspaugh had received notice he was to transfer to A Battery, greatly to his displeasure. "I sure hate to leave B Btry. I sure have become attached to some of the men in his organization and hate to bunk away but duty is duty. . . . I will just have to take it with a grin, pack up and move," he wrote on 30 July. So he was delighted when three days later Dodson told him that he was to stay in B Battery as a gun commander. "It sure was good news. I almost shouted."

Soon, however, he was transferred away from his gun and sent to the SCR section, where he would take charge as soon as the new table of organization went into effect.

Alspaugh was no complainer, and from his diary one gathers a rather favorable picture of life on Hog Island during the summer months. On 4 August the movie distributors sent them a first-class one for a change, Gary Cooper in his Academy-Award-winning portrayal of "Sergeant York." Most of the men on Hog Island went across the bay to see it.

Alspaugh went skating, climbed Ballyhoo with a buddy, attended school, worked on his gun platform, pulled guard and stood inspection, operated the SCR six hours a day, and late in August became an instructor in SCR school.

He also recorded some of the more picturesque rumors, such as: "We heard tonight that an American sub had slipped into a Japanese harbor and stayed for a month. An aircraft carrier was launched and the sub sent to [sic] torpedoes in its side sinking it."[11] Neptune only knows what started that story.

The reorganization meant a change in Drake's career. On the unfavorable side, he passed out of the orbit of Bruno Haustein, Morris Cove's excellent cook. Drake attributed the "high state of morale" among his men largely to Haustein's talents. He could even make powdered eggs palatable! Every night he prepared sandwiches and hot coffee for the lookout and radar operators. Occasionally he would go to Dutch Harbor, stay overnight, and return with "several cases of Prime-cut steaks and cans of various fruits with which to make pies." He never mentioned his source, but it was suspected that he had established diplomatic relations with someone, "probably a cook aboard one of the ships that made trips to Dutch Harbor on a regular basis."

On the plus side, on 15 August Drake and ten men left Morris Cove and returned to Ft. Mears to establish three new units of the 206th—Headquarters Third Battalion, and Batteries I and K. This reorganization was to provide additional AA power for the Regiment. "Battery I was designated a Provisional gun battery and equipped with new 90 mm state-of-the-art aircraft guns with automatic shell-loading capabilities." The commanding officer was Capt. William C. Ruchman, and Drake, having been promoted, became first sergeant—the youngest on the island. He was 20 years old. Initially Battery I consisted of 3 officers and 122 men, and was located in Unalaska Valley, some 2 miles south of the town of

Unalaska. Battery K maintained the searchlight positions and the radar site at Morris Cove. According to Drake, "The ensuing months were uneventful. . . ."[12]

The fishing season was in full swing, especially for halibut, which could reach astounding size. The men fished for food as well as for sport, because the cold storage at Dutch Harbor had been destroyed in the raids and all the frozen meat lost. "Sergeants Hooker and Arnold acquired a small boat and motor from a civilian," Jodie Jones reminisced.

> When they went to OCS, Paul Brown from Texas, Fred Gilbert from Georgia and I acquired this boat. My dad sent me a red line, etc. Other equipment was available from the supply sergeant. Between Hog Island and the main base we caught lots of halibut. While anchored out in the bay it was a common occurrence for schools of whales to come dangerously close. We ignored them and they let us alone. . . . Brown caught one halibut while fishing from the bank that was over six feet long. It fed the whole battery of 200 men. It took three men to land this fish.[13]

Weese remembered the "Hog Island Special" well. He considered halibut fishing rather tame—"just hook 'em and pull 'em in"—and preferred going after sea bass. But he remembered a spectacular halibut catch—undoubtedly Brown's feat: "Two men using a throw line on the bank at Hog caught a 120 lb. halibut abut 100 yards from the mess hall. The whole battery enjoyed that for a few days."[14]

Pack was not a fisherman, but one day when he and some friends were out hunting, a commercial fisherman asked if they would like a halibut he had caught, weighing 150 lbs. "We said we sure would. . . . So we went to the mess hall and the cook was so proud of that fish. He was able to feed the whole battery with that fish. Man, it was good!"[15]

The latter part of August saw the annual salmon run. On 21 August, Alspaugh and a friend crossed to Captain's Bay to watch. "There were thousands of salmon fighting their way upstream to spawn. The water was about a foot or a foot and a half in depth and clear and cold." A week later Alspaugh went back, and found the salmon "just as thick now as they were a week ago." But he saw more dead salmon this time.[16] During the run, fishing for salmon was even easier than catching halibut. One simply waded into the stream and stabbed them with a bayonet or hunting knife.[17]

Perhaps the most unpleasant feature of summer in the Aleutians had come and gone. In early summer, mosquito larvae emerged from the tundra and around early July the larvae became full-fledged mosquitos, and, as Drake put it, "a mass invasion of the islands began. The mosquito phenomenon lasted about two weeks," he added, "and after mating and laying eggs in the ground, they all die, thus completing their life cycle until another year."[18]

They lasted rather longer on the Alaskan mainland. "The snow was hardly gone before the mosquitoes were out in force," stated Campbell. "These were not the usual size mosquitoes that we were accustomed to, they were very, very large, their legs being one-half inch long." He glued one onto a letter to his mother to show the home folks just how big these insects were.[19] Wilson remarked that at Ladd Field "mosquitoes hovered in 'clouds,' and one attracted their attention at one's peril." The 206th men at Fairbanks would soon move to Ford Richardson at Anchorage, where Wilson would find mosquitos to be no problem.[20]

For a brief time, however, they had contact with what, to them, was an exotic form of life, namely Russians. Arrangements had been made to supply the Soviet Union with aircraft, but Stalin would not permit U.S. personnel to fly over Soviet territory. So the Americans ferried the planes as far as Ladd Field, where Soviet crews took over.[21] S. Sgt. Gaines Parker remembered them as hard-drinking men ready to take dare-devil risks. He recalled that the money they used was the old, large U.S. bills.[22]

In his ferrying days, Colonel, then Lt. James F. Brewer, met many Russians and Canadians. "The former seemed quite ill-trained, poorly dressed and only marginally equipped to be flying in that area of the world," he remarked. "Their losses were excessive. Their crew supervisors were a surly lot, I'm sure because of envy over our American 'goodies.'" The Canadians were another story— "quite similar to us as to training and life style. Even the Mounties were a friendly, affable bunch."[23]

Capt. John T. Meek—probably the only man of the 206th to serve at both Dutch Harbor and Fairbanks—had to assert himself against an example of Russian arrogance. As a graduate of VMI in electrical engineering, he was pulled out of Battery H and assigned to Post Utilities. In that capacity, he was instructed "to prepare office space for the Russian Mission" by 1700 on a certain day. One hour early, a Russian colonel came in with his interpreter. The latter asked if the office was ready. "No," replied Meek, "I don't have the space cleaned up, and don't have the office equipment, but will have it by five P.M."

To this the Russian shot back, "If you don't have it ready in fifteen minutes I will report you to the Commanding Officer." This triggered Meek's temper. Striding up to the interpreter, he barked, "Get the hell out of here and stay out until five P.M.!" The two Russians left, but within fifteen minutes the interpreter returned and inquired in a much milder tone, "Don't you have part of it ready?" Again Meek answered, "No, but it will be ready at five P.M."

That night Meek related the incident to the commanding officer, who told him, "That's all right, if we don't stand up to them they will run us off the Post."

The next morning, walking along the sidewalk, Meek encountered the interpreter, who stopped, shook hands, and said pleasantly, "Let us let bygones be bygones. Some day we will help you whip the Japanese."[24]

Wilson saw the newcomers on base and in town buying watches. "They saluted everybody from U.S. privates up!" He found the Russians impressive, on the whole, despite their baggy uniforms.

He never had any direct contact with them, but witnessed a rather peculiar incident, which he recorded in his diary on 18 August 1942. He had stopped at a watch shop to pick up one of his friends' timepieces. Two Russian flyers came in to buy a watch. The shopkeeper, a Russian himself, was talking to the senior of the two fliers in their native tongue when his wife asked a question in English "about a red star decoration of some sort on his chest." According to Wilson, "he looked her right in the eye with the expression of a king being addressed by a leper. A look of cold contempt." The shopkeeper translated for her, but the Russian uttered not a word. Obviously embarrassed, the husband put the same question to the junior officer. This one "grinned good-naturedly" but he too kept silence.[25]

It would be interesting to know what there was about a friendly, natural question to trigger such a response. Perhaps they had been cautioned against appearing friendly with Americans. For those were Stalinist days. The Great Red Father was not at all averse to accepting U.S. aid, but preferred to conduct business by remote control.

In any case, H Battery's contact with the Russians was brief. Early in September 1942 the unit moved from Fairbanks to Anchorage.

27

"A Little Lift"

If the diaries of Lieutenant Miller and Sergeant Stubbs can be taken at face value, life on Umnak was considerably more dismal than at Dutch Harbor or on the mainland. Later Miller wrote:

> No Japs for the 153rd Infantry. Plenty of Japs for the Air Force, a few Japs for the Navy. None for the doughfeet. . . . On good days the Air Force takes off on the milk run. On bad days they stay home. Every day the 153rd Infantry stays home. And works on those damn positions. And builds roads and unloads more ships and stacks more rations. And stand lonely guard. They are low in morale and spirit. In August they get a little lift when they get Quonset huts to live in and depart forever their flapping tents.[1]

A good example of how the routine mixed with the tragic is Stubbs's entry for 27 June: "Had tent inspection this morning. Lt. Snyder complimented us on our tent. A P-38 plane caught fire and crashed here this morning. The pilot was killed. Had milk and corn bread for supper. Pretty good."

Throughout July Stubbs and his buddies dug foxholes with monotonous regularity. He attended various schools and occasionally went fishing. But one has the impression that the main breaks in the monotony were letters and packages from home. On 28 July he could write of their move into the Quonset huts. "We are really proud of our new home."

Death had touched this island of healthy young men several times since the June accident. Two Canadian fliers, who had crashed on Unalaska, were buried at Umnak on 23 July. Then on 7 August Stubbs served on the ceremonial firing squad for the funeral of "a man from the Quartermaster that committed suicide." Two days later, a friend substituted for Stubbs at the funeral of another quartermaster soldier who had been run over "and killed by a caterpillar." Again on 9 September, "The Company sent a firing squad to the funeral of another Air Corps man that committed suicide." The principal impression that Stubbs's diary conveys, however, is not tragedy but grinding boredom.[2]

During this period, the more articulate Miller used his diary less to record events than to sort out his opinions, ranging from self-examination to how the war effort should be run. He had what a later generation would call a love/hate relationship with his environment:

> You know something, up here the weather can reverse itself while you look at it! . . . What else can you expect in a country where islands appear and disappear at odd times, where winds from two oceans meet to batter each other, where one day are thousands of birds and the next day none, where volcanoes still smoke in terrestrial gut-rumblings and belchings? It's a great place, these Aleutians and I want to see more of them some day. . . . Alaska will be a young man's opportunity when the Defense highway is built to Fairbanks.

Yet within a few paragraphs he was disenchanted with Umnak and wanted to go somewhere else, anywhere else. "Hell, I'd go to Berlin tomorrow by parachute, I'm so fed up here. . . ."[3]

What he saw as the monumental misuse of his infantrymen frustrated him: "We could be a valiant, hardy force of troops . . . instead of a half-sick group of stevedores.

"So little of our work has been permanent. We have dug fortifications and move them and filled them up and dug others. We have done manual labor when machines sat idle. . . ."

His bitterness extended to the GIs of whom he had been so proud. On a long hike he was dismayed because "we had man after man falling out in only a few miles of walking over roads with nothing but his rifle, gas mask and ammunition. Why? What's happened to those tough young apes who galloped all over this tundra before we had roads? . . . Tough, hell—no enthusiasm, no chatter, never a song—all these hillbillies can think . . . of is getting home to the farm and never leaving it again."[4]

One prospect sent a shaft of light across this gloomy picture—the word that fifteen-day leaves to the states would be given, and those who, like Miller, had been in the Aleutians six months or longer would have priority. He looked forward to being home if only for such a short time—"I might get married even." Nevertheless, he was somewhat supercilious toward the enlisted men who also anticipated a homecoming with delight: "The word of the furloughs has spread like wildfire and it is pitiful the way these farm boys almost cry to get home to some run-down li'l ol' cotton farm and their mules. You'd think that at least a few of them would appreciate getting away from Ark. red dust but apparently they don't. And about 90% of them will marry the first thing that goes by wearing skirts if she is old enough to pick cotton. . . ."[5]

For the 206th, the difficult decision as to which of so many deserving men should be granted leave was left to a lottery.[6] "The fall of 1942 they drew names from the whole 206th from a hat for furlough and my name was drawn," Paulus remembered. He sailed to Seattle aboard *Otsego* on a somewhat unnerving voyage. "It had a hole in the bow where it had rammed a Canadian Navy boat and it was a coal burner, so it couldn't go in convoy. We went alone with a trail of black smoke following us."[7]

Corporal O'Neal was also among the lucky ones, and had five or six days in Little Rock. While waiting at Seattle to return to Dutch Harbor, he served as a guard for a radar unit.[8] Albright's name was drawn, too. He recalled that the leave consisted of fifteen days from arrival in Seattle and, of course, from home back to Seattle. He went to Little Rock "and married Maxine—still have her."[9]

According to Alspaugh, a total of sixteen men were selected. He noted on 1 September, "Sgt. Beverburg and Cpl. Dodds of my section left today on a fifteen-day furlough in the states. I sure was glad to see them go. They haven't been much good since they found out they were going." A whiff of sour grapes hovers over that comment, but a few days later he had recovered his customary good nature, writing on 4 September, "The last group of men to go home on furlough will leave tomorrow. They are an elated group of men."[10]

Both Beverburgs were among the fortunate few. Captain Beverburg had made arrangements to be married to his college sweetheart on his first trip home, and the wedding took place as planned.[11]

Corporal Anderson had an adventure on his leave, but did not recall the date. He had the usual fifteen days—"five days on train to Little Rock, five days at home, five days return to Ft. Lawton." The ship taking him back to Dutch Harbor collided with a tanker in Puget Sound. Although considerably damaged, the troop ship limped back to Seattle, and five days later Anderson was again bound for Dutch Harbor, this time aboard the old *St. Mihiel.*[12]

Meanwhile, a major project was under way. For some time, DeWitt and Buckner had urged the establishment of bases closer to the Japanese-held positions. The AAF's General Butler preferred Tanaga Island, because he believed an airfield could be built there fairly rapidly, as opposed to Theobald's choice of Adak. The latter island had a good harbor at Kuluk Bay, but it had such poor terrain that Butler estimated four months would be required to build an airfield.

The decision was left to the Joint Chiefs of Staff, who decided in favor of the navy, and on 21 August Gen. George C. Marshall instructed the army to go along. The next day, the JCS designated 30 August as D-Day. One week left precious little time to make plans and prepare for the occupation, but perhaps it was just as well—there was no time for bickering and arguments. The project was code-named Fireplace, with Rear Adm. John W. Reeves in charge of the navy's portion and Brig. Gen. Eugene H. Landrum heading the army's occupation force. Their job was to land four thousand men on Adak.[13]

The initial problem was to discover whether there were any Japanese on the island. Every once in a while they sent out small landing parties to various islands, including Adak, but no one on the American side knew whether or not the Japanese were still there. Here was a job for the Alaska Scouts, headed by two of Butler's best intelligence officers, Col. Lawrence V. Castner and Maj. William J. Verbeck. Both were old Alaska hands, and with four experienced sergeants they formed the cadre of a small but select group of volunteers. These volunteers went through a strenuous commando course; however, Operation Fireplace would be their first combat assignment.

The personnel included "anthropologists, doctors, engineers, fishermen, hunters, prospectors, Aleuts, Eskimos, Indians . . ." Most sported beards, wore parkas, carried knives and rifles, and altogether looked like they had been rounded up by a Hollywood casting director for a war movie starring Errol Flynn. Evidently they had two things in common—they knew Alaska and the Aleutians as few men did, and they had scant respect for military discipline. Someone had christened them "Castner's Cutthroats," and the name stuck.

Two officers and thirty-five men boarded the submarines *Triton* and *Tuna* on the night of 28 August. When about a mile off Adak, they piled into rubber boats, entered Kuluk Bay, and beached the rafts. For the remainder of the night they fine-combed the island, finding neither Japanese nor any sign of a recent Japanese expedition. Evidently the enemy had decided to leave Adak to its normal population of bald eagles and ravens. The next morning Castner posted an agreed-upon "all-clear" signal for a PBY. As soon as the reconnaissance aircraft had cleared Adak's air space, it radioed the news to Kodiak.[14]

Landrum's invasion force was waiting aboard two transports, and units of the 807th Engineer Aviation Battalion with their equipment were distributed on an assortment of miscellaneous craft including fishing scows, barges, tugs, even a yacht. They landed as scheduled on 30 August and promptly set to work.

That same day, Buckner's senior engineer, Col. Benjamin Talley, his immediate subordinate, Lt. Col. Leon B. deLong, and Gehres flew to Adak aboard a PBY, but the weather did not permit landing, and Gehres directed that they go to Atka, where the seaplane tender *Casco* lay at anchor in Nazan Bay. As the storm seemed unlikely to lessen, Gehres asked that *Casco*'s guard destroyer, *Reid*, take Talley and deLong to Adak. The storm made a submarine attack almost impossible.[15]

This questionable decision almost cost Gehres his seaplane tender and his own life, for a Japanese submarine was already in Nazan Bay. *RO-61* had slipped in early the previous morning, intent on torpedoing *Casco*. Then *Reid* had appeared and effectively if unwittingly cut off the submarine's escape route. Her skipper settled her on the bottom, where she had to remain until her air was on the verge of choking the crew.

The skipper was trying to decide between surrendering or making a desperate attempt to sink both ships with *RO-61*'s two torpedoes when he received word that the destroyer was pulling out. *Reid* had barely cleared the horizon when *RO-61* surfaced and fired her torpedoes. The first missed the target and beached harmlessly. The second, however, smashed amidships on *Casco's* port side, killing five men and inflicting serious damage. Quantities of fuel oil and gasoline surged overboard. One of the life buoys activated its flare.

It was a nasty moment. If the flames touched off the fuel, *Casco* would be trapped in a sea of flame. Then came one of those incidents men remember and talk of for years. Aviation Ordnanceman J. Cobean dived overboard, struggled through the oil slick to the buoy, and held the flare under water until it went out. *Casco's* skipper beached her for future repair.

PBYs from Dutch Harbor sought and found *RO-61;* their bombs did not sink her, but opened seams through which oil escaped. *Reid,* en route back to Atka, followed the slick and sank her, taking five prisoners.[16]

Alspaugh took due note of this feat in his diary entry for 1 September: "The navy sunk a sub on the other side of Atka. Five survivors of the sub were captured and are to be brought here."[17] Massey noted their arrival but not the date beyond the month of September.[18] Bowen gave a longer account in his entry for 3 September: "A Japanese sub was sank near Unimak today. It torpedoed a tender and was reported. A PBY picked up the message and dropped depth charges, making one hit. The PBY radioed for a destroyer which finished the job and ran the sub on the rocks. Five of the crew were picked up and were brought here as prisoners of war."[19]

Obviously the sinking of a Japanese submarine and the capture of five survivors was a definite break in routine for the men of the 206th.

Meanwhile, a minor miracle was under way at Adak. Landing had not been easy in the howling gale, and many tons of valuable equipment went to the bottom, including the steel mat intended for the runway. The job of bringing order out of chaos fell to Carl "Squeaky" Anderson, captain of the Fort at Dutch Harbor, "said to be the only sailor alive who really knew Aleutian waters." In an amazingly short time, Squeaky had the beach organized, with a place for everything and everything in its place. Within eighteen hours, Landrum had landed his men, ordnance, and equipment and had them set up.

Before the landing had even been completed, engineers and scouts were searching for an airfield site. One of the latter suggested, half-jokingly, that the lagoon in Sweeper Cove might do. The officers seized upon the idea. Testing proved the basin to be flat. The fact that it flooded at high tide was a minor detail to the engineers. They constructed a dam, dikes, and a gate made from anything available. The next day, the engineers left the gate open until the tide pulled out, then slammed shut the gate.

Butler had estimated four months would be required to finish an airport on Adak; the 807th completed it in ten days. On 10 September, Eareckson—who else?—was the first to land on the new strip, code-named Longview. He deserved the honor, for he and his bombers had kept the Japanese too busy at Kiska to send out any reconnaissance missions that might have discovered the activity at Adak.[20]

Henry Swanson crossed swords with a colonel who was inspecting outposts, including a small radio shack at a spot off Adak. The site had no beach. "We used to land in the crack in the cliff with a dory," Swanson explained. "They'd put down a rope and haul the stuff up." On this particular day, the sea was much too rough for this maneuver, which under the best of conditions must have been rather like threading a needle, with a damaged dory the price of failure. Nevertheless, the colonel ordered, "Run the boat in there and I'll jump off." Swanson countered, "You can jump off if you want but I'm not going in with the boat." And he offered to move on to another bay.

The colonel was furious, and when they returned to Adak he reported Swanson to the officer in charge of the Army Tug and Barge Company, a major. The major heard him out, then said mildly, as befitted a major disagreeing with a colonel, "If Henry said you couldn't land there, you couldn't land." In a huff, the colonel went up the line to Squeaky Anderson, a good friend of Swanson's. Squeaky's reply was almost identical to the major's, but delivered much more forcefully. Pounding on his desk, he thundered in his odd accent, "When Henekee says you can't land, YOU CAN'T LAND!"

Later, after the colonel lost three men trying to land in big surf, "[he] got real tame. . . . He just wouldn't land anywhere, even if it was calm. . . ." Swanson added thoughtfully, "He might have been a good colonel, doing colonel's business, but he was a dumb colonel doing sailor's business."[21]

Oddly enough, at this time the Japanese were also engaged in a major move. Their current strategy was to hold their Aleutian garrisons only until winter, when they would move to the Kuriles. In this context, Hosogaya's mission was strictly a temporary holding one, so he decided that the Attu garrison was redundant. On 27 August he began its transfer to Kiska, completing the operation on 16 September. The Americans did not discover this move until the 1,500 Attu troops had reached Kiska. Hosogaya gambled that the Americans would be so absorbed in neutralizing Kiska that they would not bother about Attu. In this he was correct, unfortunately for his opponents. Soon the Japanese would change their minds and reoccupy Attu, but for about six weeks the Americans could have taken Attu and garrisoned it strongly at no loss of human life. As it was, recapture of Attu in 1943 would be an exceedingly costly operation in terms of manpower.[22]

All this activity had little or no effect upon the men of the 206th. "Weather socks in, wind terrific and cold bringing snow," noted Massey. "Several pieces of tin sucked from our Quonset hut, this damn weather is worse than the war. . . . I miss the sunshine and sunrise." But there was one compensation: "The northern lights are beautiful. . . ." This unit went on alert when unidentified planes were sighted, but they turned out to be P40s—"beautiful and graceful."[23]

Two earthquakes shook the Dutch Harbor area early in September. "There was a slight earthquake here this afternoon," wrote Bowen, "but we all thought it was dynamite until a bulletin came out on it. However, we commented at the time that it must have been a heavy charge."[24] Alspaugh confirmed this early mistaken impression: "They set off a charge of dynamite at Ballyhoo this morning. It was a nice blow job."[25]

There could be no question, however, about the second tremor. "We had an earthquake this afternoon," Alspaugh recorded. "It lasted for several seconds and shook tons of rock loose from Ballyhoo. The landslide lasted for 3 or 4 minutes. I believe it was the strongest quake we have had here."[26]

"Had a pretty strong earthquake this afternoon," Bowen confirmed. "I was in the shop working when it started and felt the hut begin to shake so I ran out the back door to look around No damage was done but it was a funny feeling. A large landslide was started on the steep side of Ballyhoo but it all fell in the Bay."[27]

A heavy storm on 15 September destroyed the dory. Heavy rollers smashed two docks to splinters and washed away the causeway that had just been started from Ballyhoo to Hog Island.[28]

In mid-September both of the diarists went to the harbor to see a transport and a destroyer that had collided in a fog on the night of the eighteenth. Alspaugh was mainly interested in the transport, which had "quite a hole in her side." He continued, "One or two holds were full of water and she was down past the water mark on the stern end. They are going to weld some plates on her and take her back to Bremerton."[29] Bowen noted that both ships would have to go into drydock. What is more, "the destroyer was new, had not even been commissioned."[30]

Storms, earthquakes, collisions in the fog—no doubt about it, the brief Aleutian summer had ended, and the 206th would have to brace itself for another subarctic winter.

28

"The Worst Storm of the Tour"

We bombed hell out of Kiska yesterday and today," wrote Miller jubilantly, "with fleets of bombers and fighters from our new field at Atka. They blew the place apart today, getting 7 ships, 2 or 3 subs, several aircraft, and 30 fighters strafed the camp. Two of our 38s collided—one pilot saved by PBY. . . ."[1]

While thirteen B-24s and one B-17 do not exactly qualify as "fleets of bombers," and the raid sank two minesweepers rather than seven ships, in the main Miller was surprisingly correct.[2]

At this time the volatile lieutenant was quite happy. The weather had been beautiful, Umnak was "no longer the last outpost," and Miller had been transferred to H Company, "the heavy weapons company as 2nd in command." The men of H Company impressed him: "They come from a different section of Ark. and many are college men. They've a different spirit than the farm lads."

But a few days later he was fulminating, "I wonder when an army is going to justify its existence? It seems to me that an army created to do a specific job should spend most of its efforts in attaining that objective. Instead, we see today the bewildering and slightly odorous picture of a machine so bound up in red tape and restrictions of its own making that it is likely that it spends 75% of its effort in maintaining itself. . . ."[3]

It is true enough that the army in Alaska suffered from an overabundance of red tape, thanks to the complicated command channels. Craven and Cate cite as an example, "a recommendation that a certain bomber be sent to the States for overhaul was turned down because securing permission for this simple operation would eat up a month of valuable time."[4]

Nevertheless, elsewhere the war was hotting up. The struggle for Guadalcanal, with the attendant naval action, was in full swing; bombers stationed in the United Kingdom were striking strategic targets in Europe; the 10th Air Force was harassing the Japanese in China; Operation Torch would soon begin in North Africa.[5]

Miller's diary indicates that this officer was not free of race prejudice: "Despite all I know to the contrary, I can't keep from feeling that they [the Japanese] are just apes in trousers, monkey-men who have somehow stumbled onto the secrets of modern 'civilization.'"[6]

Of more direct interest to Stubbs was the fact that on 26 September Bob Hope, Frances Langford, and the rest of Hope's little troupe visited Umnak. "Frances may be the only woman to ever set foot on this island," Stubbs noted.[7] The next day, Alspaugh recorded, "Many of the men went across the bay today to see Bob Hope. He is here for a short visit."[8] Several other men remembered Hope, but the lack of follow-up comment indicates that he did not establish with these troops the same rapport as had Joe E. Brown.

In the latter part of September Miller had another grievance: "We have a brand new BG here who is some stuff if you ask him and together with his Ex O he has made life a living hell for any honest Infantryman. . . . The Man is cute. He sees the extreme unlikelihood . . . of a Jap attack and so is concentrating his efforts to building a pretty post rather than on something as intangible as training. We are actually using our supplies of defensive barbwire ONLY to build neat fences around our company areas." (Miller's capitals.) Yet the base still lacked such essentials as electricity or running water. What is more—and this particularly grated on Miller—there had never been an American flag flown over the post. "If we are to fight in some desolate spot for America, Lord let us at least have a piece of bunting to occasionally remind us of the land we love."[9]

Stubbs's diary confirms that the 153d had fallen into the hands of someone overly concerned with the superficialities of military life. Stubbs spent days "graveling walks and sodding the area." On 15 October he wrote, "We have 30 minutes of Military Courtesy school every night now." He added in indignant italics: *"A hell of a note."* Five days later he observed, "Sgt. Keeter and I went out and punched holes in the bayonet course so the Colonel would think we had been using it." To add to the woes of the men on Umnak, wind, rain, and snow were becoming the rules rather than the exception.[10]

Over on Hog Island, on 1 October Alspaugh and his friend Whalen "finally made sergeants. It took us quite a while but there just weren't any gun sergeants' openings in the Battery." The next evening the men in his hut had a little celebration of the occasion.[11]

On 3 October Bowen visited two Russian submarines. He tried to talk to some of the men but did not have much luck. One or two could speak a little English. "They turned out wholesale for the show and all of them were clean, well barbered and well dressed."

Five days later, while Bowen was eating dinner, a man from K Battery borrowed Bowen's Cat and trailer without permission. "About two o'clock he called up and said it was stuck." Bowen and another man went to see what could be done. "The trailer had been turned over and the Cat was stuck. Before it was over, we had the Cat out but lost the trailer down a 200' embankment and it was a total loss. Tomorrow we will salvage the remains. I told Lt. Langley about it and he was swell under the conditions of about $100,000 gone for the U.S." So the next day they spliced two cables together and pulled the trailer back up the hill, but Bowen didn't think it was worth the trouble. He added rather gloomily, "We are behind in everything and losing ground every day. We are going to have to move the SCR to the top of the hill which will be a big job."

Bowen's last entry was a routine one dated Sunday 18 October.[12] On Tuesday the twentieth, this fine, intelligent young soldier lost his life in line of duty, along with a comrade, Sgt. James Allen. Bowen was well liked and respected, and his accidental death "was very hard on all the members of B Battery," as Weese said.[13] His death hit Alspaugh particularly hard, and he paid tribute to his friend in his diary:

We lost one of the best men that has ever been in the battery today. John Bowen was drowned down on the beach this afternoon trying to save some of our dock that was about to float off. Sgt Allen of G Btry also lost his life in attempting to tie the dock down.

It came so suddenly the whole island was shocked when they learned of the disaster. A large wave came in, knocking the men down and washing them and the approach out in the bay. There was no available means at our disposal to rescue them.

John was, without a doubt, one of the finest lads I have ever known. He and I lived together for several months in the same hut and I learned to like John more and more the longer I knew him.[14]

Sergeant Weese "was watching from a distance as were others— John jumped on the debris with the cable but the wave action caused him to lose his balance and fall in the water on the side away from the beach. He was wearing his boots and a heavy lined parka and once he went under he never appeared on the surface. All around were helpless to do anything." He added a comment that makes the tragedy more acute: "The men were using their own initiative to salvage the debris and could just as easily [have] ignored it."[15]

Joseph C. Johnston, who was working with Allen and Bowen that day, later gave Massey an eyewitness account which Massey relayed as follows:

> The dock was on pilings but not secured very good. Stormy waves washed the dock off the pilings and was slamming it against the island shore. The men thought they could secure it by using a 6x6 truck cable winch. They made a loop on end of cable and when the wave went back out the three ran to the dock (which was floating) and tried to put loop around the dock but was not quick enough. The next wave caught them. Allen and Bowen were on end of cable. Johnston was third man up from the end and was able to hang on cable. The other two was washed out with wave. One came up briefly but no one could tell which one. They were never seen again. The tragedy happened on north side of the pilings.[16]

Jodie Jones was in the truck repair shop when a sergeant rushed in with the news. "We ran to the scene but there was nothing we could do. In minutes they were gone. Navy rescue boats patrolled the site until there were no hopes of survival." Jones added rather bitterly, "The weather was bright and clear the next morning. The bay was as calm as a lake." Jones "searched the beach around the island but to no avail."[17]

During this period, over on Amaknak, a williwaw, striking on 18 October, had forced four navy men to seek shelter with the Battery A soldiers at Hill K-7, located between the Natukan and Makusin rivers. These were two pilots—Lieutenant Mione and Ensign Blakeley—with two enlisted men, who "had been out goose hunting and their small boat broke down." They asked to stay until the

244 THE WORST STORM OF THE TOUR

weather cleared. Of course, Battery A was happy to extend its hospitality, especially as the visitors shared their geese with their hosts, "and were they good!"

The navy men stayed at K-7 for three days. Thenceforth, whenever they went up on a flying mission, "they came over our position and really put on a show for us," wrote Luster Tate. Some two weeks later, however, Mione called Tate on the field phone to tell him they were leaving. That was all the information he could give. That afternoon, they "buzzed us a couple of times," Tate recalled, "and headed out to sea." Tate and his companions often wondered if their navy friends survived the war.[18]

Alspaugh made no diary entries from 25 October through 17 November. Miller, too, found nothing to write about between 24 September and 27 November. But plenty was going on in the upper echelons. The landing of American forces on Adak, then Atka, Sequam, and Tanaga in the Andreanofs seemed to threaten the Japanese home islands, so the Japanese High Command reversed its Aleutians policy. Rather than pull out for the winter, the Japanese would keep their foothold in that archipelago.

Lt. Col. Hiroshi Yanekawa would head a group to regarrison Attu and if possible build an airfield. An infantry battalion was scheduled for nearby Shemya, and another battalion would take Amchitka, also in the Rat Islands. On 29 October the Japanese landed on Attu, and the forces were soon in position. They had enough time, for the Americans did not know of this development until 7 November* when an aircraft spotted the Japanese on Attu.

Meanwhile, Hosogaya's ships conveyed the other landing parties toward Shemya and Amchitka. But the sight of a B-24 overhead, plus a message from headquarters warning that "a strong U.S. Navy task force had recently moved into the Aleutians" changed his mind for him, and he took the convoy back to the Japanese base at Paramushiro.[19]

This was quite unnecessary. Japanese intelligence had misinterpreted bits and pieces of U.S. messages. Nimitz was simply directing Theobald to ready the North Pacific Force to oppose the Shemya and Amchitka landings. Far from having a powerful new

---

* Coincidentally, the day the invasion of North Africa began.

task force at his disposal, Theobald had even less than his usual slim complement. *Honolulu, Louisville,* and *St. Louis* had been transferred to the Guadalcanal Theater, while six of his destroyers had been whisked away to the Pacific Coast, there to be converted into transports. Hosogaya's convoy was modest, but in a showdown probably could have defeated Theobald's force handily.[20]

Late in October, Meek transferred from Fairbanks to Dutch Harbor, and met with Massey's approval: "We got a new Battery C.O., Capt. Meeks [sic]. . . . Meeks is different, I like him, he's stern and fair."

A freighter limped in, having been rammed by a destroyer. "Boy, what a hole in that baby!" was Massey's awe-struck comment. The dock officers told the men they could have anything they unloaded, and Massey's outfit fell heir to a five-gallon can of good coffee, enough to supply the entire battery.

A williwaw set in, forcing the men to lean far over against it to walk. "A small piece of plywood comes out of nowhere," wrote Massey, "hits me across the back and sends me sprawling. If that thing had hit me edgeways it would have cut me in two. A man just has to cuss once in a while in this place!"[21]

One of the disadvantages of Hog Island became painfully evident at this time. It was wholly dependent logistically upon supply boats and barges from Amaknak, which in turn depended upon the arrival of supplies from the lower forty-eight. In these November days, this presented a serious situation. "When we were on Hog Island, coal and supplies were a problem when storms kept us from unloading supply boats," recalled Paulus. "At these times we went without. The men wouldn't eat sauerkraut so the cook pushed the cans back on the shelf. During one two-week storm we ran out of coal and finally got down to two meals a day of cold sauerkraut."[22]

On 20 November, Alspaugh noted, "We are having a big storm today. There is a big wind blowing and much snowfall. All of our equipment has to be tied down to keep it on the ground." The next day several PBYs blew over and were damaged. "We are eating two meals a day now (at 10 and 4) because of the shortage of supplies on this island."

Sunday 22 November brought good news in the shape of the U.S. announcement that French forces in Africa and the Western Hemisphere had capitulated. But there was no let-up in the storm

246 THE WORST STORM OF THE TOUR

that had been raging for four days. By 24 November, gasoline and coal were alarmingly low, and the temperature was well below zero. "We are not using much coal as it is almost all exhausted," Alspaugh wrote the next day. He added with commendable restraint, "Our food is getting a little rough . . . we had sauerkraut for breakfast this morning as well as corn cakes. Our coffee has no sugar these days."[23]

Many men of the 206th remembered all holidays as being just so many work days, but Thanksgiving in 1942 "was memorable," wrote Alspaugh. "Our Thanksgiving meal consisted of sauerkraut and corn cakes."[24] Gill recalled the menu as "pancakes for breakfast, lunch and evening meal." Jodie Jones remembered that Thanksgiving as being "in the midst of about the worst storm of the tour. The Navy could not get our rations to us so we had two meals only that day. They consisted of hot cakes and sauerkraut." Both men stressed, however, that as soon as they bay calmed down they had their belated turkey dinner with all the trimmings.[25]

Fuel, however, continued to be in short supply. "Most of my men are visiting huts where fires are permitted," Alspaugh observed on 28 November. "Unfortunately we are not allowed to build a fire here." He spent most of that weekend in bed reading Damon Runyon's short stories.

Monday the thirtieth, he and his hutmates went to the beach "and cut up some old wooden crates and timbers that had washed ashore up on the beach. We cut a whole truckload so we can build a fire now when we need one."[26]

Perhaps the same storm hit Umnak, where the main problem was snow. "We had the most snow on the ground we have ever had here," wrote Stubbs on 19 November. "Strong winds help in keeping it from getting too deep." The snow continued for the next two days, and it was so heavy that the men in Stubbs's hut had to scramble out through the windows and dig it away from the door. Then for a few days the weather broke sufficiently to permit a few outdoor details, and the men on Umnak enjoyed "a nice turkey supper" on Thanksgiving. They were, however, on alert status, and the storm played a return engagement the next day.[27]

"A Jap task force of 10 transports is operating in the Aleutians," recorded Miller, "and as usual they are picking bad weather to do it. It is a nasty day, with a real Montana blizzard blowing. . . ." He added pessimistically, "This one is only a day old so will probably last long enough for the Japs to get their force ashore and their fleet headed homeward." Miller did not anticipate any local action. "The force is suspected to be composed of engineers coming to build an air base in the Rat Is. If so it seems they are determined to maintain Kiska and now try to put a stop to us bombarding it. . . ."[28]

This was essentially correct. The Japanese recent reoccupation of Attu plus the completion of the new U.S. primary air base on Adak had given Eareckson's bombers a broader scope for their talents. For Attu was now within six hundred miles of Adak. When one target was socked in, the other might be fairly clear. By this time the bombers had done enough damage to Attu to point up the desirability of other Japanese bases to Japan's military planners. So Hosogaya brought another task force to the Aleutians, headed for Shemya and Amchitka. In view of Eareckson's raids, however, Hosogaya decided that rather than divide his ships he would steam to Kiska and reinforce that island. This he did on the night of 2 December. Just as Miller had predicted, the storm permitted the admiral to land his men safely and take his ships homeward before the weather allowed the Eleventh Air Force to catch him.[29]

Samuel Eliot Morison saw the silver lining in his reinforcement, pointing out that otherwise these 1,115 troops might have been sent to strengthen the Japanese at Guadalcanal. Once again, it is just as well that no naval engagement ensued, for by this time Theobald had only two cruisers—*Detroit* and *Raleigh*—four destroyers, some motor torpedo boats, and a few miscellaneous small craft. The spunky little PT boats had been something like glamor boys in the south, but at Adak the Aleutian winter proved a sore trial for them. Spray froze topside, adding dangerous weight, and frost as deep as two inches lined the hulls. On land, Adak was exceedingly busy, both the Seabees and the army engineers were working under floodlights to complete base structures, including quarters for fifteen thousand men.[30]

It was probably during this period of intense activity that Private Nixon had a serious run-in with his sergeant. For a short time, Nixon "was attached to a harbor company and all they did was unload ships." At the time of the trouble, these men were unloading five-hundred-pound bombs from a ship. "Our routine was to work twenty straight hours, with four hours off each day," explained

Nixon. "We slept three hours. The fourth hour we could take a bath and eat breakfast, then we reported to work for another twenty hours."

After five or six days of this insane routine, Nixon was exhausted beyond reason and beyond fear. He refused to get up, whereupon his sergeant pulled him out of his bunk and slapped him. Nixon hit him with every ounce of strength he had left. "When he got up he took off," related Nixon. "Soon, two MPs came and ordered me to the master sergeant's office. After threatening to have me shot or court martialed if I didn't return to work—I still refused—he turned me over to a lieutenant colonel."

"Did you hit the sergeant?" asked the colonel.

"Yes, after he hit me," replied Nixon.

"Do you still refuse to work?" was the next question.

"Yes, sir," Nixon answered wearily.

The colonel summoned the MPs, who put Nixon on a barge and sent him back to his own outfit. There Nixon told his story to his captain. "He informed me the next day that it looked pretty bad for me," wrote Nixon, "but I never heard any more about it."[31]

Probably what saved Nixon from court-martial was the fact that the sergeant slapped him—very definitely a no-no in the U.S. Armed Forces. Then, too, it may have dawned on someone that to expect men to work twenty straight hours for days on end unloading five-hundred-pound weights was just a mite on the unreasonable side.

29

"A White Christmas"

The winter of 1942–43 was the region's worst in thirty-four years. That December the temperature dropped to -67° at Fairbanks. In the usually milder Aleutians, crews had to thaw aircraft engines with blowtorches. The whole air community was shocked and saddened when Col. Everett S. Davis, chief of staff of the Eleventh Air Force and "pioneer genius of Alaska military aviation," flying a C-47 from the Alaska mainland to the Aleutians, was blown off course and crashed into a mountain.

On the other hand, no GI in Alaska mourned when on 9 December the daily weather aircraft flew into a snow squall and crash-landed on Attu. It had as a passenger Maj. Gen. William E. Lynd, a visiting inspector general. He had been giving "a bad time" to pilots in Alaska, for suspicion still circulated in the states that the senatorial evaluation of Alaskan weather was the truth. The day after the accident, the aircraft was sighted on the west end of Attu, "its fuselage broken off aft of the wings." All hands were rescued, the crew none the worse, while Lynd escaped with a broken collarbone. After that incident, no more was heard about exaggerated Alaskan weather reports.[1]

The navy, too, had its problems. On 27 December, a gale and racing waters shook the destroyer-minelayer *Wasmuth* so furiously that two of her depth charges broke away, exploding so close that she broke in two. The tanker *Ramapo* rescued all hands, but *Wasmuth* was beyond help.[2]

The sauerkraut Thanksgiving dinner was only one example of weather-related shortages. Kee's outfit on Gobler's Knob was snowbound for two weeks and supplied by helicopter. "I would only have a fire in the hut for one hour a day," he remembered. "We were burning coals but were about out of coal and they did not drop us any. When they got to us (we were all okay) and we saw a newspaper where the unions were on strike in the coal mines for four cents an hour more it made us sick and I'll bet until this day not one of my men joined a union."[3]

Several men recalled with some bitterness instances of strikes in the lower forty-eight. "The only time I remember any problem with food," wrote Spud Clark of C Battery, "was when labor unions called a strike at the ports in the US causing us to be out of meat for about thirty days. This caused much anti-union attitudes to develop. The unions struck for more pay per hour *increase* than we were getting for a full day." (Clark's italics.)[4]

"Once we were down to two meals a day," reminisced Garrett. "This was the first or breakfast: ½ cup of water (no coffee), 2 hotcakes (no butter or syrup), and one serving of kraut."[5]

Weese also remembered that particularly hard winter. "I recall one period when we were down to our last food and had to eat canned sweet potatoes and sauerkraut for two days. Coal supplies ran low and crews were doubled up in huts to conserve fuel. During that time men stayed in bed a lot to keep warm."[6]

Major Oehrig, at the time executive officer of B Battery, likewise entertained by no means fond memories of that period of "only pancakes and sauerkraut for two weeks."[7] What stuck in Sergeant Beverburg's mind was the period when the Hog Island contingent subsisted on canned tomatoes and bread stew.[8]

All of which was unusual, because in general Hog Island had a reputation as quite a pleasant place. "Headquarters officers and others liked to come to the island and stay a few days—said it was like a leave," wrote Weese. "Especially one doctor spent most of his time with us—he could always find a reason to stay over."[9]

What the men missed most were fresh fruit, fresh vegetables, and fresh milk. These shortages existed regardless of the weather.[10]

Meanwhile, the upper echelons were busily preparing to garrison Amchitka. On 17 December Buckner ordered Eareckson to send an air raid to determine if, after all, Japan had managed to land troops on the island. Typically, Eareckson piloted the bomber himself. His orders called for him to flatten the unoccupied Aleut village, including the church. The bombardier was exceedingly accurate, and soon had leveled the homes. Eareckson, a decent man, was so reluctant to hit the church that several times he pulled up before the bombardier could get a bead on it. But orders were orders, so eventually he permitted the bombardier to do what had to be done. That night Eareckson couldn't sleep; he played poker until morning. Then, without rest, he flew at the head of his planes providing air cover for the first landing on Amchitka.[11]

The small party was under Col. Benjamin Talley of the Engineers and Lt. Col. Alvin E. Hebert, scheduled to command the air base on Amchitka should one be feasible. The two-day survey reported that a steel-mat fighter strip could be laid in two to three weeks. There were suitable sites for a main airfield; construction would take three or four months. On 21 December, the Joint Chiefs of Staff authorized the occupation of Amchitka, to take place two weeks later.[12]

None of which as yet made any changes in the even tenor of life on Umnak. Evidently the effort to civilize the installation was still under way. "Colonel Dwyer visited our Company today," Stubbs noted in his diary on 16 December. "K. O. Johnson met him and failed to salute. The colonel didn't like it." In consequence, the next day, "All N.C.O.'s of the 3rd platoon and Pvt. Johnson had to go a military courtesy school tonight for one hour, with Lt. Jeroux, because Johnson failed to salute the colonel yesterday. That is a hell of a note in a combat zone."

From 20 December until Christmas, the men had to be in their slit trenches from 0930 until 1000 each morning for "practice air raid drills." Various work details and school sessions continued until Christmas Eve, when most of the day was free. "Santa was in the mess hall tonight. Everyone got a small present of some kind."

Christmas Day they awoke to find everything snowed under, and only twenty men turned up for breakfast. "We had a good supper tonight," Stubbs recorded. "This has been the whitest Xmas I have ever seen."[13]

Miller did not spend Christmas with his men. He returned on 15 December from helping establish an outpost to find his leave orders awaiting him. "What a daze I was in then!" Suddenly on 21 December he and two other infantry officers were given twenty minutes to be on the beach. They made it with five minutes to spare, then had to wait almost three hours for the barge to Chernofski. There they boarded *St. Mihiel*, which shipped for

Dutch Harbor the next morning. So Miller spent Christmas Day on the seas, but he didn't care—he was going home.

St. Mihiel docked at Seattle on December 29. Miller and one of his traveling companions picked up friends and went to the Press Club, almost overcome by the wonder of "our first civilized drink in a year, sitting in a soft chair, where water runs from a tap and the toilets flush!"

The next day, after a session at a barber's, after purchasing railroad tickets and checking their luggage, two euphoric lieutenants ate a good dinner and got "hell-roarin' drunk." They barely made their train and fell asleep, "stony broke." Miller awoke with "the worst hangover in military history," but it had worn off by the time the train pulled into the station. There stood his father—"straight, proud, happy and just as fine as ever." At home his mother made some breakfast, which Miller was "too excited to eat." Then he made a New Year's Eve date with his childhood sweetheart, Jo. After some persuasion on his part, she said "Yes, you big lug" to his proposal, and they were married on 5 January.[14]

This was the second Christmas away from home for the 206th. "Many boys cry during Christmas, listening to Bing Crosby's 'White Christmas' record," noted Massey. "Boy, do we have a white Christmas!"[15] A dentist, Capt. Hugh Moseley, Jr., remembered that "Christmas was a hard time," but did not recall what he did on the holiday.[16]

"Sometimes I was so homesick I could cry—most of all at Christmas," Taylor admitted. "So I would find something to do to take my mind off it, like go to the shop and work on some truck—anything to keep busy."[17]

"Christmas of 1942 was spent on Hog Island," Oehrig recalled. "We all had two cans of 3.2 beer and listened to 'White Christmas.'"[18]

On Christmas Eve, the commanding officer of B Battery on Hog Island "sent his own boat over to Ballyhoo with two cases of 24 pints each (80 proof bourbon) with one case designated for officers and one case for the men," remembered Captain Langley. They had two meals that Christmas Day—breakfast at 0900 and supper at 1600. As the men went through the chow line, each received about one-and-a-half jiggers. The teetotalers could give their ration to anyone they chose. "This situation met with 100% approval."[19]

Weese recalled that the doctor who spent so much time on

Hog, Captain Kelley, came over, bringing "enough liquor for everyone to have about two ounces apiece. There was some real bargaining for the two ounces for people who did not drink."[20]

In the spirit of the season, Pfc Earle Phillips slipped a one-dollar bill under every man's plate on Christmas morning. Tate was so touched he never spent his dollar, but kept it as a souvenir of the comradeship that helped make bearable these difficult times.[21]

In accordance with military tradition, Alspaugh and the other noncoms pulled voluntary KP on Christmas to "let some of the privates off for the day." Alspaugh pulled the "pots and pans" detail. "It was about eight o'clock when we got through. I really had a good time in the kitchen," he assured his mother. "I ate more turkey than I have since I have been in the army."[22]

December 1942 was memorable for Fitzhugh. He wanted to become an officer, but realized that since he had "only a high school education," his chances of being selected for OCS were slim. Therefore, in July 1942 he had taken the test for warrant officer, and in December he received his appointment.[23]

Late in December, Pat Patterson, who owned the foxes on Hog Island, came over to trap the Arctic blue and white foxes now in full pelt. He stayed in the hut with Garrett and Beverburg. "He was appreciative of anything he did to help him and tried to do his part in keeping our programs going," wrote the latter. When he left in January, he gave Garrett several fifths of whisky.[24]

Alspaugh's diary for 1942 ended on 23 December, and later diaries—if he kept them—are not available. But his letters home continued. "They have trapped almost all the fox here in the last few days," he wrote on January 6. "They have (the fox) beautiful fur now. There are about sixteen more to be trapped."[25] Obviously the appearance of someone from the outside world, for whatever purpose and however briefly, was a real event in the men's lives.

As the year moved to its close, Private Alex Thompson of F Battery expressed some of his thoughts in poetry:

Memorials

An Aleutian moon is shining
Over islands frozen white,

> On the graves of heroes sleeping
>> Through the still Alaskan night.
>
> The silent mountains glisten
>> With an iridescent glow
> From the stars of northern heavens
>> Reflecting in the snow.
>
> No monuments more fitting
>> Can be raised above their sod
> Than those monuments of nature:
>> The memorials of God.[26]

Appropriately enough, 1943 began with major changes at high level. First came the temporary loss of Eareckson. The colonel was a prime example of a type that occasionally surfaces under combat conditions—adored by his subordinates, valued by those superiors with sense enough to give him latitude, and a perpetual burr under the saddle of the top brass who do not quite know how to handle an officer who doesn't care that he remains a colonel while other wing commanders are major generals, and who would rather lead his aircraft into combat than preside over a staff meeting. Butler had several times complained of Eareckson to Buckner, and now Butler informed the latter that he was sending Eareckson stateside.

Buckner knew that a ZI assignment for his bomber commander would be a criminal waste, but one of Butler's complaints made sense—Eareckson needed a rest. So Buckner sent Eareckson to the states, informing him that he would return as the Eleventh Air Force's deputy chief of staff.

A measure of Eareckson's worth is the fact that when the Japanese noted his absence, Tokyo Rose gloated, "Our very good friend, Colonel Eareckson, is no more. He was shot down in the sea on January 13."

"Why, the little bitch!" Eareckson exclaimed when he heard of this untimely obituary. "Wait till I get back up there!"[27]

The next shakeup was in the navy. From the first, Buckner and Theobald had been a classic case of oil and water—each a valuable commodity in itself but incapable of combining. On one point they agreed: Fuzzy wanted a transfer quite as badly as Buckner wanted to get rid of him.

A quick visit from Vice Adm. Frank Jack Fletcher, commander of the Northwestern Sea Frontier, an equally quick report from Fletcher to Nimitz, and Theobald was relieved. On 4 January his replacement, Rear Adm. Thomas C. Kinkaid, took over. At the same time, Rear Adm. Charles H. "Soc" McMorris replaced Rear Adm. W. W. "Poco" Smith as commander of the cruiser-destroyer strike group.

Intellectually, Kinkaid stood several notches below Theobald, but he possessed what may be the most valuable weapon in a commander's arsenal—an instinctive feel for what action to take when. And having reached a decision, he went all out. Acutely aware of how small his force was, Theobald had hesitated to engage the enemy, much to Buckner's disgust. On the other hand, Kinkaid took the position that the force, although weak, was all he had, so he would make the best of what was available.[28]

From an abstract standpoint, Theobald's strategy made considerable sense. The Japanese presence in the Aleutians was a nuisance, but by no means a threat to national security. With the Allied victory, however long delayed it might be, the intruders would have to pull out. Japan had nothing in the islands worth the loss of a cruiser or even a destroyer, not to mention lives. Nevertheless, Theobald's cautious philosophy, however defensible, is not the spirit that wins wars.

McMorris made an excellent foil for Kinkaid. He was considered to be one of the brainiest officers in the Fleet, probably the homeliest, and certainly one of the most likeable.[29] "Soc" could leaven Kinkaid's practicality, and Kinkaid could tone down McMorris's mental pyrotechnics.

Kinkaid wasted no time. On 5 January, one day after he took over, he ordered landings on Amchitka. Reconnaissance and photographic flights took off over that island, and bombers headed for Kiska and Attu to keep the Japanese busy. These bombers promptly sank two freighters loaded with troops and weapons—*Montreal Maru* at Kiska, *Kotohiro Maru* off Attu. A task force of three cruisers, four destroyers, and four transports under McMorris were ready to land Brig. Gen. Lloyd E. Jones and his engineers. Then came an unavoidable delay—the Aleutian weather had no more respect for admirals bent on major operations than it had for GIs shivering on guard duty. For a week the task force pitched helplessly off Amchitka in blizzard conditions.[30]

While the Amchitka invasion perforce marked time, the 206th lost another good man in a weather-related accident. Drake's history of A Battery recorded the details:

> On 9 January 1943, Sgt Cecil K. Dix, Battery K, lost his life by drowning. He and S/Sgt Clyde T. Hill were making a communication line check between K-8 and K-9. While walking on a path at the base of Table Top Mountain, a snow slide completely enveloped both men and carried them into the bay some 50 feet below. Hill managed to gain the shore but Dix, apparently from shock of the extremely cold water, continued swimming out from shore and was soon lost. His body was never recovered. Hill, after tremendous effort and suffering from extreme hypothermia, managed to walk to the K-8 position where help was given.[31]

K Battery's history added a word of tribute: "Cecil was an amiable fellow that none could deny wasn't every inch a man's man. I sincerely doubt if there ever was such a word as CAN'T in his vocabulary."[32]

On 11 January, the storm at sea eased off from the impossible to the merely intolerable, and McMorris decided that the troops would land on the morrow, no matter what. Around midnight he sent the destroyer *Worden* into Constantine Harbor to land the Alaskan Scouts detachment. Somehow *Worden* got into the harbor, the scouts piled into whaleboats, and their second-in-command, Lt. Col. William J. Verbeck, led them ashore. On her way back to rejoin her sisters, the current swept *Worden* "onto a pinnacle rock, which punctured her hull at an engineroom." The destroyer *Dewey* tried to pull *Worden* clear, but the cable broke, and all hands had to abandon ship. *Dewey* rushed to pick up crewmen; however, fourteen drowned, and *Worden* was a total loss. The army troops landed safely.[33]

The venture had cost a valuable destroyer and fourteen priceless lives, but the Americans were on Amchitka—some forty miles from Kiska.

30

"Out There When Conditions
Were Rough"

Mid-January, during a blizzard, is not the most propitious time to attempt to establish a garrison on an Aleutian Island. However, the transports managed to land their some 2,100 troops with only one minor incident—a man was injured when he fell from the net. The attack transport *Arthur Middleton* recalled her boats after landing the first wave, and sent them to the sinking *Worden*, rescuing about 200 men. A *Middleton* crew member, Lansing S. Laidlaw, "really cried tears" when the destroyer sank. "We had so few ships and they were so badly needed."

Naval artist Lt. William F. Draper had been given a hop on *Middleton* so that he might paint the action on Amchitka. He never forgot the sight of *Worden*'s survivors boarding the transport. "They were in terrible shape; covered with oil from head to foot, just black with oil and stiff with cold. . . . When I saw them coming in they had this glazed look in their eyes and I wouldn't have been surprised if they all had died."

Then it was *Middleton*'s turn to suffer. Early that evening, an 84-knot gale blew her on shore a good 1000 feet from the beach. There she sat for weeks. The same storm damaged other landing boats, which made it difficult to get necessary supplies ashore. Oil from *Worden* and *Middleton* coated the harbor to a depth of six inches, further hampering the landing. As a result, that night the men had only cold rations and no shelter. Soon matters brightened up as far as food was concerned. *Middleton*'s cold storage system broke down, so the food was distributed to the men, who thus dined for several days on chicken, turkey, and steak.

It was probably during this period of initial confusion that Capt. Theodore Bouchette of the 37th Infantry, helping to clean up the beach, found "a large bag full of U.S. currency." He suspected this might have been a payroll, and turned it over to "higher authorities." He received no feedback, not even a commendation on his honesty. Perhaps the upper echelon considered this only to be expected.[1]

On the morning of 13 January, a group of Alaska Scouts set out on foot, although the storm still raged. Within a week, they had completed the thirty-mile hike and established an observation post on the northwest end of Amchitka. From that point, on a clear day—or in a clear hour—the peaks of Kiska were visible.

Base construction was much more difficult than it had been on Adak. Here no convenient easily drained lagoon offered a ready-made site. Here it was a case of leveling hills and filling in gullies. However, the engineers were just as efficient as Amchitka as at Adak, and despite terrain and weather they had finished an airstrip plus huts and some other buildings in approximately two weeks.

Events in the air were far less satisfactory. On 18 January, four B-24s, four B-26s, one B-25, and six P-38s took off from Adak, intent upon bombing two ships in Kiska harbor. Mechanical trouble forced two of the B-26s to return to base. No bombs were dropped, and fog closed in on both Kiska and Adak. A B-24, landing in a downwind, crashed into two P-38s; three other B-24s were missing. The next day, one of these bombers was located where it had crash-landed on Great Sitkin Island, and a navy tender rescued the crew.

The run of bad luck continued on 21 January when two B-17s from Umnak, en route to Adak, collided in mid-air. One was able to land, badly damaged; the other disappeared. On the same day, a P-40 crashed into Kuluk Bay. And two days later, two B-25s "tangled in a fog and went down." In six days, the Eleventh Air Force had lost thirteen aircraft, not one to enemy action.[2]

The Japanese did not discover the American presence on Amchitka until 23 January, and promptly sent over two aircraft that inflicted no damage. A raid by two floater Zeros (Rufes) killed three engineers and bombed the runway on 26 January, and the next day six Rufes again hit the airstrip. Except for the loss of the three men, these raids had only nuisance value, and in mid-February they ceased.[3]

The only unit of the 206th sent to Amchitka was the new Battery A. "We were out there when conditions were primitive and had to put up huts, build positions, and all the other things that go along with developing a base," Bill Jones recalled. "We . . . could see Kiska on a clear day. . . . Was nice to be on a base that had fighter planes for protection and also bombers coming and going so we could at least feel a part of the war."[4]

Cathey remembered that when Battery A reached Amchitka they "were in dense fog for nine days." Each ship in the convoy blew its whistle every five minutes to keep together. Even so, their ship nearly ran aground on Amchitka's rocky beach. They set up camp "near a rather large but shallow lake." To get some water, one of the men dug a hole near the lake. "The next morning the lake was completely dry. All the water had drained through the volcanic ash which had been covered with mud."[5]

Amchitka turned out to be a great place for gamblers, principally because the men had no place to spend money on anything else. "I saw and was in dice games where thousands of dollars were at stake and the pile of money in the circle looked half knee deep," declared Sisk. "One fellow came to the poker game I was in and asked his friend for just $20 more [on] loan. His friend said yes, but please not to ask for any more. In twenty minutes his buddy came back from a dice game and paid his debt and had over $6,000 left. . . . All of us were not that lucky," Sisk added somewhat unnecessarily.

As at Dutch Harbor and Umnak, some could not stand the strain. "On Amchitka, some outfit was having an inspection in ranks, and this lieutenant went haywire and shot five of the men, then killed himself," Sisk stated. "As I understood, he had not been in the island very long, but it was just too much for some."[6]

For the men left at their usual stations, life went on as usual, a mixture of the tragic, the comic, and the humdrum. "On 19 January 1943," wrote Drake in his history of Battery A, "Pvt. Roy L. Schantzenbach, Battery K, a recent arrival at the battery, was accidentally killed while fulfilling his duties as a sentry at the K-10 position on Mt. Ballyhoo. While on duty, and during a williwaw, the wind tore off a portion of the roof housing the searchlight and struck Schantzenbach. As a result, he died from the accident."[7]

Battery K's history had kind words for this newcomer: "Pvt. Roy L. Schantzenbach, a recent arrival to this battery, was accidentally killed while fulfilling his duties as a sentry.

"Owing to his late arrival, Roy wasn't as well known, but those who worked with him and shared his thoughts paid him the highest of tributes."[8]

At the other end of the emotional scale, an accident turned out well, and Massey's men had a good laugh at the expense of "Dollar" Dyllar from Texas. According to Massey's notes, Dyllar "went to our outhouse built on the edge of the water. A large wave took the outhouse, Dyllar and all. We heard him screaming for all he was worth, got a rope to him. He is skinned up from one end to the other. Crap-house all in pieces. Must build another."[9]

About mid-January, the men of Company F, 153d Infantry, received word that they would be shipping out of Umnak. They did not know where they were going. Stubbs spent much time on detail at the U.S. Engineer Depot while he and his friends prepared for transfer. "Our company is getting ready to leave here," he wrote on 23 January. "Everybody is working at something either day or night." They packed their barracks bags on the 25th, and two days later the bags left. On the 28th, the men sent "the last of our equipment to the beach today." But they did not pull out until the fourteenth of February. In the meantime, they attended various training films and lectures, including two, incredibly, on jungle warfare.[10]

Air missions in late January and early February produced stepped-up action against Kiska and Attu, dampened by the usual aborts due to weather, and two comic incidents. On 30 January, a B-17 dropped four depth charges and one bomb on what the crew thought was a Japanese submarine, only to see a whale break water, as if to identify itself and say "Knock it off!" Then in mid-February Amchitka resounded with alarms—a sentry reported thirty planes in V-formation headed toward Kiska. Then a sharp-eyed navy pilot remarked that this was "the first time he had ever seen Japanese airplanes flapping their wings." An echelon of geese had caused all the excitement.[11]

On Hog Island, Alspaugh attended another gunnery school, and on 12 February he was promoted to staff sergeant. That meant an increase in salary to the dizzy sum of ninety-six dollars a month base pay.[12] In his letters to his mother, Alspaugh seldom complained, so it is impossible to be sure how he and his buddies on Hog were making out. Massey's notes, however, reveal that in February conditions at his location were grim: "Rations ran out, all we have is flour and cauliflower, no salt. Get rations for first time in two weeks, boys about half sick. Damn rats invade our position, they are bigger than I've ever seen. . . . It is awfully lonesome and tiresome during these long dark nights. Our cards, dominoes, checkerboard and records about worn out. Making record needles out of safety pins."[13]

No wonder someone who experienced these winter days wrote a small essay on "The Aleutian Stare." This, he explained, was

> . . . caused by missing too many ships . . . it was kind of a lockjaw of the eyes . . . your eyes became focused on two points, one for each eye, directly in front of you . . . in this position your mind was free to wonder [sic] willy nilly anywhere it chose . . . it had varying stages . . . you began by staring at your right foot . . . later you extended this to include both feet . . . after sixteen months you began to have lapses between the start and finish of a forkful of spam . . . of course, the mate next to you would bring you around with a nudge so you wouldn't starve to death . . . at eighteen months you began discussing personal matters with the seagulls . . . at any time after that the birds began to talk back . . . it was positively amazing what some of those gulls had to say.[14]

On Amchitka, *Middleton* was still beached. "An 8-foot rock sticking up through the double bottom" thwarted all attempts to float her. Meanwhile, she was a sitting duck for the Rufes. "We wonder how long it will be until they score a hit," wrote Laidlaw. Indeed, the Japanese failure to do so was almost miraculous. The transport's crew listened to Japanese radio reports of putting on the rocks "a battleship type of freighter," obviously meaning *Middleton*. Actually, she had been beached a good two weeks before the first Japanese plane flew over. Rumors abounded, including one that *Middleton* had been sunk with only four survivors. With completion of the airstrip on 16 February and the arrival of some fighter aircraft, the atmosphere lightened. "We are all so overjoyed for now morning and evening raids will not be dreaded."[15]

In fact, as Craven and Cate remarked, "Occupation of Amchitka, while producing no immediate spectacular results, helped make the Japanese hold on the Aleutians eventually hopeless. Systematic supply of the enemy garrisons by surface craft became hazardous, requiring a powerful task force to drive a convoy through the air and naval blockade."[16]

No one realized this better than Lt. Gen. Hideichiro Higuchi, in command of Japan's ground forces in the northern Pacific. He knew he must either withdraw or heavily reinforce Attu and Kiska, while the Japanese navy must cut the U.S. supply lines to Adak and Amchitka. That meant submarines, which the Japanese navy consistently mishandled. The Japanese placed considerable faith in their undersea branch, but although Germany's U-boats had nearly brought Great Britain to her knees by attacking merchant ships, Japan persisted in using her subs against warships and even as supply boats. Stuck with this policy, Hosogaya could promise no help in that regard. Nor would the army high command approve pulling out. Instead, they ordered their northern commanders "to hold the western Aleutians at all costs." How that could be done was mainly up to the unfortunate Higuchi and his still more unfortunate troops.[17]

If anyone in the Aleutian theater was reasonably content during these months, it probably was the U.S. naval personnel. Nothing lifts the heart of the fighting man like the knowledge that his commander is a solid, combat-tested veteran who believes in action. Just such a man was Kinkaid. His orders were to establish a naval blockade, take offensive action whenever possible, and eventually drive the Japanese from the Aleutians. These instructions he intended to carry out to the best of his ability.

He promptly sent McMorris's striking force to soften up the approaches to Attu. On 18 February, he received a report that several Japanese ships were in Holtz Bay. The Eleventh Air Force got the same message and sent out a bombing mission, timed to reach Attu before McMorris's ships. Unexpectedly, the weather lifted and the strike force was able to proceed at full speed. As a result, they and the bombers reached the target area simultaneously. A veteran chief petty officer, riding in Capt. Frederick Ramputi's B-17 to verify ship identifications, assured him that the vessels below were Japanese. Ramputi made two bomb runs, but for once malfunctions worked to the Americans' benefit—"the normal, emergency and manual rack released all failed to function." McMorris's flagship, *Richmond*, could not raise the B-17 over the radio, so the admiral had no choice but to direct *Richmond* to open fire on the aircraft. Fortunately, she made no hits and Ramputi returned to Adak. After that incident, all Bomber Command flying officers were "thoroughly briefed in surface ship identification . . ."

Finding no enemy vessels—they had already gone—"Soc" shelled Attu, inflicting little damage. Then he proceeded westward. With only six ships, he could not blockade both Kiska and Attu from nearby, since they were hundreds of miles apart. His strategy was to move near Japanese waters and catch supply ships en route to the Aleutians.

He struck pay dirt almost immediately—*Akagane Maru*, loaded with infantry troops, airfield construction items and other materiel. *Indianapolis* struck her, and the cruiser's captain ordered the destroyers to torpedo the transport. There followed one of those fiascoes featuring torpedo malfunction all too common in the first two years of the Pacific War. *Coghlan* tried three times—the first failed to explode, the second went off before reaching the target, the third passed harmlessly astern of the transport. *Gillespie* had no better luck. One torpedo did not explode, "a second frolicked on the surface like a porpoise and missed." Then *Coghlan* tried shelling but failed to sink the target. Again the destroyer sent off a torpedo; it "prematured." At last, a little more than an hour after midnight, gunfire sank *Akagane Maru*. Two other Japanese army transports had set out, and the Americans did not spot them; nevertheless, they turned back to Japan without trying to land their troops and cargoes.[18]

These developments did not affect the Arkansas men on Umnak, if indeed they knew anything about them. Finally, on 14 February, they boarded a power barge and set out for Chernofski Bay on Unalaska. "The roughest thing I ever rode," Stubbs noted. "I think everyone got sick except the skipper." The next morning they boarded the troopship *Branch*. As he came aboard, the officer in charge, Major Abraham, received a sealed envelope marked "Secret." Hoping at last to know their destination, he ripped it open. "It contains a report of the unit's equipment shortage at Umnak!"

They reached Dutch Harbor that afternoon and stayed in harbor several days forbidden to leave the ship. "Another day spent aboard ship at Dutch Harbor and no one seems to know when and where we are going . . . ," commented Stubbs. "We are getting tired of this." The transport pulled out at 1700 on 19 February. "We all rushed to the chow line to get a meal before we hit rough water." This proved a wise precaution, for the voyage was rough and seasickness rampant. "Pulled in at the dock at Adak at 1:00 P.M. and got off the ship," Stubbs wrote on 21 February. "Looks like here is where we are going. Trucks hauled us about 3 miles from the dock back into the snow-covered mountains. We pitched pup tents, ate type C rations and went to bed for the night."

It would be pleasant to record that this move meant that these combat infantrymen, acclimated to the Aleutians, were to see the action they craved. But that is not what happened. Later, Miller summed up the situation bitterly:

> The 153rd lands at Adak and takes up its old chores, unloading boats, building roads, guarding planes, building houses. Now they are 450 miles closer to the Japs, but all it means is they see more bombers headed for Kiska and more infantrymen walking around in the grass with nothing to do. They slump way down, and stay slumped. This is a hell of a way for Arkansas' finest to fight a war.[19]

31

"The Japanese Could Have Sunk
Salt Lake City with a Baseball"

February ended on Adak on a pleasing note of camaraderie. "Lt. Miking lost a billfold yesterday with $200 of Sgt. Taylor's money in it," Stubbs recorded on the 28th. "We are making up tonight to replace it."

Stubbs was not a complainer, but his starkly factual record sketches its own design of monotony and shortages. He and his fellows dug the foundations for huts, put up the huts, worked on road detail. "Took a bath in a gallon can this morning," he wrote on 3 March. "Washed underwear and sox in the same can this P.M." Eventually some of the men rigged up "a shower in one hut made from an oil drum, small pipe and a tin can."

Movies had come to Adak. Occasionally—very occasionally—a reasonably good one turned up, but most were what are charitably called B pictures. Stubbs and his companions could not be choosy, and went to most if not all of them. There was one bright spot—the food on Adak had taken a turn for the better. "Had steak for dinner and fried chicken for supper," Stubbs remarked with satisfaction on 8 March. "Eating pretty good now."[1]

The improvement in the mess probably resulted from the transfer to Adak from Kodiak of Alaska's army, navy, and air force headquarters. The move made considerable sense. It placed the nerve centers one thousand miles nearer the Japanese and permitted daily, even hourly, consultation between the leaders of the ground, sea, and air operations. And all commanders received promotions—Buckner to lieutenant general, Kinkaid became a vice admiral, Butler got his second star, and Gehres was made a commodore. The latter rank, the equivalent of brigadier general, is not in normal use in the U.S. Navy, but occasionally it is activated.

While the propinquity worked well in the case of Buckner and Kinkaid, who were compatible personally and professionally, it pointed up certain weaknesses in their subordinates. Butler had little tactical experience and was a sore trial to his subordinate commanders now that he was in a position to breathe down their necks. At times they had to go to the length of canceling some pet mission of Butler's that "would have left their planes out of fuel hundreds of miles from base." Gehres, too, although a different type from Butler, occasionally seemed out of touch with reality. He telephoned Capt. Oswald Colclough at Amchitka one day, demanding to know why his PBYs weren't airborne. Amchitka happened to be socked in with a particularly ferocious williwaw, and Colclough replied with commendable restraint, "Nothing around here flying but a few Quonset huts."[2]

The nadir of morale in the entire Aleutian experience seems to have been reached on Amchitka during these early months of 1943. Sisk recalled that a show featuring Martha O'Driscoll came to the island, and he "didn't bother to go . . . , for by that time I think some of us were bitter about our plight and didn't believe in much of anything," he explained. "We were separated from civilization for so long that people from the states didn't seem real, and most certainly didn't think, act or speak our language. . . . We, in short, were slowly but surely losing something. It seemed our government had abandoned and betrayed us. But," he added, "we didn't totally lose all faith for we were made of stuff that called for loyalty and dedication to God and country. These things kept us going. Some were overcome to the point of suicide and chose that course."[3]

Despite his extenuating comments, Sisk's words paint an appalling picture. When men have reached the stage where they would rather wallow in self-pity than alleviate their boredom, they are in very sad shape indeed. In his valuable book, Garfield makes it clear that Sisk and his buddies of Battery A were far from alone in their misery. A few psychologically hardy souls took up such hobbies as photography, but they were in the minority. All too many "turned inward to feed on their own acids, and retired from reality." They would drink anything containing alcohol and pay anything for it. The suicide rate increased; homosexuality was rife and resulted in many courts-martial. Illness, psychosomatic and real, as well as self-inflicted wounds, kept the medics busy and lowered unit efficiency.

Some men did not even bother to read their mail—a military man's morale could sink no lower.[4]

Work conditions were terrible. Several times Sisk had charge of a detail of some twenty-five men for twelve-hour shifts unloading cargo vessels. "The ship's crew never did feed us. We went without food unless we happened to have a can of C rations." On one occasion, wind-driven sleet actually cut his face. And of course there were the inevitable snafus. "On one shift . . . we unloaded nothing but WAC's clothing and effects—shoes, blouses, skirts, gloves, stockings and purses—and laid the whole mess on the ground and covered it up with tarps which blew away. . . . There was not a WAC in the whole string of the Aleutians that I know of."[5]

Such mixups took place throughout the Aleutians. One doctor was exasperated to receive a large shipment of obstetric forceps when there was not a pregnant woman within a thousand miles. He also became the dumbfounded recipient of cases of antisnake venom. While the Aleutians abounded in wild animals, snakes were not among them.[6]

The bomber officers and crews had a special morale problem. They resented, almost hated, the man who had replaced Eareckson. The whole military command structure offers no more delicate task than succeeding a popular, inspirational leader. One could feel a pang of pity for Col. Earl H. DeFord, except that he seemed almost pathologically bent upon being as different from Eareckson as possible. He visualized his role as primarily that of administrator, planner, and issuer of orders, whose place was behind his desk. He had an exalted idea of his importance, dining alone at the front of the air officers' mess at a table complete with tablecloth. His subordinates had to see him eating steak and other delicacies as they walked by to their own more modest meals.

The incident that solidified the fliers' dislike came when he rode along on a bomber flight to Kiska. When the plane reached tiny Rat Island he ordered the pilot to circle. "I want to observe the action when they go over." The stunned pilot could only stare at him. Did the colonel really mean to use a fully loaded bomber as an observation post instead of letting it complete its mission? He did. "Keep circling, I want to watch," he repeated. After this incident, DeFord was known as The Mayor of Rat Island.[7]

Matters appear to have been somewhat better at the older

establishments. The founding of the 206th Officers' Club at Dutch Harbor was a case in point. In January 1943, Maj. O. L. "Pat" Greening was at Seattle awaiting transport to Dutch Harbor following an emergency leave when he encountered Col. George Tillery, Robertson's second-in-command. During a pleasant three-week wait, Greening suggested that they organize a 206th officers' club. Tillery agreed and immediately appointed Greening club officer. The two men sought out a wholesale liquor distributor whom they conned "into selling us about $3,000 worth of assorted booze and ship it to Dutch Harbor."

Knowing that Robertson disapproved of drinking, Greening was a little uneasy, but figured that Tillery would be there "to take the heat . . ." Predictably, Tillery's orders were changed and he did not return to Amchitka, leaving Greening holding the bag. Reflecting philosophically that his superiors could not do much to him except make him pay for the whiskey, not too much of a hardship as he was single and had newly been promoted to major, Greening returned to his duty station to await the day of reckoning.

It came some four weeks later when the adjutant told him to report at once to Colonel Robertson. "He had received an invoice for $3,000 worth of whiskey charged to the 206th Officers' Club," signed by Greening as club officer, and wanted to know what this was all about. Greening told him the whole story. Robertson gave the major "a good chewing out for taking his action without authority." Then he directed Greening "to find a building, set the club up and figure out how to pay for the whiskey." This turned out to be an easy task. "With everybody willing to help, by the time the shipment arrived we had a double Quonset hut with a bar, plus furniture—the best bar and lounge at Dutch Harbor." The battery officers saw to it that a share of the stock made its way to the troops.[8]

Somewhere around this time certain changes took place. On 13 November 1942 the cruiser *Juneau* had been sunk at the naval battle of Guadalcanal with heavy loss of life. Among the dead were five brothers named Sullivan. This tragedy made a deep impression on the American people. The loss of any young lives was bad enough, but mingled with sympathy for the bereaved parents was an almost atavistic sense of doom. The deaths of all the sons of one family at one time seemed to bring the possibility of mass disaster very near. One result was that the military decided that it had been a mistake to permit brothers to serve together, and those doing so should be separated. This policy touched the 206th. The Parker brothers, for example, split up, with James going to Amchitka and Alford to Battery B on Hog Island, where he made many good friends. "Most were students from Monticello College. F and D Batteries had college students from Russellville and C Battery were students from Jonesboro."[9]

Meanwhile, the Japanese were having their own troubles. Their living conditions had been good, as Aleutian accommodations go. At Kiska their quarters were underground, at Attu above, and in both locations not too crowded. They dined well on Japanese-style food, and, like their American counterparts, they augmented their diet by fishing. But their tactical position was worsening. Despite the number of aborts due to weather, U.S. bombers were heavily damaging their installations, and by spring the Americans had complete control of the air.

No convoy had reached either island since December, and both food and ammunition were low. Higuchi and his men took heart when on 9 March a large convoy slipped into Attu under cover of the fog, bringing much-needed troops and materiel. The next day, a transport reached Attu, destined to be the last. Within the next week Kinkaid's blockade had frustrated all further attempts. In desperation, Hosogaya decided on a bold stroke—he would form and personally command a super convoy. So he ordered three large transports filled to capacity and placed other supplies on the decks of four destroyers. The most powerful ships in his northern force, two light and two heavy cruisers, would act as escorts. This force left Paramushiro on 22 March, with Hosogaya in the heavy cruiser *Nachi*.[10]

Soc McMorris's search-and-destroy mission had taken him so far westward that by the early morning of 26 March he was nearer the Soviet Komandorski Islands than the Aleutians. He was in his flagship, light cruiser *Richmond*, with Destroyer Squadron 14 (*Bailey, Coghlan, Dale, Monaghan*). The heavy cruiser *Salt Lake City*, known as "Swayback Maru," for its "pronounced sheer," had relieved *Indianapolis*, which had been assigned to the North Pacific Force on 11 March, after only a week's intensive firing practice and with a new crew, "almost half of them fresh from boot camp."

The day promised to be fair, with temperatures above freezing. Visibility was so good "that lookouts reported fish broaching many miles away." The ships were zigzagging at fifteen knots, and the crews had just finished breakfast when radar picked up five vessels seven-and-a-half to twelve miles due north, evidently "transports or cargo carriers screened by destroyers or perhaps one light cruiser." The cargo vessels were exactly what McMorris was looking for, and he anticipated no trouble with the escort. Preparations for action were routine. Gunners made sure the ready boxes were filled. "Prisoners were released from the brig, messmen sliced bread for sandwiches, cooks put coffee on to boil. . . ."[11]

Soon, however, illusions of a light engagement faded. First one, then another heavy cruiser appeared, followed by two light cruisers. This was no ordinary convoy; the Americans had stumbled on Hosogaya's entire force. McMorris's four destroyers matched Hosogaya's, but in cruisers it was two to one, and no unprejudiced observer would have given old *Salt Lake City* a chance against *Maya* alone, let alone *Maya* and *Nachi*. However, among several alternatives Soc decided to accept battle. He informed Capt. Bertram J. Rodgers of *Salt Lake City* that the flagship, *Richmond*, would conform to *Salt Lake City*'s movements. He also notified Kinkaid of the situation and requested that Adak and Amchitka send him air support.

Hosogaya also ordered his force to engage, and he sent the *Marus* on their way. The Japanese opened fire on *Richmond*, then changed the target to the heavier *Salt Lake City*. The latter's return shots started a fire on *Nachi* that her crew soon controlled. In a frighteningly short time the Japanese had closed to the point where McMorris was retiring toward the southwest with Hosogaya "in hot pursuit."[12]

Nachi sent eight torpedoes toward *Salt Lake*; with superb seamanship Rodgers avoided them all, although some exploded close enough to pour frigid seawater over the bridge. Then, at about 0850, *Salt Lake*'s eight-inch guns found *Nachi*'s range and scored three hits. One struck the bridge, and Hosogaya narrowly escaped death; three officers were killed a few yards away. *Nachi* had already suffered one power failure; now for the second time the main battery was out of commission so she lost precious minutes of firing time. During this hiatus *Maya* and *Salt Lake* slugged it out, and at 0910 *Maya* scored the first hit on the old cruiser. It killed two men but the material damage was not severe.

Nachi returned to the fight, but soon the Americans noted that she had slowed down, smoking heavily. A destroyer shell had gone through the No. 1 gun turret, where it exploded, killing the gun crew. Still other shells burst above the main deck, where they killed still others.

At 0920 McMorris ordered a wide turn in an attempt to reach his prime targets, the transports. At 0930 *Nachi, Maya,* and their four destroyers charged after the Americans, both sides blazing away.[13]

If the admiral had had the opportunity or the inclination to consider anything but the imperatives of the moment, he must have wondered when the army's air support would show up. Post-attack inquiry into that point produced a real tale of woe. The bombers had been armed to strike ground targets at Kiska; their GP bombs had to be removed and armor-piercing (AP) projectiles and torpedoes substituted.* This meant pulling men off other jobs and sending them to get the bombs from their dumps, which were scattered all over Adak, and the missiles, which were frozen to the ground. Bomb-bay tanks had to be installed on the medium bombers.

Four hours passed before the bombers were loaded; then, as if on cue, a snowstorm struck, reducing ceiling and visibility to zero. This lasted two hours, and at last the planes headed out. By the time they spotted McMorris's ships, the battle was over. The snow squall, at least, was beyond human power, nevertheless, Butler received a three-pronged chewing out—from Hap Arnold, Buckner, and Kinkaid. Fortunately for the Americans, Hosogaya likewise received no air support—at 0950 his superiors advised him that no aircraft were available.[14]

By this time matters were looking very unpromising for the Americans. *Salt Lake*'s steering mechanism had been damaged, not by the Japanese but by the "shock of her own gunfire." This limited her ability to evade, and *Maya* and *Nachi* were still pouring it in her direction. Many times witnesses thought she was done for, but amazingly she suffered only one hit. It "penetrated her main deck and passed out through her hull below the waterline." McMorris could no longer think in terms of the Japanese transports; he had to save his ships, and he was about a hundred miles nearer to the Japanese base at Paramushiro than to Adak. So he ordered a smoke-screen and a southward turn.

---

* A similar incident aboard Nagumo's carriers contributed to the Japanese defeat at Midway.

At 1103 *Salt Lake* took her last hit. By 1155 she was dead in the water; her ammunition supply had been 85 percent expended; *Maya* and *Nachi* were closing rapidly. As Kinkaid said later, "The Japanese could have sunk *Salt Lake City* with a baseball." At that very moment, with a resounding victory minutes away, Hosogaya broke off the engagement. He had his reasons—fuel and ammunition were low; for all he knew, U.S. bombers might show up at any time; his flagship had been hit by "effective shots from an outstandingly valiant United States destroyer . . . ,"* in the generous words of a Japanese participant. Quite possibly Hosogaya did not realize that *Salt Lake* had dropped to speed zero, for she was behind the smoke screen.

Such incidents occasionally happen in military history, and, however rational from the point of view of the retiring commander, those spared cannot but feel a chill of thankful awe. Thus on 26 March, Ens. F. R. Lloyd, USNR, wrote in *Salt Lake City*'s log: "This day the hand of Divine Providence lay over the ship. Never before in her colorful history has death been so close for so long a time. The entire crew offered its thanks to Almighty God for His mercy and protection."

Salt Lake was only dead four minutes. Gradually she got up steam, and Soc headed for Dutch Harbor, whence both she and *Bailey* retired to Mare Island for repairs. American casualties were almost miraculously low—seven killed, seven hospitalized, thirteen with minor injuries. The Japanese, too, got off lightly—fourteen killed, twenty-seven injured. No ship on either side was sunk or permanently damaged.

The Battle of the Komandorskis has its special place in military history. It was the last major naval engagement of the Pacific War fought entirely between surface ships, with no support from either aircraft or submarines. It cost Hosogaya his command; his superiors could not forgive him for not having sunk *Salt Lake City*. To the Americans McMorris and his gallant little fleet had brought a significant if unspectacular victory. No more convoys made the run from Japan to the Aleutians; the stage had been cleared for the next action, already well along in plans and preparations.[15]

---

*   He referred to *Bailey*.

32

"Charged with a Herculean Task"

The battle of the Komandorskis seemingly made little impression on the men from Arkansas. Stubbs's entry for 26 March read: "Started putting up a hut for the 1st platoon today. It snowed most all day. We hear there is a naval battle going on now near Attu Island. Our bombers went out this P.M. Nine B24 bombers just returned at 8:15 P.M. Had steak and french fried potatoes for supper tonight." He added the next day, "Our bombers failed to find the Jap fleet yesterday. Weather too bad."[1]

Battery K of the 206th was even less concerned with strategy and tactics on 26 March: "Battery K enjoyed its first official beer bust in the mess hall this evening with entertainment being provided by the battery's comedian, T. 5 Charles L. Van Dien.

"An appropriate musical atmosphere was furnished by the jazz section of the Regimental Band."[2]

A number of men remembered such self-entertainment projects—a healthy contrast to the attitude on Amchitka. "Our regimental band would come to our mess hall and play music and do skits," recalled Sergeant Caldwell of Battery D.[3] Nixon of Battery H never forgot the occasion when one of the soldiers came on stage, delivered a soulful recitation of Joyce Kilmer's poem, "Trees," then "took his bow. The audience cracked up, especially me—this was on Adak."[4]

In contrast to the routine activities of the 206th and 153d, the upper echelons were alive with plans and preparations to drive the Japanese out of the Aleutians. These activities had been under way for months. Nimitz was favorably disposed, because the ships and men tied up in the North Pacific Force were badly needed elsewhere, and he did not believe air power alone could clear out the Japanese. To accomplish this, the United States would have to take

Kiska and Attu, so he recommended that the army begin training for the mission.

General DeWitt promptly submitted a plan to occupy Kiska, using troops already in Alaska, the War Department to supply replacements. If Washington turned down this proposal, he would agree to using troops from the states. In either case, he would need the "the equivalent of a division, trained and equipped for amphibious operations . . ." which later could be used against Attu. Admiral Ernest J. King, commander in chief, United States Fleet, agreed to the use of troops already on the spot, but thought the project required more study. Transports couldn't be ready until January or February 1943.

General Marshall saw no need for haste; in his opinion, there would be plenty of time to train the necessary troops "in the United States where facilities for amphibious training already existed." Nor did he believe the Japanese presence on Kiska constituted any real danger. So he turned down DeWitt's proposal.

By mid-November 1942 the navy had selected 15 May 1943 as the most favorable D-Day. Marshall tentatively agreed, but insisted that no final decision be reached until March. On 19 December DeWitt submitted his estimated troop needs—one division, two infantry regiments, and service and supply troops, the whole totaling some twenty-five thousand men. Marshall would only agree to a division, but that was a beginning.[5]

DeWitt's instinct was to invade Kiska with Buckner's men already on the spot, and no really satisfactory explanation has ever been forthcoming as to why this was not done. Garfield offered a few suggestions: The troops were widely scattered, morale was poor, the men had no training in amphibious operations, "and it would be impossible to strip Alaska's outposts of enough men to make up a full combat division . . ."[6] All very well—but in retrospect one wonders why stateside troops could not have been brought in to man the outposts, while the climate-hardened veterans formed at least a cadre of the assault force. As for morale, the principal reason it was low was because the men felt their government had sent them to the backyard of nowhere with no part in the war. Had they been given a real combat assignment, one would have heard much less about low morale.

Be that as it may, DeWitt requested that he be given the 35th

Infantry Division. Both its commander, Maj. Gen. Charles H. Corbett, and his deputy, Brig. Gen. Eugene M. Landrum, were experienced Aleutian hands. Instead, the War Department gave him the 7th Motorized Division. It would be difficult to make a more inappropriate choice. The Seventh consisted of national guardsmen from the West and Southwest. Many were Californians, "among them an unusually large percentage of Mexicans and Indians." Although sound, brave men, many had never so much as seen snow. Their commander, Maj. Gen. Albert E. Brown, had last served in combat in World War I.

The Seventh had been training in the California desert for assignment to North Africa. Of course, the tactics, tanks, other motorized equipment, even the clothing suitable for engaging Rommel's Afrika Corps would be not only useless, but they would be heavy liabilities in the Aleutians. Naturally, DeWitt and Buckner protested; it did no good. The Desert Fox was in retreat, so the North African Theater could spare the Seventh, which, the War Department claimed, was more advanced in readiness than the Thirty-fifth. A second protest brought a reply that could be summed up as "Take it or leave it."

CinCPAC and both Alaskan commanders contributed experienced, valuable officers to the discussions at San Diego. For once, the arguments that arose were not interservice arguments; the problem was an equally ancient one, that of the theorist versus the experienced personnel. All too often the former ignored the latter.[7]

A drastic change of plans took place on 3 March. Rear Adm. Francis W. Rockwell, in charge of the assault, did not believe that the ships the navy had promised him would be enough for a successful attack. So, while on a brief visit to San Diego, Kinkaid proposed that the target be Attu rather than Kiska. He believed that the available shipping would be sufficient. He also estimated that "one reinforced infantry regiment" could take Attu. Once this was done, Kiska would be isolated and the Japanese might have to evacuate. This seemed logical to Washington, so Attu became the objective. Thus Kinkaid was the father of the "island-hopping" strategy, destined to prove so successful elsewhere in the Pacific.

Kinkaid's suggestion was based upon erroneous estimates of the Japanese strength on Attu and Kiska. He believed the Japanese had a mere five hundred troops on Attu, and he overestimated their force on Kiska by over three thousand. This was hardly Kinkaid's fault. Military intelligence concerning the Japanese on the two islands was virtually nonexistent. It was limited in general to air reconnaissance, which was severely hampered by fog.[8]

The green light from Washington did not signal an orderly procession forward. The Seventh had been split into two regimental combat teams, training in amphibious landings at San Diego and at Fort Ord, near Monterey. They had a good instructor, Maj. Gen. Holland M. "Howlin' Mad" Smith, USMC, but the geographical conditions were almost ludicrously unrelated to those on Attu. Indeed, no location in the lower forty-eight came close to approximating the Aleutians. This helps to explain the serious rift that developed between what we may call the "Alaskans" and the "statesiders," a rift so wide that at one point Rockwell threatened to scrap the project. How to explain a place where neither food nor fuel was available, where the earth's crust could break under a man's weight, and a seasoned infantryman might, if he was lucky, make as much as a mile-and-a-half in an hour? It was like trying to describe the color blue to a blind man.

DeWitt and Brown did not get along—Brown distrusted DeWitt's belief in a quick victory; DeWitt thought Brown a wet blanket. The mutual misunderstandings worked downward. The sensible suggestions of Castner and Eareckson were set aside in favor of those of Lt. Col. Carl Jones. Although a member of Buckner's staff, he had never gone further along the Aleutian chain than Kodiak, and his recommendations fell far short of the mark.[9]

Buckner asked Brown to include his troops in Alaska; Rockwell said he did not have the shipping space. DeWitt countered by chartering a commercial vessel for that purpose. Rockwell declared he could not land extra troops quickly enough for their safety. Brown came forth with another objection: The Seventh was "a close-knit division" strangers would not fit in. The upshot was that Buckner was given the job of logistical support while his 4th Infantry Regiment remained prepared to attack Attu if it became necessary. So it was not until 18 April, after a revised intelligence report estimating Japanese strength on Attu as 1,600 rather than 500, that Rockwell decided to commit "the entire 7th Division and its reinforcements"—some 10,000 men—to the mission.

This was an even more significant date for the Japanese than for the Americans. At faraway Bougainville Island, a P-38 piloted by Capt. Tom Lanphier shot down a bomber with the charismatic Admiral Yamamoto aboard. The Japanese Navy had no officer of his caliber to step into the slot thus abruptly vacated. Garfield credited the ensuing disruption at high level with some of the "Japanese indecisiveness during the Battle of Attu . . ."[10]

On this same day, Alspaugh wrote to his mother, "My O.C.S. papers have been canceled for an indefinite period . . ." This was a big disappointment, because appointment to Officer Candidate School could not only lead to a commission, but it also represented a way to escape the Aleutian treadmill honorably and move on to a more active theater. "Sometimes I think I'm better off just staying here and sweating the war out," he continued resignedly, "and then other times I wish I could get away from here and get in the middle of things and do something besides wait."[11]

Weese was more fortunate. After being passed over once because he was ten pounds overweight, he received his appointment in the same mouth of April 1943.[12]

Lieutenant Miller had returned from his home leave to find that his unit had moved, not to Amchitka as he had heard, but to Adak. He had to "fool around Umnak almost a month" before he was able to arrange transportation. He reached Adak on 10 April "in the usual welcoming storm." Still, he found the weather better than at Umnak, and the base was "lots farther ahead than at Umnak." He added, "The 4th Infantry Regiment is going to the Semichis soon. That is the next place."[13]

From that comment it took no military genius to figure out the target; the Semichis being a tiny group of islands just off Attu, across the Agattu Strait. Stubbs, however, was still under the impression that Kiska was the objective. "We are taking over the duties of the 4th Infantry," he noted on 8 April. "I think they may be going to Kiska soon." On 10 April he and a detail of his buddies "saw some amphibian tanks unloading on the beach." He added with satisfaction, "Kiska better look out for trouble pretty soon."[14]

Kiska was already having plenty of trouble. After the storm that Miller mentioned, the weather cleared and allowed what, for the Aleutian Theater, were heavy bombing strikes. There were two reasons why Kiska rather than Attu took the brunt. The first was tactical, to keep Japanese attention focused on Kiska. The second was sheer necessity. While the weather over Kiska was comparatively favorable, Attu was often fogged over, so that missions intended for that island had to turn back and unload their bombs on Kiska.[15]

On 21 April, Kinkaid issued his order for Operation Landcrab, the capture of Attu. This placed all army and navy air forces as Task Group (TG) 16.1 under Butler. The Army Air Striking Unit (the Eleventh Air Force) became Task Unit (TU) 16.1.1, while the Naval Air Search Unit (PatWing 4) was designated TU 16.1.2. Nimitz had given Kinkaid's Task Force (TF) 51 three of the navy's older battleships—the former flagship *Pennsylvania*, the *Idaho*, and the *Nevada*, once more operational after the beating she suffered at Pearl Harbor. He also gave Kinkaid the escort carrier *Nassau* for close air support. Cruisers comprised the Southern and Northern Covering Groups. Before the main assault, two large submarines would land scouts on Attu.[16]

The spirit of reorganization spread even to units not directly concerned with Landcrab. The 206th's Battery K diary entry for 24 April read:

> Under new reorganization which makes 'I' Battery a 90 mm gun unit, old 'K' battery is once again charged with a herculean task of doing the work previously required of two batteries without any appreciative [sic] increase in strength.
>
> True to the tradition of the outfit, the fellows sprang to the task and completely occupied the tactical positions of its former colleague in record time thus relieving them that much sooner to tackle the important job of mastering the workings of their new equipment.[17]

Massey's unit experienced a shuffle of NCOs in early May, and he was transferred to the big guns of Battery D. "The C.O. called, said not to move, my orders would be changed." Sure enough, they were.

"Weather somewhat better for a few days," he wrote. "We stepped up training and target practice." The men were "edgy, homesick, and a few arguments and fights" broke out. One wonders whether these men sensed pre-battle tension in the air. One soldier transferred out, no loss to Massey, for the man was a troublemaker. "Got one man in his place, name Zero. Had to give him a G.I. bath, he smelled so bad. He's just a kid," Massey added tolerantly, "never been away from home. He is a fanatic on concert music."[18]

While the rest of the Seventh continued their amphibious training, the initial landing party, the 7th Scout Company, was being organized and trained under thirty-four-year-old Capt. William H. Willoughby, in civilian life a dairy farmer. General Brown placed much trust in Willoughby and gave him "*carte blanche* to raid every platoon in the division for top soldiers." Not only from the Seventh, but from other sources, including the Fort Ord guardhouse, Willoughby picked men with special skills and in top physical condition. He armed them with the most suitable weapons he could find, and plenty of them.

Like the rest of the Seventh, they rendezvoused at San Francisco, clad in summer uniforms. They received the medical lectures on tropical diseases customary for troops embarking for the south Pacific, so the men decided they were going to the Solomons. Arctic clothing and equipment were loaded in sealed containers.

The scouts sailed in *Narwhal* and *Nautilus*, two of the United States' largest submarines that had hastily added bunks. *Narwhal's* were of wood and canvas, a foot high by eighteen inches wide. Once a man had crammed in, he could not turn over. The scouts were not looking forward to the voyage, many having suffered from seasickness in test runs.[19]

They reached Dutch Harbor where they had a week's on-the-spot practice. Amaknak's metropolis did not impress the newcomers: "Dutch Harbor was an awful-looking place; just very high snow-capped mountains towering all about us. The roads were mud and slush, knee deep. It rained and snowed all the time, and the winds blew a gale. It was miserable. It's inconceivable that troops could have lived there for two years. There were no women and no liquor. Ham and eggs cost $1.50. A wrist watch which would have cost $20 in the States cost $70."[20]

At least these men could move about; the rest of the Division had reached Cold Bay on 30 April in unbelievably crowded transports. Since there were no shore facilities, the men had to stay aboard, sleeping in shifts, and in too close quarters by day to permit proper exercise.

The submarine-borne scouts would constitute the first wave to land on Attu; a second wave of 165 men would land from a destroyer. Their stay at Dutch Harbor gave the first wave the opportunity to practice beach landings.[21]

On one such occasion they ran afoul of Massey's men. Writing as he often did in the historical present, Massey related, "Two large subs come in, anchor off the spit. They are loaded with Rangers, they start to come ashore on rubber rafts, we hold them off the with loaded weapons until cleared from Hq. They have little to say, none wearing any identification as to rank or unit."[22]

Willoughby had devised a clever landing tactic. His men would land on enemy-held territory at night and in silence. This would not be possible if his men followed the usual method of jumping off the submarines' decks into the rafts. Therefore, he arranged that when the submarines surfaced, his men would inflate their rafts, place them on the afterdeck, and climb in carefully, so that their gear would make no noise. When they were ready, the subs would submerge, leaving the fully-manned rafts afloat. Of course, this could only come off if the seas at Attu were calm, which was by no means a certainty.

Meanwhile, at last the Americans began a heavy naval and air bombardment of Attu, and scout planes returned to Adak with some photographs that, while technically clear, contained disquieting information: Japanese strength on Attu seemed to be some 2,600—a good thousand over the last estimate. And neither the army nor the navy had any more men or equipment to spare for Brown. It did not augur well; Attu would be no pushover.[23]

33

"Sweating the Attack"

Everyone is sweating the attack on the Japs . . . ," Miller wrote in his diary on 6 May. "Well, we have just had a good storm and the weather is clearing which will be good for operations but will remove any element of surprise. The Attu garrison is expected to be about 1800 with some big headquarters there, so two regiments of infantry can expect to have trouble, but not a hopeless job. . . . There is no reason to believe, however, that the Nip won't fight to hold his fingerhold in the Aleutians . . . Attu shouldn't be too tough but Kiska will be a hornet's nest."[1]

All concerned were indeed "sweating the attack," with D-Day scheduled for 7 May. After some opposition from Rockwell, who wanted to make a single mass landing at Sarana Bay, the plan Brown favored was adopted. This specified two major landings of one regiment each at Holtz Bay and Massacre Bay. A third regiment would be reserved until events determined which of the two sites needed its presence. The scouts under Willoughby would come ashore at Beach Scarlet west of Holtz Bay and work their way eastward. The strategy was for the three groups to meet between the two bays.

Thus Brown hoped to cut off the main Japanese base at Chichagof Harbor. This, in effect, was the classic pincers movement with its centuries-long history of successful operations. In this case, however, it was based entirely on theory; none of the planners had ever engaged in an amphibious assault, and none of them seem to have had any real conception of what they were up against in the way of terrain and weather.[2]

The 7th Regiment, waiting at Cold Bay, was prepared and outfitted for "a battle so rapid that there would be no need for the men to carry blankets ashore, an occupation so fast that they were to have hot food ashore the first night." Junior officers declared the whole operation would be over in thirty-six hours. "Terrain meant nothing. The doubts of local guides meant nothing."[3]

One man who had no illusions about what an attack on Attu would involve was Eareckson, back in the picture to coordinate air and ground operations. He expressed his sentiments in verse:

> In viewing Attu's rocky shores
> While planning how to take it,
> This thought impresses more and more;
> The Nips should first forsake it.
> Since Attu ain't worth a hoot
> For raising crops or cattle,
> Let's load with booze and take a cruise
> And just call off the battle.[4]

Eareckson could have put it more sedately, but in its essence the colonel's sassy verse was probably the most sensible suggestion made at the time.

The American force was preparing to sortie when Naval Intelligence reported that the Japanese knew the strike was coming against Attu, not Kiska. Col. Yasuyo Yamasaki, an able and courageous officer who had been in command on Attu for about a month, could look for no immediate help. On 4 May he had received word from Vice Adm. Shiro Kawase, Hosogaya's replacement, that for various reasons he would have to withhold reinforcements until late May, by which time the fog season would be under way, and Japanese transports would have received radar. Until then, Attu would have to take its chances.[5]

The operation was already twenty-four hours behind schedule when Rockwell's twenty-nine ships sortied at daybreak on 4 May. It was a thoroughly miserable voyage through seas "so rough that the battleships had to elevate their forward guns so the breaking waves would not rip off their muzzle bags and bloomers . . ." The ships followed the south side of the Aleutians and entered the Bering Sea by Amutka Pass. They kept well north of Kiska to their "run-in point 115 miles NE by N of Attu." Air scouting reports from over Attu predicted dangerously high surf for 7 May, the projected D-Day, so Rockwell postponed the landing for two days. Meanwhile, anticipating that the Japanese, aware of the American intention, would have sent a respectable fleet to Attu's aid, Rockwell dispatched his battleships westward. Fresh from the Komandorski victory, they set off in a spirit of anticipation, but found no enemy. *Kimikawa Maru*, bringing a few scout aircraft to Attu, was at sea, but her path did not cross that of the battleships.

The next day the weather was, if anything, worse than on the seventh, and a dense fog had settled down. Once more Rockwell postponed D-Day, this time to the eleventh, and the ships fueled at sea. That evening the battleships rendezvoused with the task force. A typical Aleutian fog made ship movements dangerous; the destroyer-minelayer *Sicard* rammed the destroyer *MacDonough*. There were no casualties and both returned to port safely, but, as Morrison wrote, ". . . their absence was keenly felt, since *Sicard* was to have been control vessel for the landing and *MacDonough* had a special fire control mission." All of this delayed operations three hours, then Rockwell headed for Attu with a troop landing scheduled for 1040 11 May.[6]

It was late when Willoughby's scouts aboard *Nautilus* and *Narwahl* heard of the new date. These men had been cooped up in the submarines for days and suffered terribly from seasickness. "We were getting close to our destination," wrote Stan Hasrato, "and we all wondered how in the world we could fight when we had been vomiting for three weeks. We were damned weak and every man had lost an average of ten pounds." When they arrived off Attu they were "pretty nervous"; for hours their group of some 244 men would be the only Americans on the island and might have to fight off the entire Japanese garrison. Hasrato was one of five men selected to pick off Japanese sentries at Beach Scarlet and to cut their telephone lines.

Each man carried somewhere between ninety and one hundred pounds of equipment, but their only food was "one box of K rations." Thus equipped, they climbed into their boats. The submarine had actually begun to submerge when word came to delay until the next day, 11 May. The scouts exploded: "I have never heard so much swearing in all my life."[7]

They finally got off at 0100. One reason they had so little food was because these husky young men had to scramble through a twenty-five-inch hatch, and many, including Willoughby, had to leave the bulk of their food behind. The unconventional launching went off perfectly; within two hours the scouts had landed on Beach Scarlet. There snow-covered mountains came almost to the water-line; the temperature stood at 27° Fahrenheit. But as the sun rose it looked like this would be a beautiful day. Then, before the men had moved well upward, they heard aircraft engines, looked back, and watched in furious stupefaction as F4Fs from *Nassau* strafed the beached rubber boats, cutting off any hope of escape if the Japanese struck. Three men left behind to guard the boats barely escaped with their lives.[8] As obviously the navy pilots did not intentionally maroon their army comrades, one can only conclude that they thought the boats belonged to the Japanese. That suggests they had received a criminally poor briefing as to what might be expected at Beach Scarlet.

Some hours after Willoughby's little force landed, the destroyer transport *Kane* put ashore another four hundred soldiers. These joined forces with the scouts and moved up the mountain, seeking the pass to Holtz Bay. The promise of the early morning had not been fulfilled; fog had clamped down. The going was indescribable. Either tundra or heavy snow can make walking excruciatingly difficult; combine the two and the forward pace could be measured in inches rather than yards, even for élite troops like Willoughby's. When darkness fell, they had reached a mountaintop, but the temperature had fallen to 10° and a gale was blowing. Willoughby had to call a halt, lest they be blown into some invisible crevasse or canyon.[9]

The major northern force, meanwhile, had the same experience with the fog. "At seven the fog was light," wrote correspondent Howard Handleman. "We could see battleships and destroyers. . . . At eight, the fog was like a wall again; we couldn't see from one end of our ship to the other."

Col. Frank L. Culin, commanding the 32d Infantry Regiment, knew how eager his men were for the feel of solid earth beneath their feet. They had been cooped up for weeks aboard the transport *J. Franklin Bell* under conditions that would have caused a public outcry in the United States had they existed on murderers' row in a maximum security prison. "There were calisthenics topside," Handleman recalled, "But the deck was so thick with landing barges, guns and gear that only small groups of men could exercise at a time. It was so crowded men had to read leaning against other men's backs."[10]

Culin decided to reconnoiter the landing site, fog or no fog. Culin, Capt. Robert Thompson with the latter's group of "Castner's Cutthroats," including some Aleuts, and the invaluable Squeaky Anderson took off in two landing craft, towing plastic dories. The destroyer *Phelps* guided them through the fog. Half a mile offshore, the advance party entered the dories and cautiously rowed to the beach. A glance sufficed to determine that whoever selected Beach Red had chosen well. The beach was less than 100 yards wide, and an 800-foot-high cliff hemmed it in. Had the Japanese elected to defend it, a few machineguns on the height could have done the job, but evidently they considered this spot impossible for a landing. No defenses had been positioned, although Beach Red was a short four miles or so from the major installation at Holtz Bay.

Sending his Aleuts to search the hills in case any Japanese might be lurking in wait, Culin signaled *Phelps* that it was safe to land the men of the Assault Company, 1st Battalion Combat Team. These troops were aboard six boats following *Phelps*. As fast as they landed, Culin hurried them inland. Squeaky Anderson kept the matériel in order, and throughout the operation he would provide an object lesson in the importance of an efficient beachmaster to an amphibious assault.[11]

Meanwhile, the rest of the northern force, under Lt. Col. Albert V. Hartl, waited. They were impatient to land, and also they were worried about Culin and his party. Finally the word came from the commander of the attack transports, "Land when ready." The time was about 1300. "Our circling barges churned up the water in great swells which splashed over us," reminisced Handleman, "and finally strung out single file behind a destroyer which bobbed ahead like a mother hen." The destroyer and its brood of barges were enveloped in fog as if packed in cotton wool. According to Garfield, "Soldiers had to be lowered over the sides by their heels; fingertips trailing in the water, they guided the landing force through the foggy shoals and began to unload." There was no enemy in sight, and the loudest sound was Anderson's voice, screaming directions in the loud, high-pitched tones that had given him his nickname. By the time Handleman's boat had landed, the men were already hard at work, stacking food and ammunition, pulling at the guns.

Sundown had not yet come when the advance began up a ravine, on hands and knees. At one spot a rope had to be lowered so that the soldiers could pull themselves up. Having reached the top of the cliff, the men dropped in their tracks, too spent to move without rest.

The first report of contact with the enemy reached Hartl* at 1800. A patrol from B Company to the rear close to the sea had encountered a Japanese patrol of four. The Americans killed one and wounded another, but two got away. Thus the Japanese would know that an American force had landed north of their position. Sure enough, the first Japanese shell whistled over at 2028. Their fire was wild, but the invaders fell down and stayed down. Hartl decided to bivouac. He had little choice, because darkness had fallen and his maps were unreliable. The men spent a miserable night, wet and half frozen; they had no sleeping bags. The delay, although unavoidable, was unfortunate; it gave the Japanese the opportunity to dig in on the hill overlooking Holtz Valley, Hartl's objective.[12]

While all this was going on, the largest of the landing parties, the southern force under Brown's personal command, approached Massacre Bay. This group consisted of three transports, nine destroyers, and the battleship *Nevada*. Landing had been scheduled for 0740, but the ubiquitous fog necessitated postponement, and the men had to spend the morning in open boats. Fortunately the temperature stood at 48°—quite balmy by Attu's standards—but it was uncomfortable enough for unprotected men in a state of suspense. Under such conditions, even the least superstitious may respond to omens, and the name "Massacre Bay" did nothing to lift morale.

During this morning, *Pennsylvania* and *Idaho* bombarded Chichagof Harbor with no visible result. Off Massacre Bay, the fog gave no hint of lifting, so Brown and Rockwell decided to proceed and take their chances, with launch time of 1530. At that time the overcast thinned slightly and the first group of landing craft (LC) set off. One capsized; one struck a rock. The first troops went ashore unopposed at 1620. Another accident marred the second wave; an LC was swamped and a dozen men drowned.[13]

---

* Culin had returned to his ship, suffering from exposure.

But 1st Lt. H. D. Long always remembered that it was quiet—"coldly, bitterly, viciously quiet." Throughout their training, noise had been their constant companion. "Guns roared, men yelled, battleships thundered, and planes zoomed over our heads." And now the real thing "was completely, utterly quiet . . . Attu seemed devoid of life. Not a tree, an animal, or anything else that moved. And yet we knew that death lurked in the fog." The uncanny silence seemed to spook the men. According to Long, they prayed "for noise, any kind of noise. Dear God, please make a noise of some kind."

Relief came in the form of a sparrow. "He sat on a bump above the beach and sang his lungs out, and an explosive gasp shushed out of hundreds of throats. The spell was broken, the world hadn't died around us. The first DSC from Attu should go to that bird. He saved lives that day. His song changed us from a tight, tense, hypnotized, unrelated group of human beings to a relaxed, laughing, cohesive combat force."[14]

Long and his patrol headed for "Artillery Hill," held by four Japanese with two 20mm guns. By all odds they should have picked off Long's men or at least extracted a heavy price; instead, for some reason, they fled, leaving behind their weapons and ammunition.[15] Possibly they had been instructed to do so. Elsewhere it would be a standard Japanese tactic to allow U.S. amphibious forces to land, then "lure" them inland. This ploy seldom if ever worked, but at Attu Yamasaki had little choice. Once he knew where the Americans had landed, no Napoleon was needed to figure out their attack plan. Yamasaki did not have the power to drive the invaders back into the sea; he could only deploy his forces on the heights and make the Americans pay a bloody price for every foot of Attu. In fact, two companies of the 303d Infantry Battalion, under Lieutenants Honna and Goto*, were interested witnesses to the landings at Massacre Bay. By a trick of the fog, these Japanese could look down and see what was going on, but the invaders could not see upward.

By 1730, Col. Edward P. Earle had begun to move inland. It was scarcely a triumphal procession. His foot soldiers had to contend with the same indescribable combination of snow and tundra that clutched at the men of the northern landing parties. The predictions

---

* Full names not available.

of the "old Alaska hands" began to come true with frightening speed. Cat tractors towing the 105mm howitzers broke through the tundra and halted the 48th Field Artillery Battalion's Battery C after an advance of seventy-five yards. The artillery commander, Brig. Gen. Archibald V. Arnold, had his artillery mounted on sleds, but his tractors, too, bogged down.

His soldiers somehow turned the guns manually. Shortly after 1800, Lt. William Kimball, commanding Battery C, reached forward observer Lt. James West, who reported a Japanese mortar's location. Battery C's first shot went wild, but soon they found the range, and the battle of Attu began in earnest.

At 1900 Earle's infantry had been on the move for a good hour-and-a-half, but had advanced only a mile-and-a-half. A pace of a mile per hour is one of those statistics that can be so enlightening; under anything like normal conditions, a troop of Cub Scouts could have done better. The infantry's slogging hike had been frustrating in itself; now enemy fire pinned them down for an hour. Then, under ineffective covering fire from the beach, they charged, only to be met by Japanese fire so accurate that the inexperienced Americans paused in frightened confusion. Earle urged them on, but his second try also collapsed, so the colonel had to go on the defensive.

In contrast to Squeaky Anderson's efficient operation at Beach Red, the beach at Massacre Bay became a bottleneck, clogged with the mechanized equipment so valuable elsewhere, so useless on Attu. Supplies had to be hand carried, and some advance units went for at least twenty-four hours with neither food nor ammunition.

At 2200, Brown came ashore with his staff and established a headquarters.[16]

DeWitt had predicted that Attu could be taken in three days. One of the three had passed. The Americans had landed, had even made a little initial progress, but had ground to a halt, as much because of the weather and terrain as because of the defending Japanese.

34

"Get the Damned Thing Over With"

Massey had an intimation that something big was under way when he reported to the hospital, as instructed, to have his tonsils removed. The doctor told him the operation would have to be postponed and gave Massey some pills to tide him over. "The small hospital has new beds set up everything, even in some of the corridors," Massey recorded. "That can spell only one thing—an invasion."[1]

On Attu it was becoming all too evident that hospital beds would be needed; this would be no three-day cakewalk but a grim, costly campaign. Willoughby's scouts rose at 0400 on 12 May and later that morning reached the top of the mountains. Around 0800 they moved downward. The First Platoon had worn tracks in the snow; the rest of the group used these as toboggan slides and reached the valley in record time.

The Japanese, having reinforced the ridges, opened fire, and by afternoon the two forces were quite close. There matters stood for three days. The scouts were keeping the Japanese troops away from the northern force, but at a considerable cost in lives, wounded, and suffering. "Our legs were getting worse and worse," wrote Hasrato. "The men were constantly falling down. Many were sent to the command post hospital, which consisted of holes dug into snowbanks." They had no water, and slaked their thirst by eating snow. Nor did they have food. They had bitter cause to regret the rations left behind in the submarines. Supply planes had been unable to locate the scouts, although the men could hear them roaring overhead.[2]

At Beach Red, *Bell* discharged cargo, and aircraft from *Nassau* and the air force attacked Holtz Bay. *Pennsylvania*, *Idaho*, and *Phelps* continued to shell. *Pennsylvania* had a narrow escape when the Japanese submarine *I-31* fired a torpedo at her, which she dodged. All evening destroyers hunted the sub and thought they had sunk her, but she was around until 13 June when *Frazier* sank her.

Action at Massacre Bay began with the boom of *Nevada*'s guns. The fog lifted, but only far enough up the hills to conceal the Japanese. Earle ordered a battalion forward at Jarmin Pass.* After a few yards, Japanese fire sent them back. That afternoon Earle and an Alaska Scout went out in search of his front lines, for radio contact had been lost. Several hours later a patrol located them; the scout was badly wounded, the colonel dead, victims of a sniper.

The loss of this gallant officer was a blow, but there was no time to grieve. As soon as he received word, Brown sent off his chief of staff, Col. Wayne C. Zimmerman, as Earle's replacement. Brown himself reconnoitered the front lines, and sent off three messages to Rockwell, each asking where the transports *Grant* and *Chirikoff* were, with two battalions, that had been due to land that morning. Evidently Rockwell never received these inquiries for he did not reply. The peculiar air conditions in the Aleutians made radio communications chancy, and they would play a baneful role in the campaign.

Meanwhile, the *Perida* reached Massacre Bay, only to hit a rock, destroying much-needed radio equipment, and was beached for repairs.[3]

In the north, fire was intense. Late in the afternoon, Hartl again ordered an attack. The men had to advance straight up the mountain in single file, a process that consumed almost an hour, with many falling down and sliding in the snow. "They finally reached the crest, in a saddle between two peaks," Handleman recorded. "The next day they were to name that saddle 'Bloody Point,' but this afternoon it was a nameless mountain, filled with fear of the unknown."

An officer who had been slightly wounded gave a briefing on Japanese fire tactics. He added that many men of A Company were still in the gully. "Their feet are frozen. They'll have to be carried back," he said.

"That was the first word of the worst mistake of the expedi-

---

* Like several of the positions, Jarmin Pass received its name later. It was so named in honor of the ranking officer killed there.

tion," stated Handleman. "The men were equipped with fine heavy black-leather hunting boots; but on ordinary days in the Aleutians rubber is the only thing that can protect feet against the eternal wetness . . . scores suffered frozen feet in their beautiful, black boots which got wet and wouldn't dry."[4]

There can be no doubt that improper footwear caused untold misery and many amputations. The Seventh "eventually became so foot-conscious that, on Leyte, soldiers demanded and received 46,000 pairs of new shoes. They learned on Attu that bad shoes meant poor fighting. . . ." Fortunately, the army as a whole learned the same lesson. As Garfield wrote, "In the next two years' global fighting, the experience of Attu would save thousands of limbs and lives." But that was too late for the soldiers on Attu who paid for this mistake with gangrene and lost feet.[5]

The thirteenth was another frustrating day. Zimmerman's southern force men almost took Jarmin Pass, but had to roll back to their foxholes under heavy Japanese fire. Brown, with Arnold and several staff officers, was only "a few hundred yards" behind. Once more he urged Rockwell to send him the reserves, stating baldly that "the troops on hand could not budge the enemy." This message got through but, incredibly, Rockwell didn't know the whereabouts of the transports *Grant* and *Chirikoff*. Within the hour, however, he sent back word that these ships would land troops that afternoon. True to his promise, *Grant* arrived at Massacre Bay and sent a battalion plus a field hospital ashore. Brown hustled the former up to the front. At Beach Red, Japanese fire kept *Chirikoff* from landing her battalion until late afternoon, and Culin, back in command although still suffering from chills, sent these men straight to the front.

Well into their second day without food, Willoughby's scouts fought a sharp engagement, drove the Japanese from the summit, and dug in a snow cave for the night. They lit a pitifully small fire, fed with anything flammable, to warm their fingers and heat their last packets of coffee.[6]

On 14 May Eareckson was hovering over Attu, as he had every day of the campaign, regardless of weather, when Kinkaid radioed him. Rockwell had advised the admiral that poor visibility was holding up Brown's attacks, and Kinkaid asked just how bad it was. Eareckson told him that "Attu was socked in solid," whereupon Kinkaid instructed Eareckson to return.

This hint that Kinkaid required confirmation of Rockwell's advice concerning Brown's situation might be considered the opening gun of the campaign that raged for several days on the flag officer level. As time passed with no appreciable advance, the upper echelon became increasingly unhappy with Brown. For his part, Brown was disillusioned with Rockwell, whom he suspected of being more interested in saving his ships than in supporting the army. Indeed, by the afternoon of the fourteenth the capital ships had expended all their bombardment ammunition.

Lack of communication exacerbated the situation. Radios that could have clarified matters were hung up in *Perida*; an important dispatch from Brown, fully explaining the situation, was never delivered; the messenger PBY dropped it in the bay instead of on *Nevada*; static continued to play havoc. When on 15 May Brown visited the flagship and talked to Rockwell face to face, their misunderstandings disappeared, and for the balance of the leadership crisis Rockwell supported Brown loyally.

A similar direct meeting with Kinkaid might have worked as well. On the other hand, support for Brown in the higher echelon was already prejudiced. DeWitt had disliked Brown from the beginning, and Brown's failure to make good on DeWitt's estimate of a three-day conquest did not endear him further. Buckner thought Brown's problem was his lack of Alaskan background, and he suggested Maj. Gen. Eugene M. Landrum to command at Attu—which was what he had wanted in the first place. Governor Gruening would observe later of Brown, "Not only did he know nothing about Alaska, but it appeared to those who flew down from Alaska to Southern California to inform him of his appointment, that he could not be told anything."

Kinkaid had never met Brown, but went along with the recommendations of DeWitt and Buckner. With Nimitz's concurrence, he relieved Brown in favor of Landrum, who took over on 16 May. Landrum seems to have been somewhat embarrassed by the situation; he could find no fault with Brown's actions and decided to follow Brown's tactics. In later days, when Brown appealed his case and was acquitted of wrongdoing, Landrum backed him up, writing, "Your strategy paid big dividends."[7]

Meanwhile, the actual fighting pursued its grim course. The Third Battalion again tried to take Jarmin Pass and retreated in disorder. Casualties were heavy, including the four company commanders, two of whom were killed, and two were so badly wounded they had to be evacuated.

That morning Willoughby's scouts repulsed a Japanese attack and spent the day in an exchange of machine-gun and sniper fire. "The cold was intense and some of the men were vomiting green bile from their empty stomachs. . . . No one was talking." By evening, nearly half were wounded, sick, or half frozen. Yet they fought with such valor that a Japanese medical lieutenant noted in his diary, "Enemy strength must be a division." The next day, a supply plane managed a small drop. A soldier brought Hasrato's platoon three cans of beans—their first food in four days. He rationed the three cans among the thirty-six men—some thirty beans per man.[8]

Lieutenant Long was badly wounded at Massacre Valley. His men, he wrote, "were ready to fight the whole goddam Jap army right away if I said the word. This was the only time I ever saw extreme emotion of any kind. Several boys cried like babies when they saw me rather badly battered up and unable to walk." He was a bit out of his head and put up a fight, believing them to be Japanese. Then his platoon sergeant "made a classic speech. 'Lieutenant,' he said, 'you told me if I ever thought you were hurt so bad that you were mentally unfit to command I was to take over. O.K., I think so now. I command now, and you don't, and if you don't pipe down I'll slug you.'" At this Long managed a weak laugh. But throughout his speech and after, the sergeant was carrying the lieutenant "like a little baby," covering him up and making him as comfortable as possible. Another man knelt down and "said a very sincere little prayer . . ."[9]

Back on Adak, Miller and his men had been listening in on the tactical radio—"quite an experience—like hearing a series ball game. Can hear pilots talking to ground and ships and spotting targets for artillery. . . . We can just about hold our own there on the ground and we'll have to not count on air. Last two days have been socked in so tight event he Navy can't see its targets. Land forces are yelling for supplies—naturally."[10]

At one position on the fifteenth, a Japanese machine gun opened up on an American infantry platoon, and the men dropped in the mud. Then U.S. guns on the beach began to shell the same area. Literally caught between two fires, the lieutenant called out to a man on his right, "Take a couple of men, work up behind the gun and knock it out." The man neither moved nor gave any indication of having heard the order. So the lieutenant repeated it, this time to his platoon sergeant. He drew the same result. A sort of paralysis seemed to have settled over the whole platoon. So the officer himself, with one man following "at a safe distance," personally silenced the gun. Then the platoon moved forward, only to drop again when a second gun opened up. It was the same story—the lieutenant gave the order; nobody moved; so once more he did the job himself. The third time the platoon was pinned down, he didn't bother with orders, just started forward on his own. But this time the platoon sergeant touched his arm. "You shouldn't be doing this, lieutenant. That's my job." Their paralysis broken, the squad disposed of the machine-gun nest and captured the gun.[11]

On the morning of the fifteenth, Culin's men began advancing on Holtz Bay. But there was no battle; the Japanese had retreated to a ridge across the valley, leaving behind food, many weapons, and much ammunition. Unfortunately some of the equipment was useless to the Americans: Tubes didn't fit their radios, field phones didn't work on U.S. lines. But the soldiers helped themselves to the abandoned clothing. The Japanese withdrawal freed Willoughby's scouts. They were in bad shape. Evacuation of the seriously wounded left Willoughby with 165 men out of his original 420, and most of these were wearing bandages.[12]

On 16 May Alspaugh wrote home, "We have finally gone to work in earnest on the Jap in this theater of operations. I don't think it will take long for us to exterminate him up in these parts."[13]

From the calendar standpoint, it didn't take long. But time can be highly relative, and for the men on Attu every day was a dragging eternity. That same day, Culin's men occupied the ridge at Holtz Valley. Unaware that the Japanese were no longer in possession, *Nassau*'s aircraft bombed and strafed the 32d Infantry, "who had no ground panels to indicate front lines." Fortunately no grave harm was done. A few men were wounded, American radio operators turned the air blue cursing *Nassau* heartily, and the attack was called off.

As soon as Kinkaid heard of this incident, he radioed Eareckson, who as usual was aloft over Attu, "to report to General Landrum and take direct control of all air operations," coordinating air and ground operations. That evening Eareckson reported to Landrum aboard

Pennsylvania, and soon thereafter was flying a Navy Kingfisher (OS2U scout observation plane) off *Casco*. Typically, Eareckson interpreted his order as a personal mandate and in the days to come would put himself constantly in harm's way as what would later be called a "Forward Air Controller."[14]

By the afternoon of the seventeenth, Culin's men had taken the second ridge to the east of Holtz Bay; moreover, the Japanese who had been holding Jarmin Pass withdrew and headed for Chichagof Harbor. Kinkaid now decided that he could safely move Rockwell's ships to less dangerous waters, leaving behind the destroyer *Phelps*, gunboat *Charleston*, and *Casco*.

Finally, on the eighteenth, Attu received reinforcements in the form of the First Battalion, 4th Infantry. These were the Alaska-stationed troops who had been awaiting the summons. Being inured to the climate, they would suffer less than many, but they were soon in action. At the moment, however, they could barely walk, having been held for three weeks on their transport with no exercise.[15]

They had arrived just in time for the second phase of the campaign, which promised to be tough and costly. The Japanese had retired in good order, and steep, snow-covered heights protected the valley. Landrum permitted his subordinate commanders a day to make the necessary arrangements, and they would need it. Incredibly, of the ninety-three landing craft and small cargo boats that began the operation, only three were operational. "Ninety craft had gone down, victims of Attu shoals, reefs, williwaws, and surf." Rockwell moved his transports as close as he dared, and PT boats and PBYs brought supplies to the beaches.

One of the mountains at Chichagof was called Point Able, and there the Japanese held out for three days under the able direction of the same Lieutenant Honna who had done so well at Jarmin Pass. Buckner, visiting the combat zone, had Eareckson fly him and Castner over the front, including Point Able. There the general machine-gunned the Japanese positions. The weather precluded further flying, so as soon as they had returned to the tender *Casco*, Eareckson went ashore with Buckner. There the colonel found a rifle, went up to Point Able, and commenced firing. A Japanese sniper's bullet struck his back a glancing blow, whereupon Eareckson, more indignant than hurt, fired off the remaining bullets in his weapon, and some said he killed the sniper. After having his wound dressed, he returned to the beach. There Buckner some-how scared up a Purple Heart and pinned it on Eareckson. Then he swung him around and delivered a good swift kick, explaining that this was "for being where you had no business being."[16] No one was there with enough rank to do the same for Buckner, who equally had risked his life unnecessarily that same morning.

During the evening of 21 May, E Company of the 32d Infantry took Point Able. "The Japs weren't driven from the mountaintop," wrote Handleman. "They were killed there." Every Japanese, includ-ing Honna, died at his post.

The next morning found the Americans up against an equally formidable Japanese position atop the peak named Sarana Nose. Here the attackers had excellent fire cover from ordnance on the spot and from the heavy guns on the beaches. Cpl. Dan H. Manges of L Company, 17th Infantry, killed two Japanese behind a heavy gun and tried to turn it around. He couldn't manage alone, so called for Sgt. Lester B. Thistle to help. Between them they turned the gun and added it to the U. S. artillery attack.

The Japanese holding Sarana Nose comprised a rifle company of less than two hundred men against over two battalions of Americans, including the 4th Infantry. In any case, the result was inevitable, but what broke the Japanese resistance was the second artillery bombardment that afternoon. Within hours, Zimmerman's men had taken Sarana Nose.[17]

To proceed with the objective of taking Chichagof, the Americans first would have to take Fish Hook Ridge, an ice-covered, Japanese-held position. This could well be the last major engage-ment of the campaign, but that did not mean it would be easy. The further Yamasaki had to withdraw his troops, the more concen-trated would be his defense. One Japanese machine gun pinned down two American companies. "No one moved for a long time." Suddenly Pvt. Fred M. Barnett "just got all fed up and disgusted . . ." He decided he would "get the damned thing over with." Arming himself with an M-1 and some hand grenades, he approached the circle of emplacements around the gun. Nine times he walked up to one, peered inside, "stepped back and fired or tossed a grenade." Then he signaled for his buddies to advance.

That day saw the only air engagement of the Attu invasion. Colonel DeFord, who had been participating for a month or so in bombing missions—thereby revising his pilots' poor opinion of him—had to scratch the bomber attack due to weather. But when radar signaled sixteen planes approaching Attu, Lt. Col. James R. Watt took off at the head of five P-38s. The targets proved to be Mitsubishi Zero-1 medium bombers (Bettys). In the ensuing dogfight, the Japanese lost nine aircraft, the Americans lost two P-38s and one pilot.[18]

The air force did less well on the twenty-fourth. Ground troops of the 32d Infantry were delighted to see the big bombers. "Everyone cheered the planes and put out the orange panels to mark friendly front lines." But twice, on their way back from hitting the Japanese position, they mistook their targets and clobbered the 2nd Battalion. Miraculously, no one was hurt. "One machine gunner in Company H was dug out, along with his gun, from under a couple of tons of mud and tundra; and a boy from Company E had a slight tendency to stagger for a few hours afterward."

The Fish Hook was not completely taken until 28 May. On the twenty-sixth, Pvt. Joe P. Martinez of K Company, 32d Infantry, won the only Medal of Honor awarded in the Attu campaign by killing five Japanese single-handed and by clearing the sharp ridge of the Fish Hook before dying of wounds. After taking the Fish Hook, American troops entered Chichagof Valley.[19]

It was all over except for the final push. In an effort to spare needless bloodshed, Landrum had a load of pamphlets urging surrender dropped over Yamasaki's camp. Yamasaki, however, was not the surrendering type. His attitude was somewhat similar to that of Marshal Ferdinand Foch at the second battle of the Marne: "My center is giving way, my right is pushed back, situation excellent, I am attacking." With fewer than eight hundred able-bodied men left, he had one chance: a night assault to break through the weakest American position, to capture the American guns on Engineer Hill, then to take the U.S. supply camp. With his own supplies thus replenished and the American supplies taken or destroyed, he could retire into the hills. Perhaps the Americans would have to retreat; in any case, such a victory would give the Japanese Navy time to come to the rescue in one way or another. Thus the last Japanese resistance was not just a suicide charge; it was in accordance with a bold plan. And it came frighteningly near success.[20]

Company B of the 32d Infantry was headed for the battalion

kitchen when Yamasaki's soldiers fell on them, howling "Banzai!" while firing their guns and brandishing bayonets, some lashed to sticks. The Americans did not even try to resist; they fled in confused terror form what must have seemed like a host straight out of the Pit. Yamasaki did not pursue; he had a plan and stayed with it. His men charged up Engineer Hill, overran two command posts, and slaughtered the wounded and a chaplain at the medical station. A few of the wounded saved themselves by playing dead.

Atop the hill were sections of the 50th Engineers and several noncombatant units. General Arnold rallied them; he pointed out targets himself. The battle raged back and forth, but the Japanese could not take the summit. With defeat inevitable, five hundred Japanese committed suicide with their own grenades. Yamasaki tried once more, but this final charge, too, failed, and the colonel died of a bullet wound.[21]

It was all over except for mopping-up exercises. U.S. burial patrols counted 2,351 Japanese bodies, but thought that several hundred others must have been killed and buried during the campaign. Only 28 prisoners were taken. Total U.S. casualties were 3,829—549 killed, 1,148 wounded, the rest due to various illnesses and other causes.

The Battle of Attu was not highly publicized at the time, and eventually it was almost forgotten. One veteran remarked cynically, "No Marines—otherwise it would have been world history." Certainly Attu deserves to be remembered, for its mistakes perhaps more than for its successes. For these were studied carefully and put to good use. As Garfield remarked, "The 'A-frame' cargo boat, developed in Massacre Bay; Eareckson's Forward Air Control; and dozens of other makeshift Attu experiments soon became standard in the increasingly sophisticated weaponry of the continuing war."[22] The march of events left the Battle of Attu behind, and perhaps the army and navy were not sorry to downplay an engagement that, for all its ultimate success, had contained quite a few embarrassments.

35

"We Think We Will Be Seeing
Action Soon"

The Battle of Attu had little direct impact upon the men stationed on the other Aleutian Islands. They were primarily concerned with their own activities. On Amchitka, fire broke out in the ammunition dump in the area of Headquarters Company, 2nd Battalion, 37th Infantry, on 16 May. Captain Bouchette, a second lieutenant, and a staff sergeant were charged with negligence. All were cleared eventually, although it had been determined that the sergeant had been guilty of using gasoline in the area, which was against regulations. But recognizing that the fine he normally would have been assessed would be uncollectible for the duration of the war, the army authorities acquitted him along with the officers.[1]

On 22 May, the Battery K historian recorded, "T/4th Toney W. Dremer reduced to the Grade of Private because of misconduct." The writer added tolerantly, "Dremer is a good man and we are confident he will work his way up again." On the thirty-first, Lt. George E. Hayward replaced Capt. Orlando L. Greening as commander of Battery K. "We all regretted to see the Skipper go."[2]

Massey ended his comments for May: "After 18 days of fighting [on Attu] the Japs are on their knees, they dug into the mountains. Those bastards made one last effort and slaughtered some of our men. I hear only eight prisoners taken so far."[3]

On Adak, Miller had received his transfer orders and was experiencing to the full one of the prime disadvantages of military life—the prospect of losing good friends. "It is bad enough to leave loved ones at home," he observed in his journal, "but that is expected and of course we can always plan to rejoin them . . . With buddies it is different. There is something very fine about men who work and fight and come to love each other deeply. Then when they are separated something cuts deep between them and usually they go separate ways. . . . Chances are too good that you'll never see them again. . . ."

He continued gloomily, "That is happening to me now and I am finding it very hard to get up any enthusiasm for going back to the States. . . . If it weren't for the fact that I will have a chance to see my lovely wife again I would be tempted to turn down the proposition."[4] Comments about Attu wove through Stubbs's diary for May. On the twelfth, he noted overoptimistically, "Our troops hit Attu Island yesterday. We hear they have already taken the garrison and the Japs fled to the mountains." But principally he recorded the events of everyday life on Adak—typhus shots, hikes, reconnaissance, CG, policing the area, working on the huts, and of course the movies. He saw *Desperate Journey* with Errol Flynn and Ronald Reagan, and no doubt would have been incredulous had anyone told him he was watching a future president of the United States.

"We don't hear much about Attu," he remarked on the twenty-first. Two days later he recorded, "The Japs tried to bomb Attu again today. Our P-38s got 5 of their planes. We lost one plane but the pilot was saved." After a series of second-raters, the men got to see a top movie, James Cagney in *Yankee Doodle Dandy*. This was Stubbs's main comment on 30 May. The next day he ended the month with the comment, "We have two Jap prisoners from Attu here now."[5]

The Battle of Attu had not yet ended when the Engineers embarked upon further airfield construction. Men of the 4th Infantry and 18th Engineers landed on the small island of Shemya, "the only flat one in the Aleutian Chain," to survey it as the site of "the first attack air field expressly designed for the experimental new long-range B-29 Superfortress bomber." By 8 June, the first AAF aircraft, a C-47, landed on a new airstrip at Alexai Point on Massacre Bay and discharged fighter crews. A fighter strip was completed on Shemya on 21 June.[6]

Kiska was next on the agenda, with target date of 15 August. It was fully expected that Operation Cottage (the Kiska invasion) would be, as Morton put it, "a costly one and the island once taken would require a large garrison." Japanese forces were estimated at seven thousand to eight thousand men, entrenched in strong positions. So the invaders would total thirty-four thousand ground troops, of which five thousand were Canadians. And the navy lined up a formidable support force.

Kinkaid had instructed the Eleventh Air Force to bomb Kiska daily—an order far easier to issue than to obey. The weather over Kiska during June could scarcely have been worse. Indeed, for one period the target was socked in for ten straight days. Only 407 sorties got off for the entire month. The Eleventh dropped 270 tons of bombs, encountering "plentiful but ineffective" flak.[7]

The 8 July 1943 issue of *The Aleutian*, a service magazine, gives a number of glimpses into daily life in the Dutch Harbor area during this period. An entertainment had been held there featuring "Sgt. Bob Coner of the Arkansawyers of his ballad, 'The Bombing of Dutch Harbor.'" Far and away the favorite local entertainers were The Aleutian Five, a group of five navy enlisted men who started playing popular music together while at Bremerton awaiting shipment to the Aleutians. They arrived just before Christmas 1942, and soon they were so popular that their fans voted them "the nation's third greatest band led only by Glenn Miller and Tommy Dorsey."

Nor were the lovers of more serious music forgotten. The radio broadcast classical selections every Sunday evening. Of the orchestral works, Beethoven's Fifth Symphony was the favorite, followed by two other symphonies—Dvorak's "From the New World" ranked number two with Tschaikovsky's Fifth in third place. The most popular vocal selection was "Un Bel Di" from *Madame Butterfly*. It may seem odd that these men engaged in war with Japan should prefer a Japanese woman's touching avowal of faith in a faithless American, but the idea that "one fine day he'll come" may have struck a responsive chord in homesick hearts.

Sports of course continued, and the Arkansas contingent had something to brag about when their representatives took the Golden Gloves award, clobbering the Navy's best by an impressive 34 points to 12. In another area, Don Drake starred. He had been working toward a high school diploma, and finally received the necessary credits, formally graduating from Little Rock High School on 21 May 1943.

A contest that aroused intense interest was to select the "Sweetheart of Dutch Harbor." Soldiers, sailors, and marines submitted pictures of wives, girl friends, movie starlets, even babies. The title went to Billie Jean Fitzgerald of Peoria, Illinois, who was engaged to a marine. Runner-up was Ruth A. Ziegenhorn, sponsored by the 206th's Bill Jones. They had "lived on neighboring farms near Fisher, Arkansas." Looking at the pictures of these two girls, one notes that while both were exceedingly pretty, they were not the sultry, glamorous type typical of pinups. They looked like what they were—"the girls next door."[8]

Wherever Americans gather for any length of time, there will be dogs, and Adak was no exception. Buckner had several hunters, Butler a springer spaniel, Eareckson a husky, and so on down the chain of command to a seaman who had a canine of dubious ancestry that he taught to stand on its hind legs and salute officers.

Adak, in fact, was fairly civilized by Aleutian standards. Quonset huts housed no more than four men apiece, and some soldiers were trying to grow flowers.[9] Stubbs's diary reveals the improved conditions. Huts kept going up, four "USO girls put on two shows" in the mess hall, and Adak received two first-class movies—*The Invaders* and *Casablanca*. On 7 June Stubbs observed, "The Chaplain came to our mess hall tonight to hear our troubles. I don't know of anyone that has any to tell him about."[10]

Yet in some respects the war pressed closer. Two more Japanese prisoners arrived on 3 June; by the sixth, eleven POWs were on Adak, two of them in the hospital. On the eighth, Stubbs wrote, "Rumors are pretty strong that we are leaving here soon. Our Co. Commander told us tonight that we will be in the next battle here." In token of which, Stubbs and his buddies participated in marksmanship training and many hikes. On 28 June, he and three men of his platoon "put up two gas alarms and two water barrels for fire at the mess hall." He added, "Today has been the prettiest day we have had on Adak. Just like summertime in Ark." And by way of anticlimax, "Had gas school at 6:30 P.M." His last entry for June ended, "We think we will be seeing action soon."[11]

On 7 June, Miller recorded excitedly,

> Our outfit has been alerted to begin combat training for umpteen weeks preparatory for active operations! I have put in a request to be allowed to stay with the gang. If they are going to do any fighting I want to be right there with them. I've come to think a hell of a lot of this bunch of razorbacks. We don't know where we are going but it's a cinch to be a real fight and I believe will signal the beginning of U.S. throwing a Sunday punch in the Pacific— hitting Japan from 4 sides. We are having a great time sweating out our final destination.

So he and others due for rotation requested through channels that they remain "with the gang." But higher headquarters could not see it their way, ". . . so we're going to have to leave our buddies to fight alone and go back to the States. That is a real blow to all of us. But my conscience feels better for having made the effort at getting to stay. I don't know what else could have been done. Do you?" With that Miller closed his record.[12]

Massey's notes for June remark, "Lots of wounded in the small hospital here now. . . . A rotation system started for all that's been here a year or more, few good men get a shot, just the no-good dead-heads."

He added a grim paragraph that revealed all too clearly the continuing presence of an old problem: "A body found up in Captain's Bay. I hear he was stabbed to death. I also heard a sailor stood at the edge of the dock, cut his throat and fell in the water."[13]

The weather in July was a considerable improvement over June, and air force records show many and heavy bombings of Kiska. The navy, too, got into the act. The first bombardment of Kiska in eleven months came on 6 July from Rear Adm. Robert C. "Ike" Giffen's task group of three heavy cruisers, one light cruiser, and four destroyers. The net result of all this firepower was negligible. Observed Morison, "Probably more effective were five 'nuisance' night bombardments by destroyers *Aylwin* and *Monaghan* between 8 and 20 July."[14]

Such bombings and bombardments constituted routine softening-up measures. Of much more interest, especially to the airmen, were the preparations under way for attacking the Japanese home islands for the first time since the Doolittle raid of 18 April 1942. This project was the brainchild of Lt. Lawrence Reineke, newly assigned to the 21st Bomber Squadron as assistant intelligence officer. He was surprised to discover that the air force knew little about the important Japanese base at Paramushiro, much less had any plans to bomb it. So he secured maps and charts from the navy and pored over Japanese diaries captured at Attu. The result was "an amazingly complete chart of the Japanese bases at Paramushiro."

Reineke reaped the standard chewing out for having gone out of channels, but to their credit his superiors took him seriously. Kinkaid in particular favored an attack on Paramushiro, took the idea up the line, and eventually the Joint Chief of Staff approved the strike.[15]

The first group of six B-24s headed out on 10 July—the same date the Allies invaded Sicily. However, a Navy Catalina sighted four Japanese transports apparently headed for Kiska. Such shipping took priority, so Butler sent off some B-25s from Attu to catch the transports and, much to their disgust, also directed the B-24 pilots to divert from course and join the mission. Two of the Japanese ships were sunk. Meanwhile, eight B-25s left Attu on their own initiative, headed for Paramushiro. Lacking either Reineke's briefings or charts, it is questionable whether they ever reached their destination. Over whatever target they found, solid clouds necessitated "dead-reckoning runs . . ." They dropped their bombs "presumably on the southern part of Shimushu and the northern part of Paramushiro . . ."

The key word is "presumably." The Japanese reported no bombings, and the B-25s encountered neither Japanese aircraft nor flak. In fact, the surprise the raid of 18 July would achieve indicates strongly that the effort of 10 July did not hit Japanese territory.[16]

Stubbs's diary for the first eighteen days of July signals that combat was anticipated in the near future. Except for noting turkey on the Fourth of July and an occasional softball game, his entries concern military preparations. "Had school on Jap weapons this A.M.," he wrote on 5 July. "Some that were taken on Attu. We fired them this P.M. I fired the knee mortar, rifle, light machine gun and hand grenade. Our new Colonel made a talk to us today and left the impression that we may be going to Kiska." On the fourteenth, "Had security of small units, bayonet training, first aid and a talk on Jap tactics by Lt. Neff today. The Colonel gave a 3 hour talk to all N.C.O.'s of the Bn tonight." And on 18 July, the situation solidified: "We are preparing to leave here soon."[17]

Apparently no such activities stirred the 206th. Massey's notes for July were routine. And on the eleventh Alspaugh wrote to his mother, "This place is getting mighty pretty again. The grass and tundra is green and about a foot thick. Flowers are all in bloom now. Most of the flowers are purple, but some of them are white or violet colored."[18] This letter gives the impression that censorship had relaxed a bit, for the mention of tundra left little question that the writer was somewhere in Alaska.

The Eleventh had its second shot at Paramushiro on 18 July. It was not a large operation—only six B-24s from the 36th, 21st, and 404th Bombardment Squadrons participated—but its objective was important. Not only was Paramushiro a major air and naval base, but Japan's northern commands all had their headquarters there. In addition to their missiles, the bombers carried an intangible cargo: If successful, this raid would prove that the Japanese homeland was vulnerable to direct attack.

As the flight approached Siberia's heavily wooded Kamchatka peninsula, for a moment the men were caught up in the wonder of real trees, a sight some had not enjoyed for at least a year. The day was warm, and for a wonder the weather was perfect. Three aircraft dropped bombs on Kataoka naval base on Shimushu, a small island north of Paramushiro; the others concentrated on ships in the strait between Kataoka and Kashiwabara on Paramushiro.

Surprise was total. The dismayed Japanese got off some ineffectual AA fire; a few Zeros rose to the challenge, but being neither fully armed nor fueled had to turn back. Accounts of the damage inflicted differ. Craven and Cate note only "Near misses, but no direct hits were reported." Garfield claims, "The bombs blew up one ship and damaged two or three others." And he declared, "Rush prints of the strike photos showed that the raid on Paramushiro had inflicted more damage than the Japanese had inflicted on Dutch Harbor in June 1942."

Such discrepancies are the rule rather than the exception in military history. In any case, the six Liberators (B-24s) had jolted the Japanese psyche; the "sacred soil" was vulnerable. And strategy had to be altered to meet the new menace. Unless Japan was prepared to more or less write off Paramushiro, and by extension the northern islands, men, aircraft, and ships and all the matériel of war would have to be sent there from the southern fronts, which could ill spare them.[19]

For the rest of July, Stubbs and his buddies prepared for the anticipated move. On the nineteenth they turned in their sheets and extra clothing, the next day their "overage equipment." They practiced climbing landing nets, "creeping and crawling," map reading, using the compass, and bayonet training.[20]

All of which would prove profitless, for the Japanese had decided to evacuate Kiska. They had already begun evacuating, using submarines, but this type of evacuation proved costly and inefficient. By 21 June, they had taken off 820 men at a cost of 7 of the 13 submarines assigned to the mission. And of the 820 evacuees, 300 had been lost at sea. So on that date Kawase canceled the submarine evacuations. He decided on an evacuation by surface ships, Operation *Ke*. He assembled a fleet with the light cruiser *Tama* as flagship, two other light cruisers, the oiler *Nippon Maru*, escort vessel *Kunashiri*, about a dozen destroyers, and began sortie on 21 July.[21]

The twenty-second was an unusually busy day. Kawase's evacuation fleet completed its sortie, and Kinkaid took advantage of remarkably beautiful weather to give Kiska a thorough going-over. He assigned the battleships *Mississippi* and *New Mexico* with the cruiser *Portland* to Rear Adm. Robert M. Griffin, not to be confused with Rear Adm. Robert C. Giffen, who was also on the mission with three heavy cruisers and one light cruiser. These two groups of ships dumped 212 tons of high explosives on Kiska Harbor, South Head, and Gertrude Cove. The Japanese offered no return fire; what they shot off they directed at aircraft. As soon as the bombardment fleet pulled out, the AAF took over with 26 B-25s, 17 B-24s, 13 P-40s and 20 P-38s. These struck North Head, the main camp, and the submarine base and coastal defenses. They encountered heavy flak that damaged 18 aircraft and downed a B-25, but its crew was saved.[22]

The next day, one of the strangest incidents of the Pacific War began when the radar of a Catalina registered blips that resembled ships some 200 miles southwest of Attu. To this day, no one knows what they were, but Kinkaid believed they reflected a Japanese reinforcement convoy headed for Kiska. So he dispatched to the scene Griffin and Giffen, with their fleets plus the destroyers *Aylwin* and *Monaghan*, which had been blockading Kiska Harbor. He sent four PT boats to fill this vacancy but bad weather with heavy seas made the PT boats useless, and Kinkaid had to return them to Amchitka. This left Kiska Harbor free of any sort of blockade for several days.

When by the afternoon of 24 July there was no sight of Japanese ships in the Attu area, Kinkaid ordered the searching fleet to return to Kiska waters at top speed. He also ordered the oiler *Pecos* to rendezvous with the battleships. By evening of the twenty-fifth, Griffin and Giffen were some ninety miles south-southwest of Kiska.

About an hour after midnight, *Mississippi*'s radar "reported radar contacts fifteen miles on the port bow." *Idaho*, *Wichita*, and *Portland* also claimed radar sightings. When the blips' distance closed to eight miles from the cruisers and twelve from the battleships, the fleet "altered course to 340° to clear enemy torpedo water." The battleships opened fire and continued for twenty minutes, when the blips vanished.

It is significant that *Wichita's* radar had made contact with the peak of Kiska volcano. As Garfield wrote, "The image was easily distinct from the seven moving pips at which her main batteries were shooting." In other words, the pips were not reflecting stationary objects.

Wichita sent out a second plane over the area, and it found nothing—no disabled ships, no debris. It was all very mysterious, and Morison later expressed what seems to have been the official navy position: "What had shown up on the radar were return echoes from the mountains of Amchitka and other islands 100 to 150 miles distant."

This explanation is not satisfactory. As Garfield pointed out, radar can give false distances, never false bearings. Nearly all the American ships had been pointed away from any mountains. "Nor would a distant mountain give seven pips, or change course and speed."

Triangulation revealed that all the pickups "converged on one point 22,000 yards off *Mississippi's* bow," a fact that nothing could explain but the actual presence there of 7 objects. They could not have been Japanese surface ships, for the evacuation fleet was about 400 miles to the south. There were, however, several I-class submarines on the surface in the area of the pips. One indeed reported the sound of fire and flashes of guns, at which the subs submerged.

Whatever the targets, the so-called Battle of the Pips was unfortunate for the Americans. The fleet had used up a huge quantity of oil and ammunition and had to rendezvous with *Pecos*. Refueling took some twenty-four hours, and during that time the evacuation fleet moved on Kiska undiscovered.[23]

36

"A Great Big, Juicy, Expensive Mistake"

On 25 July, King Victor Emmanuel of Italy announced the fall of Mussolini's government. It was the first major political crack in the Axis, presaging Italy's rapid removal from the scene as a partner of Hitler's Germany.* This was good news, but it had little if any impact on the troops in the Aleutians. Italy was far away, and in general Americans had regarded Mussolini as an enemy, at best, in half-amused contempt.

During the period of the Battle of the Pips and to the end of July, the Eleventh had pounded Kiska steadily. The twenty-sixth saw the heaviest one-day bomb concentration so far. The weather was beautiful, and 32 B-24s, 38 P-40s, and 24 P-38s took full advantage of it to dump over 104 tons of bombs on various targets at Kiska.[1]

All of which convinced the Japanese, both on Kiska and in the evacuation fleet, that the Americans were planning to invade, probably in a matter of days. The Japanese on Kiska were understandably unhappy. In addition to enduring massive air assaults, their stock of food was dangerously low, and it did not seem that rescue could reach them before the American invasion.

Rescue, however, was moving steadily nearer. Admiral Kawase himself was present aboard the light cruiser *Tama*. Rear Adm. Shofuku Kimura commanded two other light cruisers and six destroyers, while some five other destroyers under Capt. Shigetaka Amano acted as screen. Also present was the oiler *Nippon Maru* and an escort vessel, *Kunashiri*. While they were awaiting the order to

---

* On 13 October 1943, Italy declared war on Germany.

close in, two destroyers were damaged in collisions. *Kakaba* limped back to Paramushiro. No longer combat-capable, *Hatsushimo* joined *Nippon Maru*'s screen.

At last, on 28 July, Kimura started his fifty-mile run, and Kiska received the welcome word to prepare for evacuation. About halfway in the final dash, *Tama* left the formation and took position as rear guard. The evacuees had little to do by way of preparations, having been ready for days. They "prepared demolition charges, set booby traps and scrawled insults to American on barracks walls." By the time Kimura's fleet had anchored, all that remained was to set off the charges, set fire to buildings and matériel. Because of the loss of two destroyers, space was at a premium, so Kimura ordered that small arms be abandoned. These the men dumped into the water near shore.

Carrying only a few personal items, they began loading. In exactly 55 minutes, the entire garrison of 5,183 officers and men, including Rear Adm. Shozo Akiyama, had crowded on board. It was a tight squeeze, with each cruiser taking 1,200 and each of six destroyers 470 each. The fog that had covered Kimura's approach dissipated as he and his ships departed with their human cargo and rejoined *Tama*. On 31 July/1 August, they reached Paramushiro. The only shot fired had been at Little Kiska, which someone thought was an American ship. The whole operation went off without a single casualty.[2]

Just as they had at Guadalcanal earlier in the year, the Japanese had evacuated an entire garrison practically under the noses of the besiegers. Operation *Ke* had been brilliantly conceived and carried out; both the fleet and the defenders of Kiska did their part smoothly and effectively. All concerned merited an ungrudging "Well done!" As an unnamed colonel later remarked, "How I hate those bastards but I've got to give them credit for the most masterly evacuation by any army at any time and I'm not forgetting Dunkirk."[3]

Yet we believe that Kawase and Kimura would be the first to admit that good fortune had sailed with them. Several factors contributing to their success were beyond the ability of even the most clever Japanese planners to arrange. For example, the Griffin-Giffen fleet, which could have pulverized Kimura's lightweight ships, had been directly in their path. At the precise time best-calculated to serve the Japanese purpose, the Battle of the Pips had pulled the Americans out of position. Two fine, battle-wise destroyers, *Monaghan* and *Aylwin*, had been patrolling off Kiska Harbor; these, too, had been pulled to join the Griffin-Giffen force. Had they been on station, it is almost a certainty that one or both would have spotted the incoming Japanese ships and sent off an immediate alert. As for aircraft, according to Craven and Cate, after releasing twenty-two tons of bombs over Kiska on 27 July, "Four idle days followed."[4] So no aircraft were aloft to sight and attack the ships.

Still, the Japanese high command had much to ponder. True, they had rescued valuable men and gotten back much-needed vessels without an enemy-inflicted scratch. The fact remained, as Churchill had reminded the British after Dunkirk, that wars were not won by evacuations.

Meanwhile the Americans, unaware that they were shadow boxing, prepared for what they expected would be a major campaign, probably more difficult and costly than the capture of Attu. Early in 1943, journalist Corey Ford had written, ". . . Kiska is a tough nut to take. Forget those stories of a few bewildered Nips clinging by their finger tips to a slippery cliff; here is a veritable Bering Sea Malta, its sheltered harbor protected by enfolded hills, its base honeycombed by underground passages, its approaches guarded by antiaircraft as powerful as that of a full-size task force."[5]

So the air force continued to hammer installations on Kiska and the navy bombarded the island with vim and vigor. On 1 and 2 August, the bombing was not particularly heavy, but excellent photographs were obtained on the latter date. Then on 4 August the Eleventh dumped 153 tons of bombs on Kiska, a new one-day record. That day also produced some fine photographs.

Analysis of this aerial intelligence should have engendered serious second thoughts at the command and planning levels. More than thirty craters pockmarked the Kiska runway, and the Japanese had made no effort to fill them in. Many buildings had been destroyed or severely damaged, yet they showed "no sign of having been bombed or shelled . . ." That in itself pointed to one conclusion, namely, the Japanese themselves had set fire to their installations.

Other evidence indicated evacuation: Radio Kiska had not been heard from since 28 July. Trucks, normally dispersed, were bunched together near the shore at Kiska Harbor. U.S. destroyers had been bombarding at will, with no return fire from Japanese coastal defenses. The week before, some twenty barges had been in the harbor; now only one remained.

To counter all this clear evidence of evacuation, air crews had reported AA and small arms fire, although "meager and inaccurate"; some reported seeing tracers, and one pilot declared that he had strafed a Japanese soldier and had seen him "fall flat." Maj. Gen. Holland M. Smith, USMC, sensibly pointed out "that the green aviators alone saw things." These reports had indeed originated with the A-24 pilots of the 407th Bomber Squadron, newly arrived from the lower forty-eight, and a few veterans who "were conceded to be flak happy . . . Most of the veterans . . . reported a complete lack of enemy opposition."

Morison has suggested that the Americans might have reached the correct conclusion had the enemy been "conventional," but that we always expected trickery from the Japanese. "Weren't they hiding to make us think the landing would be easy, or saving ammunition against the invasion?"

Smith asked Kinkaid to send scouts with rubber boats for a night reconnaissance. Both Buckner and Verbeck, acting commander of the scouts, agreed.[6] It is most difficult to understand why Kinkaid did not act upon this practical suggestion, which would appear to be a normal precaution even without Smith's sponsorship. He had an excellent opportunity to have sent off a scouting expedition then and there, for from the fifth to the eighth of August Kiska was socked in, and the fog would have been an excellent cover. Had this been done, an enormous amount of effort, matériel, fuel, ammunition, and not a few lives would have been saved.

According to Garfield, Kinkaid decided on the planned invasion because, if the Japanese had evacuated, "the troop landing 'would be a good training exercise, a super dress rehearsal, excellent for training purposes.'" If they had dug in, they might have annihilated the scouts.[7]

Again, this is a most puzzling rationale. Certainly the scouts would have been in danger if the Japanese were still in position, but such reconnaissance missions were the reason for their existence. And to allow an exercise the size of the Kiska invasion to go forward because it would be good training seems, in retrospect, little short of frivolous. Training for what? No other theater of operations offered a climate or terrain remotely similar to Kiska. Training for Europe or the South Pacific at Kiska made about as much sense as the Seventh preparing for Attu in California. Moreover, this was a major force that Kinkaid decided to unleash. Combat troops totaled 34,426, of whom 5,300 were Canadians, with some 100 ships to protect the transports.[8] Every man, every ship, every aircraft, every gun was urgently needed elsewhere.

One could well argue that, Japanese or no Japanese, the invasion was redundant. In June, Eareckson had declared that Kiska had no strategic value and wasn't worth a single life. Governor Gruening had asked Kinkaid if invasion was really necessary. Couldn't they just starve and bomb the Japanese off the island? Kinkaid answered that that would to too slow, "that American prestige was involved and we would have to drive them out."[9]

The decision made, preparations for invasion proceeded apace. The Eleventh continued to bomb, and the fleet kept on bombarding. On 12 August, no fewer than two heavy cruisers, three light cruisers and five destroyers blasted the island with sixty tons of shells.[10]

Among the troops fine-tuning for the invasion were the men of the 153d on Adak. Miller wrote some years later,

> Now there is firing, combat maneuvers, creeping and crawling. So what are they pulling on us this time? We've been ready to fight a half dozen times but they never let us. . . . The rumor now is the Kuriles to be the next objective. But a good majority holds out that it will be Kiska. Fights start over who knows the most, and money changes hands over whether it will be Kiska or Paramushiro. Nobody really cares, as long as they go some place where there are Japs so they can fight their way out of the Aleutians.[11]

The question of where was resolved on 5 August. "Got word today that we will leave here for Kiska Island Sunday," Stubbs informed his diary. The next day he and his buddies "threw hand grenades and fired rifle grenades . . ." On the seventh, they turned in their barracks bags and cots—"sleeping on the floor tonight." The eighth brought a lecture "on how we would operate on Kiska . . ."

At 0430 on 10 August the men awoke to be ready to leave at 0600. Predictably, they had to stand around until noon, and did not board their transport, *Doyan*, until night. "It is a nice, new ship," wrote Stubbs. They had two more days to wait before leaving on a the thirteenth, which, as Stubbs noted, was "Friday the 13th."[12]

The force that embarked was truly formidable—15,000 Californians, about half of whom were Attu veterans; 5,000 of the Alaskan 4th Regiment; another 5,000 of the 87th Mountain Combat Team; the 2,500 paratroops of the First Special Service Force; and the Canadians, as mentioned. Many of the officers were veterans of the Battle of Attu, and would hold similar positions in the Kiska venture, such as Rockwell, Zimmerman, Hartl, Eareckson, and Squeaky Anderson. The major change was in command of the ground forces; Maj. Gen. Charles H. Corbett replaced Landrum. Some distinguished brass went along—DeWitt, Smith, and Assistant Secretary of War John J. McCloy.[13]

During the two-day voyage from Adak, the Arkansas men of the 153d enjoyed themselves thoroughly. "This ship is the nicest one I have ever been on," Stubbs wrote on the thirteenth. "The morale of the men is high. Our hopes are that we will soon be going to the States after this operation is finished." He added the next day, "All the men are as happy as can be tonight like we were going on a picnic or something."[14]

To the amazement of the sailors, the soldiers from Arkansas caroled away, singing a version of "Bury Me Not on the Lone Prairie," written by Lt. Jack Moyer of Pittsburgh:

> O, bury me not in the Bering Sea,
> Where the williwaws howl
> And the seals swim free.
>
> O, when I die, don't bury me
> On the slippery rocks
> By the Bering Sea.
>
> Now I like the girls
> And the girls like me—
> But there ain't no girls
> By the Bering Sea!
>
> I wanna go home,
> It's home for me
> Never more to roam
> By the Bering Sea.[15]

The first troops to reach shore were Alaska Scout patrols, Colonel Verbeck at their head, and the Mountain Infantry under Col. Robert T. Frederick. The scouts found nothing but abandoned and destroyed equipment, and some bamboo gin that they confiscated.

The main beach proved no problem, the only signs of life being half a dozen dogs. Ens. William C. Jones got the surprise of his life when one of the dogs trotted up to him, wagging its tail. It was "Explosion," the mascot he had given the weather station over a year before, none the worse for his months with the Japanese.[16]

Stubbs's team entered their landing barge at 0645 on 15 August, but they could not land until 1300 "because of reef rock all along the shoreline." They encountered no opposition, and that night dug in on top of Knee Hill.[17]

Eareckson, on his forward air control mission, saw no sign of the enemy, "and muttered into his radio that he would give a case of good Scotch to anybody who could find one single Japanese on the island." But the troops were still jittery—those tricky Japanese might be biding their time, waiting to pounce when the invaders moved close enough. Occasionally a booby trap went off, and the men began, as nervous soldiers will, to shoot at anything that moved.[18]

Stubbs's unit sent out "a patrol from each platoon" on 16 August. He noted that, returning to their camp, "We were afraid to go through the 87th Inf. area at night. They have already shot 5 of their own men." Two days later, Stubbs's patrol "got shot at by the 87th Inf."[19]

All casualties were not on land. At 0134 on the eighteenth, *Abner Read*, on a routine patrol, ran into a Japanese mine. The stern broke off, plunging many men into the water. As a result of this accident, *Abner Read* lost seventy dead or missing and forty-seven wounded. The destroyer *Bancroft* towed her to Adak.[20]

Other Americans fell victim to the habit of picking up souvenirs. "Some of the men are collecting Jap ammunition and some are getting killed with it," Stubbs wrote on 22 August. "The Japs left lots of mines." Two days later, MPs brought in "a man that got killed with a Jap hand grenade."[21]

By this time, it was obvious that the Japanese had indeed vacated the island, and routine measures of setting up camp were instituted. In the course of various patrols, someone discovered that, along with booby traps, mines,and jeering inscriptions, the Japanese had left at least one bit of evidence of soldierly chivalry. After shooting down a P-40, they had buried the pilot, Joseph Levi, and placed a marker reading, "Sleeping here a brave American who lost youth and happiness for his motherland, July 25, Nippon Army."[22]

Kinkaid had said that "American prestige was involved" at Kiska. It was indeed, but not exactly as the admiral had visualized. As Buckner remarked, "To attract maximum attention, it's hard to find anything more effective than a great big, juicy, expensive mistake." For once, the Alaska Theater got plenty of publicity, most of it the wrong kind. There were the usual wisecracks and bits of doggerel such as the one Morison quoted, with its refrain:

> O here's to mighty ComNorPac
> Whose kingdom lay at cold Adak,
> Whose reign was known to fame for fog
> And capture of two couple dog.

At Paramushiro, the Japanese enjoyed a good laugh at American expense.

But there was nothing funny about the 313 casualties incurred—in addition to the count from *Abner Read*, 24 soldiers had been shot by trigger-happy comrades, and 4 were lost to mines. The same causes resulted in 50 wounded, while 130 suffered from trenchfoot. And, as Morison observed, "Admiral Halsey could have used some of those ships and men to speed up the capture of New Georgia; General MacArthur, at the end of the line, might have employed a few of them to help drive the Japanese from Huon Gulf and the Bismarcks Barrier."[23]

Kiska was American again; the Aleutians were free of Japanese. But the United States paid dearly for the failure to send an Alaska Scouts party to confirm what was already fairly obvious—that the enemy had evacuated and the invasion was unnecessary.

37

"The War Had Gone By"

On 11 August, during the pre-invasion phase of the Kiska operation, the Eleventh sent in B-24s from Attu for a strike on Paramushiro. They divided nineteen tons of bombs between the army staging area at Kashiwabara and Kataoka naval base on Shimushu. Defense was vigorous, with strong AA fire and forty Japanese fighters rising to challenge. Five were reported shot down, but not before the Japanese had disposed of two B-24s and damaged three others. This, out of nine starters, was a heavy casualty percentage. Obviously Paramushiro's defenses were ready and effective.[1]

The retaking of Kiska seems to have made little impression on the men left behind. Massey's comments for August remarked, "Our forces land on Kiska, the Nips have fled. I hear two of our units met and threw a few rounds at each other before being stopped. . . ."

Then he turned his attention to the local scene: "A soldier built a little raft out of scrap pieces of lumber, tied it behind a freighter during the night. The ship pulled out and the raft turned over, nearly drowned the man before he was found." Massey added disgustedly, "Some nuts will do anything."[2]

From the sixteenth to the seventeenth of August Battery K participated in a field exercise. "This organization was engaged in the defense of installations at Position K-13. Most of the defensive action occurred in the Pyramid Valley Pass when our patrols made contact with the enemy (I Battery). A long line of defense was established about midway of the Pass. Complete destruction of the enemy was recorded at about 0230. Surprise and effective firepower decided the situation."[3]

The next day, the battery historian could describe a very different happening. The battery held an anniversary party, complete with sandwiches, drinks, and music by the band. The star of the occasion was Colonel Robertson, who, toward the end of the festivities, "high-lighted the afternoon with a speech that only those that were there know anything about—however," the battery historian continued enthusiastically, "we will go so far as to say that it was strictly music to our ears—applause of course nearly brought down the roof during his speech. What news! Afterwards, a troupe of USO entertainers (women, just imagine) slipped into the scene. . . ."[4] Of course, we can't be absolutely sure, but it seems a safe bet that the colonel's news concerned a fixed rotation date—what else could have brought such a reaction?

Almost as soon as the Americans determined that the Japanese had indeed abandoned Kiska, action began to reduce the force in Alaska. On 26 August, four of the Eleventh's Bomb Squadrons—the 36th, 73d, 21st, and 406th—received orders to prepare for transfer to the ConUS (Continental United States). The 36th in particular had been heavily involved in the action. During their twenty-eight months in Alaska, the men had had no leave, had lost four out of ten of their original complement, "had dropped 1,500,000 pounds of bombs and earned 300 combat decorations."[5]

Stubbs's diary indicates that considerable "moonlight requisitioning" was going on at Kiska. On 21 August, some ships in the bay were unloading. "We couldn't resist the temptation to swipe some 5-in-1 rations at the beach tonight," he admitted. The next day he recorded, "I swiped another box of rations this A.M. We are eating pretty good now. Each man cooks for himself." Nor was food the only item thus "liberated." "We were issued three tents and we swiped two more today for the Co.," noted Stubbs on 23 August. Three days later he wrote, "The main thing is rations and we have a hard time stealing them at the beach. We find more M.P.s than we do rations."

By 27 August the first rumors of departure had begun. "We are in hopes of getting relieved but nobody knows what we are going to do." By the next day the scuttlebutt had solidified: "Got a rumor today that we are leaving Kiska within a month."[6]

At high levels, considerable debate went on as to what future action, if any, would be appropriate in the Aleutians. DeWitt wanted to carry the war to Japan and proposed a plan to invade Paramushiro, using the current forces plus reinforcement. The suggestion made a certain amount of sense, so much so that the Joint Chiefs of Staff considered DeWitt's plan for ten days. Pursuit of a fleeing foe is a time-honored tactic of war, and Paramushiro was a major complex; its loss would be a serious blow. On the other hand, cogent arguments could be lined up against an invasion. Considerations of geography and climate were as compelling as ever. The Aleutians could not adequately support a force of the size and strength needed to capture a heavily defended base on Japanese home soil. And if by some chance the Americans did take Paramushiro, how could they hold it, surrounded on all sides by Japanese territory? The project might be feasible with the cooperation of the Soviet Union, whose Kamchatka Peninsula was only minutes away by air from Paramushiro and Shimushu. But the Soviets had managed to stay out of the Pacific War, and they showed no inclination to jeopardize their neutrality unless and until it was very much to Moscow's advantage to do so. Lacking Soviet assistance, or use of Soviet territory, the cost in men and matériel would far outweigh the strategic gain. Japan's source of strength lay to the south; the Japanese Kuriles were, in their way, no more productive than the Aleutians.

Still, the Joint Chiefs did not flatly turn down the proposal. They instructed Buckner and Kinkaid to work up detailed plans and to prepare for the green light should the Soviet Union declare war on Japan. Target date was 1 June 1944.[7]

Nevertheless, strength continued to dwindle in the Aleutians. By 9 September, the RCAFs 14th Fighter Squadron at Umnak was preparing to return to Canada. On the 11th, Butler transferred to Europe, and two days later Maj. Gen. Davenport Johnson replaced him in command of the Eleventh. Almost Butler's final act as commander was to order a large-scale bombing of Paramushiro on 11 September.

In retrospect one can see that the project was ill-advised. The Eleventh's strength was so depleted that Butler could scare up only nineteen bombers—twelve B-25s and eight B-24s. Astoundingly, Craven and Cate make no mention of fighter escort, so one can only presume that there was none. The folly of sending unescorted bombers over a Japanese base bristling with efficient fighter aircraft should have been self-evident; if escort planes were not available, the mission should have been canceled.

The project was not a total loss. Weather over the target was perfect, and the aircraft dropped twenty tons of bombs on the Kashiwabara staging area, shipping in the harbor and straits. Claimed results were one freighter and one large transport sunk; another transport and two cargo ships damaged; possible hits on two more cargo vessels. On land, they hit two buildings and an AA battery on Shimushu. At least forty Japanese fighters swarmed up; the Eleventh claimed thirteen were shot down, with three other probables.

So far so good—but the cost was horrendous. Of the nineteen bombers sent out, only nine returned, and seven of those were damaged. Three had been shot down over the target; seven were so shot up they had to crash land at Petropavlovsk, Kamchatka. The Soviets eventually released the crews but impounded the aircraft, which thus were as much a loss to the United States as if they had been destroyed. *Combat Chronology* truly called this the "most disastrous day for the Eleventh." In one raid the organization had lost half its striking clout, and five months would elapse before it could launch another strike against Paramushiro.[8]

Meanwhile, on 5 September, Stubbs celebrated his birthday on Kiska and received the best of presents: "Got orders today to have our B bags packed by 9:00 A.M. tomorrow. We are leaving out." Accordingly, he and others of the 153d turned in their barracks bags, cots, and rucksacks the next day, anticipating departure that night.

The call came at 0300. Two hours later, they piled into a barge and boarded the transport at 0600. The ship left Kiska harbor at 1700 bound for Adak. "We got some rumors that we are going to the States."

The voyage was pleasant, and they docked at Adak at 1700 on 8 September. "We are right back where we started from," Stubbs wrote in disgust. "All of us are mad because we didn't stay on the ship and go to the States." So the men of Stubbs's platoon were somewhat disgruntled and suspicious as they went on detail hauling barracks bags on the ninth. "We are hearing some furlough and cadre rumors now but afraid to believe it."[9]

Still, Adak was a pleasant contrast to Kiska. On the tenth, all the NCOs of Stubbs's platoon moved into a hut. "We have a light bulb and [are] living high now." By the next day, they had three lights. But soon they went back to candles pending receipt of a generator. Then the Arkansas men settled down into the old Adak routine—details, digging trenches, policing the area, playing card games, working on the roads. Civilization reached a high point when Stubbs could record, "We have china ware in the mess hall now."

A U.S.O. team, including three women, came to Adak to give a few shows. Unfortunately, some joker spoiled things for his fellow soldiers. "The U.S.O. girls wouldn't put on their show today because someone had stolen their clothes," Stubbs wrote on 27 September. The next day the entire company was searched for the missing costumes but without result.[10]

This period seems to have been one of little interest to the men of the 206th. Massey's comments were routine, and that other dependable writer, Alspaugh, had been hospitalized for two weeks with a hemorrhoid operation. But he was up and about by 22 August when he wrote to his mother, "The flowers up here are really beautiful now. . . . The hillsides are just covered with flowers and they really are fragrant."

All this beauty was fleeting. "The flowers have all died," he informed her on 12 September, "and the grass is rapidly turning brown . . ." He had been digging for ivory. "There is a deposit of old walrus and sea lion skulls and skeletons on this place. . . . The deposit is about two feet under soil so there is quite a bit of digging involved."[11]

Around this time, "probably September 1943," Everett Carnes "was awaiting orders for transfer to Air Force Cadet training." He and a good friend, Sgt. "Moose" Ruthuon, were "horsing around" with jujitsu when Ruthuon's arm gave "a sound like a shotgun blast with accompanying pain." Carnes rushed his friend to the base hospital for X-rays. After what seemed an interminable wait for the results, a doctor came to them and announced, "No break." Remembering that sickening snap, Carnes blurted out, "You're crazy as hell!" As he remarked later, that was the only time he "voiced those sentiments to a full colonel." Actually, both were right. Ruthuon's arm wasn't broken, but he had "a dislocated elbow which probably took longer to heal than if it had been broken."[12]

Fitzhugh remembered the autumn of 1943 as the time when the famous bartender, Blackie, "was forced through political pressure to sell his establishment and leave." Fitzhugh continued, "The U.S. commissioner there, a one-armed bandit—and I mean that literally, as he took everyone for all he could and had only one arm—bought out Blackie as the commissioner owned the only other bar in the place. Blackie said that if he was not paid on time for this sale that he would return and kill the S.O.B. Less than a month after his departure the bar burned down in the night. The next morning one could still smell kerosene around the place." Fitzhugh departed Dutch Harbor before learning the ultimate outcome of this incident.[13]

The shrinking of the Aleutian forces continued. On 23 September, Kinkaid issued Operational Plan 9-43, reorganizing his army and navy air strength as Task Force 90 (TF 90) under the commanding general, Eleventh Air Force, which became Task Group 90.1 (TG 90.1), the Air Striking Unit, consisting of twelve heavy bombers, sixteen medium bombers, and one hundred fighters. TG 90.2 was the navy air arm, an Air Search Group of two squadrons each of Venturas (PV-1 medium bombers) and Catalinas (PBYs).

For the rest of 1943, the air branch worked hard "to reduce operational hazards, which between 3 June 1942 and 30 September 1943 had claimed 174 aircraft, as opposed to only 40 lost in combat." Training, too, was stepped up and refined. TG 90.2 conducted a number of reconnaissance missions over the Kuriles, just in case the Paramushiro project should be dusted off.[14]

Early in October, Tokyo Rose was bragging that the Japanese were about to recapture the Aleutians. And in that month the Japanese made what could have been considered softening-up raids. Twelve bombers attacked Attu on the ninth, and on the thirteenth nine four-engine bombers conducted another bombing raid, striking Massacre Bay and the area of the airfield. One of the eleven P-40s that rose to the challenge flew into American AA fire and had to make a forced landing. The other ten fighters lost the Japanese in the fog. No major damage was done, and the incident put Attu on the alert; however, this was the last Japanese attack on the Aleutians.[15]

Stubbs's diary gives a rather dismal picture of Adak during October 1943. That stoical soul very seldom made a direct complaint, but a sense of boredom emerges from his account. "Fifteen men from my platoon on the gravel haul today," he wrote on 1 October. "Had a show in the mess hall tonight but the machine broke down." They hauled gravel for days and "dug hut holes for the Engineers," As Stubbs explained, "Every building is put into a deep hole in the side of hill. We are lucky that it is easy digging here."

Stubbs and his buddies took their amusement where they could find it, and they contrived to enjoy themselves fairly well in their off-duty hours. Apparently Stubbs never missed a movie, and while the October crop was pretty sad it helped to pass the time. Signs of winter appeared. "We had ice on the ground when we got up this morning," he noted on 26 October. "It snowed and sleeted a little today."[16]

Familiar names began to disappear. Vice Adm. Frank Jack Fletcher replaced Kinkaid on 11 October, and the latter transferred to assume command of the Seventh Fleet, popularly known as "MacArthur's Navy." Butler became deputy commander, Allied Expeditionary Air Force in Europe, and DeFord went to England with him. DeFord became air chief of staff in the Mediterranean Theater. Smith took command of the marines soon to invade Tarawa. Eareckson let for the South Pacific, touching base at Pearl Harbor long enough for Nimitz to add a Navy Cross to Eareckson's well-earned crop of medals. Then Eareckson became support air controller in the New Guinea operation. Eventually Squeaky Anderson took his beach expertise to Iwo Jima.

Buckner remained in position until June 1944, when he departed for Hawaii to organize the Tenth Army. He hoped and planned to return to Alaska when he retired to live on property he had bought there, and he seems to have toyed with the idea of becoming territorial governor some day. But fate would have it otherwise. On 18 June 1945, on Okinawa an observation post he was visiting was hit by Japanese shells. A large block of coral was torn loose and struck Buckner. He died in a few minutes.[17]

The last quarter of 1943 and the ensuing months of the Pacific War were a particularly hard time for the men stationed in the Aleutians. It is easy to understand why. These men were a prey to one of the most dismal of human emotions—the sense of being useless. As Garfield put it, "The war had gone by; . . . there was nothing to do and nothing to look forward to."[18] The situation would have been morale lowering anywhere; it was doubly so in the Aleutians, granted the climate and the isolation. The men from Arkansas were better off than many, for they could look forward to leaving in the foreseeable future.

The high point of the autumn of 1943 for Alspaugh came on 12 October when his dog had a litter of puppies, "half mongrel and half Husky." By the first week of November he had found homes for the newcomers in "the different sections of the battery."[19]

For Stubbs, a change in his job assignment enlivened November. Fifteen NCOs, including Stubbs, moved to the Fort Battalion to take over those duties. "My job is detail spotter at the beach. We have a few days to break in for our new jobs." The hours were difficult—a straight twelve hours, then off for twenty-four. The docks operated all day every day, and Stubbs and his fellow workers were so tired at the end of their twelve-hour shift that they slept most of their off-duty time. Stubbs skipped many meals in favor of sack time, and his faithful attendance at the movies was a thing of the past. On Thanksgiving, they had two hours off for the traditional turkey dinner. Stubbs "didn't know it was Thanksgiving until we got the two hours off." Nevertheless, he liked his new job, which was a responsible one.

Snow fell steadily. "It is about the deepest on the ground now that I have seen since we have been in the Aleutians," Stubbs noted on 19 November. He added, "A Russian ship came in today loaded with Russian lumber. They had women and small boys as part of the crew."[20]

No doubt that this was the same vessel that Massey mentioned in his notes for November. "Russian transport comes in, it gets washed upon reef, has to be towed off after storm, has some women in crew." Massey shared Stubbs's opinion about the weather—"I believe it's the worst we've had." His situation was complicated by the fact that he had injured his back so badly that he had to spend a week in bed. And he had tragic news to record: "One of our battery men, a draftee, commits suicide, shoots himself. He is in 'Peanut' Coolidge's section."[21]

Christmas Eve found Stubbs at work. "We are unloading beer now. . . . The merchant marines that work on the Liberty ships bring whiskey and sell it for $360 a case or $35 a quart. Some of our men got tight last night and more tonight. I'm staying sober because I have to work tomorrow." For Christmas, he and his men split their shift, so he was able to take off at 1600 to enjoy "a big dinner" at which everyone received a present.[22]

Joe Sisk retained enjoyable memories of this, his last Christmas on Amchitka. In the early days there, the cooks, "had to steal or hijack some food to cook. They were good guys and we were proud of them." Now, however, the troops on Amchitka "had a mess hall, and had a turkey dinner with all the trimmings. We had one heck of a kitchen force. . . . That last Christmas our NCOs did KP so that the men got a break and they appreciated it."[23]

On 24 December, the men of Battery K of the 206th had their first real Christmas party of their Aleutian tour. "In previous years," explained the battery historian, "the course of the war necessitated the lads pay strict attention to their military duties and temporarily forget the pleasure of Christmas.

"Assembling after chow in a set of double quonsets situated in Sleepy Hollow," he went on, "amidst one of Mother Nature's best performances of a williwaw, the men were surprised to find that the huts had been transformed . . . into a cheerful Christmas setting," including a tree. "The tree occupied a place of prominence on the improvised stage where all could feast their eyes on it to the heart's content." It was a fun day with skits, etc. "As a grand finale to a perfect afternoon the remainder of the beer was served while the fellows gathered around to chew the well-known rag in typical G.I. style, with the hot tunes from the instruments of 'The Aleutian Five' drifting through the room."[24]

So these men, at least, had a pleasant memory to sustain them during the short period remaining before they could leave the Aleutians.

38

"Back to Civilization"

On New Year's Day, 1944, Stubbs discovered that he had been a technical sergeant since 29 December. The promotion made no difference in his duties. "We had another busy day at the sorting area," he wrote on 3 January. "Another Russian shipload of lumber is in now. The Co. gave each man three bottles of beer tonight." Three days later the ration rose to five bottles, after another hard session in the sorting area. "The Quartermaster shipped lots of cargo back to Seattle today and it kept us busy."

The eleventh was the second anniversary of Stubbs's departure from Seattle, and an unfortunate development marked the occasion. "We got orders today to turn in all diaries, and no more diaries will be kept."[1] Thus this fine soldier and faithful diarist left the scene just when his account of his unit's final period on Adak would have been invaluable.

January found Massey somewhat nervous. "We get a new C.O., Capt. Wople, they say he is the devil. I haven't met him yet. I hate to see Capt. Meeks [sic] go, he is a good C.O." When Wople showed up in February, however, Massey found he didn't "seem to be so bad." He consulted Massey about who in the battery would make the best first sergeant and accepted Massey's recommendation of S. Sgt. Frank Greco. "Everyone calls the new C.O. King Wople."

The latter promptly tested the battery's mettle by ordering a hike to the top of Mt. Ballyhoo, promising that "the N.C.O. that doesn't make it will be busted." Everyone succeeded, Massey was the second man to reach the top. "Even the battery mess sergeant, Chas. Clark, made it; Capt. Wople makes it too."[2]

Pfc Mode Clayton Crow of the 153d's Medical Detachment had a final little adventure by which to remember Adak. When Crow reached the Aleutians, he had been assigned duty as a barber, although he had never cut a man's hair before; he was a cosmetologist specializing in women's hairdressing. But he soon got the knack of it and was allowed to charge twenty-five cents a haircut. To this fee his officer clients often added tips. With nothing on which to spend money, he sent his earnings to his sister for deposit in his bank account. All those quarters and tips added up, so when he was discharged he had "a nest egg which he used to purchase a beauty salon and later a cosmetology school in Little Rock."

Meanwhile, as Adak became more civilized, nurses were assigned to the hospital. Crow "cut and styled their hair and gave them machineless permanent waves." In 1944 Olivia de Havilland came to Adak to entertain the troops and stayed in the nurses' quarters. Unaware "that Crow was on the premises doing the nurses' hair," Miss de Havilland mistook him for an intruder and "let out a piercing scream."[3] One may speculate that Crow was almost equally disconcerted at coming face to face with the unforgettable Melanie of *Gone With the Wind*.

At last came the long-awaited word: "We got orders to crate up, are being released after two years in this damn place. The whole unit moves over to Unalaska Island to wait for our transport which is out at Attu now."

But the Aleutians had not yet quite finished with the 206th. "The ship we are supposed to leave on is wrecked, the Liberty ship *Greenleaf*," wrote Massey. "It is caught in a williwaw, tossed on reefs and broke in two. Most of the crew loses their life. I hear it was 34 men.

"We wait two more weeks for another ship. . . ."[4]

A few other men remembered what they believed to be the *Greenleaf* incident, but were vague about details, including the name of the ship and the length of the ensuing delay. Captain Wall recalled a ship that broke in two. "The *SS Christopher Greenup* was the ship's name. It happened off Cold Bay, Alaska."[5]

"It is possible that the *Greenleaf* was the ship that was to have picked up my unit, Battery A, up at Amchitka," wrote lst Sgt. Oscar Jones. "We were the only battery that was reassigned from Dutch Harbor. This caused us to have to wait an additional 30 days for transportation back to the US."[6]

The vagueness is not surprising, for more than one accident

occurred during the relocation to the lower forty-eight and most of the men did not remember the name of their ship. As they had come out, so they returned, in a variety of vessels ranging from the frankly terrible to the almost luxurious. Massey's transport turned out to be "the *Gorgas*, an old World War I blockade runner. It looks and smells like hell." But that didn't matter. "I would have rode a swimming horse back if he would have made it. . . ."

Gorgas had been "shelled by a Jap sub before it got here," Massey continued. "One shot hit a stack and another put a nice hole in its port side. The ship's captain was in a foul mood."[7]

Another passenger on *Gorgas* was Pfc Edward Fitzhugh. He remembered "nine days of tough weather and the last night out of Seattle there was a Jap sub nearby. A Canadian PBY came out to flashlight signals to us telling us where the sub was situated. We made it OK."[8]

Some returned aboard *Otsego*. Croom's memory of the return trip was placid. "We did not have an escort and the waters were not as rough as going to the Aleutians."[9] But lst Sgt. Haskell Cathey remembered a narrow squeak. A destroyer asked *Otsego* to identify herself, and the vessel was a little slow in replying. A chief who had been aboard the destroyer later told Cathey that "they had manned guns and readied torpedo #1 to fire . . ." when the destroyer's captain ordered his men to try again. This time *Otsego* responded.[10]

In retrospect, Joe Sisk was thankful that his group "did not come back on the ship we were originally scheduled to board." That had been a Liberty ship loaded with "mostly empty oil drums." Sisk explained how this had led to disaster. "The Truman Commission later found that these ships were end heavy when not under heavy cargo. So this ship did not have enough weight midship so it broke in half out at high sea. I don't know what the losses were," he added, "but one half of the ship sank, the other half didn't. Later they poured concrete in the mid-part of these Liberty ships to help equalize or distribute their weight more evenly.

"I still shiver to think about the ship that broke in two and was to be our transportation back to civilization," he reminisced. "Was that nickel that was tossed back at Ft. Bliss still doing its part to form our destiny?"[11]

As might be expected, ill fortune plagued James Burke to the last. His leg and back gave him trouble throughout his tour of duty.

He was in the hospital when the 206th "got their orders to pull out." He related, "I was supposed to go back on a hospital ship, but none came through. My chance came and I slipped out of the hospital with some other guys who were shipping out and went to the docks. Everybody got their name called but me." However, several men told him to come aboard. So he went back to the hospital for his shipping papers. He got them, along with a warning: ". . . if the ship had to take on anyone from submarines that I may have to give up my bed."

Burke went aboard and stayed below for eighteen hours before he ventured topside. "Then we hit a storm and had to take the inside passage to get down to Seattle. Some places in the passage were so tight you could hear the ship scraping rocks."[12] Ryals "came back on the *S.S. Thompson* and had to bathe in salt water, but it didn't matter. I was going back to the States and civilization."[13] Cowell did not remember the name of his ship, but he vividly recalled being seasick for fourteen days, causing him to lose fifty pounds. "We were ship-wrecked," he added. "We were hit by another ship at night in very cold, thick fog."[14]

This may have been the same incident that Burris described in detail. They had left Dutch Harbor during a storm, in a vessel whose name he did not remember. The weather had been very rough for a week. While Burris was not exactly seasick, he had little inclination for food. Then one evening when night was just begin-ning to fall, the ship entered smooth water near the Inland Passage. Suddenly Burris was hungry and headed for the mess hall.

"I had gotten a tray and gone through the chow line and walked over to stand-up tables we had and started to set the tray down, and at that point we hit something. At first we thought we had been tor-pedoed," he wrote. Three of four men who had been standing at Burris's table "were over by the wall in a pile lying on the floor." Burris knelt down, still holding the tray. He set it on the table, "looked down and saw a piece of sponge cake." This he grabbed, "ducked under the table and up the stairs to the main deck. Our ship had plowed into the side of an American Oil tanker. It knocked a hole in our ship just above the water line that was large enough for 4 men to walk out side by side. We were lucky in that we were entering the Inland Passage of Alaska and there were no waves to cause us to take on water. We hobbled on into Seattle and the ship was put in drydock for repair."[15]

In contrast, Anderson enjoyed a pleasant voyage: "I was part of the last unit to leave Dutch Harbor. Boarded one of the Alaskan Steamship Line vessels for the trip to Seattle through the inside passage. Nice staterooms and all!"[16] His accommodations were probably aboard *Yukon*, which brought Pedersen from Adak to Seattle.[17]

Almost everyone had a submarine story to tell. "After five days out a Jap sub is sighted trailing us," Massey reported. "The ship zigzagged all night and day, can't sleep. A flying radar plane comes out from Canada to give us added protection."[18]

Fox Conway had a rather disjoined recollection of "sub attacks—stormy weather—had to wear life jackets 2 or 3 days—said navy had spotted sub and we had drills in case of an attack."[19]

Pfc Odell Hammond condensed what must have been quite a story into a single sentence: "Ship was chased by Jap sub and sunk and we were picked up by another ship."[20]

McKinistry's trip home was roundabout. "I went from Dutch Harbor out to Adak, to Amchitka, and then back to Seattle." On this last leg they received the unnerving word "that by all calculations a Jap submarine was directly beneath us."[21]

Sisk remembered that "a Jap sub followed us all the way from Amchitka to near Dutch Harbor." He added, "The sea was rough and the fog very dense."[22] Bill Jones confirmed, "On our return from Amchitka in 1944 we were followed by a sub for the first night and part of the next day but no contact."[23]

"We were on an old troop steamer with one boiler gone with a sub between us and home," remarked Thatcher. "I put on a vest that ripped open when the gas was applied, so I just hoped for the best."[24]

Eason was a sergeant on the guard on his transport when "a sub alert occurred. Orders were to keep everyone below deck, which was a full-time job because everyone wanted to see what was going on."[25]

Hargrave was aboard "an old, slow ship . . . without an escort. About two days out of Seattle we were told that a Jap sub had been reported in our area, which left us feeling rather insecure."[26] That last phrase may be listed under the heading of understatement.

Sergeant New returned aboard the *U.S.S. Grant*. "They said a Jap sub was after us, so the one destroyer we had shot off a few depth charges and it felt like the ship had been hit with a torpedo. So everyone on the ship tried to get topside. It made the Navy personnel get sore at the Army boys."[27]

At least two such scares turned out to be false alarms. Some aboard the Libby McNeil freighter upon which Barron sailed "thought a Jap sub was after us, but it was a whale."[28]

Early one morning before Cpl. Udell R. Tarpley had left his bed, Battle Stations sounded. "I hesitated until I heard a 3" deck gun fire," he wrote. "We went to battle stations quickly. The submarine that surfaced in front of the ship turned out to be friendly."[29]

Second only to submarines, the most abiding memory of the voyage home was the same malady that had plagued the men on their way out—seasickness. "The Bering Sea was calm when we left Dutch Harbor," Alspaugh related. "The Pacific was very rough. We came through the pass at lunchtime and the priorities of many of the men aboard changed from eating to discharging the food that they had just consumed. I think about 50–80% of the passengers were seasick."[30]

The weather was "rough beyond belief," according to Newton. "The ship bounced like a ball on the waves."[31] Dale agreed "that the water was very rough and there were times when I thought we might sink."[32] Sgt. E.F. "Bebe" Paulus, Sergeant O'Neal, and Corporal Clodi admitted to being ill throughout the entire trip. Clodi "lived on tomato juice and chocolate bars."[33] Pook Parker "threw up for about six days." Then a sailor from the boiler room took him below decks, telling him he could stay there if he could shovel. So Parker shoveled, finding it more comfortable below because the motion wasn't so noticeable.[34]

Abell was aboard *Fillmore*, and two or three days out of Dutch Harbor a williwaw struck. The ship "was stalled in heavy seas and winds in one area" for several days. "Even the ship's crewmen were sick."[35]

Patrick was so ill he could not get out of bed; ". . . the water was so rough and so many sick men [were] vomiting that it was very bad."[36] Neither Garrett's rank as a first sergeant nor his own queasy stomach on the first day out saved him from a most unpleasant assignment: "1st Sgt. O'Rear and I had the duty to clean the head in the forecastle. As fast as we could mop out an area someone vomited in it. . . ."[37]

Carnes remembered "one terrible storm. A thousand or so seasick men and a real messy ship. Finally a beautiful uneventful trip through the inland passage."[38]

Some hardy souls rose superior to submarines and seasickness. "When we returned from Amchitka to Seattle we were in a heavy storm for 3 or 4 days and no one (was) allowed on deck" George Cathey remembered. "High waves rolled across the ship. Gambling was real heavy on the way back. Both craps and poker. One boy owed me over $200 by the time we arrived at Seattle and I never collected it. As soon as we arrived in the U.S. we all went to a nice restaurant to a good meal."[39]

For Quimby, the high spot of the trip home was a four-hour layover at Seward where he enjoyed his "first glass of milk in a year."[40] Nothing bothered John Davis. "I was so happy to come home, I just tried to enjoy myself."[41]

When Burke's ship reached Seattle, he transferred to a hospital in Walla Walla "for medical evaluation and discharge." There fate had a final snafu for him. "During this time in the hospital I wasn't getting paid. Come to find out, a Canadian soldier with the same name as mine was getting my paycheck. The Canadian said he wondered why he was getting more pay." At last this problem was resolved, and Burke was discharged and on his way home.[42] Parker's ship docked on 27 February to the sound of a band playing "Mares Eat Oats." This catchy nonsense tune was inescapable in the states, but Parker and his fellow soldiers had never heard it before.[43]

Gorgas docked at Seattle "after 12 days of a rough trip." Massey and his companions were whisked off to Ft. Lewis. "The Alaskan clothes we have are so greasy and dirty they can stand up by themselves. We are quartered for five days. I heard a train whistle during the night, it was a lonesome sound. I got real homesick for the first time in two years."

Most of the NCOs in Massey's battery could not resist the temptation to "slip out and go to Seattle. They are caught sneaking in that night by M.P.'s. Capt. Wople busted all of them." That left only four senior sergeants, including Massey, with their stripes intact.[44]

Shortly, however, the men received new uniforms and leave to go to Seattle. Then came the day to board a troop train headed for Ft. Bliss, the 206th's original point of departure. "Our train is a doubleheader, moves at high speed," Massey recorded. "As we go through Spokane, Wash., there is a freighter on the main line, we hit. I am thrown across the seat, got skinned up." Several men were injured but none seriously.[45]

Thomason remembered this incident as "a slight accident. . . . Our engine hit a standing train protruding on our track which moved some of our baggage around a bit. No one was hurt, so not important." Wayne Parker was on that train but uninjured. "I don't even know where it happened—night and I was lost."[46]

Ballew was in a train wreck which may or may not have been the same one. "My car did not turn over but I helped get some guys out of overturned cars." He located this happening in Montana, remarking, "Colder in Montana than in Dutch Harbor."[47]

Two other men were involved in minor mishaps. Cpl. Robert G. Pylant's train "jumped track somewhere between Denver and El Paso."[48] According to Carnes, "The engine hit a cow causing a slight delay while the carcass was removed."[49]

Massey took up his account: "Engineer and firemen hospitalized. All steam pipes on the 14-car train are broken, no heat. We are delayed for 24 hours. A small engine limps away with its load. . . ." The train worked its way along until it reached some mountains, where another engine was attached to the rear to help push the train over the elevation. Somewhere in New Mexico they received "two more big locomotives" and moved on to El Paso. "The cars were cold and uncomfortable until we reached warmer climate in New Mexico."

By that time April had come, and everyone received a twenty-day leave. After his leave, Massey transferred to Battery B, 54AARTC under a Captain Doolittle, a former 202d AA Regiment Officer. "We hit it off fine." Massey was promoted to staff sergeant and took over the duties of first sergeant.[50]

The 206th ceased to exist as such, and its men were scattered. Pylant wound up "in Europe, fighting the Germans, nothing very important."[51] As many of his comrades had, Alspaugh transferred to the infantry and spent the last six months of the European War as a noncom in Company B, 328th Regiment, 26th Infantry Division, Third Army. "The European experience was quite a contrast to the Aleutian tour. We were constantly moving, moving forward, and being shot at about every day."[52]

From Wyre Mitchell we have a good account of those later developments. The 206th was split into three battalions. Men from all of them went to the 86th Infantry in Louisiana or to the 87th Infantry in South Carolina; the 2d Battalion went to Europe as a weapons battery. No one knew where they were going when they boarded the troop train at El Paso. Six hundred men were dropped off in Louisiana. The rest, about eight hundred men, including Mitchell, went on to Ft. Jackson, South Carolina. There Mitchell with many others "was busted to a private for they didn't need sergeants . . ." He resented this not only for himself but for his buddies who were thus downgraded through no fault of their own. They remained in Ft. Jackson from May to September 1944, when the 87th Infantry, consisting of the 345th, 346th, and 347th Regiments, entrained for New York where they boarded a liner to Glasgow, Scotland. Then they moved by train to the Manchester area, where Mitchell's 347th "lived in a big castle with a lot of ground . . ."

They remained over Thanksgiving, then were transferred to Le Havre via Southampton. They day after debarking they boarded a cattle train and eventually reached the front, where they relieved the 35th Division. They were in battle the next day. They took the town of Walsheim, Germany, but pulled out on Christmas Day. "The breakthrough has come and they call us up to help solve it." They went to the Argonne, and after taking their objective they went to St. Hubert, Belgium, where Mitchell was injured and spent two weeks in the hospital. Among other sections, the 347th was in the battle around Bastogne and on "to the Czechoslovakia border where the Germans surrendered so fast we could not handle it . . . We finally told them to go home. We in all took 65,633 prisoners."

Mitchell was intensely proud of his colleagues from the 206th, who had fewer killed and wounded than the "regular 87th boys. We think that it was the 206th boys that carried and made the 87th what it was."[53]

The men of the 206th, therefore, served well in both the Pacific and European theaters, and even as members of other units, honorably exemplified the 206th motto: "Never Give Up."

39

"A Learning Experience"

Every once in a while, over the past two years, someone would ask, "What are you working on now?" We would reply, "the story of an Arkansas unit during the war in the Aleutians." If the questioner's age was under fifty the comeback usually was a blank *"What* war in the Aleutians?"

This leads to another question—just how important was a campaign so obscure that many intelligent, well-read people had either forgotten it or had never heard of it? Certainly there were many negative features about the war effort in Alaska. The basic strategy, that it would be feasible to attack Japan through the Aleutians, was questionable, to put it mildly. The belief that the United States could be attacked through the Aleutians seemed equally questionable. Yet the concept that the Aleutians were a strategic point was taken very seriously, and not only in military circles. When Governor Gruening was in Washington in March 1942, Secretary of the Interior Harold L. Ickes suggested that the governor leave his wife in the lower forty-eight because of the threat of a Japanese invasion. Ickes was quite surprised when Gruening promptly answered that Dorothy "wanted to be with him and that his place was in Alaska . . ." Ickes informed his diary that "this showed more physical courage than I thought Gruening capable of and I liked him for it."[1]

After the American victory in the Aleutians, Ickes asked Gruening "to prepare a critical summary of the Alaskan military situation." The governor complied with alacrity, for he had been building up a head of steam and welcomed the chance to get many things off his chest.

He opened his remarks with the withering statement that "the battle of Alaska has ended and it may be reasonably contended that the Japs won it." He based this conclusion upon the fact that a small number of Japanese had "immobilized American forces about 50 times more numerous," as well as tying up vast amounts of matériel and shipping.[2]

Gruening had a low opinion of the military bureaucracy and zeroed in on a number of what he considered stupid mistakes in the field of logistics. He pointed out that installations that were built at the outbreak of war failed to consider air power. Buildings were crammed together with no attempt at concealment, and in the event of a Japanese attack would have been vulnerable targets.

He also remarked that the three naval bases at Sitka, Kodiak, and Dutch Harbor were under construction "before it was realized that the Army would have to be located somewhere" to defend the bases. This blunder greatly increased the cost of these projects "and never produced as satisfactory a result as if allowance for a joint Army-Navy base had been made in the original plans."

Gruening was particularly caustic about the situation at Sitka. To locate the army garrison, the tops were blown off eight rocky islands extending into the harbor, and the rock used to build a connecting causeway "at a cost of some 15 times the contemplated expenditure." Moreover, the straight lines made camouflage impossible. He added sourly that plenty of nearby sites were available. "Creating land in Alaska at tremendous cost will always rank as one of the most fantastic follies of the war." One must agree that adding more land to Alaska was carrying coals to Newcastle with a vengeance. Gruening added that every naval officer at Sitka with whom he consulted declared that the site was "cockeyed."

As for Dutch Harbor, everything there had to be duplicated at Umnak. "Dutch Harbor with no airport and Umnak with no seaport, is like a team composed of a lame man and a blind man—the lame carrying the blind on his back."[3]

He pointed out that despite the long planning for the Attu invasion, bad mistakes were made. Some of his strictures we have already cited. To summarize, his complaints covered the folly of training troops for the Aleutians in the hot, dry terrain of the Mojave when already there were troops *in situ* acclimated to the locale; the selection as commander of a general who had never been in Alaska, who made no attempt to familiarize himself with the terrain, and who apparently would not take advice; the heavy casualties. Gruening had a medical degree and was especially upset over the number of men suffering from frozen feet, which the right footwear would have prevented.

Gruening was only a little less irritated over Kiska. Attempts had been made to sugarcoat the fiasco on the grounds that the Japanese had fled, not daring to fight. The governor, however, considered that the escape of the enemy reflected no credit upon the Americans. And he failed to understand why, lacking Japanese opposition, Americans had fired upon each other "on a little island like Kiska, especially at the time of the year when there is virtually no darkness."[4]

Gruening cited as a horrible example of military stupidity the Excursion Inlet project. Construction of an embarkation port there, some sixty miles west of Juneau, for use in the Attu invasion, was not completed in time to serve that purpose, although work was under way between the autumn of 1942 and the summer of 1943. Gruening had argued against the project, urging instead the establishment of this post on the Gastineau Channel at Juneau. There docks and warehouses were already available, as were such utilities as light, power, and water. At Excursion Inlet all these facilities would have to be "built from scratch." DeWitt rejected Gruening's recommendation on the grounds that "the contract had been signed and he couldn't change his mind." Now that Attu had been retaken, DeWitt still insisted on finishing the installation. When Gruening asked why this was being done, the commanding officer of the post told him it was "for the next war." The governor inquired as to whom this next enemy might be, and was informed rather vaguely that "perhaps Russia would be the next opponent."

What happened next is almost beyond belief. After the base had been completed in 1944, "the Army brought in German prisoners of war who dismantled all the facilities. The Army then shipped the salvaged material elsewhere."[5]

Government mismanagement was also responsible for much unnecessary suffering on the part of the Aleuts and the near destruction of their culture. To their credit, both Guening and Buckner opposed the most ill-advised evacuation of the Aleuts. When they were finally allowed to return, they found that servicemen had thoroughly looted and wrecked their homes. These Aleuts never received adequate recompense. Recently surviving Nisei received twenty thousand dollars each by way of apology for their unjust incarceration during the war years. We are unaware of any move to offer a similar apology to the Aleuts who survived their evacuation.[6]

Of course, from the military standpoint the campaign had its positive side. If the Japanese pinned down American resources, the opposite was also true. In 1944, when the only U. S. offensive actions in the theater were nuisance air raids against the Kuriles, this "small harassing campaign . . . tied up 500 Japanese planes (toward the end, this was one-sixth of the combined Imperial air forces) and 41,000 troops, who deployed against the threat of an invasion in the Kuriles," Garfield wrote. "The invasion never did take place, but its threat was enough. The Kurile campaign was of far greater value than the bored Aleutian servicemen imagined."[7]

The U.S. Strategic Bombing Survey agreed that the Japanese were "desperately concerned over an amphibian advance" against the Empire from the direction of Kuriles and estimated the air strength "in the Hokkaido-Kurile Area in the summer of 1944" at about 500 planes. By the spring of 1945, however, urgent needs in other areas had reduced the number of aircraft in the Kuriles to some 18 army fighters at Paramushiro and 12 navy dive-bombers "divided between Shimushu and Etorofu."

The figure of 41,000 represented the peak of army strength in the Kuriles; in 1945 it decreased to 27,000. As the Survey pointed out, these men saw no action "except in defense against harassing air raids, or against sporadic shore bombardment by light United States naval forces." Nevertheless, the high number of Japanese soldiers in the Kuriles—no doubt as bored and disgruntled as their opposites in the Aleutians—meant that many Japanese soldiers were "unavailable for combat assignment elsewhere. Moreover," continued the Survey, "Their supply and movement afforded excellent shipping targets for aggressive United States submarines. This resulted in a heavy loss of ships to Japan as well as a loss at sea of about 10 percent of the total personnel deployed to the islands." The Aleutian campaign's cost to Japan in men and matériel was light compared to that experienced in other theaters, but for a nation so limited in manpower and resources, the loss of every ship, aircraft and man carried a price tag far out of proportion to what a similar loss meant, in the military sense, to the United States.[8]

One of the lessons of the Aleutian campaign was the fact that air power, for all its might, had its limitations. Efforts to bomb the Japanese off Kiska proved fruitless. "With thrice the original air strength and two air bases as close as 60 and 200 miles respectively from Kiska, air effort alone did not suffice to drive the Japanese from their honeycomb defense." It took the capture of Attu and the prospect of massive amphibious attack to convince the Japanese to leave Kiska.

The survey remarked that "the Aleutians ranked high as a school for the rapid building of air fields." The one on Umnak had taken four months—not bad at all—but that on Adak required only fifteen days. "In the dead of winter on the island of Amchitka, a fighter strip was in operation a little over a month after the initial landing."

Thanks to the dreadful weather, "the Aleutians early became an experimental and proving ground for airborne search radar." In the Survey's opinion, "Without radar the effectiveness of air search would have been reduced to practically nothing." The Japanese, who did not have radar in the Aleutians, had to abandon search missions out of Kiska by flying boat.

The Aleutian campaign exploded the myth of the northern route as a natural avenue of attack on Japan. In terms of mileage, it was much the shortest pathway, but it proved tactically impractical. The conditions of weather and terrain were well known, but somehow "it was not fully appreciated" just how powerful an effect these factors would have on military operations. One figure suffices to underline this: The Eleventh Air Force's ratio of total theater loss to combat loss of aircraft was 6.5 to 1, whereas the ratio in the Pacific Theater as a whole was 3 to 1.[9]

Alaska as such benefited from the war years. Indeed, it may not be too much to say that she attained statehood long before she would have in the normal course of events. Before Alaska's strategic position was recognized, her needs and wishes had stood well down on the government's priority list, while to many citizens she was still "Seward's Icebox," as remote as the craters of the moon.

The war changed all that. The military descended upon Alaska, technology in its wake. The signal corps ran two thousand miles of telephone line between Fairbanks and the lower forty-eight—the Alcan line. The Alaska Scouts worked wonders. On foot and by dogsled, they mapped every mile of the Alaskan coastline and conducted "a pipeline survey from Fairbanks to Point Barrow."[10]

Above all, U. S. Army Engineers and Canadian construction workers completed "the long-visualized, often-postponed, finally-decided Alaska Highway," running for 1,500 miles through British Columbia, the Yukon Territory, and central Alaska. Transportation had long been a problem in that area where the population averaged 1 per 8 square miles. The only railroad was "a one-track 470-mile line between Seward and Fairbanks . . ." Only two highways, totaling 534 miles, could be considered "well built modern roads."

The problems that had to be faced were monumental, and who knows how long the project would have taken without the prod of perceived military necessity. Ground had to be thawed before the construction equipment could make a dent in it. In places "six feet of volcanic ash had to be removed . . ." In summer the thermometer hit 90°, "and for long weeks vast stretches of land became groundless swamps." Sometimes rain pelted down in torrents, and the men had to build a roof over the site before they could pour the concrete. Labor and logistics problems plagued them—"workers quit their jobs; planes carrying foodstuffs were grounded in bad weather; boats were late." But at last it was done, and the Alaskans had a direct land link with their fellow Americans. An unidentified clipping hints that not all their fellow Alaskans were thrilled, fearing that the highway would bring an influx of "tin can tourists."[11]

Perhaps of equal importance were the personal ties forged. While the veterans agree almost unanimously that only a native could love the Aleutians, it was far otherwise with those stationed on the Alaskan mainland. Buckner was not the only serviceman to fall in love with this magnificent land and to hope to return after the war. Thousands of men from all over the United States had been exposed for long periods to Alaska's mighty mountains, majestic forests, clear streams, pure air, and hospitable people. Alaska could never be remote again; she had been woven into the national consciousness.

For the men of the 206th, the Aleutian campaign was a highly personalized, sharply localized experience. A few—a very few—

retained favorable memories. "It was an interesting short time in my life and I enjoyed it," was Beasley's reaction.[12] Colonel Dodson agreed. "It was interesting and I really enjoyed it."[13] Pfc Wayne L. Lindley remarked rather wistfully, "I believe I enjoyed life more as a PFC with all my friends than I did as an officer in Hawaii."[14]

Tate hoped to visit the Aleutians again some day. "Made some friends that I love very much and cherish them and my experiences in Alaska."[15] Fitzhugh agreed that his recollections were positive. "I would not trade my experience in Dutch Harbor for anything. It gave me a much broader outlook on human nature and behavior. . . . I made many life-long friends. I have no complaints. Those who got so bored that they would go off the deep end did not know how to entertain themselves."[16]

A second, rather more numerous minority found the Aleutian years totally negative. "Only a very young man with a pretty stable mind could have stayed as long as we did without going nuts," declared Bebe Paulus.[17] Chief Costley observed bluntly, "It was absolutely the worst duty that I ever served and I spent 27 years in the army."[18] Burris and Massey were both emphatic and laconic. "It was hell," said the former, and "Two years of hell," summarized the latter.[19] "I would call my experience there a terrible nightmare that still haunts me," wrote Joe Sisk. "I have but few pleasant memories about our stay there. I am sure it was a venture I could endure only once and still have a degree of sanity left."[20] Dale summarized morosely, "I would just say that from my point of view the Aleutians should be given back to the Eskimos."[21]

Most of the men had mixed reactions. For many, the fate of their comrades in the 200th helped reconcile them to their lot. "We were lucky to go there," stated Fox Conway. "We could have went to the Philippines. The flip of the coin saved us."[22] Pack remarked, "I believe the Lord was on Col. Robinson's [sic] side when he called the coin. I read the teletype news on them each day. They really got a beating. . . ."[23] Haskell Cathey said, "I would thank God for us being sent to the Aleutians instead of the Philippines. I had some friends in the 200th that never came back."[24]

The most general reaction to the Aleutian tour of duty, however, was that it had been what Caldwell termed "One terrific learning experience."[25] Mused Weese, "I grew up and matured a lot. Learned how to deal with people—both enlisted men and officers.

This served me well in OCS and in the remainder of my military career."[26] Sergeant Robertson remarked, "It was a learning experience. We left as a bunch of boys and came back as men."[27]

Nevertheless, once was enough! "I would not want to have missed this experience," said Faulhaber, "but I certainly hope that I never have to do it again."[28] Captain Beverburg observed, "It was a great experience, but I have no desire for a second time around."[29] Stout spoke for many when he declared, "As of now, wouldn't take a million to do it again."[30]

O'Neal paid a striking tribute to his outfit which may well serve as a parting toast:

> If I had to go again under the same set of circumstances I would hope it could be with the same men and officers that departed Seattle in August 1941. We did the job assigned and while that job did not make headlines I feel it was important in its own little way. I was proud of my Country, I was proud of my Regiment, I was proud of the men who served in her ranks and I'm thankful to be one of those men who can look back and say we NEVER GAVE UP.[31]

Epilogue: Return to Yesterday

The flight came in low and slightly to the left of the runway. All of a sudden we felt the plane shudder as the pilot pushed the engines' throttles forward and the plane began to climb. We were going around. We all looked at one another in anticipation and, frankly, with some fear. There were six of us—four veterans, one wife, and myself. We were making a pilgrimage of sorts to the place where these guys had lived almost fifty years ago, and which, after all that time, they could not forget. Charlie Williams so ably put it: we were going to Mecca.

The party consisted of Donnel Drake, the old first sergeant who probably knows as much about the 206th in Alaska as anyone in the unit; Mason Patrick, who had served there as a very young man, and you could see that he was excited, although he was the quiet type; Charlie Williams, who looked as trim as ever; Bill and Peggy Arbaugh. Bill was slightly heavier than in the old days, quite knowledgeable about the war and the area. Of course, Peggy had not served there, but she was as well versed as any of us and kept us all honest in our tales of yesterday. Her good humor and cheerful disposition added greatly to our enjoyment of the trip. Finally there was Monroe Massey, whose notes you have followed through this whole story, and who was to pass away one year later.

As the plane circled, Drake assured me that this was SOP (standing operating procedure). He told me that many times in the old days, because of the high winds, aircraft had to turn around and go back to the mainland. Often during the war planes could not land at all and there would be no aircraft in or out for days.

As we approached the runway, I could see the beauty and majesty of the area—Eiders Point, Mt. Ballyhoo, Hog Island, the

Spit, Morris Cove, Signal Hill, Captain's Bay, Otter Point, Beaver Inlet, Fort Mears, Power Hill, Bunker Hill, Mt. Makushin—all with World War II dugouts, gun emplacements, pits for eight-inch guns, concrete pill boxes, 166-mm gun emplacements, trenches still intact.

On the final approach, Hog Island was on the left and beautiful Mt. Ballyhoo on the right. The sky was cloudy, but fortunately there was not much wind. As the plane lined up to land, I could see that it was much lower. When we came over the runway the wheels touched at the very end, giving the pilot full coverage.

The runway itself was a 2,500- to 3,000-foot gravel strip with much sand on it, and the plane was fitted with special equipment to keep the gravel from tearing it up. On the edge, we could see a few old oil drums and a couple of old buildings. Arbaugh told me that it looked much as it did when he served there years ago.

The airport was a fancy Quonset hut built during the war. There were only two scheduled flights in a day, and both left within an hour of landing. Prices at the airport were out of sight. Shirts sold for seventy dollars, dolls for sixty dollars, and hats for one hundred dollars. A sandwich and a coke were ten dollars at the Ballyhoo Bar. The building had been built by the Navy Seabees during the war and was in very good shape.

We ordered a cab and to our surprise one came quite quickly. The fee was two dollars. Later we found that this was the fee no matter where we went on the island. An old Vietnamese refugee named Dong ran the cab company, and we quickly hired from him for fifty dollars a day an old World War II pickup truck. We had taken it out for ten minutes and about three miles from the hotel when it ground to a halt and refused to start again. Dong had to come and tow us in because we had no battery for it. After an hour's worth of wrangling and gnashing of teeth, we finally got a vehicle that would work, and it was our savior, for we drove that thing all over the island at all times of day.

As we drove along the roads, each member of our party recalled some of the anecdotes and tales that we have recounted in this book. "There's Hog Island," shouted Massey. Williams was interested in the hill where he had spent not too many pleasant days, but now talked about it like it was heaven. Massey and Patrick were looking for the Spit and their little foxholes on the side of

Mt. Ballyhoo, Arbaugh looked for his old dugout, and Drake for Morris Cove.

We passed wreck after wreck along the side of the roads. Old cabs were lying all over the place. Even though it was July, snow still clung to the tops of Mts. Makushin and Ballyhoo and other high peaks. All the roads were bad but some were worse than others. The roads to the mountain passes were so bad that the roads going to them seemed like modern superhighways, even though they were almost as bad. A new car would not last very long in Unalaska.

After getting our vehicle, we drove to the Unisea Inn, a very nice complex, built where the old subpens used to be. Ironically, the Japanese own the hotel and the whole complex. The Unisea is a pleasant place, run by a former madam, with nice people, good food, and it is relatively inexpensive. A no-nonsense place. If you behave badly, make too much noise, or are otherwise obnoxious, you get kicked out. No fooling around at the Unisea!

Since it was summer, the sun was still shining at one o'clock in the morning, and it hardly set before it was up again. We found it hard to get used to this, and we stayed up all hours wandering around the area. The natives, however, appeared to sleep during normal hours.

The Unisea complex has a bank, a small church, a travel agency, and a store run by the Alaska Commercial Company that sells everything from groceries and soft drinks to toilet articles, clothes, televisions, radios, etc. This big complex has a monopoly on the island and is not cheap. The customer pays $8.16 for a gallon of milk, $2.98 for a loaf of bread, $1.69 for a candy bar, $2.50 for some cigars. At the nearby Italian restaurant and Chinese restaurant the prices were reasonable.

Driving up from the old subpen to the junction of the first road, you can see Margaret Bay directly ahead. To the right you drive past what was once Fort Mears. A few buildings are left, such as the old commissary, but of all the areas on the islands, Fort Mears has lost the most. At other installations such as Signal Hill, Morris Cove, and Mt. Ballyhoo, the visitor can still see signs of where the 206th and other units had been. Fort Mears is almost gone. Continuing down the road, you can reach the airport.

Leaving the Unisea and turning left, you head to Unalaska. The

Iluilick River now has a bridge to cross rather than the old ferry, and this bridge connects Dutch Harbor to Unalaska. The old army chapel is now the Parks and Recreation building. There is a new school and a TV station. Thanks to the satellite, this station brings the viewer super stations from New York, Atlanta, Chicago, and Denver, as well as HBO, Showtime, CNN, etc.

Looking down the main street, called Broadway, we could see a myriad of businesses and stores, small buildings built mainly of wood. Many of the features associated with the war were located at the northwest edge of the village. Today a fish processing plant, which we visited, stands on the site of the Coast Guard bunkhouse. The offices at the Unalaska dock have been removed as well as the naval hospital. We saw a big building, the headquarters for the native Aleutians. A general store called Carl's provides some competition for the Unalaska Commercial Company.

There was a roller rink, a small city park with a gazebo, several rows of houses, a post office where Blackie's Bar used to be, and a new bar next to it called the Elbow Room. Incidentally, *Playboy* magazine voted this bar the third toughest one in the country. After a couple of hours in it, anyone could see why.

Across from the post office stood a restaurant, and across from the Elbow Room was a variety store called Nicki's. Down from Nicki's was the Bishop house, and next to it the old Russian church that had been the cornerstone of the town for years. It can be seen from almost any part of the area.

The church looked badly in need of paint from the outside, but its gold dome shone all over the island, and the inside was beautiful. The Sunday mass in the church was in Russian with some English. The Russian Orthodox priest gave the same ritual that had been practiced, with some modifications, for years. All the congregation were natives; no fishermen or Caucasians except us stood for the two-hour mass. Next to the church was a monument to all those who have gone down to the sea in ships.

A recent development, Iliuliuk Lake Subdivision, occupies the site of the old joint cemetery. No trace remains of the cemetery—no fences or monuments.

Two old wartime docks, two warehouses and ammunition magazines, and a few cabanas still stand along Captain's Bay road. One cabana is the office of the Maritime Company. Pecker Point was still there, but the old house of ill repute is long gone and no ferry serves the point. The town has a ball field and a nice-looking school. The remains of the old prison and the general's quarters were still there. The chimney to his fireplace was visible for several hundred yards. There were still remains of old military installations on Signal Hill. The road to Ballyhoo was rough, but the trip was worth it, and the men were able to see many of the remains of buildings and gun turrets still there.

The Spit has been built up with refineries, and ships were docked nearby. After a little hunting, Massey and Mason Patrick were able to find their old foxholes. They were quite ecstatic about it. Perhaps none was more happy about finding his old holes than Charlie Williams, who climbed hill and dale and walked our feet off to find one of them, and then he took us to the old gold mine camp to find another. Arbaugh was cool about all this, but he also was thrilled to find his hole.

Looking out over Captain's Bay close to the gold mine camp, we could see the hull of the half-sunk, *Northwestern* still proudly standing in view. We rented a boat and Earl Meadows, a veteran of the Islands, took us past the *Northwestern*. We could see her name plainly written on her side. We went looking for Drake's place at Morris Cove, but although we walked and walked until we were dead tired, we could not locate it. However, the next day Drake commandeered an old LST in which he and Charlie Williams went to Morris Cove and saw where years ago Drake had spent those many dreadful days.

Except for the Unisea Inn, there is not much to do on the island, but the Elbow Room goes strong. We went there twice and once got caught in a riot. Natives and fishermen frequent the bar, and while Kiska Kate is no more, there are several others who could pass for her. The natives there were very nice to us, but we could see that much tension exists.

They feel, with much justification, that they were never treated right. They were interned and kept from their homes for three years. As the danger had passed as early as 1943, they should have been able to return to their homes much earlier than they did. When they returned, they found extensive evidence of widespread

and wanton vandalism and destruction of property. GIs had ran-
sacked the contents of closed packing boxes, trunks, and cupboards.
They had left clothing scattered all over the floors, trampled and
fouled. Dishes, stoves, radios, books, and many other personal items
were broken or damaged, many others were stolen. When the GIs
pulled out, they left many fine buildings and places which the
natives could have used, but they were never allowed to, and the
buildings have since decayed.

The natives now own most of the land, but they are bitter about
the past and do not want to cooperate with the fishermen and the
Anglos on the island. On the other hand, the Anglos believe that
the natives should help them develop the place. The natives want
no part of this development.

Recently, at the request of some of the Arkansas veterans and
with the help of several Alaskan officials, this author tried to per-
suade the natives to change the name of Hog Island to Arkansas
Island, in honor of those who served there. When the idea was presented to the natives of the town, they promptly voted it down.
While they had nothing against the men from Arkansas, they had
had enough of the white man changing their life style. Despite this
feeling, the natives and their families joined with us for all the
Fourth of July festivities, including a big fireworks display and a
typical American barbeque.

We spent hours with Henry Swanson*, whom we have quoted
extensively in our story, and who has become a living legend to both
natives and other islanders. He was well and quite articulate as he
told us tales of the Fox Islands and the war. Also of much help to us
was the Unalaska librarian, Jan Duncan. And the local TV station
had us on the air to discuss the old days and what it was like, and
how things have changed.

To us, Unalaska today seemed quite prosperous. Fishermen at
one of the best ports in the country have been doing quite well.
There used to be an old joke in the islands that a woman was behind
every tree, but there were no trees. Nowadays there are women on
the island—teachers, secretaries, housewives, as there are in any
other American community.

---

* We were saddened to learn that Henry Swanson died shortly after the completion of this
manuscript.

The area is as beautiful as ever. The williwaws still howl; the fog and clouds still hang low; the old hills still hold stories of yesteryear with relics of gun emplacements, worn-out buildings, and foxholes.

While a joint monument has been erected at the entrance to the airport honoring the Americans, Canadians, and yes, the Japanese, who died in the Williwaw War, the hulk of the old *Northwestern* and the places where some of the men of the 206th died stand as the real monuments.

They say "You can't go home again," but for a few days, five guys did just that as they completed what for some would be the last trip to a home far away from their native land.

Notes

1: "Well Above the Average"

1. "History of Battery 'K,' 206th CA (AA), January 6th, 1941 to March 31st, 1943." Hereafter Btry K History. This battery was "A" until a reorganization of 18 August 1942; Donnel Drake, "History of Battery A." Hereafter Btry A history. Drake prepared this history for Goldstein's use.

2. Papers of Col. Elgan C. Robertson. Hereafter Robertson papers.

3. Scrapbooks of Louis E. Taylor, Book 1. Hereafter Taylor scrapbooks. Taylor served with Battery E.

4. 206th C.A. (AA) Historical Survey Data Sheets submitted by former members of the organization.

5. Btry K history.

6. Taylor scrapbooks; Robertson papers.

7. Reply to questionnaire from Goldstein by T. 4 Nathan R. Patrick. Hereafter Patrick questionnaire.

8. Reply to questionnaire from Goldstein by T. Sgt. John H. Harp. Hereafter Harp questionnaire.

9. Reply to questionnaire from Goldstein by WO Bernard E. Stout. Hereafter Stout questionnaire.

10. Btry K history; Btry A history; Donnel Drake, "Arkansas National Guard: A Military History 1781–1939." Hereafter "Arkansas National Guard." Drake prepared this document for Goldstein's use, his source being *National Guard of the United States: State of Arkansas 1938*, Baton Rouge, La., 1938.

11. Reply to questionnaire from Goldstein by S. Sgt. Murrel W. Buzzan. Hereafter Buzzan questionnaire.

12. Reply to questionnaire from Goldstein by Pvt John W. Davis. Hereafter Davis questionnaire.

13. Reply to questionnaire from Goldstein by Pfc Lawrence Richardson. Hereafter Richardson questionnaire.

14. Stout questionnaire.

15. Btry K history.

16. Undated letter from Alford "Pook" Parker to Goldstein, postmarked 14 November 1989. Hereafter Parker letter.

17. Brochure on the 39th CAA Brigade, Fort Bliss, TX, 18 April 1991, fiftieth anniversary. Hereafter 39th Brochure. Reply to questionnaire from Goldstein by Cpl. R. R. "Dick" Ballew. Hereafter Ballew questionnaire.

18. Btry A. history.

19. Taylor scrapbooks.

20. Notes of Sgt. James M. Massey. He did not keep a formal diary, but made periodic jottings, which he kindly placed at Goldstein's disposal. Hereafter Massey notes.

21. Reply to questionnaire from Goldstein by Sgt. Earl Gill. Hereafter Gill questionnaire.

22. Letters of Cpl. David Alspaugh to his family, 21 January 1941. Alspaugh generously provided Goldstein with a number of letters addressed to various members of his family. Hereafter Alspaugh letters.

23. Taylor scrapbooks. These and other typical prices of the period come mainly from *The New York Times*.

24. Reply to questionnaire from Goldstein by Cpl. Neal P. Kinney. Hereafter Kinney questionnaire.

25. Taylor scrapbooks.

26. Reply to questionnaire from Goldstein by Pfc Dennis P. Abell. Hereafter Abell questionnaire.

27. Reply to questionnaire from Goldstein by 2d Lt. Raymond Byergson. Hereafter Byergson questionnaire.

28. Alspaugh letter.

29. Parker letter.

2: "Training Began to Pick Up"

1. Massey notes.

2. 39th Brochure.

3. Btry K history.

4. Gill questionnaire.

5. Reply to questionnaire from Goldstein by Cpl. Joseph G. Jones. Hereafter Jones questionnaire.

6. Btry A history.

7. Massey notes.

8. Taylor scrapbooks.

9. Alspaugh letters.

10. Jones questionnaire.

11. Stout questionnaire.

12. Alspaugh letters.

13. Massey notes.

14. Alspaugh letters.

15. Ballew questionnaire.

16. Reply to questionnaire from Goldstein by 1st Sgt. John W. Weese. Hereafter Weese questionnaire.

17. Reply to questionnaire from Goldstein by 1st Sgt. Donnel J. Drake. Hereafter Drake questionnaire.

18. Taylor scrapbooks.

19. Kinney questionnaire.

20. Taylor scrapbooks; Alspaugh letters.

21. Alspaugh letters.

22. Taylor scrapbooks; reply to questionnaire from Goldstein to Cpl. Earl P. Hargrave. Hereafter Hargrave questionnaire; Alspaugh letters.

23. Gill questionnaire.

24. Alspaugh letters.

25. Taylor scrapbooks.

26. Alspaugh letters.

27. Jones questionnaire.

28. Drake questionnaire.

29. Gill questionnaire.

30. Kinney questionnaire.

31. Reply to questionnaire from Goldstein to 1st Sgt. Robert D. Garrett. Hereafter Garret questionnaire.

32. Reply to questionnaire from Goldstein to T. Sgt. W. L. McKinistry. Hereafter McKinistry questionnaire.

33. Weese questionnaire.

34. Reply to questionnaire from Goldstein by Pfc Lawrence R. Henderson. Hereafter Henderson questionnaire.

35. Reply to questionnaire from Goldstein by M. Sgt. James W. Keeton. Hereafter Keeton questionnaire.

36. Taylor scrapbooks.

3: "Who Knows Our Destiny . . . ?"

1. Drake questionnaire.

2. Undated statement by James W. Burke. Hereafter Burke statement.

3. Taylor scrapbooks.

4. Reply to questionnaire from Goldstein by 1st Sgt. Bill E. Jones. Hereafter B. Jones questionnaire.

5. Alspaugh letters.

6. Massey notes.

7. Alspaugh letters.

8. Parker letter.

9. Alspaugh letters.

10. Taylor scrapbooks.

11. Btry K history.

12. Ibid.

13. Reply to questionnaire from Goldstein by Pfc Edward B. Fitzhugh. Hereafter Fitzhugh questionnaire.

14. Btry K history.

15. Parker letter.

16. At a reunion of the 206th in 1960, Colonel Robertson confirmed that this unlikely event did in fact take place. Reply to questionnaire from Goldstein by S. Sgt. S. P. "Fox" Conway. Hereafter Conway questionnaire.

17. Reply to questionnaire from Goldstein by Maj. John T. Meek. Hereafter Meek questionnaire.

18. Hargrave questionnaire.

19. Reply to questionnaire from Goldstein by S. Sgt. Charles "Spud" Clark. Hereafter Clark questionnaire.

20. Reply to questionnaire from Goldstein by Cpl. Luster V. Tate. Hereafter Tate questionnaire.

21. Reply to questionnaire from Goldstein by S. Sgt. Robert M. Proffitt. Hereafter Proffitt questionnaire.

22. Kinney questionnaire.

23. Reply to questionnaire from Goldstein by Pfc James L. Pack. Hereafter Pack questionnaire.

24. Massey notes.

25. Reply to questionnaire from Goldstein by Col. Minot B. Dodson. Hereafter Dodson questionnaire.

26. Reply to questionnaire from Goldstein by 1st Sgt. Oscar H. Jones. Hereafter O. Jones questionnaire.

27. Weese questionnaire.

28. B. Jones questionnaire.

29. Parker letter.

30. Garrett questionnaire.

31. Reply to questionnaire from Goldstein by T. 4 Joe B. Sisk. Hereafter Sisk questionnaire.

32. Drake questionnaire.

33. For a brief description of the debate in the House over this issue, see Gordon W. Prange, *Pearl Harbor: The Verdict of History*, pp. 28–32.

34. William M. Franklin, "Alaska, Outpost of American Defense," *Foreign Affairs*, October 1940, p. 246.

4: "A Sometimes Difficult Situation"

1. Btry K history; Drake questionnaire.

2. Weese questionnaire.

3. Letter, 10 July 1989 from James Earl Wilson to Goldstein. Wilson was a Pfc in Btry H. Hereafter Wilson letter.

4. Taylor scrapbooks.

5. 39th brochure.

6. Drake questionnaire; Alspaugh letters.

7. Ballew questionnaire.

8. Alspaugh letters.

9. Reply to questionnaire from Goldstein by Pfc Sheldon L. Radney. Hereafter Radney questionnaire.

10. B. Jones questionnaire.

11. Massey questionnaire.

12. Alspaugh letters.

13. Burke statement.

14. Btry K history.

15. Alspaugh letters.

16. *National Guard of the United States; State of Arkansas*, pp. 27–29, 171.

17. Parker letter.

18. Alspaugh letters. The 39th did not go to Alaska. On 1 September 1943 it transferred back to Fort Bliss, and on 10 July 1944 was assigned to the Replacement and School Command. On 24 October 1944 it moved to Camp Maxey, TX, where it was deactivated two days later. 39th Brochure.

19. Burke statement.

20. Btry K history.

21. Reply to questionnaire from Goldstein by Pfc James L. Pack. Hereafter Pack questionnaire.

22. Reply to questionnaire from Goldstein by S. Sgt. Louis Taylor. Hereafter Taylor questionnaire.

23. Drake questionnaire.

24. Jones questionnaire.

25. Taylor questionnaire.

26. Sisk questionnaire.

27. Garrett questionnaire.

28. Btry K history.

29. Drake questionnaire.

30. Reply to questionnaire from Goldstein by Sgt. Harry K. Dougherty. Hereafter Dougherty questionnaire.

31. Reply to questionnaire from Goldstein by T. 5 Lawrence G. Eheman. Hereafter Eheman questionnaire.

32. Reply to questionnaire from Goldstein by Pfc Wayne L. Lindley. Hereafter Lindley questionnaire.

33. B. Jones questionnaire.

34. Reply to questionnaire from Goldstein by Cpl. Thomas P. O'Neal. Hereafter O'Neal questionnaire.

35. Reply to questionnaire from Goldstein by Cpl. Thomas Quimby. Hereafter Quimby questionnaire.

36. Proffitt and Sisk questionnaires.

37. Ballew questionnaire.

38. Conway questionnaire.

39. Reply to questionnaire from Goldstein by T. Sgt. George B. Faulhaber. Hereafter Faulhaber questionnaire.

40. Hargrave questionnaire.

41. Drake questionnaire.

42. Reply to questionnaire from Goldstein by S. Sgt. Herman F. Beverburg. Hereafter Beverburg questionnaire.

43. Reply to questionnaire from Goldstein by Sgt. William S. Newton. Hereafter Newton questionnaire.

44. Drake questionnaire.

45. Reply to questionnaire from Goldstein by Pfc Paul D. Beasley. Hereafter Beasley questionnaire.

46. Pack questionnaire.

47. Ibid; Taylor scrapbooks.

48. Wilson letter.

49. Reply to questionnaire from Goldstein by Cpl. Lewis W. Allen. Hereafter Allen questionnaire.

50. Reply to questionnaire from Goldstein by Sgt. Wesley Campbell. Hereafter Campbell questionnaire. Campbell was supply sergeant of Battery H.

51. Ibid.

52. Reply to questionnaire from Goldstein by Sgt. Gaines F. Parker. Hereafter Parker questionnaire.

53. Reply to questionnaire from Goldstein by S. Sgt. Leonard S. Brown. Hereafter Brown questionnaire.

54. Campbell questionnaire.

5: "Is this Alaska?"

1. Drake questionnaire.
2. Taylor questionnaire.
3. O'Neal questionnaire.
4. Reply to questionnaire from Goldstein by Sgt. Forrest N. Laubach. Hereafter Laubach questionnaire.
5. Reply to questionnaire from Goldstein by 1st Sgt. Haskell J. Cathey. Hereafter Cathey questionnaire.
6. Eheman questionnaire.
7. Lindley questionnaire.
8. Reply to questionnaire from Goldstein by Sgt. E. F. Paulus. Hereafter Paulus questionnaire.
9. Beverburg questionnaire.
10. Proffitt questionnaire.
11. Jones questionnaire.
12. B. Jones questionnaire.
13. Reply to questionnaire from Goldstein by Capt. Alvin L. Beverburg. Hereafter A. Beverburg questionnaire. He was a second lieutenant at the time.
14. Btry K history.
15. Henderson questionnaire.
16. Jones questionnaire.
17. Written by a Coast Artillery soldier stationed on top of Mt. Ballyhoo, Dutch Harbor, July 1941.
18. Cuttlefish VII, *People of the Aleutian Islands*, Unalaska, Alaska, 1986, pp. 1–4. Hereafter *People of the Aleutian Islands*; Cuttlefish VI, *The Unknown Islands: Life and Tales of Henry Swanson*, Unalaska, Alaska, 1982, pp. ix–x. Hereafter *Unknown Islands*. These books are projects of the Unalaska City School District.
19. See for example "The Aleutians: They are Barren Links between Two Worlds," *Life*, p. 71. Hereafter "Barren Links."
20. Herb Hilscher, *Alaska, U.S.A.*, Boston, 1959, pp. 6–7; Herbert H. Rasche, "Alaska Purchase Centennial 1867–1967" *Arctic*, p. 63.
21. *People of the Aleutians*, pp. 20–21.
22. *People of the Aleutians* relates many such incidents.
23. Ibid., pp. 26–31.
24. Herb Hilscher, *Alaska Now*, Boston, 1948, pp. 7–8.
25. *People of the Aleutians*, pp. 65–70.
26. *Alaska Now*, p. 8.
27. Joseph Driscoll, *War Discovers Alaska*, New York, 1943, pp. 16–17.
28. *Alaska Now*, pp. 9–10.

29. *People of the Aleutians*, p. 96

30. *Alaska, U.S.A.*, p. 13.

31. Ernest Gruening, ed., *An Alaskan Reader, 1867–1967*, New York, 1966, pp. 61–62.

32. *Alaska, U.S.A.*, p. 13.

33. Ernest Gruening, *The State of Alaska*, New York, 1954, pp. 107–12.

34. Ibid., pp. 129–33.

35. Donnel Drake, "Brief History of Dutch Harbor, Unalaska Island." Hereafter "Dutch Harbor." Drake prepared this study for Goldstein's use.

36. Charles Hendricks, "The Eskimos and the Defense of Alaska," *Pacific Historical Review*, 1986, p. 273. Hereafter "Eskimos and Defense."

37. "Dutch Harbor."

38. A. Randle Elliott, "U.S. Defense Outposts in the Pacific," *Foreign Policy Reports*, March 15, 1941, pp. 1–4. Hereafter "Defense Outposts."

39. Wesley F. Craven and James L. Cate, *The Army Air Force in World War II, Vol. IV, The Pacific: Guadalcanal to Saipan, August 1942 to July 1944*, Chicago, 1950, pp. 360–63. Hereafter *Guadalcanal to Saipan*.

6: "Officially Named Fort Mears"

1. D. Colt Denfield, *The Defense of Dutch Harbor, Alaska from Military Construction to Base Cleanup*, Anchorage, Alaska, 1987, pp. 33–34. Hereafter *Defense of Dutch Harbor*.

2. Ibid., pp. 32–34.

3. Ibid., p. 35.

4. Ibid., pp. 38–40.

5. Ballew questionnaire.

6. Sisk questionnaire.

7. Reply to questionnaire from Goldstein by Cpl. Virgil L. Clodi. Hereafter Clodi questionnaire.

8. Reply to questionnaire from Goldstein by S. Sgt. David B. Alspaugh. Hereafter Alspaugh questionnaire.

9. Reply to questionnaire from Goldstein by Sgt. James M. Massey. Hereafter Massey questionnaire.

10. A. Beverburg questionnaire.

11. *Defense of Dutch Harbor*, pp. 42–45.

12. Btry A history.

13. Alspaugh letters.

14. *Defense of Dutch Harbor*, p. 43.

15. Alspaugh letters.

16. Ibid.

17. Btry A history.

18. Weese questionnaire.

19. Quimby questionnaire.

20. Patrick and Radney questionnaires.

21. Abell questionnaire.

22. Alspaugh letters.

23. Ibid.

24. Reply to questionnaire from Goldstein by Sgt. William L. Young. Hereafter Young questionnaire; Clodi questionnaire.

25. Reply to questionnaire from Goldstein by Cpl. James D. Costley. Hereafter Costley questionnaire.

26. Reply to questionnaire from Goldstein by Maj. Henry A. Oehrig. Hereafter Oehrig questionnaire.

27. Reply to questionnaire from Goldstein by Capt. David M. Wall. Hereafter Wall questionnaire.

28. B. Jones questionnaire.

29. Weese questionnaire.

30. Davis questionnaire.

31. Henderson questionnaire.

7: "Early On in Our Story"

1. Alspaugh letters.

2. Wall questionnaire.

3. Garret questionnaire.

4. Reply to questionnaire from Goldstein by T. 4 Troy E. Burris. Hereafter Burris questionnaire.

5. Fitzhugh questionnaire.

6. Ballew questionnaire.

7. Reply to questionnaire from Goldstein by WO Ernest W. Pedersen. Hereafter Pedersen questionnaire.

8. Reply to questionnaire from Goldstein by Sgt. Oliver F. Raney. Hereafter Raney questionnaire.

9. Davis questionnaire.

10. Alspaugh letters.

11. Ibid.

12. Samuel E. Morison, *History of United States Naval Operations in World War II, Vol. IV, Coral Sea, Midway and Submarine Actions*, Boston, 1949, pp. 164–65. Hereafter *Coral Sea*.

13. *People of the Aleutian Islands*, pp. 305–06.
14. "Eskimos and Defense," p. 281.
15. *Guadalcanal to Saipan*, p. 363.
16. Alspaugh letters.
17. A. Beverburg questionnaire.
18. Fitzhugh questionnaire.
19. Massey questionnaire.
20. Sisk questionnaire.
21. Reply to questionnaire from Goldstein by Sgt. Russell R. Haden. Hereafter Haden questionnaire.
22. Sisk questionnaire.
23. Ibid.
24. Reply to questionnaire from Goldstein by Lt. Col. Voris O. Callaway. Hereafter Callaway questionnaire.
25. Fitzhugh questionnaire.
26. Reply to questionnaire from Goldstein by Col. Walton L. Hogan. Hereafter Hogan questionnaire.
27. Otis R. Holmes letter.
28. Haden questionnaire.
29. Drake questionnaire.
30. Buzzan questionnaire.
31. Kinney questionnaire.
32. Clodi questionnaire.
33. Drake questionnaire.
34. Costley questionnaire.
35. Paulus questionnaire.
36. Jones questionnaire. Among others who recalled that alcohol was available at the PX and on Unalaska were Bill Jones, Sisk, Cathey, and Sergeant Beverburg.
37. Reply to questionnaire from Goldstein by Sgt. Aubrey T. Albright. Hereafter Albright questionnaire.
38. Fitzhugh questionnaire.
39. Drake questionnaire.
40. Newton and Henderson questionnaires.
41. Davis questionnaire.
42. Reply to questionnaire from Goldstein by T. Sgt. Frank Leeder. Hereafter Leeder questionnaire.
43. Jones questionnaire.
44. Conway questionnaire.
45. Beverburg questionnaire.
46. Massey questionnaire.
47. Hargrave questionnaire.

48. Burris questionnaire.

49. Davis questionnaire.

50. Clodi questionnaire.

51. Weese questionnaire.

52. Reply to questionnaire from Goldstein by S. Sgt. Wayne D. Parker. Hereafter W. Parker questionnaire; Albright and Ballew questionnaires.

53. Cathey questionnaire.

54. Weese questionnaire.

55. Conway and Beasley questionnaires.

56. Ballew questionnaire.

57. Reply to questionnaire from Goldstein by T. 3 James O. Barron. Hereafter Barron questionnaire.

58. Fitzhugh questionnaire.

59. Alspaugh letters

60. Btry K history.

8: "Still Just a Big Adventure"

1. Reply to questionnaire from Goldstein by Pfc James E. Wilson. Hereafter Wilson questionnaire.

2. Taylor scrapbooks. The newspaper article did not give Cawthron's rank.

3. Brown questionnaire.

4. Wilson questionnaire.

5. Brown questionnaire.

6. Ibid.

7. Wilson questionnaire.

8. Brown questionnaire.

9. Wilson questionnaire.

10. Brown questionnaire.

11. Wilson questionnaire.

12. Brown questionnaire.

13. Wilson questionnaire.

14. Taylor scrapbooks.

15. G. Parker questionnaire.

16. Taylor scrapbooks.

17. Otis E. Hayes, Jr., "When War Came to Seward," *Alaska Journal,* Autumn 1983, pp. 107–08. Hereafter "War Came to Seward."

18. Taylor scrapbooks.

19. Ibid.

20. Reply to questionnaire from Goldstein by Pfc Walter C. Rybel. Hereafter Rybel questionnaire.
21. McKinistry questionnaire.
22. Weese questionnaire.
23. McKinistry questionnaire.
24. Burke statement.
25. Taylor scrapbooks.
26. Gill questionnaire.
27. Beverburg questionnaire.
28. O. Jones questionnaire.
29. O'Neal questionnaire.
30. Davis questionnaire.
31. Jones questionnaire.
32. Hargrave questionnaire.
33. Henderson questionnaire.
34. A. Beverburg questionnaire.
35. Jones questionnaire.
36. Reply to questionnaire from Goldstein by T. 4 Wiley H. Croom. Hereafter Croom questionnaire.
37. Garrett questionnaire.
38. Albright questionnaire.
39. Barron questionnaire.
40. Stout questionnaire.

9: "It Really Looks Serious Now"

1. *Hearings Before the Joint Committee on the Investigation of the Pearl Harbor Attack, Seventy-ninth Congress,* Washington, D.C., 1946, Part 14, p. 1329. Hereafter *PHA.*
2. Ibid., p. 1407.
3. Ibid., pp. 1330–31.
4. "War Came to Seward," p. 110.
5. Gordon W. Prange, *At Dawn We Slept,* New York, 1981, pp. 430–31. Hereafter *At Dawn We Slept.*
6. Dodson questionnaire.
7. Alspaugh letters.
8. A. Parker letter.
9. Fitzhugh, A. Beverburg, and Alspaugh questionnaires.
10. Stout questionnaire.
11. Paulus questionnaire.

12. Weese questionnaire.

13. Hargrave questionnaire.

14. Radney questionnaire.

15. McKinistry questionnaire.

16. Paulus questionnaire.

17. Davis questionnaire.

18. Weese questionnaire.

19. Hargrave questionnaire.

20. Reply to questionnaire from Goldstein by T. 5 Everette C. Carnes. Hereafter Carnes questionnaire.

21. Haden questionnaire.

22. Costley questionnaire.

23. Stout questionnaire.

24. Sisk questionnaire.

25. Jones questionnaire.

26. Garrett questionnaire.

27. O'Neal questionnaire.

28. Alspaugh questionnaire.

29. Beverburg questionnaire.

30. Reply to questionnaire from Goldstein by Capt. James A. Langley. Hereafter Langley questionnaire.

31. Jones questionnaire.

32. Dodson questionnaire.

33. Alspaugh questionnaire.

34. Haden questionnaire.

35. Proffitt questionnaire.

36. Reply to questionnaire from 1st Sgt. John A. Thomason, Jr. Hereafter Thomason questionnaire.

37. Beverburg questionnaire. O'Neal and Captain Wall expressed similar opinions.

38. Stout questionnaire.

39. Costley questionnaire.

40. Burris questionnaire.

41. Weese questionnaire.

42. Wesley F. Craven and James L. Cate, *The Army Air Forces in World War II, Vol. I, Plans and Early Operations*, Chicago, 1948, pp. 166–67. Hereafter *Plans and Early Operations*.

43. Ibid., pp. 169–70.

44. Ibid., pp. 167–68.

45. Fletcher Pratt, "Campaign Beyond Glory," *Harper's Magazine*, November 1944, p. 559. Hereafter "Campaign Beyond Glory."

46. Taylor scrapbooks.

10: "This Is It!"

1. Btry A history.
2. Ibid.
3. Reply to questionnaire from Goldstein by Cpl. Robert L. Walkup, Sr. Hereafter Walkup questionnaire.
4. Sisk questionnaire.
5. Alspaugh questionnaire.
6. Alspaugh letters.
7. Tate questionnaire.
8. Taylor questionnaire.
9. Cuttlefish V. *The Aleutian Invasion: World War II in the Aleutians,* Unalaska, Alaska, 1981, pp. 32–33. Hereafter *Aleutian Invasion.*
10. Laubach questionnaire.
11. Weese questionnaire.
12. Fitzhugh questionnaire.
13. Jones questionnaire.
14. Reply to questionnaire from Goldstein by Pfc Devoe H. Cowell. Hereafter Cowell questionnaire.
15. Massey notes.
16. Btry K history.
17. Callaway questionnaire.
18. Henderson questionnaire.
19. Beverburg questionnaire.
20. Gill questionnaire.
21. Conway questionnaire.
22. O'Neal questionnaire.
23. Reply to questionnaire from Goldstein by S. Sgt. Clifford C. Caldwell. Hereafter Caldwell questionnaire.
24. *Arkansas Gazette,* 4 August 1980.
25. Wall questionnaire.
26. Walkup questionnaire.
27. Garrett questionnaire.
28. Reply to questionnaire from Goldstein by Sgt. Cleo J. Eason. Hereafter Eason questionnaire.
29. Taylor questionnaire.
30. Reply to questionnaire from Goldstein by T. Sgt. Alfred F. Nichols. Hereafter Nichols questionnaire.
31. "War Came to Seward," p. 108, 111.
32. For an in–depth analysis, see Gordon W. Prange, *Pearl Harbor: The Verdict of History,* New York, 1986.
33. Campbell questionnaire.

34. Wilson questionnaire.

35. Corey Ford and Alastair MacBain, "Sourdough Army," *Colliers,* 25 April 1942, pp. 13, 54.

36. Haden questionnaire.

37. Reply to questionnaire from Goldstein by Sgt. James H. Ryals. Hereafter Ryals questionnaire.

38. Costley questionnaire.

39. Patrick questionnaire.

40. Reply to questionnaire from Goldstein by Maj. Pat M. Kee. Hereafter Kee questionnaire.

41. Reply to questionnaire from Goldstein by Sgt. James M. Simmons. Hereafter Simmons questionnaire.

42. Burris questionnaire.

43. Kinney questionnaire.

44. Keeton questionnaire.

45. Meek questionnaire.

46. Campbell questionnaire.

47. "War Came to Seward," p. 111.

48. Claus-M. Naske, "The Relocation of Alaska's Japanese Residents," *Pacific Northwest Quarterly,* July 1983, pp. 125–26. Hereafter "Relocation of Japanese."

49. "War Came to Seward," pp. 111–12.

11: "Under Trying Conditions"

1. Btry A history.
2. Sisk questionnaire.
3. Croom questionnaire.
4. A. Beverburg questionnaire.
5. Dodson questionnaire.
6. Weese questionnaire.
7. O'Neal questionnaire.
8. Massey questionnaire.
9. Raney questionnaire.
10. Jones questionnaire.
11. Rybel questionnaire.
12. Stout questionnaire.
13. Costley questionnaire.
14. Gill questionnaire.
15. Ryals questionnaire.

16. Kinney questionnaire.
17. Brown questionnaire.
18. "Campaign Beyond Glory," pp. 558–59.
19. Btry A history.
20. Fitzhugh questionnaire.
21. Btry K history.
22. Weese questionnaire.
23. O. Jones questionnaire.
24. Cathey questionnaire.
25. Reply to questionnaire from Goldstein by Cpl. Bernard W. Anderson. Hereafter Anderson questionnaire.
26. Haden questionnaire.
27. Btry A history.
28. Leeder questionnaire.
29. Reply to questionnaire from Goldstein by S. Sgt. George M. Cathey. Hereafter G. Cathey questionnaire.
30. Proffitt questionnaire.
31. Taylor questionnaire.
32. Weese questionnaire.
33. Garrett questionnaire.
34. Hargrave questionnaire.
35. B. Jones and Henderson questionnaires.
36. Gill questionnaire.
37. O'Neal questionnaire.
38. Proffitt questionnaire.
39. Reply to questionnaire from Goldstein by S. Sgt. Doss D. Dale. Hereafter Dale questionnaire.
40. Weese questionnaire.
41. Stout questionnaire.
42. Jones questionnaire.
43. B. Jones questionnaire.
44. Taylor scrapbooks.
45. Ibid.
46. Ibid.
47. Alspaugh letters.
48. Btry K history.
49. Burris questionnaire.
50. Keeton and Leeder questionnaires.
51. Caldwell questionnaire.
52. Tate questionnaire.
53. Haden questionnaire.

54. Reply to questionnaire from Goldstein by Cpl. James M. Kimberlin. Hereafter Kimberlin questionnaire.

55. Langley questionnaire.

56. Keeton questionnaire.

57. Beasley questionnaire.

58. Langley questionnaire.

59. Tate and Beasley questionnaires.

60. Keeton questionnaire.

61. Haden and Croom questionnaires.

62. Reply to questionnaire from Goldstein by Woodrow C. Trimble. Hereafter Trimble questionnaire.

63. Keeton questionnaire.

64. Tate questionnaire.

65. Kinney questionnaire.

66. Keeton questionnaire.

67. Langley questionnaire.

68. Caldwell questionnaire.

69. Kinney questionnaire.

70. Burris questionnaire.

71. Walkup questionnaire.

72. Trimble questionnaire.

12: "Snafu!"

1. Alspaugh letters.

2. Ballew questionnaire.

3. Quimby questionnaire.

4. Taylor scrapbooks.

5. Alspaugh letters.

6. Clodi questionnaire; *Defense of Dutch Harbor*, p. 114.

7. Burris questionnaire.

8. Pedersen questionnaire.

9. Diary of S. Sgt. David B. Alspaugh. Hereafter Alspaugh diary; Alspaugh letters.

10. Alspaugh diary.

11. *Plans and Early Operations*, pp. 304–06.

12. Diary of Lt. Robert H. Miller. Hereafter Miller diary.

13. Diary of Cpl. Willie Stubbs. Hereafter Stubbs diary.

14. Miller diary.

15. Stubbs diary.
16. Miller diary.
17. Stubbs and Miller diaries.
18. Miller diary.
19. Ibid.
20. Stubbs diary.
21. Miller diary.
22. Ibid.
23. Stubbs diary.
24. Diary of John Bowen. Hereafter Bowen diary.
25. Miller diary.
26. Ibid.
27. Proffitt questionnaire.
28. Bowen diary.

13: "This Country Gets You"

1. Bowen diary.
2. Alspaugh diary.
3. Bowen diary.
4. Caldwell questionnaire.
5. Wall and Fitzhugh questionnaire.
6. Ballew questionnaire.
7. Oehrig questionnaire.
8. McKinistry questionnaire.
9. Anderson questionnaire.
10. Sisk questionnaire.
11. Weese questionnaire.
12. Alspaugh questionnaire.
13. Cowell questionnaire.
14. Reply to questionnaire from Goldstein by T. Cpl. Tony Junevitch. Hereafter Junevitch questionnaire.
15. Eheman questionnaire.
16. Reply to questionnaire from Goldstein by Sgt Leo L. New. Hereafter New questionnaire.
17. Reply to questionnaire from Goldstein by Sgt. Jean D. Thatcher. Hereafter Thatcher questionnaire.
18. Keeton questionnaire.
19. Costley questionnaire.

20. Ryals questionnaire.

21. Sisk questionnaire.

22. McKinistry questionnaire.

23. *The Aleutian*, 8 July 1943.

24. Bowen diary.

25. Brown questionnaire.

26. Wilson questionnaire.

27. G. Parker questionnaire.

28. Brown questionnaire.

29. Alspaugh diary.

30. Bowen diary.

31. Wilson letter.

32. Wilson questionnaire.

33. Alspaugh diary.

34. Bowen diary.

35. Brown questionnaire.

36. Bowen diary.

37. O'Neal questionnaire.

38. Alspaugh diary.

39. Sisk questionnaire.

40. Reply to questionnaire from Goldstein by Cpl. Frederick H. Raymond. Hereafter Raymond questionnaire.

41. Thomason questionnaire.

42. Kinney questionnaire.

43. H. Beverburg questionnaire.

44. Langley questionnaire.

45. *Unknown Islands*, p. 60.

46. Alspaugh diary and questionnaire.

47. Bowen diary.

48. Miller diary.

49. Stubbs diary.

50. Miller diary.

51. Stubbs diary.

52. Miller diary.

53. Stubbs diary.

54. Miller diary.

55. Proffitt questionnaire.

14: "We Plowed On"

1. Reply to questionnaire from Goldstein by Pvt. Edgar L. Nixon. Hereafter Nixon questionnaire.
2. Massey notes.
3. Ryals questionnaire.
4. Thomason questionnaire.
5. Ryals questionnaire.
6. Massey notes.
7. Bowen diary.
8. Alspaugh diary.
9. Massey notes.
10. Ibid.
11. Bowen diary.
12. Alspaugh diary.
13. Kee questionnaire.
14. McKinistry questionnaire.
15. Costley questionnaire.
16. Garrett questionnaire.
17. Fitzhugh questionnaire.
18. McKinistry questionnaire.
19. Wall, New, Clodi, and Radney questionnaires.
20. See for example Raney, Ryals, New, etc., questionnaires.
21. Wall questionnaire.
22. Reply to questionnaire from Goldstein by Pvt. Martin D. Cibich. Hereafter Cibich questionnaire. See also O. Jones and Rybel questionnaires.
23. Reply to questionnaire from Goldstein by Sgt. Charles D. Robertson. Hereafter Robertson questionnaire.
24. Alspaugh diary.
25. Samuel E. Morison, *History of the United States Navy in World War II, Vol. I, The Rising Sun in the Pacific*, Boston, 1950, pp. 342–75. Hereafter *Rising Sun in the Pacific*.
26. Alspaugh and Bowen diaries; Burris questionnaire.
27. Bowen diary.
28. Alspaugh diary.
29. Bowen diary.
30. Langley questionnaire.
31. Pedersen questionnaire.
32. Caldwell questionnaire.
33. Ballew questionnaire.
34. Jones questionnaire.
35. Keeton questionnaire.

36. *People of the Aleutian Islands*, pp. 227–28.
37. Miller and Stubbs diaries.
38. Miller diary.
39. Stubbs diary.
40. Miller diary.
41. Stubbs diary.
42. Ibid.
43. Miller diary.
44. Stubbs diary.
45. Ibid.
46. Miller diary.
47. Stubbs diary.
48. Miller diary.
49. *Coral Sea*, p. 164; Gordon W. Prange, *Miracle at Midway*, New York, 1982, p. 156. Hereafter *Miracle at Midway*.

15: "A Dangerous Game"

1. Alspaugh diary.
2. Bowen diary.
3. Alspaugh diary.
4. Keeton questionnaire.
5. Bowen diary.
6. Alspaugh diary.
7. Bowen diary.
8. Massey notes.
9. Stubbs diary.
10. Miller diary.
11. Ibid.
12. Stubbs and Miller diaries.
13. Alspaugh diary.
14. Bowen diary.
15. Btry A history.
16. Drake material.
17. Ibid.
18. Ibid.
19. Btry A history
20. Drake questionnaire.
21. "Relocation of Japanese," pp. 126–32.
22. Alspaugh diary.

23. Stubbs diary.
24. Miller diary.
25. Miller and Stubbs diaries.
26. Stubbs diary.
27. Reply to questionnaire from Goldstein by Sgt. Frank Snellgrove. Hereafter Snellgrove questionnaire.
28. Kee questionnaire.
29. Alspaugh diary.
30. Pack questionnaire.
31. Laubach questionnaire.
32. H. Beverburg questionnaire.
33. Caldwell questionnaire.
34. Abell questionnaire.
35. Alspaugh diary.
36. Massey notes.
37. Bowen diary.
38. Alspaugh diary.

16: "Tomorrow May Bring Untold Things"

1. Bowen diary.
2. Massey notes.
3. Alspaugh diary.
4. Bowen diary.
5. Massey notes.
6. Bowen diary.
7. Stubbs diary.
8. Alspaugh diary.
9. Stubbs diary.
10. Miller diary.
11. Stubbs diary.
12. Lt. Robert H. Miller, "The Aleutian Island Campaign, Co. E & F, 153d Inf., Mortar Plat Co. H." Hereafter "Aleutian Island Campaign."
13. Miller diary.
14. Alspaugh diary.
15. *Miracle at Midway*, pp. 40–45. For a detailed account of this battle, see *Coral Sea*, pp. 21–64.
16. *Defense of Dutch Harbor*, pp. 60–62.
17. *Unknown Islands*, p. 161.
18. Ibid., pp. 166–67.

19. Miller and Stubbs diaries.

20. "Aleutian Island Campaign."

21. Alspaugh and Bowen diaries.

22. Bowen diary.

23. Miller diary.

24. Miller and Alspaugh diaries.

25. Alspaugh and Bowen diaries.

26. *Coral Sea*, pp. 173–74; *Miracle at Midway*, p. 155.

27. Alspaugh diary.

28. Miller diary.

29. *Coral Sea*, pp. 172–73; *Miracle at Midway*, pp. 108–09.

30. Bowen diary.

17: "It's the Damn Japs!"

1. Miller diary.

2. Stubbs diary.

3. *Arkansas Gazette*, 4 August 1980.

4. Bowen diary.

5. *The Aleutian Invasion*, p. 39.

6. Unpublished article by Dennis Pike Abell, "The Japanese Air Attacks, Dutch Harbor, Aleutian Islands, Alaska, June 3 and 4, 1942." Hereafter "Japanese Air Attack."

7. Miller scrapbooks. This was from one of a number of articles date-lined Seattle, 25 June, presumably 1942.

8. Massey notes.

9. Btry A history; Albright questionnaire.

10. Miller scrapbooks.

11. Ibid.

12. *Coral Sea*, pp. 167–72; *Miracle at Midway*, pp. 156–58.

13. William Clemmens, "Report on the Aleutians," *Reader's Digest*, March 1943, p. 96.

14. *Miracle at Midway*, p. 157; *Coral Sea*, pp. 168–70.

15. *Defense of Dutch Harbor*, p. 73.

16. List of flash messages received at Btry B. Courtesy of Dolph B. Kulbeth. Hereafter "Flash messages."

17. B. Jones questionnaire.

18. Cowell questionnaire.

19. Miller scrapbooks.

20. *Coral Sea*, pp. 175–76; *Miracle at Midway*, pp. 151–52.

21. *Defense of Dutch Harbor*, pp. 73–74; *Coral Sea*, pp. 175–76.
22. *Defense of Dutch Harbor*, p. 76; *Coral Sea*, p. 176.
23. Miller scrapbooks.
24. "Campaign Beyond Glory," p. 561; *Defense of Dutch Harbor*, p. 77.
25. *The Aleutian Invasion*, p. 39.
26. Sisk questionnaire.
27. Davis questionnaire.
28. Fitzhugh questionnaire.
29. Jonesboro (Arkansas) *Sun*, 27 May 1987.
30. Ryals questionnaire.
31. Taylor questionnaire.
32. Junevitch questionnaire.
33. Reply to questionnaire from Goldstein by S. Sgt. Wyre T. Mitchell. Hereafter Mitchell questionnaire.
34. Pack questionnaire.
35. B. Jones questionnaire.
36. Pedersen questionnaire.
37. Henderson questionnaire.
38. Snellgrove questionnaire.

18: "Friendly Planes, Hell!"

1. Massey notes; Massey questionnaire.
2. Cathey questionnaire.
3. Bowen diary.
4. Garrett questionnaire.
5. Langley questionnaire.
6. Croom questionnaire.
7. Miller scrapbooks.
8. Keeton questionnaire.
9. Burris questionnaire.
10. Snellgrove questionnaire.
11. Cathey questionnaire.
12. Parker letters.
13. Flash messages.
14. Fitzhugh questionnaire.
15. *Aleutian Invasion*, p. 34.
16. *Defense of Dutch Harbor*, pp. 90–91.
17. Gill questionnaire.
18. *Defense of Dutch Harbor*, pp. 76–78.

19. Massey notes.
20. Bowen diary.
21. Miller scrapbooks.
22. *Aleutian Invasion*, p. 30.
23. Ibid., p. 29.
24. Massey notes; Massey questionnaire.
25. Henderson questionnaire.
26. *Arkansas Gazette*, 4 August 1980.
27. Massey notes.
28. Btry A history.
29. "Japanese Air Attack"
30. Jonesboro (Arkansas) *Sun*, 27 May 1987.
31. Btry A history.
32. Hargrave questionnaire.
33. Parker letter.
34. Alspaugh diary.
35. Massey notes.
36. Nixon questionnaire.

19: "The Waiting Is Torment"

1. *Defense of Dutch Harbor*, p. 78.
2. Ibid., p. 90.
3. Ibid.; *Coral Sea*, p. 176.
4. *Coral Sea*, p. 176; *Defense of Dutch Harbor*, p. 91.
5. *The Aleutian Invasion*, pp. 43–44.
6. *Defense of Dutch Harbor*, p. 91; *Coral Sea*, p. 176; *Plans and Early Operations*, pp. 466–67.
7. Miller diary.
8. "Aleutian Island Campaign."
9. Miller scrapbooks.
10. "Japanese Air Attack."
11. Btry A history.
12. A. Parker letter.
13. Massey notes.
14. *The Aleutian Invasion*, p. 35.
15. Sisk questionnaire.
16. Davis questionnaire.
17. Keeton questionnaire.
18. G. Cathey, Weese, and Kinney questionnaires.

19. Keeton questionnaire.
20. Burris questionnaire.
21. Croom questionnaire.
22. G. Cathey questionnaire.
23. Fitzhugh questionnaire.
24. Taylor scrapbooks; Jonesboro (Arkansas) *Sun*, 27 May 1987.
25. "Japanese Air Attack."
26. Taylor scrapbooks.
27. Weese and Radney questionnaires; Alspaugh diary.
28. Massey notes.
29. Taylor scrapbooks.
30. Clodi questionnaire.
31. Taylor scrapbooks.
32. "Japanese Air Attack."
33. *Defense of Dutch Harbor*, pp. 74–75.
34. Flash messages.
35. Taylor questionnaire.

20: "Like a Big Bunch of Mosquitos"

1. Flash messages.
2. Pedersen questionnaire.
3. Costley questionnaire.
4. Callaway questionnaire.
5. *Coral Sea*, p. 117.
6. *Plans and Early Operations*, p. 468; *Defense of Dutch Harbor*, pp. 91–92.
7. *Defense of Dutch Harbor*, p. 92.
8. A. Parker letter.
9. *Defense of Dutch Harbor*, p. 92.
10. *Plans and Early Operations*, p. 468; *Defense of Dutch Harbor*, pp. 92–93.
11. Flash messages.
12. Jonesboro (Arkansas) *Sun*, 27 May 1987.
13. Flash messages.
14. *Plans and Early Operations*, p. 467; *Coral Sea*, p. 177.
15. Flash messages.
16. Btry A history.
17. See for example Simmons, Patrick, Clodi, and Fitzhugh questionnaires.
18. "Japanese Air Attack."
19. A. Parker letter.

20. Btry A history.
21. *The Aleutian Invasion*, pp. 35–36.
22. Cowell questionnaire; Flash messages.
23. Davis questionnaire.
24. Henderson questionnaire.
25. Bowen diary.
26. Alspaugh diary.
27. Burris questionnaire.
28. Raney questionnaire.
29. Massey notes.
30. *Plans and Early Operations*, pp. 469, 721.

21: "They Sure Did Some Damage"

1. *The Aleutian Invasion*, pp. 30–31.
2. "Japanese Air Attack."
3. *Defense of Dutch Harbor*, p. 94.
4. Btry A history.
5. *Defense of Dutch Harbor*, p.94.
6. Proffitt questionnaire.
7. *Defense of Dutch Harbor*, pp. 94–95.
8. Ibid., p. 95; Proffitt questionnaire.
9. *Seattle Post-Intelligencer*, 18 July 1942, quoted in *The Aleutian Invasion*, pp. 27–28.
10. "Japanese Air Attack."
11. Massey notes.
12. Alspaugh diary.
13. Bowen diary.
14. *Defense of Dutch Harbor*, p. 95.
15. Robertson questionnaire; 206th GO #10, 8 July 1942.
16. *Defense of Dutch Harbor*, p. 95.
17. Massey notes.
18. Coral Sea, p. 178; *Defense of Dutch Harbor*, p. 96.
19. Stubbs diary.
20. "Aleutian Island Campaign."
21. Miller diary.
22. "Aleutian Island Campaign."
23. Ibid.; Miller diary.
24. *Defense of Dutch Harbor*; Miller diary.
25. *Plans and Early Operations*, pp. 468–69; *Defense of Dutch Harbor*, p. 93.

26. Ibid.; Miller diary.
27. *Coral Sea*, pp. 178–79; *Miracle at Midway*, pp. 296–97, 299.

22: "We Calmed Down Some"

1. Burris questionnaire.
2. Harp questionnaire.
3. Pedersen questionnaire.
4. McKinistry questionnaire.
5. Massey notes.
6. Btry A history.
7. Keeton questionnaire.
8. Proffitt questionnaire.
9. Reply to questionnaire from Goldstein by S. Sgt. Wayne D. Parker. Hereafter W. Parker questionnaire.
10. Cathey questionnaire.
11. Reply to questionnaire from Goldstein by M. Sgt. Clarence P. Williamson. Hereafter Williamson questionnaire.
12. Faulhaber questionnaire.
13. Albright questionnaire.
14. Burris questionnaire.
15. Ryals questionnaire.
16. Flash messages.
17. Henderson questionnaire.
18. Flash messages.
19. Hargrave questionnaire.
20. Quimby questionnaire.
21. Henderson questionnaire.
22. Eheman questionnaire.
23. Jonesboro (Arkansas) *Sun*, 27 May 1987.
24. Ryals questionnaire.
25. Albright questionnaire.
26. Raney questionnaire.
27. Oehrig questionnaire.
28. Proffitt questionnaire.
29. Cathey questionnaire.
30. Barron questionnaire.
31. Henderson questionnaire.
32. *Defense of Dutch Harbor*, p. 96.
33. Alspaugh diary.

34. *Defense of Dutch Harbor*, p. 96.

35. Burris questionnaire.

36. *Defense of Dutch Harbor*, pp. 96–97, 95.

37. *Plans and Early Operations*, p. 469.

38. For a full account, see *Miracle at Midway*.

39. *Defense of Dutch Harbor*, p. 97.

40. Jim Reardon, "The Akutan Zero," Part I, *Alaska Magazine*, September 1987, pp. 1–7.

41. Ibid., p. 6; Masatake Okumiya and Jiro Horikoshi, with Martin Caidin, *Zero!*, New York, 1956, pp. 115–16.

42. "The Akutan Zero," p. 7.

43. Raney questionnaire.

44. Pack questionnaire.

45. Beverburg questionnaire.

46. "The Akutan Zero," pp. 3–4; *Miracle at Midway*, p. 154; *Zero!*, pp. 115–16; Joe Mizraki, "Samurai," *Wings*, December 1977, pp. 26–28.

47. "The Akutan Zero," Part II, *Alaska Magazine*, October 1987, pp. 8–12; *Zero!*, pp. 116–17.

48. Burris questionnaire.

49. Alspaugh questionnaire.

50. Sisk questionnaire.

23: "The Japs Are Here!"

1. *Coral Sea*, p. 182.

2. Brian Garfield, *The Thousand-Mile War: World War II in Alaska and the Aleutians*, New York, 1969, p. 43. Hereafter *1000-Mile War*; Kit C. Carter and Robert Mueller, comp., *The Army Air Forces in World War II: Combat Chronology*, Washington, 1975, p. 190. Hereafter *Combat Chronology*.

3. *1000-Mile War*, p. 82; Bowen diary; *Unknown Islands*, p. 165.

4. *Coral Sea*, pp. 168, 172.

5. Ibid., p. 168; *1000-Mile War*, p. 80.

6. *Coral Sea*, pp. 168, 172–73.

7. Ibid., p. 168; *1000-Mile War*, p. 76.

8. The United States Strategic Bombing Survey, Naval Analysis Division, *The Campaigns of the Pacific War*, Washington, D.C., 1946, p. 80. Hereafter *Campaigns*; *1000-Mile War*, pp. 76, 79.

9. Jim Reardon, "Kiska: One Island's Moment in History," *Alaska Magazine*, January 1986, p. 18. Hereafter "Kiska." *1000-Mile War*, p. 80.

10. *Aleutian Invasion*, p. 59; *1000-Mile War*, p. 80.

11. *Aleutian Invasion*, p. 60; *1000-Mile War*, p. 80.

12. "Kiska," pp. 20–21, 49; *1000-Mile War*, pp. 80–81.

13. *Aleutian Invasion*, p. 47; *1000-Mile War*, p. 79.

14. *Coral Sea*, pp. 180–81.

15. *Aleutian Invasion*, p. 46.

16. Ibid., pp. 46, 48.

17. Ibid., p. 48; *1000-Mile War*, pp. 81, 310.

18. Corey Ford, "They Came to Attu," *Colliers*, 8 August 1942, p. 42. Hereafter "They Came to Attu." *People of the Aleutian Islands*, pp. 286–88. Ford spells Hodikoff's name Hudakof.

19. "They Came to Attu," pp. 42–43.

20. Ibid., p. 43.

21. *Aleutian Invasion*, pp. 46–49; *People of the Aleutian Islands*, p. 288.

22. *1000-Mile War*, p. 81; *Coral Sea*, pp. 181–82.

24: "Settled on Hog Island"

1. Bowen diary.

2. Massey notes.

3. *Combat Chronology*, pp. 20–23.

4. *1000-Mile War*, pp. 89–92.

5. Btry A history.

6. Ibid.

7. Ibid.

8. Ibid.

9. Ibid.

10. Bowen diary.

11. Alspaugh diary.

12. Bowen diary.

13. Alspaugh diary.

14. Bowen diary.

15. Alspaugh diary.

16. Bowen diary. After this entry, Bowen mislaid his diary and did not find it for two months. He covered the intervening period with a narrative.

17. Alspaugh diary.

18. Bowen diary.

19. Croom questionnaire.

20. Jones questionnaire.

21. Weese questionnaire.

22. Sisk questionnaire.

23. Weese questionnaire.

24. Bowen diary.

25. Alspaugh letters.

26. Weese questionnaire.

27. Ibid.

28. Bowen diary.

29. Ibid.

30. *Coral Sea*, p. 215.

31. *Defense of Dutch Harbor*, p. 121.

32. Haden questionnaire.

33. Wall questionnaire.

34. *Defense of Dutch Harbor*, p. 121.

35. *Coral Sea*, pp. 214–19.

25: "Unfit for Pigs"

1. John C. Kirtland and David F. Coffin, Jr., *The Relocation of and Internment of the Aleuts During World War II*, Vol. II, Anchorage, 1981, pp. 323–24. Hereafter *Relocation and Internment*.

2. Ibid., pp. 324–25; *Defense of Dutch Harbor*, pp. 114–15.

3. *Relocation and Internment*, pp. 325–27; *Defense of Dutch Harbor*, pp. 114–15.

4. *Defense of Dutch Harbor*, p. 119.

5. *Relocation and Internment*, pp. 328–29; *Aleutian Invasion*, p. 101.

6. *Relocation and Internment*, pp. 329–30.

7. *Aleutian Invasion*, p. 109.

8. *Relocation and Internment*, pp. 330–31.

9. Ibid., pp. 331–32.

10. Ibid., pp. 332–33.

11. *People of the Aleutian Islands*, pp. 274–80.

12. *Aleutian Invasion*, p. 103; *Defense of Dutch Harbor*, p. 116; *Relocation and Internment*, pp. 333–34.

13. *Aleutian Invasion*, pp. 103–04; *Relocation and Internment*, pp. 335–36.

14. *Aleutian Invasion*, pp. 100, 104–05; *People of the Aleutian Islands*, p. 309.

15. *Aleutian Invasion*, p. 107.

16. *Pribilof Progress-Pribilof Pace* (Aleutian-Pribilof Island Association), quoted in *Aleutian Invasion*, p. 109.

17. *Aleutian Invasion*, p. 109.

18. *People of the Aleutian Islands*, pp. 309–10.

19. *Aleutian Invasion*, p. 107.

20. *Relocation and Internment*, pp. 338–41.
21. Ibid., pp. 343–45.
22. Ibid., pp. 345–46.
23. Ibid., pp. 347–50.
24. Ibid., pp. 350–51; *Aleutian Invasion*, p. 107.
25. *Aleutian Invasion*, pp. 107–08.
26. *People of the Aleutian Islands*, pp. 309–11.
27. *Relocation and Internment*, pp. 351–52.
28. *Defense of Dutch Harbor*, p. 117.
29. *Aleutian Invasion*, pp. 110–11.
30. Ibid., pp. 106–07.
31. *Relocation and Internment*, pp. 353–55.
32. *People of the Aleutian Islands*, p. 312.
33. *Defense of Dutch Harbor*, pp. 117–18.
34. Article by Sgt. Ray Duncan in the 18 May 1945 issue of *Yank*, quoted in *Aleutian Invasion*, pp. 112–13.
35. *Relocation and Internment*, pp. 356–57.
36. Ibid., pp. 358–59.

26: "But Duty Is Duty"

1. *Combat Chronology*, pp. 24–36.
2. *1000-Mile War*, pp. 98–100, 113; *Combat Chronology*, p. 24.
3. Samuel Eliot Morison, *History of United States Naval Operations in World War II, Vol. VII, Aleutians, Gilberts and Marshalls*, Boston, 1951, pp. 9–10. Hereafter *Aleutians, Gilberts and Marshalls; 1000-Mile War*, pp. 119–20.
4. *Aleutians, Gilberts and Marshalls*, pp. 8–12; *1000-Mile War*, pp. 120–21.
5. *Arkansas Democrat*, 22 and 24 July 1942.
6. *1000-Mile War*, p. 101.
7. Miller diary.
8. *1000-Mile War*, pp. 101–02, 122–23; *Defense of Dutch Harbor*, pp. 120–21.
9. Btry K history; Bowen diary.
10. Alspaugh diary; Bowen diary.
11. Alspaugh diary.
12. Btry A history.
13. Jones questionnaire.
14. Weese questionnaire.

15. Pack questionnaire.

16. Alspaugh diary.

17. See for example questionnaires of W. Parker, Albright, and Tate.

18. Drake questionnaire.

19. Campbell questionnaire.

20. Wilson letter.

21. *Relocation and Internment*, Vol. I, pp. 263–69.

22. G. Parker questionnaire.

23. Reply to questionnaire from Goldstein by Col. James F. Brewer. Hereafter Brewer questionnaire.

24. Meek questionnaire.

25. Wilson questionnaire.

27: "A Little Lift"

1. "Aleutian Island Campaign," p. 13.

2. Stubbs diary.

3. Miller diary.

4. Ibid.

5. Ibid.

6. Several veterans, including Paulus, O'Neal, and Albright, remembered the lottery.

7. Paulus questionnaire.

8. O'Neal questionnaire.

9. Albright questionnaire.

10. Alspaugh diary.

11. A. and H. Beverburg questionnaires.

12. Anderson questionnaire.

13. *1000-Mile War*, pp. 131–32; *Guadalcanal to Saipan*, p. 369.

14. *1000-Mile War*, pp. 132–33; *Guadalcanal to Saipan*, p. 369.

15. *1000-Mile War*, pp. 133–34; *Guadalcanal to Saipan*, p. 369–70.

16. *1000-Mile War*, pp. 135–36; *Aleutians, Gilberts and Marshalls*, p. 13.

17. Alspaugh diary.

18. Massey notes.

19. Bowen diary.

20. *1000-Mile War*, pp. 137–38; *People of the Aleutian Islands*, p. 306; *Aleutians, Gilberts and Marshalls*, p. 13.

21. *The Unknown Islands*, pp. 180–84.

22. *Aleutians, Gilberts and Marshalls*, p. 13; *1000-Mile War*, pp. 146–48; *Combat Chronology*, p. 35.

23. Massey notes.
24. Bowen diary.
25. Alspaugh diary.
26. Ibid. Alspaugh recorded this earthquake on the eighth, Bowen on the seventh.
27. Bowen diary.
28. Bowen and Alspaugh diaries.
29. Alspaugh diary.
30. Bowen diary.

28: "The Worst Storm of the Tour"

1. Miller diary.
2. *Combat Chronology*, p. 41.
3. Miller diary.
4. *Guadalcanal to Saipan*, pp. 372–73.
5. *Combat Chronology*, pp. 30–37.
6. Miller diary.
7. Stubbs diary.
8. Alspaugh diary.
9. Miller diary.
10. Stubbs diary.
11. Alspaugh diary.
12. Bowen diary.
13. Weese questionnaire.
14. Alspaugh diary.
15. Weese questionnaire.
16. Massey letter enclosed with his questionnaire.
17. Jones questionnaire.
18. Luster Tate, "History of 206th CA 'AA'."
19. *1000-Mile War*, p. 147–49.
20. Ibid., pp. 148–49; *Aleutians, Gilberts and Marshalls*, p. 14.
21. Massey notes.
22. Paulus questionnaire.
23. Alspaugh diary.
24. Alspaugh questionnaire.
25. Gill and Jones questionnaires.
26. Alspaugh diary.
27. Stubbs diary.

28. Miller diary.
29. *1000-Mile War*, p. 149.
30. *Aleutians, Gilberts and Marshalls*, pp. 15–16.
31. Nixon questionnaire.

29: "A White Christmas"

1. *1000-Mile War*, pp. 153–54; *Combat Command*, p. 67.
2. *1000-Mile War*, p. 154; *Aleutians, Gilberts and Marshalls*, p. 17.
3. Kee questionnaire.
4. Clark questionnaire.
5. Garrett questionnaire.
6. Weese questionnaire.
7. Oehrig questionnaire.
8. H. Beverburg questionnaire.
9. Weese questionnaire.
10. A number of veterans, including Quimby, Weese, and Hargrave, mentioned these shortages.
11. *1000-Mile War*, pp. 149–50.
12. Ibid., p. 150; *Guadalcanal to Saipan*, p. 374; *Aleutians, Gilberts and Marshalls*, p. 17.
13. Stubbs diary.
14. Miller diary.
15. Massey notes.
16. Reply to questionnaire from Goldstein by Capt. Hugh Moseley, Jr. Hereafter Moseley questionnaire.
17. Taylor questionnaire.
18. Oehrig questionnaire.
19. Langley questionnaire.
20. Weese questionnaire.
21. Tate questionnaire.
22. Alspaugh letters.
23. Fitzhugh questionnaire.
24. Garrett and H. Beverburg questionnaires.
25. Alspaugh letters.
26. Reply to questionnaire from Goldstein by S. Sgt. Roy S. Jackson. Hereafter Jackson questionnaire.
27. *1000-Mile War*, pp. 156–57.
28. Ibid., pp. 157–62; *Aleutians, Gilberts and Marshalls*, p. 17.

29. *At Dawn We Slept*, p. 68.

30. *Aleutians, Gilberts and Marshalls*, pp. 17–18; *1000-Mile War*, pp. 162–64; *Guadalcanal to Saipan*, pp. 374–75; *Combat Chronology*, p.78.

31. Btry A history.

32. Btry K history.

33. *Aleutians, Gilberts and Marshalls*, p. 18; *1000-Mile War*, p. 163. *Guadalcanal to Saipan*, p. 375.

30: "Out There When Conditions Were Rough"

1. *1000-Mile War*, p. 163; Lansing S. Laidlaw, "Aleutian Experiences of the 'Mad M'," *Oregon Historian* Spring 1979, pp. 36–42 (hereafter "Mad M"); Material supplied to Goldstein by Michael P. Bouchette (hereafter Bouchette material); Lael Morgan, "An Artist's War in the Aleutians," *Alaska Journal*, summer 1980, pp. 37–38.

2. *1000-Mile War*, pp. 163–64; *Guadalcanal to Saipan*, p. 375; *Combat Chronology*, pp. 84–87.

3. *Combat Chronology*, pp. 87–90; *1000-Mile War*, p. 164.

4. B. Jones questionnaire.

5. Cathey questionnaire.

6. Sisk questionnaire.

7. Btry A history.

8. Btry K history.

9. Massey notes.

10. Stubbs diary.

11. *Combat Chronology*, pp. 92–101; *1000-Mile War*, p. 164.

12. Alspaugh letters.

13. Massey notes.

14. Beasley material. The source of this item is not given.

15. "Mad M," pp. 37–43.

16. *Guadalcanal to Saipan*, p. 376.

17. *Aleutians, Gilberts and Marshalls*, p. 18; *1000-Mile War*, pp. 167–68; *At Dawn We Slept*, p. 100; *Coral Sea, Midway and Submarine Actions*, pp. 195–98.

18. *Aleutians, Gilberts and Marshalls*, pp. 19–20; *1000-Mile War*, pp. 165–67; *Combat Chronology*, p. 97.

19. Stubbs diary; "Aleutian Island Campaign."

31: "The Japanese Could Have Sunk *Salt Lake City* with a Baseball"

1. Stubbs diary.
2. *1000-Mile War*, pp.184–85.
3. Sisk questionnaire.
4. *1000-Mile War*, pp. 187–91, 315.
5. Sisk questionnaire. WACs did serve on the Alaskan mainland.
6. *1000-Mile War*, p. 188.
7. Ibid., pp. 185–86, 315.
8. Reply to questionnaire from Goldstein to Maj. O. L. Greening. Hereafter Greening questionnaire.
9. Parker letter.
10. *1000-Mile War*, pp. 168–70; *Aleutians, Gilberts and Marshalls*, p. 21.
11. *Aleutians, Gilberts and Marshalls*, pp. 22–23.
12. Ibid., pp. 23–26; *1000-Mile War*, pp. 172–73.
13. *Aleutians, Gilberts and Marshalls*, pp. 26–29; *1000-Mile War*, pp. 173–75.
14. *Guadalcanal to Saipan*, p. 377; *Aleutians, Gilberts and Marshalls*, p. 34; *1000-Mile War*, pp. 175, 314.
15. *Aleutians, Gilberts and Marshalls*, pp. 28–36; *1000-Mile War*, pp. 175–79.

32: "Charged with a Herculean Task"

1. Stubbs diary.
2. Btry K history.
3. Caldwell questionnaire.
4. Nixon questionnaire.
5. *Strategy and Command*, pp. 425–28.
6. *1000-Mile War*, p. 192.
7. Ibid., pp. 192–95; William L. Worden, "The 7th Made It the Hard Way," *Saturday Evening Post*, 22 September 1945, p. 22. Hereafter "The 7th."
8. *Combat Chronology*, p. 102; *1000-Mile War*, pp. 195–96; *Strategy and Command*, pp. 428–29; *Guadalcanal to Saipan*, pp. 377–78.
9. *1000-Mile War*, pp. 196–99; *Aleutians, Gilberts and Marshalls*, p. 37; *Guadalcanal to Saipan*, pp. 378–79.
10. *1000-Mile War*, pp. 197–98, 315. See Masataka Chihaya with Goldstein and Dillon, *Fading Victory: The Diary of VADM Matome Ugaki*,

pp. 352–63 for the only eyewitness account of the shooting down of Yamamoto's plane.

11. Alspaugh letters.

12. Weese questionnaire.

13. Miller diary.

14. Stubbs diary.

15. *1000-Mile War*, pp. 198–200; *Combat Chronology*, pp. 114–28; *Guadalcanal to Saipan*, pp. 378–80.

16. *Guadalcanal to Saipan*, p. 380; *Aleutians, Gilberts and Marshalls*, p. 38; *Combat Chronology*, p. 124.

17. Btry K history.

18. Massey notes.

19. *1000-Mile War*, pp. 199–201; *Aleutians, Gilberts and Marshalls*, p. 38; Stan Hasrato, "Heroes Rising from the Sea," *Colliers*, 4 August 1945, pp. 14, 50. Hereafter "Heroes Rising."

20. "Heroes Rising," p. 50.

21. *1000-Mile War*, p. 201.

22. Massey notes.

23. *1000-Mile War*, pp. 200–02.

33: "Sweating the Attack"

1. Miller diary.

2. *1000-Mile War*, p. 203.

3. "The 7th," p. 23.

4. *1000-Mile War*, p. 204.

5. Ibid., pp. 204, 206–07; *Aleutians, Gilberts and Marshalls*, p. 40.

6. *Aleutians, Gilberts and Marshalls*, pp. 40–41.

7. "Heroes Rising," p. 50.

8. *1000-Mile War*, pp. 208–09.

9. *Aleutians, Gilberts and Marshalls*, p. 41; *1000-Mile War*, pp. 213–14.

10. Howard Handleman, "Bridge to Victory," *Reader's Digest*, November 1943, pp. 125–27. Hereafter "Bridge to Victory."

11. Ibid., pp. 128–29; *1000-Mile War*, pp. 209–10; *Aleutians, Gilberts and Marshalls*, p. 42.

12. "Bridge to Victory," pp. 128–31; *1000-Mile War*, pp. 210, 215.

13. *Aleutians, Gilberts and Marshalls*, pp. 42–43; *1000-Mile War*, pp. 210–13; Lt. Robert J. Mitchell, ed., *The Capture of Attu: Tales of World War II in Alaska As Told by the Men Who Fought There*, Anchorage, 1944, p. 23. Hereafter *Capture of Attu*. This work is in two parts. Part I is entitled

The Battle of the Aleutians 1942–1943, by Cpl. Dashiell Hammett and Cpl. Robert Colodny; Part II is *The Capture of Attu.* This is the same Hammett who wrote such mystery classics as *The Maltese Falcon* and *The Thin Man.* He was stationed on Adak for eighteen months and edited the camp newspaper, the *Adakian.* Colodny, an historian, did the research for *The Battle of the Aleutians.*

    14. *The Aleutian,* 8 July 1943.

    15. *1000-Mile War,* pp. 212–13.

    16. Ibid., pp. 212–16; *Capture of Attu,* p. 20.

34: "Get the Damned Thing Over With"

    1. Massey notes.

    2. *Capture of Attu,* p. 38; *1000-Mile War,* pp. 216–17; "Heroes Rising," p. 54.

    3. *1000-Mile War,* pp. 216–19; *Capture of Attu,* p. 20; *Aleutians, Gilberts and Marshalls,* pp. 44–45.

    4. "Bridge to Victory," pp. 131–32.

    5. "The 7th," p. 86; *1000-Mile War,* pp. 256–57.

    6. *1000-Mile War,* pp. 220–22; *Aleutians, Gilberts and Marshalls,* p. 46; "Bridge to Victory," pp. 133–34; *Capture of Attu,* p. 38.

    7. *1000-Mile War,* pp. 222–33, 317; Claus-M. Naske, "The Battle of Alaska Has Ended and . . . the Japs Won It," *Military Affairs,* July 1985, p. 48. Hereafter "Battle of Alaska." This article is based mainly upon the papers of former Governor Ernest Gruening of Alaska; *Aleutians, Gilberts and Marshalls,* p. 46.

    8. *1000-Mile War,* pp. 223–26; *Capture of Attu,* pp. 38–39; "Heroes Rising," p. 54.

    9. *The Aleutian,* 8 July 1943.

    10. Miller diary.

    11. "The 7th," p. 86; *1000-Mile War,* pp. 227–38. Worden places this action in Massacre Valley; Garfield's description implies this was a platoon of Willoughby's Scouts. Worden does not mention the U.S. shelling—understandably in an article published in 1945.

    12. "Bridge to Victory," pp. 135–365; *1000-Mile War,* pp. 228–29; *Capture of Attu,* p. 40.

    13. Alspaugh letters.

    14. *Aleutians, Gilberts and Marshalls,* p. 48; *1000-Mile War,* pp. 233–34, 240.

    15. *Aleutians, Gilberts and Marshalls,* p. 48; *1000-Mile War,* pp. 234–36, 239; *Tacoma Times,* 9 December 1943.

16. *1000-Mile War*, pp. 237–41.

17. "Bridge to Victory," p. 138; *1000-Mile War*, pp. 241–43; *Capture of Attu*, p. 40; *Tacoma Times*, 9 December 1943.

18. *Tacoma Times*, 9 December 1943; *Capture of Attu*, p. 43; *1000-Mile War*, pp. 243–47; *Guadalcanal to Saipan*, p. 384.

19. *Capture of Attu*, pp. 47–48; *Guadalcanal to Saipan*, p. 385; *1000-Mile War*, pp. 247–50.

20. *1000-Mile War*, pp. 251–52.

21. *Aleutians, Gilberts and Marshalls*, p. 50; *Capture of Attu*, pp. 57–72; *1000-Mile War*, pp. 252–56.

22. *Aleutians, Gilberts and Marshalls*, p. 51; *1000-Mile War*, pp. 256–58.

35: "We Think We Will Be Seeing Action Soon"

1. Bouchette material.
2. Btry K history.
3. Massey notes.
4. Miller diary.
5. Stubbs diary.
6. *Combat Chronology*, pp. 144, 148; *Aleutians, Gilberts and Marshalls*, p. 53; *1000-Mile War*, pp. 59–60.
7. *Combat Chronology*, pp. 141–51; *Guadalcanal to Saipan*, pp. 387–88; *Aleutians, Gilberts and Marshalls*, p. 54; *Strategy and Command*, pp. 431–32; *1000-Mile War*, pp. 260–61.
8. *The Aleutian*, 8 July 1943.
9. *1000-Mile War*, p. 261.
10. Stubbs diary.
11. Ibid.
12. Miller diary.
13. Massey notes.
14. *Combat Chronology*, pp. 152–67; *Aleutians, Gilberts and Marshalls*, pp. 54–55.
15. *1000-Mile War*, pp. 263–64.
16. Ibid., pp. 264–66; *Guadalcanal to Saipan*, pp. 388–89; *Combat Chronology*, p. 56.
17. Stubbs diary.
18. Alspaugh letters.
19. *Guadalcanal to Saipan*, p. 389; *1000-Mile War*, pp. 266–68; *Combat Chronology*, p. 160.
20. Stubbs diary.

21. *Aleutians, Gilberts and Marshalls*, pp. 57–58; *1000-Mile War*, pp. 271–73.

22. *Guadalcanal to Saipan*, p. 389; *Aleutians, Gilberts and Marshalls*, pp. 55–56; *Combat Chronology*, p. 162.

23. *Aleutians, Gilberts and Marshalls*, pp. 59–61; *1000-Mile War*, pp. 274–80, 319.

36: "A Great Big, Juicy, Expensive Mistake"

1. *Combat Chronology*, pp. 163–67; *Guadalcanal to Saipan*, pp. 389–90.

2. *Aleutians, Gilberts and Marshalls*, pp. 57–59; *1000-Mile War*, pp. 273, 280–81.

3. "Allied Troops Retake Deserted Kiska," *Life*, 13 September 1943, p. 25. No author is given for this article.

4. *Guadalcanal to Saipan*, p. 389.

5. Corey Ford, "Mission Over Kiska," *Colliers*, 13 February 1943, p. 20.

6. *Combat Chronology*, pp. 168–69; *Guadalcanal to Saipan*, pp. 389–90; *Aleutians, Gilberts and Marshalls*, pp. 61–62; *1000-Mile War*, pp. 283–84.

7. *Aleutians, Gilberts and Marshalls*, p. 62; *Guadalcanal to Saipan*, pp. 390–92; *1000-Mile War*, pp. 284–85.

8. *Aleutians, Gilberts and Marshalls*, pp. 62–63; *1000-Mile War*, pp. 284–85.

9. *1000-Mile War*, p. 284; "Battle of Alaska," p. 150.

10. *Combat Chronology*, pp. 172–74; *Aleutians, Gilberts and Marshalls*, p. 61.

11. "Aleutian Island Campaign," pp. 14–15.

12. Stubbs diary.

13. *Aleutians, Gilberts and Marshalls*, pp. 62–63; *1000-Mile War*, pp. 285–86.

14. Stubbs diary.

15. "Aleutians Island Campaign," pp. 1, 15.

16. *1000-Mile War*, pp. 287–88.

17. Stubbs diary.

18. *1000-Mile War*, p. 288.

19. Stubbs diary.

20. *Aleutians, Gilberts and Marshalls*, pp. 63–64.

21. Stubbs diary; *The Aleutian Invasion*, pp. 124–25.

22. *The Capture of Attu*, p. 79.

23. *1000-Mile War*, p. 289; *Aleutians, Gilberts and Marshalls*, p. 64.

37: "The War Had Gone By"

1. *Guadalcanal to Saipan*, p. 390; *Combat Chronology*, pp. 172–73.
2. Massey notes.
3. Btry K history.
4. Ibid.
5. *Combat Chronology*, p. 180; *1000-Mile War*, pp. 291–92.
6. Stubbs diary.
7. *1000-Mile War*, pp. 290–91; *Aleutians, Gilberts and Marshalls*, p. 65; *Guadalcanal to Saipan*, pp. 392–93.
8. *Guadalcanal to Saipan*, pp. 390–97; *Aleutians, Gilberts and Marshalls*, p. 66; *Combat Chronology*, pp. 187–88; *1000-Mile War*, pp. 291–93.
9. Stubbs diary.
10. Ibid.
11. Alspaugh letters.
12. Carnes questionnaire.
13. Fitzhugh questionnaire.
14. *Combat Chronology*, p. 194; *Guadalcanal to Saipan*, pp. 397–98; *Aleutians, Gilberts and Marshalls*, p. 66.
15. *1000-Mile War*, p. 293; *Combat Chronology*, pp. 200–01.
16. Stubbs diary.
17. *Aleutians, Gilberts and Marshalls*, p. 66; *1000-Mile War*, pp. 291–97.
18. *1000-Mile War*, p. 294.
19. Alspaugh letters.
20. Stubbs diary.
21. Massey notes.
22. Stubbs diary.
23. Sisk questionnaire.
24. Btry K history.

38: "Back to Civilization"

1. Stubbs diary.
2. Massey notes.
3. Letter, Mrs. Gerry Crow to Goldstein, 9 April 1987.
4. Massey notes.
5. Wall questionnaire.
6. O. Jones questionnaire.
7. Massey notes.
8. Fitzhugh questionnaire.
9. Croom questionnaire.

10. H. Cathey questionnaire.

11. Sisk questionnaire.

12. Burke statement.

13. Ryals questionnaire.

14. Cowell questionnaire.

15. Burris questionnaire.

16. Anderson questionnaire.

17. Pedersen questionnaire.

18. Massey notes.

19. Conway questionnaire.

20. Reply to questionnaire from Goldstein by Pfc Odell Hammond. Hereafter Hammond questionnaire.

21. McKinistry questionnaire.

22. Sisk questionnaire.

23. B. Jones questionnaire.

24. Thatcher questionnaire.

25. Eason questionnaire.

26. Hargrave questionnaire.

27. New questionnaire.

28. Barron questionnaire.

29. Reply to questionnaire from Goldstein by Udell R. Tarpley. Hereafter Tarpley questionnaire.

30. Alspaugh questionnaire.

31. Newton questionnaire.

32. Dale questionnaire.

33. Paulus, O'Neal, and Clodi questionnaires.

34. A. Parker letter.

35. Abell questionnaire.

36. Patrick questionnaire.

37. Garrett questionnaire.

38. Carnes questionnaire.

39. G. Cathey questionnaire.

40. Quimby questionnaire.

41. Davis questionnaire.

42. Burke statement.

43. A. Parker letter.

44. Massey notes.

45. Ibid.; Massey questionnaire.

46. Thomason and W. Parker questionnaires.

47. Ballew questionnaire.

48. Reply to questionnaire from Goldstein by Robert G. Pylant. Hereafter Pylant questionnaire.

49. Carnes questionnaire.

50. Massey notes and questionnaire.
51. Pylant questionnaire.
52. Alspaugh questionnaire.
53. Mitchell questionnaire.

39: "A Learning Experience"

1. "Battle of Alaska," p. 144
2. Ibid., p. 148.
3. Ibid.
4. Ibid., pp. 145, 149–50.
5. Ibid., p. 150; *1000-Mile War*, p. 294.
6. See chapter 25 for details.
7. *1000-Mile War*, pp. 295–96.
8. *Campaigns*, p. 83.
9. Ibid., pp. 84–85.
10. *1000-Year War*, p. 295.
11. Joseph Wechberg, "Alaska, Springboard of Attack," *Canadian Geographical Journal*, April 1943, pp. 185–86; Taylor scrapbooks.
12. Beasley questionnaire.
13. Dodson questionnaire.
14. Lindley questionnaire.
15. Tate questionnaire.
16. Fitzhugh questionnaire.
17. Paulus questionnaire.
18. Costley questionnaire.
19. Burris and Massey questionnaires.
20. Sisk questionnaire.
21. Dale questionnaire.
22. Conway questionnaire.
23. Pack questionnaire.
24. H. Cathey questionnaire.
25. Caldwell questionnaire.
26. Weese questionnaire.
27. Robertson questionnaire.
28. Faulhaber questionnaire.
29. A. Beverburg questionnaire.
30. Stout questionnaire. Among those expressing similar sentiments were McKinistry, Ryals, Sergeant Beverburg, Simmons, Buzzan, and Leeder.
31. O'Neal questionnaire.

Bibliography

Books

Adams, Ben. *Alaska, The Big Land.* New York: Hill and Wang, 1959.

Carter, Kit C. and Robert Mueller, comps. *The Army Air Forces in World War II: Combat Chronology, 1941–1945.* Washington: Air University and Office of Air History, 1975.

Craven, Wesley F. and James L. Cate. *The Army Air Forces in World War II, Vol. I, Plans and Early Operations, January 1939 to August 1942.* Chicago: University of Chicago Press, 1948.

_____. *The Army Air Forces in World War II, Vol. IV: The Pacific: Guadalcanal to Saipan, August 1942 to July 1944.* Chicago: University of Chicago Press, 1950.

Cuttlefish V. *The Aleutian Invasion: World War Two in the Aleutian Islands.* Unalaska: Unalaska City School District, 1981.

Cuttlefish VI. *The Unknown Islands: Life and Tales of Henry Swanson.* Unalaska: Unalaska City School District, 1982.

Cuttlefish VII. *People of the Aleutian Islands.* Unalaska: Unalaska City School District, 1986.

Denfield, D. Colt. *The Defense of Dutch Harbor, Alaska from Military Construction to Base Cleanup.* Anchorage: Defense Environmental Restoration Program, Alaska District, U.S. Army Corps of Engineers, December 1979.

Driscoll, Joseph. *War Discovers Alaska.* New York: Cornwall Press, 1943.

Garfield, Brian. *The Thousand-Mile War: World War II in Alaska and the Aleutians.* New York: Doubleday, 1969.

Gruening, Ernest, ed. *An Alaskan Reader 1867–1967.* New York: Meredith Press, 1966.

_____. *The State of Alaska.* New York: Random House, 1954.

Hearings Before the Joint Committee on the Investigation of the Pearl Harbor

Attack, Congress of the United States, Seventy-ninth Congress,
Washington: Government Printing Office, 1946.

Hilscher, Herb. *Alaska, U.S.A.* Boston: Little, Brown & Co., 1959.

———. *Alaska Now.* Boston: Little, Brown & Co., 1948.

Kirtland, John C. and David F. Coffin, Jr. *The Relocation of and Internment of the Aleuts During World War II,* Vols. I and II. Anchorage: Aleutian/Pribilof Islands Association, Inc., 1981.

Mitchell, Robert J., coll. *The Capture of Attu: As Told by the Men Who Fought There.* Anchorage: Alaska Northwest Publishing Co., 1944.

Morgan, Murray. *Bridge to Russia.* New York: American Book-Stratford Press, 1947.

Morison, Samuel E. *History of United States Naval Operations in World War II, Vol. I, The Rising Sun in the Pacific.* Boston: Little, Brown & Co., 1950.

———. *History of United States Naval Operations in World War II, Vol. IV, Coral Sea, Midway and Submarine Actions.* Boston: Little, Brown & Co., 1949.

———. *History of United States Naval Operations in World War II, Vol. VII, Aleutians, Gilberts and Marshalls.* Boston: Little, Brown & Co., 1949.

Morton, Louis. *U.S. Army in World War II: The War in the Pacific: Strategy and Command: The First Two Years.* Washington: Office of the Chief of Military History, Department of the Army, 1962.

National Guard Historical Annual 1938. Baton Rouge: Army and Navy Publishing Co., 1938.

Okumiya, Masatake and Jiro Horikoshi, with Martin Caidin. *Zero!* New York: Ballantine Books, 1956.

Pope County History, Vol. II.

Prange, Gordon W. *At Dawn We Slept.* New York: McGraw-Hill Book Co., 1981.

———. *Miracle at Midway.* New York: McGraw-Hill Book Co., 1982.

Sherwood, Morgan B. *Exploration of Alaska, 1865–1900.* New Haven: Yale University Press, 1965.

Starr, S. Frederick, ed. *Russia's American Colony.* Durham, N.C.: Duke University Press, 1987.

Tikhmenev, Petr Aleksandrovich. *A History of the Russian-American Company.* Pierce, Richard A. and Alton S. Donnelly, trans. and ed., Fairbanks: Limestone Press, 1978.

U.S. Strategic Bombing Survey, Naval Analysis Division, *The Campaigns of the Pacific War.* Washington: Government Printing Office, 1956.

U.S. War Department. *The Capture of Attu As Told By the Men Who Fought There.* Washington: The Infantry Journal, 1944.

Articles

"Aleutian Springboard," *Popular Mechanics*, September 1943.

"The Aleutians: They Are Barren Links between Two Worlds," *Life*

"Alaska and the Far East," *The Commonweal*, 16 August 1940.

"Allied Troops Retake Deserted Kiska," *Life*, 13 September 1943.

Annabel, Russell. "Mad-Dog Hunt on Attu," *Saturday Evening Post*, 14 August 1943.

Araneto, M. T., Jr. "Japan's Eleventh Hour," *Current History*, June 1943.

Arnold, Maj. Gen. H. H. "Our Air Frontier in Alaska," *National Geographic*, October 1940.

Beaufort, John. "Bombers Are Resourceful," *Christian Science Monitor*, 20 November 1943.

Brochure on the 39th CAA Brigade, Fort Bliss, Texas, 18 April 1991, 50th Anniversary.

Clemmens, William. "Report on the Aleutians," *Reader's Digest*, March 1943.

Elliott, A. Randle. "U.S. Defense Outposts in the Pacific," *Foreign Policy Report*, 15 March 1941.

Ellis, Dan. "Springfield Rifles and Forgotten Men," *The Alaska Journal*, Autumn 1980.

Ford, Corey. "Forgotten Front," *Colliers*, 27 March 1943.

_____. "Mission over Kiska," *Colliers*, 13 February 1943.

_____. "Remember Dutch Harbor," *Colliers*, 1 and 8 May 1943.

_____. "They Came to Attu," *Colliers*, 8 August 1942.

Ford, Corey and Alaister MacBain, "Castner's Cutthroats," *Colliers*

_____. "Sourdouth Army," *Colliers*, 25 April 1942.

_____. "Uncle Sam Arms Alaska," *Reader's Digest*, January 1941.

Franklin, William M. "Alaska, Outpost of American Defense," *Foreign Affairs*, October 1940.

Gilman, William, "Kiska Mission," *Saturday Evening Post*, 19 June 1943.

Hammett, Cpl. Dashiell and Cpl. Robert Colodny, "The Battle of the Aleutians: A Graphic History 1942–1943," Adak: Intelligence Section, Field Force Headquarters.

Handleman, Howard. "Bridge to Victory," *Reader's Digest*, November 1943.

Hasrato, Stan. "Heroes Rising from the Sea," *Colliers*, 4 August 1945.

Hays, Otis E., Jr. "When War Came to Seward," *Alaska Journal*, Autumn 1980.

Hendricks, Charles. "The Eskimos and the Defense of Alaska," *Pacific Historical Review*, 1985.

Laidlaw, Lansing S. "Aleutian Experience of the 'Mad M.'," *Oregon Historian*, Spring 1979.

McGara, Ken. "Aleutian Islands Shrouded with Mystery, War Memories," *The Sunday Oklahoman*, 27 July 1986.

Mizraki, Joe. "Samurai," *Wings*, December 1977.

Morgan, Lael. "An Artist's War in the Aleutians," *Alaska Journal*, Summer 1980.

Nashe, Claus-M. "The Battle of Alaska Has Ended and . . . the Japs Won It," *Military Affairs*, July 1985.

_____. "The Relocation of Alaska's Japanese Residents," *Pacific Northwest Quarterly*, July 1983.

Pratt, Fletcher. "Campaign Beyond Glory: The Navy in the Aleutians 1942–43," *Harper's Magazine*, November 1944.

Pratt, Admiral William V., USN (Ret). "What the Japanese Are Up To in Attu," *Newsweek*, 29 June 1942.

Rasche, Herbert H. "Alaska Purchase Centennial, 1867–1967," *Arctic*.

Reardon, Jim. "The Akutan Zero," *Alaska*, September and October 1987.

_____. "Kiska: One Island's Moment in History," *Alaska*, January 1986.

Rogers, Lindsay. "National Defense: Plan or Patchwork?" *Foreign Affairs*, October 1940.

Stokesbury, James. "Battle of Attu," *American History Illustrated*, 1 November 1979.

"Trade Winds," *The Saturday Review*, 6 November 1963.

Trimble, Mike. "Alaska Battle Site Changes Little, Arkansan Finds," *Arkansas Gazette*, 4 August 1980.

Wechsberg, Joseph. "Alaska, Springboard of Attack," *Canadian Geographical Journal*, April 1943.

Wintermute, Maj. Ira F. "War in the Fog," *American*, August 1943.

"With the Alaska Jap Fighters," *Popular Mechanics*, October 1943.

Worden, William L. "The 7th Made It the Hard Way," *Saturday Evening Post*, 22 September 1945.

Magazines

Alaska

Alaska Journal

Aleutian

Aleutians

American

American History Illustrated

Arctic

Army and Navy

Business Week

Canadian Geographical Journal

Colliers

Commonweal

Current History

Foreign Affairs

Foreign Policy Reports

Harper's

Life

Military Affairs

National Geographic
Newsweek
Oregon Historian
Pacific Historical Review
Pacific Northwest Quarterly
Popular Mechanics
Reader's Digest

Saturday Evening Post
Saturday Review
Scholastics
Time
Wings
Yank

Newspapers

Aleutian Eagle
Anchorage Times
Arkansas Democrat
Arkansas Gazette
Baltimore American
Camden (Arkansas) *News*
Christian Science Monitor
El Paso Herald-Post

Jonesboro (Arkansas) *Sun*
New York Times
Pribilof Progress-Pribilof Pace
Seattle Post-Intelligencer
Seattle Times
Sunday Oklahoman
Tacoma Times

Unpublished Sources

Abell, Dennis Pike. "The Japanese Air Attacks, Dutch Harbor, Aleutian
    Islands, Alaska, June 3 and 4, 1942."
Alspaugh, David B. Letters.
Beasley, Paul. Material.
Bouchette, Michael F. Material.
Burke, James. Statement.
Crow, Mrs. Gerry. Letter to Goldstein, 9 April 1987.
Diary of David B. Alspaugh.
Diary of John Bowen.
Diary of Robert H. Miller.
Diary of Willie Stubbs.
Drake, Donnel J. "Arkansas National Guard: A Military History,
    1781–1939."
_____. "Arkansas National Guard During World War II."
_____. "Brief History of Dutch Harbor."
_____. "History of Alaska, 1741–1939."
_____. "History of Battery A."
_____. Material.

_____. "Military History of the Arkansas National Guard as of 1938."
Flash messages received at Battery B. Courtesy Dolph B. Kulbeth.
Holmes, Otis R. Letter.
Massey, James M. Notes.
Miller, 1st Lt. Robert H. "The Aleutian Island Campaign, Co. H and F, 153rd Infantry, Mortar Plat Co. H."
_____. Scrapbooks.
Mitchell, Wyse T. "206th CAA After the Aleutians."
Official Daily Report and Chronology of Action in Alaska (3 June 1942–22 August 1943).
Parker, Alford. Undated letter to Goldstein, postmarked 14 November 1989.
Robertson, Col. Elgan C. Papers.
Tate, Luster V. "History of 206th CA 'AA'."
Taylor, Louis E. Scrapbooks.
Wilson, James E. Letter to Goldstein, 10 July 1989.

Questionnaires

(The following submitted replies to questionnaires from Goldstein, without which the story could never have been told.)

Abell, Dennis Pike
Albright, Aubrey T.
Allen, Lewis A.
Alspaugh, David Brant
Anderson, Bernard W.
Ballard, Harold N.
Ballew, Rudolph
Barron, James O.
Beasley, Paul D.
Beverburg, Alvin Lorenz
Beverburg, Herman F.
Brewer, James F.
Brown, Leonard S.
Burke, James
Burris, Roy E.
Burris, Troy E.
Buzzan, Murrel W.
Byergson, Raymond
Caldwell, Clifford C.

Callaway, Voris O.
Campbell, Wesley R.
Carnes, Everette C.
Cathey, George W.
Cathey, Haskell J.
Caudle, James M.
Chambers, Paul
Chapman, Otto M.
Cibich, Martin D.
Clark, Charles
Clodi, Virgil L.
Conway, S. P.
Costley, James D.
Cothran, Robert L.
Cowell, Devoe H.
Croom, Wiley H.
Dale, Doss D.
Davis, John Warren
Dodson, Minot B.

Dougherty, Harry K.
Drake, Donnel James
Eason, Cleo J.
Edwards, Henry Bateman, Jr.
Eheman, Lawrence G.
Faulhaber, George B.
Felts, Clyde A.
Fitzhugh, Edward B.
Garrett, Robert Dee
Gartrell, Dewey W.
Gill, Earl
Greening, O. L.
Haden, Russell R.
Hammond, Odell
Hargrave, Earl P.
Harp, John H.
Henderson, Lawrence R.
Hickman, James
Hogan, Walton L.
Holmes, Otis
Horner, James Tappan
Jackson, Roy S.
Jennings, Clifton B., Jr.
Jones, Bill E.
Jones, Joseph G.
Jones, Oscar H.
Junevitch, Tony
Kee, Pat M.
Keeton, James Walter
Kimberlin, James M.
Kinney, Neal P.
Langley, James A.
Laubach, Forrest N.
Leeder, Frank
Lindley, Wayne L.
McKinistry, W. J.
Martin, Edwin C.
Massey, James M.
Mayes, Elmer
Meek, John T.
Mikels, Harold B.

Mitchell, Wyre T.
Moseley, Hugh, Jr.
New, Leo L.
Newton, William S.
Nichols, Alfred F.
Nixon, Edgar L.
Oehrig, Henry A.
O'Neal, Thomas P.
Pack, James L.
Parker, Gaynes
Parker, Wayne D.
Patrick, Nathan Ray
Paulus, E. F.
Pedersen, Ernest W.
Proffitt, Robert M.
Pylant, Robert G.
Quimby, Thomas
Radney, Sheldon L.
Raney, Oliver Chas.
Raymond, Frederick Harold
Richardson, Lawrence
Robertson, Charles D.
Ryals, James H.
Rybel, Walter C.
Simmons, James M.
Sisk, Joe B.
Snellgrove, Frank
Stout, Bernard E.
Tarpley, Udell R.
Tate, Luster V.
Taylor, Louis I.
Thatcher, Jean D.
Thomason, John A., Jr.
Trimble, Woodrow
Walkup, Robert L., Sr.
Wall, David M.
Weese, John W.
Williamson, Clarence F., Jr.
Wilson, James Earl
Young, William L.

Interviews

Abell, Dennis Pike	31 August 1987
Albright, Aubrey	1 and 2 September 1988
Alspaugh, David	1 and 2 September 1988
Arbaugh, William	2, 3, and 4 July 1989
Beasley, Paul D.	31 August and 1 September 1986
Bowen, William	1 September 1986 and 15 May 1987
Conway, S. P.	1 and 2 September 1988
Drake, Donnel L.	2, 3, and 4 July 1989
Garrett, Cyril	1 September 1988
Garrett, Robert T.	1 and 2 September 1987
Jones, James T.	2 September 1988
Jones, William	31 August 1988
Laubach, Charles	2 September 1987
Massey, James M.	2, 3, and 4 July 1989
Patrick, Mason	2, 3, and 4 July 1989
Pierce, Arley	1 and 2 September 1987
Proffitt, John	2 September 1987
Quimby, Thomas	1 September 1987
Raney, Charles	2 September 1986
Robertson, Elgan C.	1 September 1986
Stubbs, Willie	2 September 1987
Williams, Charles	2, 3, and 4 July 1989
Wilson, James E. (by telephone)	15 November 1987

Contributors

We gratefully acknowledge the financial support of the following toward this project. If any name has been inadvertently omitted or misspelled, we sincerely apologize.

The names listed below are those of members, widows, and honorary members of the 206th:

Abell, Dennis Pike
Albright, A. T.
Alspaugh, David
Anderson, B.
Ashton, Peyton

Ballard, H.
Ballard, Rowland
Ballew, Dick
Basicin, June
Beasley, Paul
Beverburg, Al
Bloom, Howard
Bowen, Bill (honorary member)
Brenner, J.
Buzzan, M.

C Battery

Cathey, George
Chambers, Paul
Cibich, Marty

Clodi, V. L.
Coleman, Harley
Coleman, William
Collier, Emma Edrington
Conway, "Fox"
Cook, J.
Cook, Mrs. James

Dees, Frank
Diemer, Tony
Dietrick, Hal
Dixon, William
Drake, Don
Drye, Robert

Eason, Cleo
Ehemann, L.
Emrich, Eleanor D.

Field, H. Wester
Fitzhugh, Ed
Foreman, Bill

Gartrell, D.
Gates, Jake
Gibson, Cecil
Gonzalez, Francisco
Greening, Pat

H Battery

Halley, Floyd
Hargraves, Earl
Harp, J.
Hayden, Russell
Henderson, Lawrence
Hendricks, Lillian
Hendricks, Owen
Hill, Ray

Ingram, Mrs. Frank

Johnson, Ralph
Jones, Bill
Jones, J.

Kirkland, T. K.
Kulbeth, Dolph

Lamp, Ed
Laubach, Chas.
Laubach, Forrest
Leeder, Frank
Little, Thomas
Love, George

Massey, J. M.
McMilian, T. E.
Medina, Oscar
Meek, J.
Metcalf, Doc
Mitchell, W. T.
Moore, Laurice
Moseley, Hugh

New, Leo
Newton, Chas.
Nichols, Al
Nicholson, P.

Oehrig, Henry
O'Neal, T. P.
Osment, Eugene
Owens, R.

Parker, "Pook"
Paulus, E. F.
Phillips, Joe
Pierce, Arlie
Porter, Robert
Pride, Richard
Prince, Melvin
Proffitt, Bob
Pylant, Bob

Quimby, Tom

Radney, Sheldon
Randall, J.
Raney, Oliver
Raymond, Pete
Richardson, Doyle
Robinson, Chas. "Whitey"
Rothenhoffer, Homer
Ruthven, Geneva
Ruthven, M. R.

Sangster, Gerald C.
Scheibner, Carl
Schrantz, Mr.
Seay, W. S.
Simmons, James
Smith, E. C.
Stokes, Bill

Thatcher, Jean

Villines, Ford
Von Kanel, Ervin

Williams, Chas.
Williamson, Gaston
Willson, Bingham

Yarbrough, W.
Young, Bruce

The following are corporations, trusts, and individual nonmembers:

Altheimer Foundation
Arkansas Endowment for
    Humanities

Arkansas-Louisiana Gas Company
Arkansas Power & Light

Bowen, Jim
Bryson, Paul

Geschwind, R. M.

Lamar Paper

McLarty Company
Murphy Foundation

Ross, Jane

Index

CPSIA information can be obtained
at www.ICGtesting.com
Printed in the USA
BVHW04*0931240818
525414BV00002B/1/P